Suzuki GSX-R & Katana (GSX-F)

Service and Repair Manual

Alan Ahlstrand
and John H Haynes Member of the Guild of Motoring Writers

Models covered

(10Y7-272-2055)

Suzuki GSX-R750. 748/749cc. 1985 through 1992
Suzuki GSX-R1100. 1052/1127cc. 1986 through 1992
Suzuki GSX600F Katana. 599cc. 1988 through 1996
Suzuki GSX750F Katana. 748cc. 1989 through 1996
Suzuki GSX1100F Katana. 1127cc. 1988 through 1996

© Haynes Publishing 1999

ABCDE
FGH

Printed in the USA

A book in the **Haynes Service and Repair Manual Series**

Haynes Publishing
Sparkford, Yeovil, Somerset BA22 7JJ, England

ISBN 1 85960 284 3

Haynes North America, Inc
861 Lawrence Drive, Newbury Park, California 91320, USA

Library of Congress Catalog Card Number 96-79015

Editions Haynes
4, Rue de l'Abreuvoir
92415 COURBEVOIE CEDEX, France

British Library Cataloguing in Publication Data
A catalogue record for this book is available from the British Library.

Haynes Publishing Nordiska AB
Box 1504, 751 45 UPPSALA, Sweden

Contents

LIVING WITH YOUR SUZUKI GSX-R/GSX-F

Introduction

Daily (pre-ride) checks

MAINTENANCE

Routine maintenance and servicing

Contents

REPAIRS AND OVERHAUL

Engine, transmission and associated systems

Chassis components

Fairing and bodywork

Electrical system

Wiring diagrams

REFERENCE

Index

Suzuki Every Which Way

by Julian Ryder

From Textile Machinery to Motorcycles

Suzuki were the second of Japan's Big Four motorcycle manufacturers to enter the business, and like Honda they started by bolting small two-stroke motors to bicycles. Unlike Honda, they had manufactured other products before turning to transportation in the aftermath of World War II. In fact Suzuki has been in business since the first decade of the 20th-Century when Michio Suzuki manufactured textile machinery.

The desperate need for transport in post-war Japan saw Suzuki make their first motorised bicycle in 1952, and the fact that by 1954 the company had changed its name to Suzuki Motor Company shows how quickly the sideline took over the whole company's activities. In their first full manufacturing year, Suzuki made nearly 4500 bikes and rapidly expanded into the world markets with a range of two-strokes.

Suzuki didn't make a four-stroke until 1977 when the GS750 double-overhead-cam across-the-frame four arrived. This was several years after Honda and Kawasaki had established the air-cooled four as the industry standard, but no motorcycle epitomises the era of what came to be known as the Universal Japanese motorcycle better than the GS. So well engineered were the original fours that you can clearly see their genes in the GS500 twins that are still going strong in the mid-1990s. Suzuki's ability to prolong the life of their products this way means that they are often thought of as a conservative company. This is hardly fair if you look at some of their landmark designs, most of which have been commercial as well as critical successes.

Two-stroke Success

Early racing efforts were bolstered by the arrival of Ernst Degner who defected from the East German MZ team at the Swedish GP of 1961, bringing with him the rotary-valve secrets of design genius Walter Kaaden. The new Suzuki 50 cc racer won its first GP on the Isle of Man the following year and winning the title easily. Only Honda and Ralph Bryans interrupted Suzuki's run of 50 cc titles from 1962 to 1968.

The T500 two-stroke twin

The arrival of the twin-cylinder 125 racer in 1963 enabled Hugh Anderson to win both 50 and 125 world titles. You may not think 50 cc racing would be exciting - until you learn that the final incarnation of the thing had 14 gears and could do well over 100 mph on fast circuits. Before pulling out of GPs in 1967 the 50 cc racer won six of the eight world titles chalked up by Suzuki during the 1960s as well as providing Mitsuo Itoh with the distinction of being the only Japanese rider to win an Isle of Man TT. Mr Itoh still works for Suzuki, he's in charge of their racing program.

Europe got the benefit of Suzuki's two-stroke expertise in a succession of air-cooled twins, the six-speed 250 cc Super Six being the most memorable, but the arrival in 1968 of the first of a series of 500 cc twins which were good looking, robust and versatile marked the start of mainstream success.

So confident were Suzuki of their two-stroke expertise that they even applied it to the burgeoning Superbike sector. The GT750 water-cooled triple arrived in 1972. It was big, fast and comfortable although the handling and stopping power did draw some comment. Whatever the drawbacks of the road bike, the engine was immensely successful in Superbike and Formula 750 racing. The roadster has its devotees, though, and is now a sought-after bike on the classic Japanese scene. Do not refer to it as the Water Buffalo in such company. Joking aside, the later disc-braked versions were quite civilised, but the audacious idea of using a big two-stroke motor in what was essentially a touring bike was a surprising success until the fuel crisis of the mid-'70s effectively killed off big strokers.

The same could be said of Suzuki's only real lemon, the RE5. This is still the only mass-produced bike to use the rotary (or Wankel) engine but never sold well. Fuel consumption in the mid-teens allied to frightening complexity and excess weight meant the RE5 was a non-starter in the sales race.

Development of the Four-stroke range

When Suzuki got round to building a four-stroke they did a very good job of it. The GS fours were built in 550, 650, 750, 850 1000 and 1100 cc sizes in sports, custom, roadster and even shaft-driven touring forms over many years. The GS1000 was in on the start of Superbike racing in the early 1970s and the GS850 shaft-driven tourer was around nearly 15 years later. The fours spawned a line of 400, 425, 450 and 500 cc GS twins that were essentially the middle half of the four with all their reliability. If there was ever a criticism of the GS models it was that with the exception of the GS1000S of 1980, colloquially known as the ice-cream van, the range was visually uninspiring.

They nearly made the same mistake when they launched the four-valve-head GSX750 in 1979. Fortunately, the original twin-shock

One of the later GT750 'kettle' models with front disc brakes

The GS400 was the first in a line of four-stroke twins

The GS750 led the way for a series of four cylinder models

to riding a GP bike. The fearsome beast could top 140 mph and only weighed 340 lb - the other alleged GP replicas were pussy cats compared to the Gamma's man-eating tiger.

The RG only lasted a few years and is already firmly in the category of collector's item; its four-stroke equivalent, the GSX-R, is still with us and looks like being so for many years. You have to look back to 1985 and its launch to realise just what a revolutionary step the GSX-R750 was: quite simply it was the first race replica. Not a bike dressed up to look like a race bike, but a genuine racer with lights on, a bike that could be taken straight to the track and win.

The first GSX-R, the 750, had a completely new motor cooled by oil rather than water and an aluminium cradle frame. It was sparse, a little twitchy and very, very fast. This time Suzuki got the looks right, blue and white bodywork based on the factory's racing colours and endurance-racer lookalike twin headlights. And then came the 1100 - the big GSX-R got progressively more brutal as it chased the Yamaha EXUP for the heavyweight championship.

And alongside all these mould-breaking designs, Suzuki were also making the best looking custom bikes to come out of Japan, the Intruders; the first race replica trail bike, the DR350; the sharpest 250 Supersports, the RGV250; and a bargain-basement 600, the Bandit. The Bandit proved so popular they went on to build 1200 and 750 cc versions of it. I suppose that's predictable, a range of four-stroke fours just like the GS and GSXs. It's just like the company really, sometimes predictable, admittedly - but never boring.

version was soon replaced by the 'E'-model with Full-Floater rear suspension and a full set of all the gadgets the Japanese industry was then keen on and has since forgotten about, like 16-inch front wheels and anti-dive forks. The air-cooled GSX was like the GS built in 550, 750 and 1100 cc versions with a variety of half, full and touring fairings, but the GSX that is best remembered is the Katana that first appeared in 1981. The power was provided by an 1000 or 1100 cc GSX motor, but wrapped around it was the most outrageous styling package to come out of Japan. Designed by Hans Muth of Target Design, the Katana looked like nothing seen before or since. At the time there was as much anti feeling as praise, but now it is rightly regarded as a classic, a true milestone in motorcycle design. The factory have even started making 250 and 400 cc fours for the home market with the same styling as the 1981 bike.

Just to remind us that they'd still been building two-strokes for the likes of Barry Sheene, in 1986 Suzuki marketed a road-going version of their RG500 square-four racer which had put an end to the era of the four-stroke in 500 GPs when it appeared in 1974. In 1976 Suzuki not only won their first 500 title with Sheene, they sold RG500s over the counter and won every GP with them - with the exception of the Isle of Man TT which the works riders boycotted. Ten years on, the RG500 Gamma gave road riders the nearest experience they'd ever get

Suzuki's GSX-R range represented their cutting edge sports bikes

The GSX-R750 and GSX-R1100

The phrase race-replica was bandied about a lot when the first GSX-R was launched in 1985. This was a mistake, the smaller GSX-R was not a race-replica, it was a racer: period. It even looked like the factory endurance racer on which various components had been developed. The GSX-R didn't make any more power than its competitors, both the Suzuki and the FZ750 Yamaha claimed to make 100 bhp and the 900 cc GPZ Kawasaki made 115 bhp, it was the fact the thing only weighed 388 lb that made it so amazing.

The old saying goes that the most expensive thing to add to a bike is lightness, but Suzuki managed it with a combination of lightweight components, oil cooling, and a decided lack of creature comforts. The frame weighed only 18 lb without the swinging arm and wrapped around a motor that was pared down to the minimum possible weight thanks to oil cooling. Five-and-a-half litres of the stuff were pumped around the cylinder head and cooled in a big radiator thus enabling all the top-end components to be as light as possible.

On the road, the GSX-R felt like a racer. A third of the power arrived between 7000 and 9000 rpm, the flat-slide carbs didn't like being snapped open at low revs, and the chassis was very, very sensitive. If you twitched so did the bike, despite the unfashionably large 18-inch front wheel. I once took my left hand off the bars on one of the first GSX-Rs to look over my shoulder and was rewarded with a lock-to-lock tank-slapper. I was on one of London's major arterial roads at the time...

By contrast the first of the 1100 cc GSX-Rs had all of the technology, lack of weight and race-track cred of the 750, but it was astoundingly civilised. The twitchiness was gone, the fussy carburation banished. In its place was a massively powerful yet very usable if slightly plain sports tourer that could hustle when asked. After all, this is still a race-track bred machine we're talking about - it just didn't seem like it.

Over the years the 750 GSX-R was tamed whereas the 1100 got less civilised. The J-model 750 of 1988 was the first to get the Slingshot designation - actually a reference to a new carburettor design - and a new short-stroke motor (73 x 44.7 mm replacing the original 70 x 48.7 mm). It also got a substantial, and very modern, restyle with more rounded lines including air ducts either side of the headlights. The 1990 L-model changed again, this time back to the original dimensions of 70 x 48.7 mm. The 1100's major changes tended to lag a year behind the 750's. It was the 1989 K-model that got the short-stroke 78 x 59 mm 1127 cc motor to replace the original 76 x 78 mm 1052 cc lump and the following year it got upside-down front forks.

Both the 750 and 1100 oil-cooled motors were superseded by new, water-cooled designs in 1992 and 1993, respectively.

The GSX600F, 750F and 1100F (Katana)

Riders who didn't need a cutting-edge sportster also benefited from the GSX-R's development, because the engines were used in a new generation of GSX models (Katanas in the US). The 750 was sleeved down for the GSX600, a budget bike that was deliberately built to a price and not intended to compete with the Supersports 600s like the FZR or CBR. All-enveloping bodywork hid the steel chassis and produced an effect that one observer likened to a teapot when it appeared in 1987.

Aesthetics aside, the GSX was astounding value for money and the following year a better looking 750 cc version was launched. In late '87 the 1100 motor was used in a GSX aimed at the sports tourer segment occupied by FJ Yamahas and CBR Hondas. It was one of those bikes that wasn't well received on its launch but as time went on it, like the GSXs, revealed itself as yet another very good motorcycle. And when you took the price into account they were seen as exceptional bikes.

The GSX750F Katana model

Acknowledgements

Our thanks are due to Joe Ortiz who suggested and arranged many of the photographs in addition to performing mechanical work. NGK Spark Plugs (UK) Ltd supplied the color spark plug condition photographs and the Avon Rubber Company provided information on tire fitting.

Thanks are also due to Redcat Marketing and Kel Edge for supplying colour transparencies, to Fred Furlong of Yeovil for supplying the GSX-R1100 on the front cover, and to Phil Flowers who carried out the front cover photography. The introduction, "Suzuki - Every Which Way" was written by Julian Ryder.

About this Manual

The aim of this manual is to help you get the best value from your motorcycle. It can do so in several ways. It can help you decide what work must be done, even if you choose to have it done by a dealer; it provides information and procedures for routine maintenance and servicing; and it offers diagnostic and repair procedures to follow when trouble occurs.

We hope you use the manual to tackle the work yourself. For many simpler jobs, doing it yourself may be quicker than arranging an appointment to get the motorcycle into a dealer and making the trips to leave it and pick it up. More importantly, a lot of money can be saved by avoiding the expense the shop must pass on to you to cover its labour and overhead costs. An added benefit is the sense of satisfaction and accomplishment that you feel after doing the job yourself.

References to the left or right side of the motorcycle assume you are sitting on the seat, facing forward.

We take great pride in the accuracy of information given in this manual, but motorcycle manufacturers make alterations and design changes during the production run of a particular motorcycle of which they do not inform us. No liability can be accepted by the authors or publishers for loss, damage or injury caused by any errors in, or omissions from, the information given.

Professional mechanics are trained in safe working procedures. However enthusiastic you may be about getting on with the job at hand, take the time to ensure that your safety is not put at risk. A moment's lack of attention can result in an accident, as can failure to observe simple precautions.

There will always be new ways of having accidents, and the following is not a comprehensive list of all dangers; it is intended rather to make you aware of the risks and to encourage a safe approach to all work you carry out on your bike.

Asbestos

● Certain friction, insulating, sealing and other products - such as brake pads, clutch linings, gaskets, etc. - contain asbestos. Extreme care must be taken to avoid inhalation of dust from such products since it is hazardous to health. If in doubt, assume that they do contain asbestos.

Fire

● Remember at all times that petrol is highly flammable. Never smoke or have any kind of naked flame around, when working on the vehicle. But the risk does not end there - a spark caused by an electrical short-circuit, by two metal surfaces contacting each other, by careless use of tools, or even by static electricity built up in your body under certain conditions, can ignite petrol vapour, which in a confined space is highly explosive. Never use petrol as a cleaning solvent. Use an approved safety solvent.

● Always disconnect the battery earth terminal before working on any part of the fuel or electrical system, and never risk spilling fuel on to a hot engine or exhaust.

● It is recommended that a fire extinguisher of a type suitable for fuel and electrical fires is kept handy in the garage or workplace at all times. Never try to extinguish a fuel or electrical fire with water.

Fumes

● Certain fumes are highly toxic and can quickly cause unconsciousness and even death if inhaled to any extent. Petrol vapour comes into this category, as do the vapours from certain solvents such as trichloroethylene. Any draining or pouring of such volatile fluids should be done in a well ventilated area.

● When using cleaning fluids and solvents, read the instructions carefully. Never use materials from unmarked containers - they may give off poisonous vapours.

● Never run the engine of a motor vehicle in an enclosed space such as a garage. Exhaust fumes contain carbon monoxide which is extremely poisonous; if you need to run the engine, always do so in the open air or at least have the rear of the vehicle outside the workplace.

The battery

● Never cause a spark, or allow a naked light near the vehicle's battery. It will normally be giving off a certain amount of hydrogen gas, which is highly explosive.

● Always disconnect the battery ground (earth) terminal before working on the fuel or electrical systems (except where noted).

● If possible, loosen the filler plugs or cover when charging the battery from an external source. Do not charge at an excessive rate or the battery may burst.

● Take care when topping up, cleaning or carrying the battery. The acid electrolyte, evenwhen diluted, is very corrosive and should not be allowed to contact the eyes or skin. Always wear rubber gloves and goggles or a face shield. If you ever need to prepare electrolyte yourself, always add the acid slowly to the water; never add the water to the acid.

Electricity

● When using an electric power tool, inspection light etc., always ensure that the appliance is correctly connected to its plug and that, where necessary, it is properly grounded (earthed). Do not use such appliances in damp conditions and, again, beware of creating a spark or applying excessive heat in the vicinity of fuel or fuel vapour. Also ensure that the appliances meet national safety standards.

● A severe electric shock can result from touching certain parts of the electrical system, such as the spark plug wires (HT leads), when the engine is running or being cranked, particularly if components are damp or the insulation is defective. Where an electronic ignition system is used, the secondary (HT) voltage is much higher and could prove fatal.

Remember...

✗ **Don't** start the engine without first ascertaining that the transmission is in neutral.

✗ **Don't** suddenly remove the pressure cap from a hot cooling system - cover it with a cloth and release the pressure gradually first, or you may get scalded by escaping coolant.

✗ **Don't** attempt to drain oil until you are sure it has cooled sufficiently to avoid scalding you.

✗ **Don't** grasp any part of the engine or exhaust system without first ascertaining that it is cool enough not to burn you.

✗ **Don't** allow brake fluid or antifreeze to contact the machine's paintwork or plastic components.

✗ **Don't** siphon toxic liquids such as fuel, hydraulic fluid or antifreeze by mouth, or allow them to remain on your skin.

✗ **Don't** inhale dust - it may be injurious to health (see Asbestos heading).

✗ **Don't** allow any spilled oil or grease to remain on the floor - wipe it up right away, before someone slips on it.

✗ **Don't** use ill-fitting spanners or other tools which may slip and cause injury.

✗ **Don't** lift a heavy component which may be beyond your capability - get assistance.

✗ **Don't** rush to finish a job or take unverified short cuts.

✗ **Don't** allow children or animals in or around an unattended vehicle.

✗ **Don't** inflate a tyre above the recommended pressure. Apart from overstressing the carcass, in extreme cases the tyre may blow off forcibly.

✔ **Do** ensure that the machine is supported securely at all times. This is especially important when the machine is blocked up to aid wheel or fork removal.

✔ **Do** take care when attempting to loosen a stubborn nut or bolt. It is generally better to pull on a spanner, rather than push, so that if you slip, you fall away from the machine rather than onto it.

✔ **Do** wear eye protection when using power tools such as drill, sander, bench grinder etc.

✔ **Do** use a barrier cream on your hands prior to undertaking dirty jobs - it will protect your skin from infection as well as making the dirt easier to remove afterwards; but make sure your hands aren't left slippery. Note that long-term contact with used engine oil can be a health hazard.

✔ **Do** keep loose clothing (cuffs, ties etc. and long hair) well out of the way of moving mechanical parts.

✔ **Do** remove rings, wristwatch etc., before working on the vehicle - especially the electrical system.

✔ **Do** keep your work area tidy - it is only too easy to fall over articles left lying around.

✔ **Do** exercise caution when compressing springs for removal or installation. Ensure that the tension is applied and released in a controlled manner, using suitable tools which preclude the possibility of the spring escaping violently.

✔ **Do** ensure that any lifting tackle used has a safe working load rating adequate for the job.

✔ **Do** get someone to check periodically that all is well, when working alone on the vehicle.

✔ **Do** carry out work in a logical sequence and check that everything is correctly assembled and tightened afterwards.

✔ **Do** remember that your vehicle's safety affects that of yourself and others. If in doubt on any point, get professional advice.

● If in spite of following these precautions, you are unfortunate enough to injure yourself, seek medical attention as soon as possible.

Frame and engine numbers

The frame serial number is stamped into a plate on the left side of the frame near the front. The engine serial number is on the crankcase near the oil filler cap. Both of these numbers should be recorded and kept in a safe place so they can be furnished to law enforcement officials in the event of theft.

The frame serial number, engine serial number and carburetor identification number should also be kept in a handy place (such as with your driver's license) so they are always available when purchasing or ordering parts for your machine.

The models covered by this manual are as follows:

Katana 600 (GSX600F), 1988 on (US)
GSX600F, January 1988 through 1995 (UK)
GSX-R750, 1986 through 1992 (US)
GSX-R750, March 1985 through 1992 (UK)
Katana 750, 1989 on (US)
GSX750F, January 1989 on (UK)
Katana 1100, 1988 through 1993 (US)
GSX1100F, October 1987 on (UK)
GSX-R1100, 1986 through 1992 (US)
GSX-R1100, March 1986 through 1992 (UK)

Model year identification

Suzuki uses a letter code to designate model years, as follows:

F - 1985	K - 1989	P - 1993
G - 1986	L - 1990	R - 1994
H - 1987	M - 1991	S - 1995
J - 1988	N - 1992	T - 1996

US

To identify the model year on a US bike, look at the first digit of the second part of the frame number. For example, the frame number JS1GR75A-G2100001 indicates a 1986 model, because G (the code for 1986) is the first digit of the second part of the frame number.

UK

On UK bikes, the model year code doesn't appear in the frame number. Instead, refer to the accompanying table, which lists the starting frame number for each model and year.

Buying spare parts

Once you have found all the identification numbers, record them for reference when buying parts. Since the manufacturers change specifications, parts and vendors (companies that manufacture various components on the machine), providing the ID numbers is the only way to be reasonably sure that you are buying the correct parts.

Whenever possible, take the worn part to the dealer so direct comparison with the new component can be made. Along the trail from the manufacturer to the parts shelf, there are numerous places that the part can end up with the wrong number or be listed incorrectly.

The two places to purchase new parts for your motorcycle - the accessory store and the franchised dealer - differ in the type of parts they carry. While dealers can obtain virtually every part for your motorcycle, the accessory dealer is usually limited to normal high wear items such as shock absorbers, tune-up parts, various engine gaskets, cables, chains, brake parts, etc. Rarely will an accessory outlet have major suspension components, cylinders, transmission gears, or cases.

Used parts can be obtained for roughly half the price of new ones, but you can't always be sure of what you're getting. Once again, take your worn part to the wrecking yard (breaker) for direct comparison.

Whether buying new, used or rebuilt parts, the best course is to deal directly with someone who specializes in parts for your particular make.

UK model	Year	Code	Starting frame number
GSX-R750	1985	F	GR75A-100001
	1986	G	GR75A-107368
	1987	H	GR75A-112130
	1988	J	GR77A-100001
	1989	K	GR77A-104392
	1990	L	GR7AA-100034
	1991	M	GR7AA-100001
	1992	N	Not available
GSX-R1100	1986	G	GU74B-100001
	1987	H	GU74B-103282
	1988	J	GU74B-106265
	1989	K	GV73B-100001
	1990	L	GV73B-103392
	1991	M	GV73B-106082
	1992	N	GV73B-108660
GSX600F	1988	J	GN72A-100001 to 103968
			GN72A-103979 to 104098
	1989	K	GN72A-103969 to 103978
			GN72A-104099
	1990	L	GN72A-106385
	1991	M	GN72A-110633
	1992	N	GN72A-115034
	1993	P	GN72A-118194
	1994	R	GN72A-121465
	1995 on	S	GN72A-123718
GSX750F	1989	K	GR78A-100001
	1990	L	GR78A-105765
	1991	M	GR78A-113118
	1992	N	GR78A-119920
	1993	P	GR78A-125061
	1994	R	GR78A-131112
	1995 on	S	GR78A-134162
GSX1100F	1988	J	GV72A-100001
	1989	K	GV72A-101093
	1990	L	GV72A-101223
	1991	M	GV72A-101584
	1992	N	GV72A-101990
	1993	P	GV72D-101019
	1994 on	R	GV72A-102304

The frame number is stamped on a plate on the left side of the frame . . .

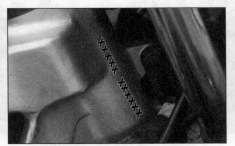

. . . as well as on the steering head

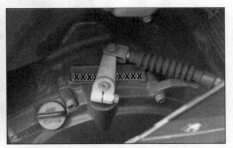

The engine number is stamped on the crankcase near the oil filler cap

1 Brake and clutch fluid levels

⚠ **Warning: Brake hydraulic fluid can harm your eyes and damage painted surfaces, so use extreme caution when handling and pouring it and cover surrounding surfaces with rag. Do not use fluid that has been standing open for some time, as it absorbs moisture from the air which can cause a dangerous loss of braking/clutch effectiveness.**

Before you start:
✔ Make sure you have the correct hydraulic fluid - DOT 4.
✔ With the motorcycle on the centerstand, turn the handlebars until the top of the front brake (or clutch) master cylinder is as level as possible. If necessary, loosen the lever clamp bolts and rotate the master cylinder assembly slightly to make it level.

Bike care:
● The fluid in the front and rear brake master cylinder reservoirs will drop slightly as the brake pads wear down.
● If the fluid level was low or requires repeated topping-up, inspect the brake or clutch system for leaks.
● In order to ensure proper operation of the hydraulic disc brakes (and the clutch on hydraulic clutch models), the fluid level in the master cylinder reservoirs must be properly maintained.
● Check the operation of both brakes before taking the machine on the road; if there is evidence of air in the system (spongy feel to lever or pedal), it must be bled as described in Chapter 6. Similarly any air in the clutch system must be bled as described in Chapter 2.

1 Look closely at the inspection window in the master cylinder reservoir. Make sure that the fluid level is above the Lower line on the reservoir.

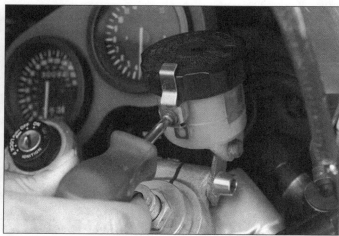

2 On models with a screw top cap (on other models the cap will be held by two screws), remove the security clamp . . .

3 . . . and remove the cap together with the rubber diaphragm.

4 Top up with DOT 4 hydraulic fluid until the level is above the lower level line.

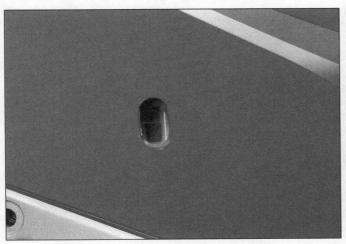

5 On some models, the rear reservoir is visible through an inspection hole in the fairing.

6 The rear reservoir is mounted to the frame. Remove the seat for access.

2 Engine/transmission oil level

Before you start:

✔ Place the motorcycle on the centerstand, then start the engine and allow it to reach normal operating temperature. Where no centerstand is fitted, support the motorcycle in an upright position using an auxiliary stand.

> Caution: Do not run the engine in an enclosed space such as a garage or shop.

✔ Stop the engine and allow the motorcycle to sit undisturbed on its stand for one minute. Make sure that the motorcycle is on level ground.

Bike care:

● If you have to add oil frequently, you should check whether you have any oil leaks. If there is no sign of oil leakage from the joints and gaskets the engine could be burning oil (see Fault Finding).

The correct oil
● Modern, high-revving engines place great demands on their oil. It is very important that the correct oil for your bike is used.
● Always top up with a good quality oil of the specified type and viscosity and do not overfill the engine.

Oil type	API grade SE or SF (min)
Oil viscosity	SAE 10W-40

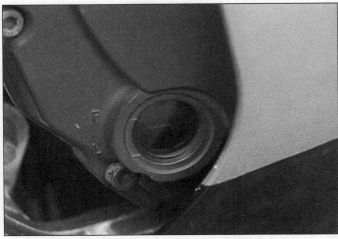

1 With the engine off and the motorcycle upright, check the oil level in the window located at the lower part of the right crankcase cover. The oil level should be between the F (full) and L (low) level marks next to the window.

2 If the level is below the Low mark, remove the oil filler cap from the right crankcase cover and add enough oil of the recommended grade and type to bring the level up to the F mark. Do not overfill.

3 Clutch operation (cable clutch)

Bike care:

● Correct clutch freeplay is necessary to ensure proper clutch operation and reasonable clutch service life. Freeplay normally changes because of cable stretch and clutch wear, so it should be checked and adjusted periodically.

● If the lever is stiff to operate and doesn;t return quickly, lubricate the cable (see Chapter 1).

● Refer to the table for freeplay measurement. Too little freeplay may result in the clutch not engaging completely (slip). If there is too much freeplay, the clutch might not release fully (drag).

● If a small amount of cable adjustment is required, use the fine adjuster at the top of the cable. If a large amount of adjustment is required, use the coarse adjuster at the lower end of the cable. If no more cable adjustment is possible, go on to check the freeplay in the clutch release mechanism as described in Chapter 1 (GSX600F and GSX750F models), or replace the clutch cable with a new one (GSX-R750 models).

Model	Freeplay
GSX600F - 1988 through 1993 models	4 mm (0.16 inch) at lever stock
GSX600F - 1994-on models	10 to 15 mm (0.4 to 0.6 inch) at lever end
GSX750F - 1989 through 1994 models	2 to 3 mm (0.08 to 0.12 inch) at lever stock
GSX750F - 1995-on models	10 to 15 mm (0.4 to 0.6 inch) at lever end
GSX-R750 models	2 to 3 mm (0.08 to 0.12 inch) at lever stock

1 Clutch cable freeplay measurement at lever stock. Pull in on the lever until resistance is felt, then note how far the lever has moved away from its stock at the pivot end.

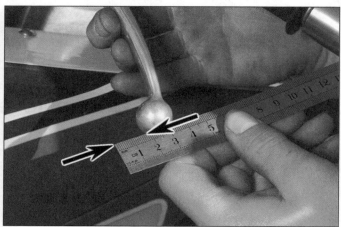

2 Clutch cable freeplay measurement at lever end. Pull in on the lever until resistance is felt, then note how far the lever ball end is from its at-rest position.

3 A small amount of adjustment can be made using the fine adjuster at the clutch lever. Always retighten the lockwheel (where fitted) once the adjustment is complete.

4 On GSX600F and GSX750F models use the cable lower (coarse) adjuster on the engine left side for large amounts of adjustment. Tighten the locknut when adjustment is complete.

5 On GSX-R750 models use the cable lower (coarse) adjuster on the engine right side for large amounts of adjustment. Tighten the locknut when adjustment is complete.

4 Tires

The correct pressures:

● The tires must be checked when **cold**, not immediately after riding. Note that low tire pressures may cause the tire to slip on the rim or come off. High tire pressures will cause abnormal tread wear and unsafe handling.

● Use an accurate pressure gauge.

● Proper air pressure will increase tire life and provide maximum stability and ride comfort.

Tire care:

● Check the tires carefully for cuts, tears, embedded nails or other sharp objects and excessive wear. Operation of the motorcycle with excessively worn tires is extremely hazardous, as traction and handling are directly affected.

● Check the condition of the tire valve and ensure the dust cap is in place.

● Pick out any stones or nails which may have become embedded in the tire tread. If left, they will eventually penetrate through the casing and cause a puncture.

● If tire damage is apparent, or unexplained loss of pressure is experienced, seek the advice of a tire fitting specialist without delay.

Tire tread depth:

● At the time of writing UK law requires that tread depth must be at least 1 mm over 3/4 of the tread breadth all the way around the tire, with no bald patches. Many riders, however, consider 2 mm tread depth minimum to be a safer limit. Suzuki recommend a minimum tread depth of 1.6 mm (0.06 inch) on the front and 2 mm (0.08 inch) on the rear.

● Many tires now incorporate wear indicators in the tread. Identify the triangular pointer or TWI marking on the tire sidewall to locate the indicator bar and replace the tire if the tread has worn down to the bar.

1 Check the tire pressures when the tires are **cold** and keep them properly inflated.

2 Measure the tread depth at the center of the tire using a tread depth gauge.

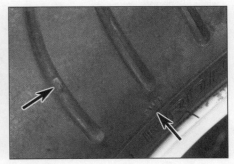

3 Tire tread wear indicator bar and its location marking on the sidewall (arrows).

Loading/speed	Front	Rear
GSX600F models	33 psi (2.27 Bar)	36 psi (2.48 Bar)
GSX-R750 - 1985 through 1989 models:		
Solo riding	36 psi (2.48 Bar)	36 psi (2.48 Bar)
With passenger	36 psi (2.48 Bar)	42 psi (2.89 Bar)
GSX-R750 1990-on models	33 psi (2.27 Bar)	36 psi (2.48 Bar)
GSX750F model - solo riding	36 psi (2.48 Bar)	36 psi (2.48 Bar)
GSX750F model - with passenger	36 psi (2.48 Bar)	42 psi (2.89 Bar)
GSX-R1100 - 1986 through 1988 models:		
Solo riding	36 psi (2.48 Bar)	36 psi (2.48 Bar)
With passenger	36 psi (2.48 Bar)	42 psi (2.89 Bar)
GSX-R1100 1989 model:		
Solo riding	33 psi (2.27 Bar)	36 psi (2.48 Bar)
With passenger	36 psi (2.48 Bar)	42 psi (2.89 Bar)
GSX-R1100 1990 model:		
Solo riding	32 psi (2.20 Bar)	36 psi (2.48 Bar)
With passenger	32 psi (2.20 Bar)	42 psi (2.89 Bar
GSX-R1100 1991-on models	33 psi (2.27 Bar)	36 psi (2.48 Bar)
GSX1100F models	36 psi (2.48 Bar)	42 psi (2.89 Bar)

5 Suspension, steering and drive chain

Suspension and steering:
● Make sure the steering operates smoothly, without looseness and without binding.

● Check front and rear suspension for smooth operation.

Drive chain:
● Make sure the drive chain isn't out of adjustment.
● Make sure the drive chain is adequately lubricated.

6 Legal and safety checks

Lighting and signalling:
● Take a minute to check that the headlight, taillight, brake light and turn signals all work correctly.
● Check that the horn sounds when the switch is operated.
● A working speedometer is a statutory requirement in the UK.

Safety:
● Check that the throttle grip rotates smoothly and snaps shut when released, in all steering positions.
● Check that the engine shuts off when the kill switch is operated.
● Check that sidestand return spring holds the stand securely up when retracted. The same applies to the centerstand (where fitted).
● Following the procedure in your owner's manual, check the operation of the sidestand switch.

Fuel:
● This may seem obvious, but check that you have enough fuel to complete your journey. If you notice signs of fuel leakage - rectify the cause immediately.
● Ensure you use the correct grade fuel - see Chapter 3 Specifications.

Chapter 1
Routine maintenance and Servicing

Contents

Degrees of difficulty

Easy, suitable for novice with little experience 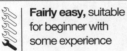	**Fairly easy,** suitable for beginner with some experience 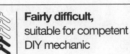	**Fairly difficult,** suitable for competent DIY mechanic	**Difficult,** suitable for experienced DIY mechanic	**Very difficult,** suitable for expert DIY or professional

Specifications

Katana 600 (GSX600F) model

Engine

Spark plugs
  Type
    1988 through 1995
      Standard .... NGK DR8ES
      Hot type (1) .... NGK DR8ES-L
    1996
      Standard .... NGK CR9EK
      Hot type (1) .... NGK CR8EK
  Gap .... 0.6 to 0.7 mm (0.024 to 0.028 inch)
Engine idle speed
  1988 and 1989 UK .... 1100 +/-100 rpm
  All others .... 1300 +/-100 rpm
Valve clearances (COLD engine)
  Screw-type valve adjusters .... 0.10 to 0.15 mm (0.004 to 0.006 inch)
  Shim-type valve adjusters
    Intake .... 0.10 to 0.20 mm (0.004 to 0.008 inch)
    Exhaust .... 0.15 to 0.25 mm (0.006 to 0.010 inch)
Cylinder compression pressure
  Standard .... 9.78 to 14.67 bars (142 to 213 psi)
  Minimum .... 7.85 bars (114 psi)
  Maximum variation .... 1.93 bars (28 psi)
Cylinder numbering (from left side to right side of bike) 1-2-3-4

Katana 600 (GSX600F) model (continued)
Miscellaneous

Brake pad minimum thickness	To limit line
Brake pedal height	45 mm (1.8 inch) below top of footpeg

Freeplay adjustments
Throttle cable	0.5 to 1.0 mm (0.020 to 0.040 inch)

Clutch cable
1988 through 1993 models	4 mm (0.16 inch)
1994-on models	10 to 15 mm (0.4 to 0.6 inch)

Drive chain
Slack
Standard	25 to 35 mm (1.0 to 1.4 inch)
Service limit	1.77 inch (45 mm)
21-pin length	319.4 mm (12.6 inch)
Battery electrolyte specific gravity	1.28 at 20 degrees C (68 degrees F)

Minimum tire tread depth (2)
Front	1.6 mm (0.060 inch)
Rear	2.0 mm (0.080 inch)

Tire pressures (cold)
Front	2.27 bars (33 psi)
Rear	2.48 bars (36 psi)

Recommended lubricants and fluids

Engine/transmission oil
Type	API grade SE or SF (minimum)
Viscosity	SAE 10W-40

Capacity
With filter change	3.8 liters (4.0 US qt, 6.7 Imp pt)
Oil change only	3.6 liters (3.8 US qt, 6.3 Imp pt)
Engine overhaul	5.0 liters (5.3 US qt, 8.8 Imp pt)
Brake fluid	DOT 4

Fork oil
Type	SAE 10 - fork oil

Amount
1988	460 cc (15.5 US fl oz, 16.2 Imp fl oz)
1989 on	478 cc (16.1 US fl oz, 16.8 Imp fl oz)

Oil level
1988	134 mm (5.28 inch)
1989 on	100 mm (3.93 inch)
Drive chain	20W-50 engine oil (not chain lube)
Cables and lever pivots	Chain and cable lubricant or 10W30 motor oil
Sidestand/centerstand pivots	Medium-weight, lithium-based multi-purpose grease
Brake pedal/shift lever pivots	Chain and cable lubricant or 10W30 motor oil
Throttle grip	Multi-purpose grease or dry film lubricant

Torque specifications

Oil drain plug	20 to 25 Nm (18 to 25 ft-lbs)

Spark plugs
New plugs	1/2 turn after gasket touches engine
Used plugs	1/4 turn after gasket touches engine
Valve cover bolts	See Chapter 2

GSX-R750 model
Engine

Spark plugs
Type
1985 through 1987
Standard type	NGK D9EA
Hot type	NGK D8EA

1988 and 1989
Standard type	NGK JR9C
Hot type	NGK JR8C
1990 on	NGK CR10EK, ND U31ETR
Gap	0.6 to 0.7 mm (0.024 to 0.028 inch)

Engine idle speed
1985 through 1990	1100+/-100 rpm
1991 on	1200+/-100 rpm

Valve clearances (COLD engine)
  Screw-type valve adjusters
    1985 through 1988 . . . . 0.09 to 0.13 mm (0.004 to 0.005 inch)
    1989 and 1990
      Intake . . . . 0.10 to 0.15 mm (0.004 to 0.006 inch)
      Exhaust . . . . 0.18 to 0.23 mm (0.007 to 0.009 inch)
  Shim-type valve adjusters
    Intake . . . . 0.10 to 0.20 mm (0.004 to 0.008 inch)
    Exhaust . . . . 0.15 to 0.25 mm (0.006 to 0.010 inch)
Cylinder compression pressure
  Standard . . . . 9.78 to 13.71 bars (142 to 199 psi)
  Minimum . . . . 7.85 bars (114 psi)
  Maximum variation . . . . 1.93 bars (28 psi)
Cylinder numbering (from left side to right side of bike) 1-2-3-4

Miscellaneous

Brake pad minimum thickness . . . . To limit line
Brake pedal height
  1985 through 1987 . . . . 60 mm (2.4 inch) below top of footpeg
  1988 on . . . . 58 to 68 mm (2.3 to 2.6 inch)
Freeplay adjustments
  Throttle cable . . . . 0.5 to 1.0 mm (0.020 to 0.040 inch)
  Clutch cable (where applicable) . . . . 2 to 3 mm (0.08 to 0.12 inch)
Drive chain
  Slack
    1985 . . . . 30 to 35 mm (1.2 to 1.4 inch)
    1986 through 1989 . . . . 25 to 30 mm (1.0 to 1.2 inch)
    1990 on . . . . 25 to 35 mm (1.0 to 1.4 inch)
  21-pin length . . . . 319.4 mm (12.6 inch)
Battery electrolyte specific gravity . . . . 1.28 at 20 degrees C (68 degrees F)
Minimum tire tread depth (2)
  Front . . . . 1.6 mm (0.060 inch)
  Rear . . . . 2.0 mm (0.080 inch)
Tire pressures (cold)
  1985 through 1989
    Front . . . . 2.48 bars (36 psi)
    Rear (single rider) . . . . 2.48 bars (36 psi)
    Rear (rider and passenger) . . . . 2.89 bars (42 psi)
  1990 on
    Front . . . . 2.27 bars (33 psi)
    Rear . . . . 2.48 bars (36 psi)

Recommended lubricants and fluids

Engine/transmission oil
  Type . . . . API grade SE or SF (minimum)
  Viscosity . . . . SAE 10W-40
  Capacity
    With filter change . . . . 3.8 liters (4.0 US qt, 6.7 Imp pt)
    Oil change only . . . . 3.6 liters (3.8 US qt, 6.3 Imp pt)
    Engine overhaul . . . . 5.0 liters (5.3 US qt, 8.8 Imp pt)
Brake fluid . . . . DOT 4
Fork oil
  Type
    1985 through 1987 . . . . SAE 15 - fork oil
    1988 on . . . . SAE 10 - fork oil
  Amount
    1985 through 1987 . . . . 456 cc (15.4 US fl oz, 16.1 Imp fl oz)
    1988 . . . . 407 cc (13.7 US fl oz, 14.3 Imp fl oz)
    1989 . . . . 416 cc (14.1 US fl oz, 14.6 Imp fl oz)
    1990 . . . . 428 cc (14.5 US fl oz, 15.1 Imp fl oz)
    1991 on
      US, Canada . . . . 452 cc (15.1 US fl oz, 15.9 Imp fl oz)
      UK . . . . 462 cc (15.6 US fl oz, 16.3 Imp fl oz)
  Oil level
    1985 through 1987 . . . . 107 mm (4.2 inch)
    1988 and 1989 . . . . 141 mm (5.55 inch)
    1990 . . . . 132 mm (5.2 inch)
    1991 on
      US, Canada . . . . 123 mm (4.8 inch)
      UK . . . . 107 mm (4.2 inch)

1

GSX-R750 model (continued)

Drive chain . . . . 20W-50 engine oil (not chain lube)
Cables and lever pivots . . . . Chain and cable lubricant or 10W30 motor oil
Sidestand/centerstand pivots . . . . Medium-weight, lithium-based multi-purpose grease
Brake pedal/shift lever pivots . . . . Chain and cable lubricant or 10W30 motor oil
Throttle grip . . . . Multi-purpose grease or dry film lubricant

Torque specifications

Oil drain plug . . . . 20 to 25 Nm (18 to 25 ft-lbs)
Spark plugs
   New plugs . . . . 1/2 turn after gasket touches engine
   Used plugs . . . . 1/4 turn after gasket touches engine
Valve cover bolts . . . . See Chapter 2

Katana 750 (GSX750F) model

Engine

Spark plugs
   Type
      Standard . . . . NGK JR9C
      Hot type (1) . . . . NGK JR8C
   Gap . . . . 0.6 to 0.7 mm (0.024 to 0.028 inch)
Engine idle speed . . . . 1100+/-100 rpm
Valve clearances (COLD engine)
   Intake . . . . 0.10 to 0.15 mm (0.004 to 0.006 inch)
   Exhaust . . . . 0.18 to 0.23 mm (0.007 to 0.009 inch)
Cylinder compression pressure
   Standard . . . . 9.78 to 13.71 bars (142 to 199 psi)
   Minimum . . . . 7.85 bars (114 psi)
   Maximum variation . . . . 1.93 bars (28 psi)
Cylinder numbering (from left side to right side of bike) 1-2-3-4

Miscellaneous

Brake pad minimum thickness . . . . To limit line
Brake pedal height . . . . 45 mm (1.8 inch) below top of footpeg
Freeplay adjustments
   Throttle cable . . . . 0.5 to 1.0 mm (0.020 to 0.040 inch)
   Clutch cable
      1989 through 1994 models . . . . 2 to 3 mm (0.080 to 0.120 inch)
      1995-on models . . . . 10 to 15 mm (0.4 to 0.6 inch)
Drive chain
   Slack . . . . 30 to 40 mm (1.2 to 1.6 inch)
   21-pin length . . . . 319.4 mm (12.6 inch)
Battery electrolyte specific gravity . . . . 1.28 at 20 degrees C (68 degrees F)
Minimum tire tread depth (2)
   Front . . . . 1.6 mm (0.060 inch)
   Rear . . . . 2.0 mm (0.080 inch)
Tire pressures (cold)
   Front . . . . 2.48 bars (36 psi)
   Rear
      Single rider . . . . 2.48 bars (36 psi)
      Rider and passenger . . . . 2.89 bars (42 psi)

Recommended lubricants and fluids

Engine/transmission oil
   Type . . . . API grade SE or SF (minimum)
   Viscosity . . . . SAE 10W-40
   Capacity
      With filter change . . . . 3.9 liters (4.1 US qt, 6.9 Imp pt)
      Oil change only . . . . 3.6 liters (3.8 US qt, 6.3 Imp pt)
      Engine overhaul . . . . 4.9 liters (5.2 US qt, 8.6 Imp pt)
Brake fluid . . . . DOT 4
Fork oil
   Type . . . . SAE 10 - fork oil
   Amount . . . . 491 cc (16.6 US fl oz, 17.3 Imp fl oz)
   Oil level . . . . 97.3 mm (3.83 inches)

Drive chain	20W-50 engine oil (not chain lube)
Cables and lever pivots	Chain and cable lubricant or 10W30 motor oil
Sidestand/centerstand pivots	Medium-weight, lithium-based multi-purpose grease
Brake pedal/shift lever pivots	Chain and cable lubricant or 10W30 motor oil
Throttle grip	Multi-purpose grease or dry film lubricant

Torque specifications

Oil drain plug	20 to 25 Nm (18 to 25 ft-lbs)
Spark plugs	
New plugs	1/2 turn after gasket touches engine
Used plugs	1/4 turn after gasket touches engine
Valve cover bolts	See Chapter 2

GSX-R1100 model

Engine

Spark plugs	
Type	
1986 through 1988	NGK J9A
1989 on	
Standard	NGK JR9B
Hot type (1)	NGK JR10B
Gap	0.6 to 0.7 mm (0.024 to 0.028 inch)
Engine idle speed	
1986 through 1988	1100+/-100 rpm
1989 on	
US (except California)	1200+/-100 rpm
UK, Canada, California	1100+/-100 rpm
Valve clearances (COLD engine)	
Screw-type valve adjusters	
1986 through 1988	0.10 to 0.15 mm (0.004 to 0.006 inch)
1989 and 1990	
Intake	0.10 to 0.15 mm (0.004 to 0.006 inch)
Exhaust	0.18 to 0.23 mm (0.007 to 0.009 inch)
Shim-type valve adjusters	
Intake	0.10 to 0.20 mm (0.004 to 0.008 inch)
Exhaust	0.15 to 0.25 mm (0.006 to 0.010 inch)
Cylinder compression pressure	
1986 through 1988	
Standard	9.78 to 13.71 bars (142 to 199 psi)
Minimum	7.85 bars (114 psi)
Maximum variation	1.93 bars (28 psi)
1989 on	
Standard	11.78 to 13.71 bars (170 to 199 psi)
Minimum	9.78 bars (142 psi)
Maximum variation	1.93 bars (28 psi)
Cylinder numbering (from left side to right side of bike)	1-2-3-4

Miscellaneous

Brake pad minimum thickness	To limit line
Brake pedal height	
1986 through 1988	55 mm (2.2 inch) below top of footpeg
1989 on	65 mm (2.6 inch) below top of footpeg
Freeplay adjustments	
Throttle cable	0.5 to 1.0 mm (0.020 to 0.040 inch)
Drive chain	
Slack	
1986 through 1988	20 to 25 mm (0.8 to 1.0 inch)
1989 and 1990	25 to 30 mm (1.0 to 1.2 inch)
1991 on	25 to 35 mm (1.0 to 1.4 inch)
21-pin length	319.4 mm (12.6 inch)
Battery electrolyte specific gravity	1.28 at 20 degrees C (68 degrees F)
Minimum tire tread depth (2)	
Front	1.6 mm (0.060 inch)
Rear	2.0 mm (0.080 inch)

1

Tire pressures (cold)
  1986 through 1988
    Front .... 2.48 bars (36 psi)
    Rear (single rider) .... 2.48 bars (36 psi)
    Rear (rider and passenger) .... 2.89 bars (42 psi)
  1989
    Front (single rider) .... 2.27 bars (33 psi)
    Front (rider and passenger) .... 2.48 bars (36 psi
    Rear (single rider) .... 2.48 bars (36 psi)
    Rear (rider and passenger) .... 2.89 bars (42 psi)
  1990
    Front .... 2.20 bars (32 psi)
    Rear (single rider) .... 2.48 bars (36 psi)
    Rear (rider and passenger) .... 2.89 bars (42 psi)
  1991 on
    Front .... 2.27 bars (33 psi)
    Rear .... 2.48 bars (36 psi)

Recommended lubricants and fluids

Engine/transmission oil
  Type .... API grade SE or SF (minimum)
  Viscosity .... SAE 10W-40
  Capacity
    1986 through 1988
      With filter change .... 3.7 liters (3.9 US qt, 6.5 Imp pt)
      Oil change only .... 3.4 liters (3.6 US qt, 6.0 Imp pt)
      Engine overhaul .... 4.7 liters (5.0 US qt, 8.3 Imp pt)
    1989 on
      With filter change .... 4.2 liters (4.4 US qt, 7.4 Imp pt)
      Oil change only .... 4.0 liters (4.2 US qt, 7.0 Imp pt)
      Engine overhaul .... 5.1 liters (5.4 US qt, 9.0 Imp pt)
Brake and clutch fluid .... DOT 4
Fork oil
  Type
    1986 through 1988 .... SAE 15 - fork oil
    1989 and 1990 .... SAE 5 - fork oil
    1991 on .... Suzuki fork oil L01
  Amount
    1986 through 1988 .... 417 cc (14.1 US fl oz, 14.7 Imp fl oz)
    1989
      US .... 453 cc (15.3 US fl oz, 15.9 Imp fl oz)
      UK and Canada .... 418 cc (14.1 US fl oz, 14.7 Imp fl oz)
    1990 .... 415 cc (14.0 US fl oz, 14.6 Imp fl oz)
    1990 .... 428 cc (14.5 US fl oz, 15.1 Imp fl oz)
    1991 on .... 398 cc (13.5 US fl oz, 14.0 Imp fl oz)
  Oil level
    1986 through 1988 .... 159 mm (6.26 inch)
    1989
      US .... 113 mm (4.45 inches)
      UK and Canada .... 146 mm (5.75 inches)
    1990 .... 145 mm (5.71 inches)
    1991 on .... 131 mm (5.16 inches)
Drive chain .... 20W-50 engine oil (not chain lube)
Cables and lever pivots .... Chain and cable lubricant or 10W30 motor oil
Sidestand/centerstand pivots .... Medium-weight, lithium-based multi-purpose grease
Brake pedal/shift lever pivots .... Chain and cable lubricant or 10W30 motor oil
Throttle grip .... Multi-purpose grease or dry film lubricant

Torque specifications

Oil drain plug .... 20 to 25 Nm (15 to 18 ft-lbs)
Spark plugs
  New plugs .... 1/2 turn after gasket touches engine
  Used plugs .... 1/4 turn after gasket touches engine
Valve cover bolts .... See Chapter 2

Katana 1100 (GSX1100F) model

Engine

Spark plugs
Type
Standard (1988 and 1989) .... NGK JR9B or J9B
Standard (1990 on) .... NGK JR9B
Cold type (UK models)(3) JR10B
Gap .... 0.6 to 0.7 mm (0.024 to 0.028 inch)
Engine idle speed .... 1100+/-100 rpm
Valve clearances (COLD engine)
Intake .... 0.10 to 0.15 mm (0.004 to 0.006 inch)
Exhaust .... 0.18 to 0.23 mm (0.007 to 0.009 inch)
Cylinder compression pressure
Standard .... 10.75 to 14.67 bars (156 to 213 psi)
Minimum .... 8.81 bars (128 psi)
Maximum variation .... 1.93 bars (28 psi)
Cylinder numbering (from left side to right side of bike) 1-2-3-4

Miscellaneous

Brake pad minimum thickness .... To limit line
Brake pedal height .... 50 mm (2.0 inch) below top of footpeg
Freeplay adjustments
Throttle cable .... 0.5 to 1.0 mm (0.020 to 0.040 inch)
Drive chain
Slack .... 20 to 25 mm (0.8 to 1.0 inch)
21-pin length .... 319.4 mm (12.6 inch)
Battery electrolyte specific gravity .... 1.28 at 20 degrees C (68 degrees F)
Minimum tire tread depth (2)
Front .... 1.6 mm (0.060 inch)
Rear .... 2.0 mm (0.080 inch)
Tire pressures (cold)
Front .... 2.48 bars (36 psi)
Rear .... 2.89 bars (42 psi)

Torque specifications

Oil drain plug .... 20 to 25 Nm (18 to 25 ft-lbs)
Spark plugs
New plugs .... 1/2 turn after gasket touches engine
Used plugs .... 1/4 turn after gasket touches engine
Valve cover bolts .... See Chapter 2

Recommended lubricants and fluids

Engine/transmission oil
Type .... API grade SE or SF (minimum)
Viscosity .... SAE 10W-40
Capacity
With filter change .... 4.5 liters (4.8 US qt, 7.9 Imp pt)
Oil change only .... 4.3 liters (4.5 US qt, 7.6 Imp pt)
Engine overhaul .... 5.5 liters (5.8 US qt, 9.7 Imp pt)
Brake and clutch fluid .... DOT 4
Fork oil
Type .... SAE 10 - fork oil
Amount
1988 .... 478 cc (16.2 US fl oz, 16.8 Imp fl oz)
1989 on .... 406 cc (13.7 US fl oz, 14.3 Imp fl oz)
Oil level
1988 .... 126 mm (4.92 inch)
1989 on .... 145.8 mm (5.74 inch)
Drive chain .... 20W-50 engine oil (not chain lube)
Cables and lever pivots .... Chain and cable lubricant or 10W-30 motor oil
Sidestand/centerstand pivots .... Medium-weight, lithium-based multi-purpose grease
Brake pedal/shift lever pivots .... Chain and cable lubricant or 10W-30 motor oil
Throttle grip .... Multi-purpose grease or dry film lubricant

1

(1) *Alternate hot-type plugs should be used if the standard plugs become carbon-fouled.*
(2) *In the UK, tread depth must be at least 1 mm over 3/4 of the tread breadth all the way around the tire, with no bald patches.*
(3) *Alternate cold-type plugs should be used if the standard plugs have white or glazed electrodes.*

Component locations on right side

1 Rear brake fluid reservoir
2 Air filter
3 Engine oil filler
4 Crankcase breather
5 Front brake fluid reservoir
6 Throttle cable upper adjusters
7 Brake pads
8 Engine oil filter
9 Clutch cable lower adjuster (early
   GSX-R750)
10 Engine oil sightglass
11 Rear brake light switch

Component locations on left side

1 Clutch fluid reservoir (hydraulic clutches)
2 Clutch cable upper adjuster (cable clutches)
3 Steering head bearings
4 Spark plugs and valves

5 Idle speed adjuster
6 Battery
7 Drive chain adjusters
8 Drive chain

9 Clutch cable lower adjuster (Katana 600/750, GSX600/750F)
10 Engine oil drain plug
11 Fork oil drain screw

1

The intervals listed below are the shortest intervals recommended by the manufacturer for each particular operation during the model years covered in this manual. Your owner's manual may have different intervals for your model.

Daily (pre-ride) checks
☐ See *'Daily (pre-ride) checks'* at the beginning of this manual

After the initial 600 miles (1000 km)
Note: *This check is usually performed by a Suzuki dealer after the first 1000 km (600 miles) from new. Thereafter, maintenance is carried out acccording to the following intervals of the schedule.*

Every 600 miles (1000 km)
Carry out all the items under the 'Daily (pre-ride) checks'
☐ Check, adjust and lubricate the drive chain (Section 1)

Every 2000 miles (3000 km)
Carry out all the items under the 600 miles (1000 km) check
☐ Clean the air filter element (Section 2)

Every 4000 miles (6000 km) or 12 months
Carry out all the items under the 2000 miles (3000 km) check
☐ Change the engine oil and filter (Section 3)
☐ Clean and gap the spark plugs (Section 4)
☐ Adjust the valve clearances (Section 5)
☐ Check the cylinder compression pressures (Section 6)
☐ Check/adjust the throttle operation/grip freeplay, and the idle speed (Section 7)
☐ Check the evaporative emission control system (California models) (Section 8)
☐ Inspect the crankcase breather (Section 9)
☐ Check the brake discs, pads, pedal position and hoses (Section 10 and Chapter 6)

Every 4000 miles (6000 km) or 12 months (continued)
☐ Check the fuel system and clean the filter (Section 11)
☐ Check and adjust the cable clutch (Section 12)
☐ Lubricate the clutch and brake lever pivots and the throttle cable upper end piece (Section 13)
☐ Lubricate the shift/brake lever pivots and the sidestand pivots (Section 13)
☐ Check the steering (Section 14)
☐ Check the tires and wheels (Section 15)
☐ Renew the fork oil (Section 16)
☐ Inspect the front and rear suspension (Section 17)
☐ Tighten cylinder head, exhaust pipe and chassis bolts and nuts (Section 18)
☐ Check battery specific gravity (Section 19)

Every 7500 miles (12,000 km) or 24 months
Carry out all the items under the 4000 miles (6000 km) check
☐ Replace the air filter element (Section 20)
☐ Replace the spark plugs (Section 21)

Every two years
☐ Change the brake fluid (Section 22)
☐ Change the clutch fluid (hydraulic clutch) (Section 23)

Every four years
☐ Replace the fuel hose (and vapor hose on California models) (Section 24)
☐ Replace the brake hoses (Section 25)
☐ Replace the clutch hose (hydraulic clutch) (Section 26)

Introduction

1 This Chapter covers in detail the checks and procedures necessary for the tune-up and routine maintenance of your motorcycle. The routine maintenance schedule is designed to keep the machine in proper running condition and prevent possible problems. The following Sections contain detailed procedures for carrying out the items listed on the maintenance schedule, as well as additional maintenance information designed to increase reliability.

2 Since routine maintenance plays such an important role in the safe and efficient operation of your motorcycle, it is presented here as a comprehensive check list. For the rider who does all his or her own maintenance, these lists outline the procedures and checks that should be done on a routine basis.

3 Deciding where to start or plug into the routine maintenance schedule depends on several factors. If you have a motorcycle whose warranty has recently expired, and if it has been maintained according to the warranty standards, you may want to pick up routine maintenance as it coincides with the next mileage or calendar interval. If you have owned the machine for some time but have never performed any maintenance on it, then you may want to start at the nearest interval and include some additional procedures to ensure that nothing important is overlooked. If you have just had a major engine overhaul, then you may want to start the maintenance routine from the beginning. If you have a used machine and have no knowledge of its history or maintenance record, you may desire to combine all the checks into one large service

initially and then settle into the maintenance schedule prescribed.

4 The Sections which outline the inspection and maintenance procedures are written as step-by-step comprehensive guides to the performance of the work. They explain in detail each of the routine inspections and maintenance procedures on the check list. References to additional information in applicable Chapters is also included and should not be overlooked.

5 Before beginning any maintenance or repair, the machine should be cleaned thoroughly, especially around the oil filter, spark plugs, valve cover, side covers, carburetors, etc. Cleaning will help ensure that dirt does not contaminate the engine and will allow you to detect wear and damage that could otherwise easily go unnoticed.

Every 600 miles (1000 km)

1 Drive chain and sprockets - cleaning, lubrication, check and adjustment

1 A neglected drive chain won't last long and can quickly damage the sprockets. Routine chain adjustment and lubrication isn't difficult and will ensure maximum chain and sprocket life.

2 The drive chain uses O-rings to permanently seal grease inside the links. Damaging the O-rings will allow the grease to leak out, ruining the chain. For this reason, it's important to use the correct cleaning and lubrication methods.

Cleaning and lubrication

3 At the recommended interval (or more often if the chain rusts), clean and oil the drive chain. Suzuki strongly recommends cleaning with kerosene, because it provides some lubrication and because other cleaners may damage the O-rings and allow grease to leak out.

4 After cleaning the chain, oil it. If you don't

have Suzuki chain lube, use 20W/50 engine oil. Don't use commercial chain lubricant, since it may damage the O-rings and let the grease leak out. Apply the oil to the area where the side plates overlap - not the middle of the rollers **(see illustration)**. After applying the oil, let it soak in a few minutes before wiping off any excess.

> **HAYNES HINT** *With the bike supported so its rear wheel is off the ground, hold the oil can tip near the edge of the chain and turn the wheel by hand as the oil emerges - repeat the procedure on the inside edge of the chain.*

Check

5 To check the chain, place the bike on its centerstand (if equipped) or support it so the rear wheel is off the ground and shift the transmission into Neutral. Make sure the ignition switch is off.

6 Push up on the bottom run of the chain and measure the slack midway between the two

sprockets **(see illustration)**, then compare your measurements to the value listed in this Chapter's Specifications.

7 As wear occurs, the chain will actually stretch, which means adjustment usually involves removing some slack from the chain. In some cases where lubrication has been neglected, corrosion and galling may cause the links to bind and kink, which effectively shortens the chain's length. If the chain is tight between the sprockets, rusty or kinked, it's time to replace it with a new one. **Note:** *Repeat the chain slack measurement along the length of the chain - ideally, every inch or so. If you find a tight area, mark it with felt pen or paint and repeat the measurement after the bike has been ridden. If the chain's still tight in the same area, it may be damaged or worn. Because a tight or kinked chain can damage the transmission output shaft bearing, it's a good idea to replace it.*

8 Remove the chain guard. Check the entire length of the chain for damaged rollers, loose links and pins.

9 Remove the cotter pin from the axle nut (if equipped). Loosen the nut **(see illustration)**.

1

1.4 Apply 20W/50 engine oil to the joints between the side plates and the rollers - not in the center of the rollers

1.6 Push up on the bottom run of the chain and measure how far it deflects - if it's not within the specified limits, adjust the slack in the chain

1.9 Remove the cotter pin (if equipped) from the axle nut, then loosen the nut

1.10a This chain adjuster design uses a nut, stud and bracket . . .

1.10b . . . this type uses a nut (arrow), a stud and a plate that fits on the end of the swingarm . . .

1.10c . . . and a third type has a locknut (arrow) which must be loosened so the adjuster bolt can be turned

10 Loosen the locknut (if equipped) on each chain adjuster. Tighten the adjusters evenly to remove all slack from the chain **(see illustrations)**, then measure the length of 21 pins along the top run. Rotate the wheel and repeat this check at several places on the chain, since it may wear unevenly. Compare your measurements with the maximum 21-pin length listed in this Chapter's Specifications. If any of your measurements exceed the maximum, replace the chain. **Note:** *Never install a new chain on old sprockets, and never use the old chain if you install new sprockets - replace the chain and sprockets as a set.*

11 Remove the shift lever and engine sprocket cover (see Chapter 6). Check the teeth on the engine sprocket and the rear sprocket for wear **(see illustration)**. Refer to Chapter 6 for the sprocket *diameter measurement procedure* if the sprockets appear to be worn excessively.

Adjustment

12 Rotate the rear wheel until the chain is positioned with the least amount of slack present.

13 Loosen the chain adjusters until the proper chain tension is obtained (get the adjuster on the chain side close, then set the

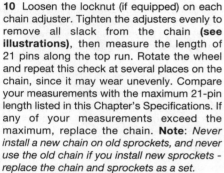

1.11 Check the sprockets in the areas indicated to see if they are worn excessively

adjuster on the opposite side). Be sure to turn the adjusters evenly to keep the rear wheel in alignment. If the adjusters reach the end of their travel, the chain is excessively worn and should be replaced with a new one (see Chapter 5).

14 When the chain has the correct amount of slack, make sure the marks on the adjusters correspond to the same relative marks on each side of the swingarm **(see illustration)**. Tighten the axle nut to the torque listed in the

1.14 When the adjuster bolts are set evenly, the adjuster marks on both sides should line up with the same marks in the swingarm, but don't rely completely on this; make a visual check of sprocket alignment as well

Chapter 5 Specifications, then install a new cotter pin (if equipped). If necessary, turn the nut an additional amount to line up the cotter pin hole with the castellations in the nut - don't loosen the nut to do this.

15 Tighten the adjuster locknuts (if equipped) securely.

Every 2000 miles (3000 km)

2 Air filter element - servicing

Katana 600 (GSX600F)

1 Remove the fuel tank and its bracket (see Chapter 3).

2 If the carburetor vent hoses are secured with tape, untape them (use new tape during installation).

GSX-R750 and GSX-R1100 (1985 through 1988)

3 Remove the seat (see Chapter 7).

4 Remove the fuel tank (see Chapter 4).

GSX-R750 and GSX-R1100 (1989 and later)

5 Remove the seat and frame covers (see Chapter 7).

6 Remove the battery (see Section 17).

7 Remove the battery case.

Katana 750 (GSX750F)

8 Remove the seat (see Chapter 7).

9 Remove the fuel tank mounting bolts, but don't remove the tank (see Chapter 3).

10 Remove the upper fairing screws and frame cover screws from both sides of the bike **(see illustrations)**.

11 Remove the mounting bracket for the fuel tank and air cleaner case **(see illustrations)**.

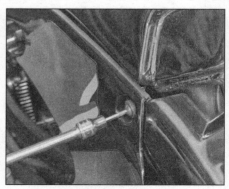

2.10a Remove the upper fairing screws . . .

2.10b ... and frame cover screws

2.11a Remove two bolts ...

2.11b ... and a screw from each side, then remove the fuel tank bracket

2.17a Remove the filter element mounting screws; disconnect the carburetor vent hoses from the clips (arrows) ...

2.17b ... and lift the filter element out of the airbox

2.19 Remove the drain plug from the air box drain hose (if equipped) and let the water drain out

12 Lift the rear end of the fuel tank for access to the air filter.

Katana 1100 (GSX1100F)

13 Remove the seat and frame covers (see Chapter 7).
14 Remove the bracket from the rear of the fuel tank (but not the tank itself) (see Chapter 3).
15 Lift the rear end of the fuel tank for access to the air filter screws.

All models

16 On 1985 through 1987 models, remove the wingnut and washer from the front side of the airbox and pull the filter out toward the rear.
17 On 1988 and later models, remove four screws and pull the element out of the airbox **(see illustrations)**.
18 Use compressed air to clean the element by blowing from the outside in (blowing from the inside out will force dirt into the pores of the filter). At the specified intervals, replace the element with a new one.

19 Clean the inside of the air box. On models equipped with an air box drain hose, remove the plug and let the water drain out **(see illustration)**.
20 Reinstall the filter by reversing the removal procedure. Make sure the element is seated properly in the filter housing before installing the cover. On 1985 through 1987 models, position the filter so the arrow on the outer portion points upward. Make sure the carburetor vent hoses are routed correctly. If the vent hoses were secured with tape, use new tape to secure them.

1

Every 4000 miles (6000 km) or 12 months

3   Engine oil/filter - change

1 Consistent routine oil and filter changes are the single most important maintenance procedure you can perform on a motorcycle. The oil not only lubricates the internal parts of the engine, transmission and clutch, but it also acts as a coolant, a cleaner, a sealant, and a protectant. Because of these demands, the oil takes a terrific amount of abuse and should be replaced often with new oil of the recommended grade and type.

HAYNES HINT *Saving a little money on the cost difference between good and cheap oils won't pay off if the engine is damaged.*

2 Before changing the oil and filter, warm up the engine so the oil will drain easily. Be careful when draining the oil, as the exhaust pipes, the engine, and the oil itself can cause severe burns.
3 Put the motorcycle on the centerstand over a clean drain pan. Remove the oil filler cap to vent the crankcase and act as a reminder that there is no oil in the engine.
4 Next, remove the drain plug from the engine **(see illustration)** and allow the oil to

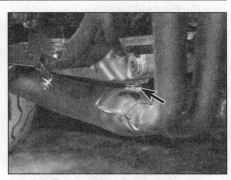

3.4 Remove the oil pan drain plug (arrow)

3.5a The oil filter is mounted on the front of the engine behind the exhaust pipes

3.5b Remove the oil filter with a filter wrench or a special socket

3.8 Tighten the oil filter the specified amount with a special socket or filter wrench - a strap-type wrench like this one can be used

drain into the pan. Discard the sealing washer on the drain plug; it should be replaced whenever the plug is removed.

5 As the oil is draining, remove the oil filter **(see illustrations)**. If additional maintenance is planned for this time period, check or service another component while the oil is allowed to drain completely.

6 Wipe any remaining oil off the filter sealing area of the crankcase.

7 Check the condition of the drain plug threads and the sealing washer.

8 Coat the gasket on a new filter with clean engine oil. Install the filter by hand until the filter gasket is felt to contact the crankcase. Now tighten the filter a full two turns using the filter wrench or a strap wrench **(see illustration)**.

9 Slip a new sealing washer over the drain plug, then install and tighten the plug. Tighten the drain plug to the torque listed in this Chapter's Specifications. Avoid over-tightening, as damage to the engine case will result.

10 Before refilling the engine, check the old oil carefully. If the oil was drained into a clean pan, small pieces of metal or other material can be easily detected. If the oil is very metallic colored, then the engine is experiencing wear from break-in (new engine) or from insufficient lubrication. If there are flakes or chips of metal in the oil, then something is drastically wrong internally and the engine will have to be disassembled for inspection and repair.

11 If there are pieces of fiber-like material in the oil, the clutch is experiencing excessive wear and should be checked.

12 If the inspection of the oil turns up nothing unusual, refill the crankcase to the proper level with the recommended oil and install the

OIL CARE
FOLLOW THE CODE
OIL BANK LINE
0800 66 33 66

In the USA, note that any oil supplier must accept used oil for recycling

Note: It is antisocial and illegal to dump oil down the drain. To find the location of your local oil recycling bank, call this number free.

filler cap. Start the engine and let it run for two or three minutes. Shut it off, wait a few minutes, then check the oil level. If necessary, add more oil to bring the level up to the Maximum mark. Check around the drain plug and filter housing for leaks.

13 The old oil drained from the engine cannot be reused in its present state and should be disposed of. Check with your local refuse disposal company, disposal facility or environmental agency to see whether they will accept the oil for recycling. Don't pour used oil into drains or onto the ground. After the oil has cooled, it can be drained into a suitable container for transport to one of these disposal sites.

4 Spark plugs - servicing

1 Make sure your spark plug socket is the correct size before attempting to remove the plugs.

2 Remove fairing panels, the seat and fuel tank as needed for access to the plugs (see Chapter 3 and Chapter 7).

3 Disconnect the spark plug caps from the spark plugs **(see illustration)**. If available, use compressed air to blow any accumulated debris from around the spark plugs. Remove the plugs.

4.3 Rotate the spark plug caps (arrows) back and forth to loosen them, then pull them off the plugs and check them for brittleness and cracking

4 Inspect the electrodes for wear. Both the center and side electrodes should have square edges and the side electrode should be of uniform thickness. Look for excessive deposits and evidence of a cracked or chipped insulator around the center electrode. Compare your spark plugs to the spark plug reading chart at the end of this manual. Check the threads, the washer and the porcelain insulator body for cracks and other damage.

5 If the electrodes are not excessively worn, and if the deposits can be easily removed with a wire brush, the plugs can be regapped and reused (if no cracks or chips are visible in the insulator). If in doubt concerning the condition of the plugs, replace them with new ones, as the expense is minimal.

6 Cleaning spark plugs by sandblasting is permitted, provided you clean the plugs with a high flash-point solvent afterwards.

7 Before installing new plugs, make sure they are the correct type and heat range. Check the gap between the electrodes, as they are not preset. For best results, use a wire-type gauge rather than a flat gauge to check the gap **(see illustration)**. If the gap must be adjusted, bend the side electrode only and be very careful not to chip or crack the insulator nose **(see illustration)**. Make sure the washer is in place before installing each plug.

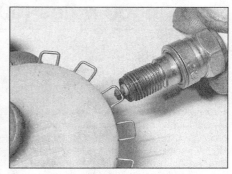

4.7a Spark plug manufacturers recommend using a wire type gauge when checking the gap - if the wire doesn't slide between the electrodes with a slight drag, adjustment is required

8 Since the cylinder head is made of aluminum, which is soft and easily damaged, thread the plugs into the head by hand.

HAYNES HINT *Since the plugs are quite recessed, slip a short length of hose over the end of the plug to use as a tool to thread it into place. The hose will grip the plug well enough to turn it, but will start to slip if the plug begins to cross-thread in the hole - this will prevent damaged threads and the accompanying repair costs.*

9 Once the plugs are finger tight, the job can be finished with a socket. Refer to this Chapter's Specifications for the correct setting. Do not over-tighten them.
10 Reconnect the spark plug caps.

5 Valve clearances - check and adjustment

1 The engine must be completely cool for this maintenance procedure, so let the machine sit overnight before beginning.
2 Remove the spark plugs (see Section 4).
3 Remove the valve cover (see Chapter 2).
4 Remove the cover from the signal generator (see Chapter 2).
5 Turn the crankshaft with a box wrench or socket on the large hex of the signal generator until the T mark on the rotor is aligned with the timing mark on the pickup coil **(see illustration)**.
Caution: DO NOT use the signal generator Allen bolt to turn the crankshaft - it may snap or strip out. Also be sure to turn the engine in its normal direction of rotation.
6 The notches in the ends of the camshafts should now be pointing away from each other and aligned with the gasket mating surface on the cylinder head **(see illustration)**. Also check the position of the no. 1 cylinder cam lobes - they should be in one of the

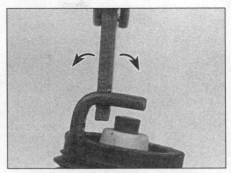

4.7b To change the gap, bend the side electrode only, as indicated by the arrows, and be very careful not to crack or chip the ceramic insulator surrounding the center electrode

acceptable positions for valve adjustment **(see illustrations)**. If the camshafts aren't positioned correctly, rotate the engine one full turn more, so the signal generator T mark and timing mark again line up. The camshafts should now be positioned correctly.
7 With the engine in this position, the following valves can be checked:
a) No. 1, intake and exhaust
b) No. 2, exhaust
c) No. 3, intake

Screw-type valve adjusters

8 Start with the no. 1 intake valve clearance. Insert a feeler gauge of the thickness listed in this Chapter's Specifications between each valve stem and cam lobe adjuster screw **(see illustration)**. Pull the feeler gauge out slowly - you should feel a slight drag. If there's no drag, the clearance is too loose. If there's a heavy drag, the clearance is too tight.
9 If the clearance is incorrect, loosen the adjuster screw locknut with a box wrench (see illustration 5.8) and turn the adjuster screw in or out as needed.
10 Hold the adjuster screw with the box wrench (to keep it from turning) and tighten the locknut. Recheck the clearance to make sure it hasn't changed.
11 Now adjust the remaining valves listed in

5.5 Turn the engine in its normal direction of rotation until the T mark and pickup coil protrusion align

A Pickup coil protrusion
B T mark
C Use this hex to turn the engine - DO NOT use the Allen bolt in the center of the hex!

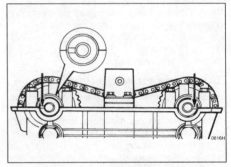

5.6a When correctly positioned for the first stage of valve adjustment, the camshaft notches should point away from each other - if they don't, turn the engine another full turn

Step 7, following the same procedure you used for the No. 1 cylinder valves. Make sure to use a feeler gauge of the specified thickness.
12 Rotate the crankshaft one full turn and again align the T mark on the rotor with the protrusion on the pickup coil (see illustration

1

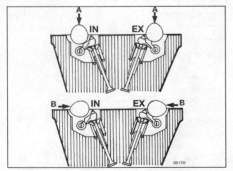

5.6b Acceptable cam lobe positions for valve adjustment (screw-type valve adjusters)

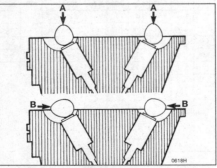

5.6c Acceptable cam lobe positions for valve adjustment (shim-type valve adjusters)

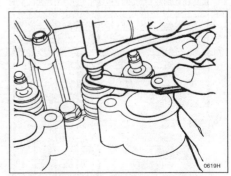

5.8 Loosen the locknut with a box wrench and turn the adjusting screw with a screwdriver to change the clearance (screw-type valve adjusters)

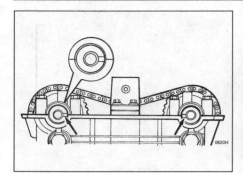

5.12 When correctly positioned for the second stage of valve adjustment, the camshaft notches should point toward each other - if they don't, turn the engine another full turn

5.14 Check valve clearance with a feeler gauge between the rocker arm and adjusting shim (shim-type valve adjusters)

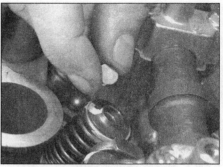

5.19 Valve clearance is changed by varying the thickness of the adjusting shim (shim-type valve adjusters)

5.5). The notches in the ends of the camshafts should now point toward each other **(see illustration)**.

13 Adjust the following valves as described in Steps 8 and 9 (see illustration 5.8):
a) *No. 2, intake*
b) *No. 3, exhaust*
c) *No. 4, intake and exhaust*

Shim-type valve adjusters

14 Start with the no. 1 intake valve clearance. Insert a feeler gauge of the thickness listed in this Chapter's Specifications between each valve stem and rocker arm **(see illustration)**. Pull the feeler gauge out slowly - you should feel a slight drag. If there's no drag, the clearance is too loose. If there's a heavy drag, the clearance is too tight.

15 If the clearance is incorrect, select a feeler gauge of a thickness that will fit with a light drag. Write down the thickness of this feeler gauge next to the number and position of the valve (for example, No. 1 left intake, 0.20 mm). This is the actual valve clearance, which you will need later to select new valve shims.

16 Check the remaining valves listed in Step 7 and write down the clearances of any that aren't within the Specifications.

17 Rotate the crankshaft one full turn and again align the T mark on the rotor with the protrusion on the pickup coil (see illustration 5.5). The notches in the ends of the camshafts should now point toward each other (see illustration 5.12).

18 Measure the following valves as described in Steps 14 and 15
a) *No. 2, intake*
b) *No. 3, exhaust*
c) *No. 4, intake and exhaust*

Write down the number and location of any of the valves that aren't within the Specifications.

19 To correct the clearances, turn the engine to the position described in Step 5. Pry the rocker arm aside with a suitable tool, lift the shim out with a magnet **(see illustration)**, and measure its thickness.

20 Select new valve shims to correct the clearances on any valves not within the Specifications. To do this, compare the clearance you've measured with the fitted shim thickness using the selection charts for intake and exhaust valves **(see illustrations)**.

MEASURED CLEARANCE (mm)	230	235	240	245	250	255	260	265	270	275	280	285	290	295	300	305	310	315	320	325	330	335	340	345	350
PRESENT SHIM SIZE (mm)	2.30	2.35	2.40	2.45	2.50	2.550	2.60	2.65	2.70	2.75	2.80	2.85	2.90	2.95	3.00	3.05	3.10	3.15	3.2	3.25	3.3	3.35	3.4	3.45	3.5
0.00-0.04			2.30	2.35	2.40	2.45	2.50	2.550	2.60	2.65	2.70	2.75	2.80	2.85	2.90	2.95	3.00	3.05	3.10	3.15	3.2	3.25	3.3	3.35	3.4
0.05-0.09		2.30	2.35	2.40	2.45	2.50	2.55	2.60	2.65	2.70	2.75	2.80	2.85	2.90	2.95	3.00	3.05	3.10	3.15	3.2	3.25	3.3	3.35	3.4	3.45
0.10-0.20	SPECIFIED CLEARANCE/NO ADJUSTMENT REQUIRED																								
0.21-0.25	2.40	2.45	2.50	2.55	2.60	2.65	2.70	2.75	2.80	2.85	2.90	2.95	3.00	3.05	3.10	3.15	3.2	3.25	3.3	3.35	3.4	3.45	3.5	3.5	
0.26-0.30	2.45	2.50	2.55	2.60	2.65	2.70	2.75	2.80	2.85	2.90	2.95	3.00	3.05	3.10	3.15	3.2	3.25	3.3	3.35	3.4	3.45	3.5	3.5		
0.31-0.35	2.50	2.55	2.60	2.65	2.70	2.75	2.80	2.85	2.90	2.95	3.00	3.05	3.10	3.15	3.2	3.25	3.3	3.35	3.4	3.45	3.5				
0.36-0.40	2.55	2.60	2.65	2.70	2.75	2.80	2.85	2.90	2.95	3.00	3.05	3.10	3.15	3.2	3.25	3.3	3.35	3.4	3.45	3.5					
0.41-0.45	2.60	2.65	2.70	2.75	2.80	2.85	2.90	2.95	3.00	3.05	3.10	3.15	3.2	3.25	3.3	3.35	3.4	3.45	3.5						
0.46-0.50	2.65	2.70	2.75	2.80	2.85	2.90	2.95	3.00	3.05	3.10	3.15	3.2	3.25	3.3	3.35	3.4	3.45	3.5							
0.51-0.55	2.70	2.75	2.80	2.85	2.90	2.95	3.00	3.05	3.10	3.15	3.2	3.25	3.3	3.35	3.4	3.45	3.5								
0.56-0.60	2.75	2.80	2.85	2.90	2.95	3.00	3.05	3.10	3.15	3.2	3.25	3.3	3.35	3.4	3.45	3.5									
0.61-0.65	2.80	2.85	2.90	2.95	3.00	3.05	3.10	3.15	3.2	3.25	3.3	3.35	3.4	3.45	3.5										
0.66-0.70	2.85	2.90	2.95	3.00	3.05	3.10	3.15	3.2	3.25	3.3	3.35	3.4	3.45	3.5											
0.71-0.75	2.90	2.95	3.00	3.05	3.10	3.15	3.2	3.25	3.3	3.35	3.4	3.45	3.5												
0.76-0.80	2.95	3.00	3.05	3.10	3.15	3.2	3.25	3.3	3.35	3.4	3.45	3.5													
0.81-0.85	3.00	3.05	3.10	3.15	3.2	3.25	3.3	3.35	3.4	3.45	3.5														
0.86-0.90	3.05	3.10	3.15	3.2	3.25	3.3	3.35	3.4	3.45	3.5															
0.91-0.95	3.10	3.15	3.2	3.25	3.3	3.35	3.4	3.45	3.5																
0.96-1.00	3.15	3.2	3.25	3.3	3.35	3.4	3.45	3.5																	
1.01-1.05	3.2	3.25	3.3	3.35	3.4	3.45	3.5																		
1.06-1.10	3.25	3.3	3.35	3.4	3.45	3.5																			
1.11-1.15	3.3	3.35	3.4	3.45	3.5																				

Optional shims

These shims are available as a set.

HOW TO USE THIS CHART:

I. Measure valve clearance.

II. Measure present shim size.

III. Match clearance in vertical column with present shim size in horizontal column.

EXAMPLE

Valve clearance is   0.23 mm

Present shim size   2.70 mm

Shim size to be used 2.80 mm

5.20a Intake valve shim selection chart

Optional shims (columns 230–245) | **These shims are available as a set.** (columns 250–350)

MEASURED CLEARANCE (mm) \ SUFFIX NO. / PRESENT SHIM SIZE (mm)	230	235	240	245	250	255	260	265	270	275	280	285	290	295	300	305	310	315	320	325	330	335	340	345	350
(shim size mm)	2.30	2.35	2.40	2.45	2.50	2.550	2.60	2.65	2.70	2.75	2.80	2.85	2.90	2.95	3.00	3.05	3.10	3.15	3.2	3.25	3.3	3.35	3.4	3.45	3.5
0.00–0.04				2.30	2.35	2.40	2.45	2.50	2.550	2.60	2.65	2.70	2.75	2.80	2.85	2.90	2.95	3.00	3.05	3.10	3.15	3.2	3.25	3.3	3.35
0.05–0.09			2.30	2.35	2.40	2.45	2.50	2.550	2.60	2.65	2.70	2.75	2.80	2.85	2.90	2.95	3.00	3.05	3.10	3.15	3.2	3.25	3.3	3.35	3.4
0.10–0.14		2.30	2.35	2.40	2.45	2.50	2.550	2.60	2.65	2.70	2.75	2.80	2.85	2.90	2.95	3.00	3.05	3.10	3.15	3.2	3.25	3.3	3.35	3.4	3.45
0.15–0.25	SPECIFIED CLEARANCE/NO ADJUSTMENT REQUIRED																								
0.26–0.30	2.40	2.45	2.50	2.55	2.60	2.65	2.70	2.75	2.80	2.85	2.90	2.95	3.00	3.05	3.10	3.15	3.2	3.25	3.3	3.35	3.4	3.45	3.5	3.5	
0.31–0.35	2.45	2.50	2.55	2.60	2.65	2.70	2.75	2.80	2.85	2.90	2.95	3.00	3.05	3.10	3.15	3.2	3.25	3.3	3.35	3.4	3.45	3.5			
0.36–0.40	2.50	2.55	2.60	2.65	2.70	2.75	2.80	2.85	2.90	2.95	3.00	3.05	3.10	3.15	3.2	3.25	3.3	3.35	3.4	3.45	3.5				
0.41–0.45	2.55	2.60	2.65	2.70	2.75	2.80	2.85	2.90	2.95	3.00	3.05	3.10	3.15	3.2	3.25	3.3	3.35	3.4	3.45	3.5					
0.46–0.50	2.60	2.65	2.70	2.75	2.80	2.85	2.90	2.95	3.00	3.05	3.10	3.15	3.2	3.25	3.3	3.35	3.4	3.45	3.5						
0.51–0.55	2.65	2.70	2.75	2.80	2.85	2.90	2.95	3.00	3.05	3.10	3.15	3.2	3.25	3.3	3.35	3.4	3.45	3.5							
0.56–0.60	2.70	2.75	2.80	2.85	2.90	2.95	3.00	3.05	3.10	3.15	3.2	3.25	3.3	3.35	3.4	3.45	3.5								
0.61–0.65	2.75	2.80	2.85	2.90	2.95	3.00	3.05	3.10	3.15	3.2	3.25	3.3	3.35	3.4	3.45	3.5									
0.66–0.70	2.80	2.85	2.90	2.95	3.00	3.05	3.10	3.15	3.2	3.25	3.3	3.35	3.4	3.45	3.5										
0.71–0.75	2.85	2.90	2.95	3.00	3.05	3.10	3.15	3.2	3.25	3.3	3.35	3.4	3.45	3.5											
0.76–0.80	2.90	2.95	3.00	3.05	3.10	3.15	3.2	3.25	3.3	3.35	3.4	3.45	3.5												
0.81–0.85	2.95	3.00	3.05	3.10	3.15	3.2	3.25	3.3	3.35	3.4	3.45	3.5													
0.86–0.90	3.00	3.05	3.10	3.15	3.2	3.25	3.3	3.35	3.4	3.45	3.5														
0.91–0.95	3.05	3.10	3.15	3.2	3.25	3.3	3.35	3.4	3.45	3.5															
0.96–1.00	3.10	3.15	3.2	3.25	3.3	3.35	3.4	3.45	3.5																
1.01–1.05	3.15	3.2	3.25	3.3	3.35	3.4	3.45	3.5																	
1.06–1.10	3.2	3.25	3.3	3.35	3.4	3.45	3.5																		
1.11–1.15	3.25	3.3	3.35	3.4	3.45	3.5																			
1.16–1.20	3.3	3.35	3.4	3.45	3.5																				

HOW TO USE THIS CHART:

I. Measure tappet clearance with engine cold.
II. Measure present shim size.
III. Match clearance in vertical column with present shim size in horizontal column.

EXAMPLE

Valve clearance is	0.27 mm
Present shim size	2.90 mm
Shim size to be used	3.00 mm

5.20b Exhaust valve shim selection chart

Make a list of the shims you need for each valve and take it to a Suzuki dealer to purchase new shims.

HAYNES HiNT *It is worthwhile noting down all the valve shim thicknesses to save time and expense when the valve clearances are next adjusted; provided they are not worn or damaged, the shims can be moved to other locations.*

21 Install the new shim in the valve spring retainer, then pry the rocker arm back into position.

6.5 A compression gauge with a threaded fitting for the spark plug hole is preferred over the type that requires hand pressure to maintain the seal

22 Recheck the valve clearance as described in Steps 14 and 15.
23 Replace shims as needed for the remaining valves.
24 Rotate the engine to the position described in Step 17.
25 Replace shims as needed and recheck clearance on the valves listed in Step 18.

All models

26 Install the valve cover and all of the components that had to be removed to get it off.

6 Cylinder compression - check

1 Among other things, poor engine performance may be caused by leaking valves, incorrect valve clearances, a leaking head gasket, or worn pistons, rings and/or cylinder walls. A cylinder compression check will help pinpoint these conditions and can also indicate the presence of excessive carbon deposits in the cylinder heads.
2 The only tools required are a compression gauge and a spark plug wrench. Depending on the outcome of the initial test, a squirt-type oil can may also be needed.
3 Start the engine and allow it to reach normal operating temperature. Place the motorcycle on the centerstand or sidestand,

remove the fuel tank, then remove the spark plugs (see Section 4, if necessary). Work carefully - don't strip the spark plug hole threads and don't burn your hands.
4 Disable the ignition by unplugging the primary wires from the coils (see Chapter 4). Be sure to mark the locations of the wires before detaching them.
5 Install the compression gauge in one of the spark plug holes (see illustration). Hold or block the throttle wide open.
6 Crank the engine over a minimum of four or five revolutions (or until the gauge reading stops increasing) and observe the initial movement of the compression gauge needle as well as the final total gauge reading. Repeat the procedure for the other cylinders and compare the results to the value listed in this Chapter's Specifications.
7 If the compression in both cylinders built up quickly and evenly to the specified amount, you can assume the engine upper end is in reasonably good mechanical condition. Worn or sticking piston rings and worn cylinders will produce very little initial movement of the gauge needle, but compression will tend to build up gradually as the engine spins over. Valve and valve seat leakage, or head gasket leakage, is indicated by low initial compression which does not tend to build up.
8 To further confirm your findings, add a small amount of engine oil to each cylinder by inserting the nozzle of a squirt-type oil can through the spark plug holes. The oil will tend

1

to seal the piston rings if they are leaking. Repeat the test for the other cylinder.

9 If the compression increases significantly after the addition of the oil, the piston rings and/or cylinders are definitely worn. If the compression does not increase, the pressure is leaking past the valves or the head gasket. Leakage past the valves may be due to insufficient valve clearances, burned, warped or cracked valves or valve seats or valves that are hanging up in the guides.

10 If compression readings are considerably higher than specified, the combustion chambers are probably coated with excessive carbon deposits. It is possible (but not very likely) for carbon deposits to raise the compression enough to compensate for the effects of leakage past rings or valves. Remove the cylinder head and carefully decarbonize the combustion chambers (see Chapter 2).

7.3 Turn the idle speed adjusting screw (arrow) in or out until the correct idle speed is obtained

times, then recheck the idle speed. If necessary, repeat the adjustment procedure.

5 If a smooth, steady idle can't be achieved, the fuel/air mixture may be incorrect or the carburetors may need to be synchronized. Refer to Chapter 3 for additional carburetor information.

Throttle operation/grip freeplay

6 Make sure the throttle grip rotates easily from fully closed to fully open with the front wheel turned at various angles. The grip should return automatically from fully open to fully closed when released. If the throttle sticks, check the throttle accelerator and decelerator (if equipped) cables for cracks or kinks in the housings. Also, make sure the inner cables are clean and well-lubricated.

7 Check for a small amount of freeplay at the cable and compare the freeplay to the value listed in this Chapter's Specifications. If it's incorrect, adjust the accelerator cable to correct it.

8 Freeplay adjustments can be made at the throttle end of the cable. Loosen the locknut on the cable where it leaves the handlebar **(see illustration)**. Turn the adjuster until the specified freeplay is obtained (see this Chapter's Specifications), then retighten the locknut.

9 If the cable can't be adjusted within specifications, replace it (see Chapter 3).

10 If the motorcycle is equipped with a decelerator cable, adjust it so there is little or no play when the throttle is closed.

7.8 Loosen the accelerator cable locknut with one wrench, then hold it and turn the adjuster with another wrench to obtain the correct throttle freeplay

  Warning: Turn the handlebars all the way through their travel with the engine idling. Idle speed should not change. If it does, the cable may be routed incorrectly. Correct this condition before riding the bike.

---

7 Idle speed and throttle operation/grip freeplay - check and adjustment

Idle speed

1 The idle speed should be checked and adjusted at the specified intervals, as well as whenever the carburetors are synchronized or when it is obviously too high or too low. Before adjusting the idle speed, make sure the valve clearances and spark plug gaps are correct. Also, turn the handlebars back-and-forth and see if the idle speed changes as this is done. If it does, the accelerator cable may not be adjusted correctly, or it may be worn out. Be sure to correct this problem before proceeding.

2 The engine should be at normal operating temperature, which is usually reached after 10 to 15 minutes of stop and go riding. Place the motorcycle on the sidestand (or centerstand, if equipped) and make sure the transmission is in Neutral.

3 Turn the throttle stop screw, located on the left side of the bike **(see illustration)**, until the idle speed listed in this Chapter's Specifications is obtained.

4 Snap the throttle open and shut a few

---

8 Evaporative emission control system - check

None of the emission control system require maintenance, other than checks for damaged or loose components (see Chapter 3).

9 Crankcase breather - inspection

1 The crankcase breather, used on some models, consists of a hose that runs from the air cleaner air box to an oil separator on the valve cover. The hose should be inspected and the separator cleaned periodically.

2 Loosen the clamp and disconnect the hose from the airbox fitting **(see illustration)**.

3 Remove the separator mounting screws and take the separator off the valve cover **(see illustration)**.

4 Remove the foam element from the separator and clean it in solvent **(see illustration)**. Replace the element if it's cracked, torn or deteriorated.

9.2 Loosen the hose clamp and disconnect the breather hose from the air cleaner air box (GSX-R1100 shown, others similar)

9.3 Remove the mounting screws (arrows) and lift the breather cover off the valve cover

9.4 Remove and clean the foam element

10.7 To adjust the rear brake light switch, raise or lower it in relation to the bracket

10 Brake system - checks

General

1 A routine general check of the brakes will ensure that any problems are discovered and remedied before the rider's safety is jeopardized.
2 Check the brake lever and pedal for loose connections, excessive play, bends, and other damage. Replace any damaged parts with new ones (see Chapter 6).
3 Make sure all brake fasteners are tight. Check the brake pads for wear (see Section 5) and make sure the fluid level in the reservoirs is correct (see Section 2). Look for leaks at the hose connections and check for cracks in the hoses. If the lever or pedal is spongy, bleed the brakes as described in Chapter 6.
4 Make sure the brake light operates just before resistance is felt when the brake lever is depressed.
5 Make sure the brake light is activated just before resistance is felt when the rear brake pedal is depressed.
6 The front brake light switch is mounted beneath the brake lever. On early models (switch fastened with two screws) the switch is adjustable. To adjust it, loosen the switch mounting screws and move the switch from side to side so the brake light comes on at the specified point. On later models (switch fastened with one screw) the switch isn't adjustable.
7 If adjustment of the rear brake light switch is necessary, turn the switch body so the brake light is activated at the correct point **(see illustration)**. If the switch doesn't operate the brake lights, check it as described in Chapter 8.

Brake pad wear

8 The front and rear brake pads should be checked at the recommended intervals and replaced with new ones when worn beyond the limit listed in this Chapter's Specifications.
9 To check the brake pads, remove the dust

10.9 The brake pads are visible once the dust cover is removed (arrow) - some rear caliper dust covers are accessible from below (rear caliper shown; front caliper similar)

cover (if equipped) from the caliper so you can see the edges of the pad lining material **(see illustration)**. The brake pads should have at least the minimum amount of lining material remaining on the metal backing plate as listed in this Chapter's Specifications.
10 If the pads are worn excessively, they must be replaced with new ones (see Chapter 6).

Rear brake pedal position

11 Rear brake pedal position should be set at the height listed in this Chapter's Specifications.
12 To adjust the position of the pedal, loosen the locknut on the adjusting bolt, turn the bolt to set the pedal position and tighten the locknut **(see illustration)**.
13 If necessary, adjust the brake light switch.

11 Fuel system - check and filter cleaning

⚠️ **Warning: Gasoline (petrol) is extremely flammable, so take extra precautions when you work on any part of the fuel system. Don't smoke or allow open flames or bare light bulbs near the work area, and don't work in a garage where a natural gas-type appliance (such as a water**

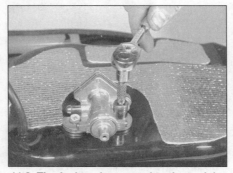

11.8 The fuel tap is secured to the tank by two screws

10.12 To adjust the brake pedal height, loosen the locknut (arrow) and turn the adjusting bolt

heater or clothes dryer) is present. If you spill any fuel on your skin, rinse it off immediately with soap and water. When you perform any kind of work on the fuel system, wear safety glasses and have a fire extinguisher suitable for a Class B type fire (flammable liquids) on hand.

1 Check the fuel tank, the fuel tap, the lines and the carburetors for leaks and evidence of damage.
2 If carburetor gaskets are leaking, the carburetors should be disassembled and rebuilt by referring to Chapter 3.
3 If the fuel tap is leaking, tightening the screws may help. If leakage persists, the tap should be disassembled and repaired or replaced with a new one.
4 If the fuel lines are cracked or otherwise deteriorated, replace them with new ones.
5 Check the vacuum hose connected to the fuel tap. If it is cracked or otherwise damaged, replace it with a new one.
6 The fuel filter, which is attached to the fuel tap, may become clogged and should be removed and cleaned periodically. In order to clean the filter, the fuel tank must be drained and the fuel tap removed.
7 Remove the fuel tank (see Chapter 3). Drain the fuel into an approved fuel container.
8 Once the tank is emptied, loosen and remove the screws that attach the fuel tap to the tank **(see illustration)**. Remove the tap and filter.
9 Take the filter off the tap **(see illustration)**.

1

11.9a The fuel filter is mounted on the tap

11.9b Replace the flange O-ring if it's brittle or deteriorated

11.11a On California models, inspect the evaporative emission hoses (arrow) . . .

11.11b . . . use the vacuum hose routing decal to follow them to their fittings

Clean the filter **(see illustration)** with solvent and blow it dry from the inside out with compressed air. If the filter is torn or otherwise damaged, replace the entire fuel tap with a new one. Check the mounting flange O-ring **(see illustration)**. If it is damaged, replace it with a new one.

10 Install the O-ring, filter and fuel tap on the tank.

California models

11 Inspect the evaporative emission system lines **(see illustrations)**. Replace any that are cracked or deteriorated.

All models

12 Install the fuel tank. Refill the tank and check carefully for leaks around the mounting flange and screws.

mechanism set in the engine sprocket cover.

3 Create slack in the clutch cable by fully backing off the locknut on the fine adjuster at the top of the cable and screwing the adjuster into the lever bracket. Do the same on the coarse adjuster set in the top of the sprocket cover (see 'Daily (pre-ride) checks' at the beginning of this Manual).

4 Back off the locknut on the release mechanism, then back off adjuster screw a few turns. Turn the adjuster screw in until resistance is felt, then back it off 1/4 to 1/2 turn **(see illustration)**.

5 Hold the adjuster screw steady and tighten the locknut.

6 Readjust the cable freeplay as described in 'Daily (pre-ride) checks' at the beginning of this Manual.

to be applied where it will do the most good, the component should be disassembled. However, if chain and cable lubricant is being used, it can be applied to the pivot joint gaps and will usually work its way into the areas where friction occurs. If motor oil or light grease is being used, apply it sparingly as it may attract dirt (which could cause the controls to bind or wear at an accelerated rate). **Note:** *One of the best lubricants for the control lever pivots is a dry-film lubricant (available from many sources by different names).*

3 The clutch cable (if equipped) should be separated from the handlebar lever and bracket before it is lubricated **(see illustration)**. This is a convenient time to inspect the Teflon bushing at the end of the cable. The cable should be treated with motor oil or a commercially available cable lubricant

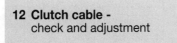

12 Clutch cable - check and adjustment

13 Lubrication - general

General

1 See 'Daily (pre-ride) checks' at the beginning of this Manual.

Release mechanism - check and adjustment (GSX600F and GSX750F models)

2 Remove the plug from the clutch release

1 Since the controls, cables and various other components of a motorcycle are exposed to the elements, they should be lubricated periodically to ensure safe and trouble-free operation.

2 The footpegs, clutch and brake lever, brake pedal, brake link, shift lever and side and centerstand (if equipped) pivots should be lubricated frequently. In order for the lubricant

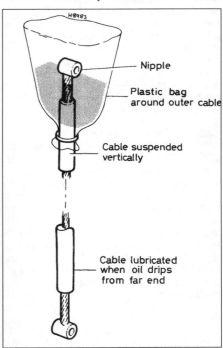

13.3b Lubricating a control cable with a makeshift funnel and motor oil

12.4 Adjusting the clutch release mechanism

13.3a Lubricating a cable with a pressure lube adapter (make sure the tool seats around the inner cable)

14.6 Loosen the upper pinch bolts on each fork (arrow)

14.7 Loosen the steering stem bolt

which is specially formulated for use on motorcycle control cables. Small adapters for pressure lubricating the cables with spray can lubricants are available and ensure that the cable is lubricated along its entire length. If motor oil is being used, tape a funnel-shaped piece of heavy paper or plastic to the end of the cable, then pour oil into the funnel and suspend the end of the cable upright **(see illustration)**. Leave it until the oil runs down into the cable and out the other end. When attaching the cable to the lever, be sure to lubricate the barrel-shaped fitting at the end with high-temperature grease. **Note**: *While you're lubricating, check the barrel end of the cable for fraying. Replace frayed cables.*

4 To lubricate the throttle cable (and choke cable if equipped), disconnect the cable(s) at the lower end, then lubricate the cable with a pressure lube adapter (see illustration 13.3a). See Chapter 3 for the choke cable removal procedure.

5 The speedometer cable should be removed from its housing and lubricated with motor oil or cable lubricant.

6 Refer to Chapter 5 for the swingarm needle bearing and rear suspension linkage lubrication procedures.

14 Steering head bearings - check and adjustment

1 This vehicle is equipped with tapered roller type steering head bearings which can become dented, rough or loose during normal use of the machine. In extreme cases, worn or loose steering head bearings can cause steering wobble that is potentially dangerous.

Check

2 To check the bearings, place the motorcycle on the centerstand (if equipped) or place a pair of jackstands beneath the front frame rails and block the machine so the front wheel is in the air.

3 Point the wheel straight ahead and slowly move the handlebars from side-to-side. Dents or roughness in the bearing races will be felt and the bars will not move smoothly.

4 Next, grasp the fork legs and try to move the wheel forward and backward. Any looseness in the steering head bearings will be felt. If play is felt in the bearings, adjust the steering head as follows:

Adjustment

5 Remove the fuel tank (see Chapter 3).

6 Loosen the fork upper pinch bolts **(see illustration)**. This allows the necessary vertical movement of the steering stem in relation to the fork tubes.

7 Loosen the steering head bolt **(see illustration)**.

8 Use a spanner wrench to loosen the steering stem locknut.

9 Carefully tighten the steering stem locknut until the steering head is tight but does not bind when the forks are turned from side-to-side.

Caution: Take care not to apply excessive pressure because this will cause premature failure of the bearings.

10 Retighten the steering head nut and the fork pinch bolts, in that order, to the torque values listed in the Chapter 5 Specifications.

11 Recheck the steering head bearings for play as described previously. If necessary, repeat the adjustment procedure. Reinstall all parts previously removed.

12 Refer to Chapter 5 for steering head bearing lubrication and replacement procedures.

15 Wheels and tires - check

Wheels

1 The cast wheels used on this machine are virtually maintenance free, but they should be kept clean and checked periodically for cracks and other damage. Never attempt to repair damaged cast wheels; they must be replaced with new ones.

2 Check the valve stem locknuts to make sure they are tight. Check the valve stem rubber for condition; have it replaced if

necessary. Also, make sure the valve stem cap is in place and tight. If it is missing, install a new one made of metal or hard plastic.

3 Check the wheel runout and alignment (Chapter 6).

Tires

4 Check the tire condition and tread depth thoroughly - see *'Daily (pre-ride) checks'* at the beginning of this Manual.

16 Fork oil - replacement

1 Place the motorcycle on the centerstand (if equipped) or place a wooden block beneath the front frame rails to securely support the front wheel off the ground.

2 Remove the fork cap bolt **(see illustration)**. Remove the fork spring.

3 Place a drain pan under the fork leg.

 Warning: Do not allow the fork oil to contact the brake discs, pads or tire. If it does, clean the discs with brake system cleaner and replace the pads with new ones before riding the motorcycle. Wipe the tire clean.

4 If the motorcycle is equipped with an anti-dive unit or a compression damping adjuster, remove it (see Chapter 5).

5 If the motorcycle is equipped with a fork

1

16.2 Lift out the fork cap bolt and inspect its O-ring

16.5a Some models are equipped with a fork drain screw at the bottom of each fork leg; it can be at the rear, as on this 750 Katana (GSX750F) . . .

16.5b . . . or on the side, as on this 1100 Katana (GSX1100F)

16.8 Use a funnel and pour the specified amount of fluid into the fork

drain bolt, remove it and allow the oil to drain **(see illustrations)**.

6 After most of the oil has drained, slowly compress and release the forks to pump out the remaining oil. An assistant will most likely be required to do this procedure.

7 Check the anti-dive unit, compression damper adjuster or drain bolt gasket for damage and replace it if necessary. Clean the threads of the drain bolt (if equipped) with solvent and let it dry, then install the bolt and gasket, tightening it securely. Refer to Chapter 5 for installation details of the anti-dive unit or compression damper (if equipped).

8 Pour the type and amount of fork oil, listed in this Chapter's Specifications, into the fork tube through the opening at the top **(see illustration)**. Remove the supports from under the motorcycle and slowly pump the forks a few times to purge the air from the upper and lower chambers.

9 Fully compress the front forks (you may need an assistant to do this). Measure the distance from the oil to the top of the fork tube. This can be done with a stiff tape measure, but a more accurate way is to make a special tool from a piece of metal tubing, rubber hose and a suction pump **(see illustration)**. Compare your measurement to the value listed in this Chapter's

Specifications. Drain or add oil, as necessary, until the level is correct.

10 Check the O-ring on the fork cap, then coat it with a thin layer of multi-purpose grease. Install the fork spring. Install the fork cap bolt and tighten it to the torque listed in the Chapter 5 Specifications. Make sure the alignment marks on cap and handlebar line up (if equipped) **(see illustration)**.

11 Repeat the procedure on the other fork.

12 Install the lower fairing.

17 Suspension - check

1 The suspension components must be maintained in top operating condition to ensure rider safety. Loose, worn or damaged suspension parts decrease the vehicle's stability and control.

2 While standing alongside the motorcycle, lock the front brake and push on the handlebars to compress the forks several times. See if they move up-and-down smoothly without binding. If binding is felt, the forks should be disassembled and inspected as described in Chapter 6.

3 Carefully inspect the area around the fork seals for any signs of fork oil leakage. If

leakage is evident, the seals must be replaced as described in Chapter 6.

4 Check the tightness of all suspension nuts and bolts to be sure none have worked loose.

5 Inspect the rear shock absorber for fluid leakage and tightness of the mounting nuts. If leakage is found, the shock should be replaced.

6 Set the bike on its centerstand (if equipped) or place it SECURELY on jackstands so the rear wheel is off the ground. Grab the swingarm on each side, just ahead of the axle. Rock the swingarm from side to side - there should be no discernible movement at the rear. If there's a little movement or a slight clicking can be heard, make sure the pivot shaft nuts are tight. If the pivot nuts are tight but movement is still noticeable, the swingarm will have to be removed and the bearings replaced as described in Chapter 6.

7 Inspect the tightness of the rear suspension nuts and bolts. Use a torque wrench and refer to the Chapter 5 Specifications.

18 Fasteners - check

General

1 Since vibration of the machine tends to loosen fasteners, all nuts, bolts, screws, etc. should be periodically checked for proper tightness.

2 Pay particular attention to the following:

Spark plugs
Engine oil drain plug
Gearshift lever
Footpegs and sidestand (and centerstand, if equipped)
Engine mount bolts
Shock absorber mount bolts
Shock absorber linkage bolts
Front axle and clamp bolt
Rear axle nut

3 If a torque wrench is available, use it along with the torque specifications at the beginning of this, or other, Chapters.

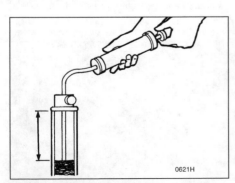

16.9 Measure oil level in the fork; this measuring tool can be easily fabricated, but a tape measure will also work; add or drain oil to correct the level

16.10 If the fork cap bolt has alignment marks (arrows), make sure they line up when it's installed

19.2a The battery may be secured by a strap . . .

19.2b . . . or a metal bracket

19.3 Detach the negative cable (left arrow) from the battery first, then detach the positive cable (right arrow); the plastic cap protects the positive terminal from accidental contact with metal

Cylinder head

4 To tighten the cylinder head nuts, refer to Valve cover removal and installation and Cylinder head installation in Chapter 2.

Exhaust fasteners

5 Periodically check all of the exhaust system joints for leaks and loose fasteners. The lower fairing will have to be removed to do this properly (see Chapter 7). If tightening the clamp bolts fails to stop any leaks, replace the gaskets with new ones (a procedure which requires disassembly of the system).

6 The exhaust pipe bolts at the cylinder heads are especially prone to loosening, which could cause damage to the head. Check them frequently and keep them tight.

19 Battery electrolyte level/specific gravity - check

⚠️ *Warning: Be extremely careful when handling or working around the battery. The electrolyte is very caustic and an explosive gas (hydrogen) is given off when the battery is charging.*

1 Remove the seat (see Chapter 7).

2 Remove the strap or bracket that secures the battery **(see illustrations)**.

3 Remove the bolts securing the battery cables to the battery terminals (remove the negative cable first, positive cable last) **(see illustration)**.

4 Pull the battery straight up to remove it **(see illustration)**. The electrolyte level will now be visible through the translucent battery case - it should be between the Upper and Lower level marks **(see illustration)**.

5 If it is low, remove the cell caps and fill each cell to the upper level mark with distilled water. Do not use tap water (except in an emergency), and do not overfill. The cell holes are quite small, so it may help to use a plastic squeeze bottle with a small spout to add the water. If the level is within the marks on the case, additional water is not necessary.

6 Next, check the specific gravity of the electrolyte in each cell with a small hydrometer made especially for motorcycle batteries. These are available from most dealer parts departments or motorcycle accessory stores.

7 Remove the caps, draw some electrolyte from the first cell into the hydrometer **(see illustration)** and note the specific gravity. Compare the reading to the Specifications listed in this Chapter. Note: *Add 0.004 points to the reading for every 10-degrees F above 68-degrees F - subtract 0.004 points from the reading for every 10-degrees below 68-degrees F. Return the*

electrolyte to the appropriate cell and repeat the check for the remaining cells. When the check is complete, rinse the hydrometer thoroughly with clean water.

8 If the specific gravity of the electrolyte in each cell is as specified, the battery is in good condition and is apparently being charged by the machine's charging system.

9 If the specific gravity is low, the battery is not fully charged. This may be due to corroded battery terminals, a dirty battery case, a malfunctioning charging system, or loose or corroded wiring connections. On the other hand, it may be that the battery is worn out, especially if the machine is old, or that infrequent use of the motorcycle prevents normal charging from taking place.

10 Be sure to correct any problems and charge the battery if necessary. Refer to Chapter 8 for additional battery maintenance and charging procedures.

11 Install the battery cell caps, tightening them securely. Reconnect the cables to the battery, attaching the positive cable first and the negative cable last. Make sure to install the insulating boot over the positive terminal. Install the seat. Be very careful not to pinch or otherwise restrict the battery vent tube **(see illustration)**, as the battery may build up enough internal pressure during normal charging system operation to explode.

1

19.4a Disconnect the vent tube (arrow) and lift the battery straight up and out of the case - note that new batteries are equipped with a plastic cap over the vent fitting; this must be removed to connect the vent tube during installation

19.4b The electrolyte level should be between the upper and lower marks on the case

19.7 Check the specific gravity with a hydrometer

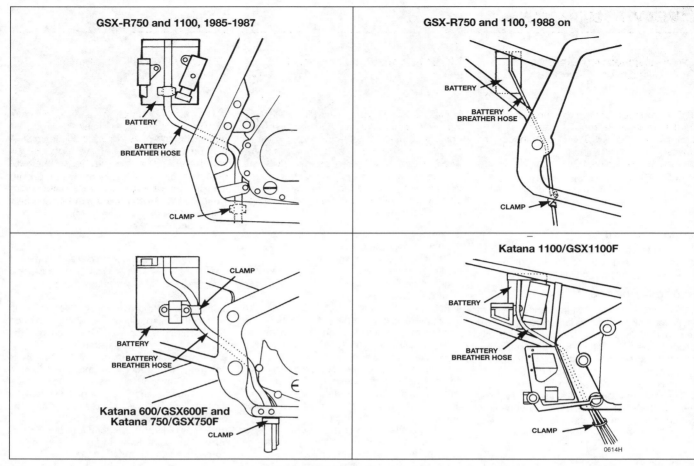

19.11 Battery vent hose details

Every 7500 miles (12,000 km) or 24 months

20 Air filter element - replacement

See Section 2 'Air filter element - servicing' under the 4000 miles (6000 km) or 12 months heading for details.

21 Spark plugs - replacement

See Section 4 'Spark plugs - servicing' under the 4000 miles (6000 km) or 12 months heading for details.

Every two years

22 Brake fluid - replacement

1 The brake fluid should be replaced at the prescribed interval, or whenever a master cylinder or caliper overhaul is carried out. Refer to the brake bleeding section in Chapter 6.

23 Clutch fluid - replacement

1 The clutch fluid should be replaced at the prescribed interval, or whenever a master cylinder or release cylinder overhaul is carried out. Refer to the clutch bleeding section in Chapter 2.

 HAYNES HiNT *Old hydraulic fluid is invariably darker than new fluid, making it easier to see when all old fluid has been expelled from the system.*

Every four years

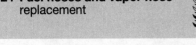

24 Fuel hoses and vapor hose - replacement

1 Over a period of time the fuel hoses may harden, crack or deteriorate, and fail.
2 Refer to Chapter 3 and disconnect the hoses.
3 Use new hose clips.

25 Brake hoses - replacement

1 The flexible brake hoses will deteriorate with age, and must be replaced with new ones, regardless of their apparent condition
2 Refer to Chapter 6 and disconnect the brake hoses from the master cylinders and calipers.
3 Fit new hoses and bleed the system (see Chapter 6). Alway use new banjo union sealing washers.

26 Clutch hose - replacement

1 The flexible clutch hose will, in time, deteriorate, and must be replaced with a new one, regardless of its apparent condition
2 Refer to Chapter 2 and disconnect the clutch hose from the master and release cylinders.
3 Fit a new hose and bleed the system (see Chapter 2). Alway use new banjo union sealing washers.

1

Notes

Chapter 2
Engine, clutch and transmission

Contents

2

Degrees of difficulty

Easy, suitable for novice with little experience	**Fairly easy,** suitable for beginner with some experience	**Fairly difficult,** suitable for competent DIY mechanic 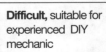	**Difficult,** suitable for experienced DIY mechanic	**Very difficult,** suitable for expert DIY or professional

Specifications

Katana 600 (GSX600F) model

General
Bore . . . . 62.6 mm (2.465 inches)
Stroke . . . . 48.7 mm (1.917 inch)
Displacement . . . . 599 cc (36.6 cubic inches)
Compression ratio . . . . 11.3 : 1

Katana 600 (GSX600F) model (continued)

Camshaft and rocker arms

Lobe height (intake)
  Standard
    1988 and 1989
      US .... 33.617 to 33.657 mm (1.3235 to 1.3251 inch)
      UK .... 33.563 to 33.583 mm (1.3214 to 1.3222 inch)
    1990 and 1991
      US .... 33.617 to 33.657 mm (1.3235 to 1.3251 inch)
      UK .... 33.900 to 33.960 mm (1.3346 to 1.3370 inch)
    1992 on
      US .... 33.632 to 33.688 mm (1.3241 to 1.3263 inch)
      UK .... 33.922 to 33.978 mm (1.3355 to 1.3377 inch)
  Minimum
    1988 and 1989
      US .... 33.320 mm (1.3118 inch)
      UK .... 33.270 mm (1.3098 inch)
    1990 and 1991
      US .... 33.320 mm (1.3118 inch)
      UK .... 33.600 mm (1.3228 inch)
    1992 on
      US .... 33.330 mm (1.3122 inch)
      UK .... 33.620 mm (1.3236 inch)
Lobe height (exhaust)
  Standard
    1988 and 1989
      US .... 32.882 to 32.922 mm (1.2946 to 1.2961 inch)
      UK .... 33.146 to 33.186 mm (1.3050 to 1.3065 inch)
    1990 through 1991 .... 32.882 to 32.922 mm (1.2946 to 1.2961 inch)
    1992 on .... 32.902 to 32.958 mm (1.2954 to 1.2976 inch)
  Minimum
    1988 and 1989
      US .... 32.590 mm (1.2831 inch)
      UK .... 32.850 mm (1.2933 inch)
    1990 and 1991 .... 32.590 mm (1.2831 inch)
    1992 on .... 32.600 mm (1.2835 inch)
Bearing oil clearance
  Standard .... 0.032 to 0.066 mm (0.0013 to 0.0026 inch)
  Maximum .... 0.150 mm (0.0059 inch)
Journal diameter .... 21.959 to 21.980 mm (0.8645 to 0.8654 inch)
Camshaft runout limit .... 0.10 mm (0.004 inch)
Camshaft chain 21-pin length (maximum)
  1988 through 1995 .... 158.0 mm (6.22 inches)
  1996 .... No maximum length specified
Rocker arm inside diameter .... 12.000 to 12.018 mm (0.4724 to 0.4731 inch)
Rocker shaft diameter .... 11.973 to 11.984 mm (0.4714 to 0.4718 inch)

Cylinder head, valves and valve springs

Cylinder head warpage limit .... 0.2 mm (0.008 inch)
Valve head thickness (margin) limit .... 0.5 mm (0.020 inch)
Valve seat width (intake and exhaust) .... 0.9 to 1.1 mm (0.035 to 0.043 inch)
Valve stem bend limit .... 0.05 mm (0.002 inch)
Valve stem length above keeper groove .... 2.5 mm (0.0098 inch)
Valve stem diameter
  Intake .... 4.965 to 4.980 mm (0.1955 to 0.1961 inch)
  Exhaust
    1988 through 1991 .... 4.945 to 4.960 mm (0.1947 to 0.1953 inch)
    1992 on .... 4.955 to 4.970 mm (0.1950 to 0.1957 inch)
Valve guide inside diameter .... 5.000 to 5.012 mm (0.1969 to 0.1973 inch)
Valve spring free length
  1988 through 1991
    Inner .... 35 mm (1.38 inch)
    Outer .... 38.4 mm (1.51 inch)
  1992 on
    Inner .... 39.1 mm (1.54 inch)
    Outer .... 41.6 mm (1.64 inch)
Valve head radial runout limit .... 0.03 mm (0.001 inch)

Cylinder block

Surface warp limit . . . . 0.2 mm (0.008 inch)
Bore diameter
  Standard . . . . 62.600 to 62.615 mm (2.4646 to 2.4652 inches)
  Maximum . . . . 62.690 mm (2.4681 inches)

Pistons

Piston diameter
  Standard . . . . 62.555 to 62.570 mm (2.4628 to 2.4634 inches)
  Minimum . . . . 62.480 mm (2.4598 inches)
Piston-to-cylinder clearance
  Standard . . . . 0.040 to 0.050 mm (0.0016 to 0.0020 inch)
  Maximum . . . . 0.120 mm (0.0047 inch)
Ring side clearance
  Top . . . . 0.180 mm (0.007 inch)
  Second . . . . 0.150 mm (0.006 inch)
Ring groove width
  Top . . . . 0.81 to 0.83 mm (0.032 to 0.033 inch)
  Second . . . . 1.01 to 1.03 mm (0.039 to 0.040 inch)
  Oil . . . . 2.01 to 2.03 mm (0.079 to 0.080 inch)
Ring thickness
  Top . . . . 0.77 to 0.79 mm (0.030 to 0.031 inch)
  Second . . . . 0.97 to 0.99 mm (0.038 to 0.039 inch)
Ring free end gap
  Top
    Standard . . . . Approximately 8.6 mm (0.34 inch)
    Limit . . . . 6.9 mm (0.27 inch)
  Second
    Standard . . . . Approximately 6.7 mm (0.26 inch)
    Limit . . . . 5.4 mm (0.21 inch)
Ring end gap (installed)
  Standard
    Top . . . . 0.1 to 0.3 mm (0.004 to 0.012 inch)
    Second
      1988 through 1991 . . . . 0.1 to 0.3 mm (0.004 to 0.012 inch)
      1992 on . . . . 0.3 to 0.5 mm (0.012 to 0.020 inch)
    Oil . . . . Not specified
  Maximum . . . . 0.7 mm (0.030 inch)

Crankshaft and bearings

Main bearing oil clearance
  Standard . . . . 0.020 to 0.044 mm (0.0008 to 0.0017 inch)
  Maximum . . . . 0.080 mm (0.0031 inch)
Main bearing journal diameter . . . . 31.976 to 32.000 mm (1.2589 to 1.2598 inch)
Crankshaft thrust clearance . . . . 0.04 to 0.09 mm (0.002 to 0.004 inch)
Right thrust bearing thickness . . . . 2.445 to 2.465 mm (0.0963 to 0.0970 inch)
Connecting rod side clearance
  Standard . . . . 0.010 to 0.020 mm (0.004 to 0.008 inch)
  Maximum . . . . 0.030 mm (0.012 inch)
Connecting rod big end thickness . . . . 20.95 to 21.00 mm (0.825 to 0.827 inch)
Crankpin width . . . . 21.10 to 21.15 mm (0.831 to 0.833 inch)
Connecting rod bearing oil clearance
  Standard . . . . 0.032 to 0.056 mm (0.0013 to 0.0022 inch)
  Maximum . . . . 0.080 mm (0.0031 inch)
Connecting rod journal (crankpin) diameter . . . . 33.976 to 34.000 mm (1.3376 to 1.3386 inch)
Oil pressure (60 degrees C/140 degrees F) . . . . 2.97 to 5.86 bars (43 to 85 psi)
Crankshaft runout . . . . 0.05 mm (0.002 inch)

Clutch

Spring free length
  1988 through 1991 . . . . 33 mm (1.30 inch)
  1992 on . . . . 47.5 mm (1.87 inch)
Friction plate thickness
  1988 through 1991
    Standard . . . . 2.65 to 2.95 mm (0.104 to 0.116 inch)
    Minimum . . . . 2.35 mm (0.103 inch)
  1992 on
    Standard . . . . 2.12 to 2.28 mm (0.083 to 0.090 inch)
    Minimum . . . . 1.72 mm (0.068 inch)
Steel plate warpage limit . . . . 0.10 mm (0.004 inch)
Release screw adjustment . . . . 1/4 to 1/2 turn back

2

Katana 600 (GSX600F) model (continued)

Transmission

Shift fork gear groove width
  No. 1 and no. 3 grooves .... 4.8 to 4.9 mm (0.189 to 0.193 inch)
  No. 2 groove .... 5.0 to 5.1 mm (0.197 to 0.201 inch)
Shift fork ear thickness
  No. 1 and No. 3 forks .... 4.6 to 4.7 mm (0.181 to 0.185 inch)
  No. 2 fork .... 4.8 to 4.9 mm (0.189 to 0.193 inch)
Shift fork to groove clearance
  Standard .... 0.1 to 0.3 mm (0.004 to 0.012 inch)
  Maximum .... 0.5 mm (0.020 inch)

Torque specifications

Engine mounting bolts
  55 mm length .... 50 to 60 Nm (36 to 43.5 ft-lbs)
  130 and 175 mm length .... 70 to 80 Nm (50.5 to 58 ft-lbs)
Valve cover bolts .... 13 to 15 Nm (9.5 to 11 ft-lbs)
Oil hose to valve cover bolts .... 8 to 12 Nm (6.0 to 8.5 ft-lbs)
Oil hose to cylinder block bolts .... 8 to 12 Nm (6.0 to 8.5 ft-lbs)
Camshaft bearing cap bolts .... 8 to 12 Nm (6.0 to 8.5 ft-lbs)
Camshaft sprocket bolts .... 24 to 26 Nm (17.4 to 18.8 ft-lbs)
Rocker arm shaft lockbolts .... 8 to 10 Nm (6 to 7 ft-lbs)
Camshaft chain idler .... 8 to 12 Nm (6.0 to 8.5 ft-lbs)
Camshaft chain top guide .... 8 to 12 Nm (6.0 to 8.5 ft-lbs)
Cylinder head bolt .... 8 to 12 Nm (6.0 to 8.5 ft-lbs)
Cylinder head nuts .... 35 to 40 Nm (25.5 to 29 ft-lbs)
Cylinder block base nut .... 7 to 11 Nm (5 to 8 ft-lbs)
Cylinder block studs to crankcase .... 13 to 16 Nm (9.5 to 11.5 ft-lbs)
Cam chain tensioner bolts .... 6 to 8 Nm (4.5 to 6.0 ft-lbs)
Cam chain tensioner spring holder bolt .... 30 to 40 Nm (21.5 to 29 ft-lbs)
Signal generator cover bolts .... 12 to 16 Nm (8.5 to 11.5 ft-lbs)
Signal generator bolt .... See Chapter 8
Starter clutch mounting bolt .... 140 to 160 Nm (101.5 to 115.5 ft-lbs)
Clutch spring bolts .... 11 to 13 Nm (8.0 to 9.5 ft-lbs)
Clutch sleeve hub nut .... 60 to 80 Nm (43.5 to 58 ft-lbs)
Oil pan bolts .... 12 to 16 Nm (8.5 to 11.5 ft-lbs)
Oil pump bolts .... 8 to 12 Nm (6.0 to 8.5 ft-lbs)
Crankcase bolts
  6 mm bolts .... 9 to 13 Nm (6.5 to 9.5 ft-lbs)
  8 mm bolts .... 20 to 24 Nm 14.5 to 17.4 ft-lbs)
Connecting rod nuts .... 33 to 37 Nm (23.9 to 27 ft-lbs)
Shift cam stopper bolt .... 15 to 23 Nm (11 to 16.5 ft-lbs)
Engine sprocket nut .... 100 to 130 Nm (72.5 to 94 ft-lbs)
Engine sprocket bolt (where fitted) .... 9 to 12 Nm (6.5 to 8.5 ft-lbs)

GSX-R750 model

General

Bore
  1985 through 1987, 1990 on .... 70.00 mm (2.756 inches)
  1988 and 1989 .... 73.00 mm (2.874 inches)
Stroke
  1985 through 1987, 1990 on .... 48.7 mm (1.917 inch)
  1988 and 1989 .... 44.7 mm (1.760 inch)
Displacement
  1985 through 1987, 1990 on .... 749 cc (45.7 cubic inches)
  1988 and 1989 .... 748 cc (45.6 cubic inches)

Camshaft and rocker arms

Lobe height (intake)
  1985 through 1987 (UK)
    Standard .... 33.563 to 33.603 mm (1.3214 to 1.3229 inch)
    Minimum .... 33.270 mm (1.3098 inch)
  1986 and 1987 (US)
    Standard .... 33.594 to 33.634 mm (1.3226 to 1.3242 inch)
    Minimum .... 33.300 mm (1.3110 inch)
  1988 and 1989
    Standard .... 33.878 to 33.918 mm (1.3338 to 1.3353 inch)
    Minimum .... 33.580 mm (1.3220 inch)

Camshaft and rocker arms (continued)

Lobe height (intake)
  1990
    Standard .... 33.876 to 33.936 mm (1.3337 to 1.3361 inch)
    Minimum .... 33.580 mm (1.3220 inch)
  1991 on
    Standard .... 33.896 to 33.944 mm (1.3345 to 1.3364 inch)
    Minimum .... 33.600 mm (1.3228 inch)
Lobe height (exhaust)
  1985 through 1987 (UK)
    Standard .... 33.146 to 33.186 mm (1.3049 to 1.3065 inch)
    Minimum .... 32.850 mm (1.2933 inch)
  1986 and 1987 (US)
    Standard .... 32.882 to 32.9922 mm (1.2946 to 1.2989 inch)
    Minimum .... 32.590 mm (1.2831 inch)
  1988
    Standard .... 33.533 to 33.573 mm (1.3202 to 1.3218 inch)
    Minimum .... 33.240 mm (1.3087 inch)
  1989
    Standard .... 33.604 to 33.664 mm (1.3230 to 1.3254 inch)
    Minimum .... 33.310 mm (1.3114 inch)
  1990
    Standard .... 32.872 to 32.932 mm (1.2492 to 1.2965 inch)
    Minimum .... 32.580 mm (1.2827 inch)
  1991 on
    Standard .... 32.906 to 32.954 mm (1.2955 to 1.2974 inch)
    Minimum .... 32.610 mm (1.2839 inch)
Bearing oil clearance
  Standard .... 0.032 to 0.066 mm (0.0013 to 0.0026 inch)
  Maximum .... 0.150 mm (0.0059 inch)
Journal diameter .... 21.959 to 21.980 mm (0.8645 to 0.8654 inch)
Camshaft runout limit .... 0.10 mm (0.004 inch)
Camshaft chain 21-pin length (maximum) .... 158.0 mm (6.22 inches)
Rocker arm inside diameter .... 12.000 to 12.018 mm (0.4724 to 0.4731 inch)
Rocker shaft diameter .... 11.973 to 11.984 mm (0.4714 to 0.4718 inch)

Cylinder head, valves and valve springs

Cylinder head warpage limit .... 0.2 mm (0.008 inch)
Valve head thickness (margin) limit .... 0.5 mm (0.020 inch)
Valve seat width (intake and exhaust) .... 0.9 to 1.1 mm (0.035 to 0.043 inch)
Valve stem bend limit .... 0.05 mm (0.002 inch)
Valve stem length above keeper groove .... 2.5 mm (0.0098 inch)
Valve stem diameter
  Intake .... 4.965 to 4.980 mm (0.1955 to 0.1961 inch)
  Exhaust .... 4.945 to 4.960 mm (0.1947 to 0.1953 inch)
Valve guide inside diameter .... 5.000 to 5.012 mm (0.1969 to 0.1973 inch)
Valve spring free length
  1985 through 1987
    Inner .... 35.0 mm (1.38 inch)
    Outer .... 38.4 mm (1.51 inch)
  1988 through 1990
    Inner .... 33.9 mm (1.33 inch)
    Outer .... 37.3 mm (1.47 inch)
  1991 on
    Inner .... 35.0 mm (37.8 inches)
    Outer .... 37.8 mm (1.49 inch)
Valve head radial runout limit .... 0.03 mm (0.001 inch)

Cylinder block

Surface warp, limit .... 0.2 mm (0.008 inch)
Bore diameter
  Nominal 70 mm bores
    Standard (1985 through 1987) .... 70.000 to 70.015 mm (2.7559 to 2.7565 inches)
    Standard (1990 on) .... 69.940 to 69.955 mm (2.7535 to 2.7541 inches)
    Maximum .... 70.080 mm (2.7590 inches)
  Nominal 73 mm bores
    Standard .... 73.000 to 73.015 mm (2.8740 to 2.8746 inches)
    Maximum .... 73.090 mm (2.8775 inches)

2

GSX-R750 model (continued)

Pistons
Piston diameter
  With 70 mm bores
    Standard
      1985 through 1987 .... 69.945 to 69.960 mm (2.7537 to 2.7543 inches)
      1990 on .... 69.940 to 69.955 mm (2.7535 to 2.7541 inches)
    Minimum .... 69.880 mm (2.7512 inches)
  With 73 mm bores
    Standard .... 72.955 to 72.970 mm (2.8722 to 2.8728 inches)
    Minimum .... 72.880 mm (2.8693 inches)
Piston-to-cylinder clearance
  1985 through 1987
    Standard .... 0.050 to 0.060 mm (0.0020 to 0.0024 inch)
    Maximum .... 0.120 mm (0.0047 inch)
  1988 and 1989
    Standard .... 0.040 to 0.050 mm (0.0015 to 0.0019 inch)
    Maximum .... 0.120 mm (0.0047 inch)
  1990 on
    Standard .... 0.055 to 0.065 mm (0.0022 to 0.0026 inch)
    Maximum .... 0.120 mm (0.0047 inch)
Ring side clearance
  1985 through 1987
    Top .... 0.180 mm (0.007 inch)
    Second .... 0.150 mm (0.006 inch)
  1988 on (top and second) .... 0.180 mm (0.007 inch)
Ring groove width
  1985 through 1987
    Top .... 0.81 to 0.83 mm (0.032 to 0.033 inch)
    Second .... 1.01 to 1.03 mm (0.039 to 0.040 inch)
    Oil .... 2.01 to 2.03 mm (0.079 to 0.080 inch)
  1988 on
    Top and second .... 0.81 to 0.83 mm (0.032 to 0.033 inch)
    Oil .... 1.51 to 1.53 mm (0.059 to 0.060 inch)
Ring thickness
  1985 through 1987
    Top .... 0.77 to 0.79 mm (0.030 to 0.031 inch)
    Second .... 0.97 to 0.99 mm (0.038 to 0.039 inch)
  1988 on (top and second) .... 0.77 to 0.79 mm (0.030 to 0.031 inch)
Ring free end gap
  1985 through 1987
    Top
      Standard .... Approximately 9.1 mm (0.36 inch)
      Limit .... 7.3 mm (0.29 inch)
    Second
      Standard .... Approximately 7.5 mm (0.30 inch)
      Limit .... 6.0 mm (0.24 inch)
  1988
    Top
      Standard .... Approximately 9.6 mm (0.38 inch)
      Limit .... 7.7 mm (0.30 inch)
    Second
      Standard .... Approximately 6.9 mm (0.27 inch)
      Limit .... 5.5 mm (0.21 inch)
  1989
    Top
      Standard .... Approximately 8.2 mm (0.32 inch)
      Limit .... 6.6 mm (0.26 inch)
    Second
      Standard .... Approximately 6.9 mm (0.27 inch)
      Limit .... 5.5 mm (0.21 inch)
  1990 on
    Top
      Standard .... Approximately 9.8 mm (0.39 inch)
      Limit .... 7.8 mm (0.31 inch)
    Second
      Standard .... Approximately 7.7 mm (0.30 inch)
      Limit .... 6.2 mm (0.24 inch)

Pistons (continued)

Ring end gap (installed)

1985 (UK)

Standard

Top .... 0.10 to 0.25 mm (0.004 to 0.010 inch)

Second .... 0.20 to 0.35 mm (0.008 to 0.014 inch)

Limit (top and second) .... 0.7 mm (0.030 inch)

1986 through 1988 (top and second)

Standard .... 0.1 to 0.3 mm (0.004 to 0.012 inch)

Limit .... 0.7 mm (0.030 inch)

1989

Standard

Top .... 0.10 to 0.25 mm (0.004 to 0.010 inch)

Second .... 0.20 to 0.35 mm (0.008 to 0.014 inch)

Limit .... 0.7 mm (0.030 inch)

1990 on

Standard (top and second) .... 0.20 to 0.35 mm (0.008 to 0.014 inch)

Limit (top and second) .... 0.7 mm (0.030 inch)

Crankshaft and bearings

Main bearing oil clearance

Standard .... 0.020 to 0.044 mm (0.0008 to 0.0017 inch)

Maximum .... 0.080 mm (0.0031 inch)

Main bearing journal diameter .... 31.976 to 32.000 mm (1.2589 to 1.2598 inch)

Crankshaft thrust clearance

1985 through 1987

Standard .... 0.04 to 0.18 mm (0.002 to 0.007 inch)

Maximum .... 0.25 mm (0.010 inch)

1988 and 1989 .... 0.05 to 0.13 mm (0.002 to 0.005 inch)

1990 on .... 0.055 to 0.110 mm (0.0022 to 0.0043 inch)

Right thrust bearing thickness

1986 and 1987, 1990 on .... 2.425 to 2.450 mm (0.0954 to 0.0964 inch)

1988 and 1989, ... 2.42 to 2.44 mm (0.095 to 0.096 inch)

Connecting rod side clearance

Standard .... 0.010 to 0.020 mm (0.004 to 0.008 inch)

Maximum .... 0.030 mm (0.012 inch)

Connecting rod big end thickness .... 20.95 to 21.00 mm (0.825 to 0.827 inch)

Crankpin width .... 21.10 to 21.15 mm (0.831 to 0.833 inch)

Connecting rod bearing oil clearance

Standard .... 0.032 to 0.056 mm (0.0013 to 0.0022 inch)

Maximum .... 0.080 mm (0.0031 inch)

Connecting rod journal (crankpin) diameter .... 33.976 to 34.000 mm (1.3376 to 1.3386 inch)

Oil pressure (60 degrees C/140 degrees F) .... 2.97 to 5.86 bars (43 to 85 psi)

Crankshaft runout .... 0.05 mm (0.002 inch)

Clutch

Spring free length

1985 through 1987 .... 34.0 mm (1.34 inch)

1988 and 1989 .... 38.1 mm (1.50 inch)

1990 on .... 47.5 mm (1.87 inch)

Friction plate thickness

1985 through 1987

Standard .... 2.92 to 3.08 mm (0.115 to 0.121 inch)

Minimum .... 2.62 mm (0.103 inch)

1988 on

Standard .... 2.12 to 2.28 mm (0.083 to 0.090 inch)

Minimum .... 1.82 mm (0.072 inch)

Steel plate warpage limit .... 0.10 mm (0.004 inch)

Transmission

Shift fork gear groove width

No. 1 and no. 3 grooves .... 4.8 to 4.9 mm (0.189 to 0.193 inch)

No. 2 groove .... 5.0 to 5.1 mm (0.197 to 0.201 inch)

Shift fork ear thickness

No. 1 and No. 3 forks .... 4.6 to 4.7 mm (0.181 to 0.185 inch)

No. 2 fork .... 4.8 to 4.9 mm (0.189 to 0.193 inch)

Shift fork to groove clearance

Standard .... 0.1 to 0.3 mm (0.004 to 0.012 inch)

Maximum .... 0.5 mm (0.020 inch)

2

GSX-R750 model (continued)
Torque specifications

Engine mounting bolts
    55 mm length .... 50 to 60 Nm (36 to 43.5 ft-lbs)
    180 and 255 mm length (early models) .... 70 to 80 Nm (50.5 to 58 ft-lbs)
    150 and 175 mm length (later models) .... 70 to 88 Nm (50.5 to 63.5 ft-lbs)
Valve cover bolts .... 13 to 15 Nm (9.5 to 11 ft-lbs)
Oil hose to valve cover bolts .... 8 to 12 Nm (6.0 to 8.5 ft-lbs)
Oil hose to cylinder block bolts .... 8 to 12 Nm (6.0 to 8.5 ft-lbs)
Camshaft bearing cap bolts .... 8 to 12 Nm (6.0 to 8.5 ft-lbs)
Camshaft sprocket bolts .... 24 to 26 Nm (17.4 to 18.8 ft-lbs)
Rocker arm shaft lockbolts .... 8 to 10 Nm (6 to 7 ft-lbs)
Camshaft chain idler
    1985 through 1987 .... 7 to 11 Nm (5.0 to 8.0 ft-lbs)
    1988 on .... 8 to 12 Nm (6.0 to 8.5 ft-lbs)
Cylinder head bolt
    1985 through 1987 .... 9 to 11 Nm (6.5 to 8.0 ft-lbs)
    1988 on .... 8 to 12 Nm (6.0 to 8.5 ft-lbs)
Cylinder head nuts .... 35 to 40 Nm (25.5 to 29 ft-lbs)
Cylinder block base nut .... 7 to 11 Nm (5 to 8 ft-lbs)
Cylinder block studs to crankcase .... 13 to 16 Nm (9.5 to 11.5 ft-lbs)
Cam chain tensioner bolts .... 6 to 8 Nm (4.5 to 6.0 ft-lbs)
Cam chain tensioner spring holder bolt .... 30 to 45 Nm (21.5 to 32.5 ft-lbs)
Signal generator cover bolts .... 12 to 16 Nm (8.5 to 11.5 ft-lbs)
Signal generator bolt .... See Chapter 8
Starter clutch mounting bolt
    1985 through 1987 .... 110 to 130 Nm (80 to 94 ft-lbs)
    1988 on .... 143 to 157 Nm (103.5 to 113.5 ft-lbs)
Clutch spring bolts .... 11 to 13 Nm (8.0 to 9.5 ft-lbs)
Clutch sleeve hub nut
    1985 through 1987 .... 50 to 70 Nm (36 to 50 ft-lbs)
    1988 on .... 80 to 100 Nm (58 to 72.5 ft-lbs)
Oil pan bolts .... 12 to 16 Nm (8.5 to 11.5 ft-lbs)
Oil pump bolts .... 8 to 12 Nm (6.0 to 8.5 ft-lbs)
Crankcase bolts
    1985 through 1987
        6 mm bolts .... 9 to 13 Nm (6.5 to 9.5 ft-lbs)
        8 mm bolts .... 20 to 24 Nm 14.5 to 17.4 ft-lbs)
Crankcase bolts
    1988 on
        6 mm bolts .... 12 to 16 Nm (8.5 to 11.5 ft-lbs)
        8 mm bolts .... 20 to 28 Nm (14.5 to 20 ft-lbs)
Connecting rod nuts
    1985 through 1987 .... 33 to 37 Nm (24 to 26 ft-lbs)
    1988 and 1989 .... 49 to 53 Nm (35.5 to 38.5 ft-lbs)
    1990 on .... 65 to 69 Nm (47 to 50 ft-lbs)
Shift cam stopper bolt .... 15 to 23 Nm (11 to 16.5 ft-lbs)
Engine sprocket nut .... 100 to 130 Nm (72.5 to 94 ft-lbs)
Engine sprocket bolt (where fitted) .... 9 to 12 Nm (6.5 to 8.5 ft-lbs)

Katana 750 (GSX750F) model

General

Bore .... 73.00 mm (2.874 inches)
Stroke .... 44.72 mm (1.761 inch)
Displacement .... 748 cc (45.6 cubic inches)
Compression ratio .... 10.7 : 1

Camshaft and rocker arms

Lobe height (intake)
    Standard
        1989 through 1995 .... 33.594 to 33.634 mm (1.3226 to 1.3242 inch)
        1996 .... 33.600 to 33.644 mm (1.3228 to 1.3246 in)ch
    Minimum .... 33.300 mm (1.3110 inch)
Lobe height (exhaust)
    Standard
        1989 through 1995 .... 32.882 to 32.922 mm (1.2946 to 1.2961 inch)
        1996 .... 32.890 to 32.934 mm (1.2949 to 1.2966 inch)
    Minimum .... 32.590 mm (1.2831 inch)
Bearing oil clearance
    Standard .... 0.032 to 0.066 mm (0.0013 to 0.0026 inch)
    Maximum .... 0.150 mm (0.0059 inch)

Camshaft and rocker arms (continued)

Journal diameter . . . . 21.959 to 21.980 mm (0.8645 to 0.8654 inch)
Camshaft runout limit . . . . 0.10 mm (0.004 inch)
Camshaft chain 21-pin length (maximum) . . . . 158.0 mm (6.22 inches)
Rocker arm inside diameter . . . . 12.000 to 12.018 mm (0.4724 to 0.4731 inch)
Rocker shaft diameter . . . . 11.973 to 11.984 mm (0.4714 to 0.4718 inch)

Cylinder head, valves and valve springs

Cylinder head warpage limit . . . . 0.2 mm (0.008 inch)
Valve head thickness (margin) limit . . . . 0.5 mm (0.020 inch)
Valve seat width (intake and exhaust) . . . . 0.9 to 1.1 mm (0.035 to 0.043 inch)
Valve stem bend limit . . . . 0.05 mm (0.002 inch)
Valve stem length above keeper groove . . . . 2.5 mm (0.0098 inch)
Valve stem diameter
   Intake . . . . 4.965 to 4.980 mm (0.1955 to 0.1961 inch)
   Exhaust . . . . 4.945 to 4.960 mm (0.1947 to 0.1953 inch)
Valve guide inside diameter . . . . 5.000 to 5.012 mm (0.1969 to 0.1973 inch)
Valve spring free length
   Inner . . . . 33.9 mm (1.33 inch)
   Outer . . . . 37.3 mm (1.47 inch)
Valve head radial runout limit . . . . 0.03 mm (0.001 inch)

Cylinder block

Surface warp limit . . . . 0.2 mm (0.008 inch)
Bore diameter
   Standard . . . . 73.000 to 73.015 mm (2.8740 to 2.8746 inches)
   Maximum . . . . 73.090 mm (2.8775 inch)

Pistons

Piston diameter
   Standard . . . . 72.955 to 72.970 mm (2.8722 to 2.8728 inches)
   Minimum . . . . 72.880 mm (2.8693 inches)
Piston-to-cylinder clearance
   Standard . . . . 0.040 to 0.050 mm (0.0015 to 0.0019 inch)
   Maximum . . . . 0.120 mm (0.0047 inch)
Ring side clearance . . . . 0.180 mm (0.007 inch)
Ring groove width
   Top and second . . . . 0.81 to 0.84 mm (0.032 to 0.033 inch)
   Oil . . . . 1.51 to 1.53 mm (0.059 to 0.060 inch)
Ring thickness (top and second) . . . . 0.77 to 0.79 mm (0.030 to 0.031 inch)
Ring free end gap
   Top
      Standard . . . . Approximately 8.2 mm (0.32 inch)
      Limit . . . . 6.6 mm (0.26 inch)
   Second
      Standard . . . . Approximately 6.9 mm (0.27 inch)
      Limit . . . . 5.5 mm (0.21 inch)
Ring end gap (installed)
   Standard
      Top . . . . 0.10 to 0.25 mm (0.004 to 0.010 inch)
      Second . . . . 0.20 to 0.35 mm (0.008 to 0.014 inch)
      Oil . . . . Not specified
   Maximum . . . . 0.7 mm (0.030 inch)

Crankshaft and bearings

Main bearing oil clearance
   Standard . . . . 0.020 to 0.044 mm (0.0008 to 0.0017 inch)
   Maximum . . . . 0.080 mm (0.0031 inch)
Main bearing journal diameter . . . . 35.976 to 36.000 mm (1.4163 to 1.4173 inch)
Crankshaft thrust clearance . . . . 0.05 to 0.13 mm (0.002 to 0.005 inch)
Right thrust bearing thickness . . . . 2.42 to 2.44 mm (0.095 to 0.096 inch)
Connecting rod side clearance
   Standard . . . . 0.010 to 0.020 mm (0.004 to 0.008 inch)
   Maximum . . . . 0.030 mm (0.012 inch)
Connecting rod big end thickness . . . . 20.95 to 21.00 mm (0.825 to 0.827 inch)
Crankpin width . . . . 21.10 to 21.15 mm (0.831 to 0.833 inch)
Connecting rod bearing oil clearance
   Standard . . . . 0.032 to 0.056 mm (0.0013 to 0.0022 inch)
   Maximum . . . . 0.080 mm (0.0031 inch)
Connecting rod journal (crankpin) diameter . . . . 35.976 to 36.000 mm (1.4163 to 1.4173 inch)
Oil pressure (60 degrees C/140 degrees F) . . . . 2.97 to 5.86 bars (43 to 85 psi)
Crankshaft runout . . . . 0.05 mm (0.002 inch)

2

Katana 750 (GSX750F) model (continued)

Clutch

Spring free length	38.1 mm (1.50 inch)
Friction plate thickness	
Standard	2.12 to 2.28 mm (0.083 to 0.090 inch)
Minimum	1.82 mm (0.072 inch)
Steel plate warpage limit	0.10 mm (0.004 inch)

Transmission

Shift fork gear groove width	
No. 1 and no. 3 grooves	4.8 to 4.9 mm (0.189 to 0.193 inch)
No. 2 groove	5.0 to 5.1 mm (0.197 to 0.201 inch)
Shift fork ear thickness	
No. 1 and No. 3 forks	4.6 to 4.7 mm (0.181 to 0.185 inch)
No. 2 fork	4.8 to 4.9 mm (0.189 to 0.193 inch)
Shift fork to groove clearance	
Standard	0.1 to 0.3 mm (0.004 to 0.012 inch)
Maximum	0.5 mm (0.020 inch)

Torque specifications

Engine mounting bolts	
55 mm length	50 to 60 Nm (36 to 43.5 ft-lbs)
130 and 175 mm length	70 to 80 Nm (50.5 to 58 ft-lbs)
Valve cover bolts	13 to 15 Nm (9.5 to 11 ft-lbs)
Oil hose to valve cover bolts	8 to 12 Nm (6.0 to 8.5 ft-lbs)
Oil hose to cylinder block bolts	8 to 12 Nm (6.0 to 8.5 ft-lbs)
Camshaft bearing cap bolts	8 to 12 Nm (6.0 to 8.5 ft-lbs)
Camshaft sprocket bolts	24 to 26 Nm (17.4 to 18.8 ft-lbs)
Rocker arm shaft lockbolts	8 to 10 Nm (6 to 7 ft-lbs)
Camshaft chain idler	8 to 12 Nm (6.0 to 8.5 ft-lbs)
Cylinder head bolt	8 to 12 Nm (6.0 to 8.5 ft-lbs)
Cylinder head nuts	35 to 40 Nm (25.5 to 29 ft-lbs)
Cylinder block base nut	7 to 11 Nm (5 to 8 ft-lbs)
Cylinder block studs to crankcase	13 to 16 Nm (9.5 to 11.5 ft-lbs)
Cam chain tensioner bolts	6 to 8 Nm (4.5 to 6.0 ft-lbs)
Cam chain tensioner spring holder bolt	30 to 45 Nm (21.5 to 32.5 ft-lbs)
Signal generator cover bolts	12 to 16 Nm (8.5 to 11.5 ft-lbs)
Signal generator bolt	See Chapter 8
Starter clutch mounting bolt	143 to 157 Nm (103.5 to 113.5 ft-lbs)
Clutch spring bolts	11 to 13 Nm (8.0 to 9.5 ft-lbs)
Clutch sleeve hub nut	80 to 100 Nm (58 to 72.5 ft-lbs)
Oil pan bolts	12 to 16 Nm (8.5 to 11.5 ft-lbs)
Oil pump bolts	8 to 12 Nm (6.0 to 8.5 ft-lbs)
Crankcase bolts	
6 mm bolts	9 to 13 Nm (6.5 to 9.5 ft-lbs)
8 mm bolts	20 to 24 Nm 14.5 to 17.4 ft-lbs)
Connecting rod nuts	49 to 53 Nm (35.5 to 38.5 ft-lbs)
Shift cam stopper bolt	15 to 23 Nm (11 to 16.5 ft-lbs)
Engine sprocket nut	100 to 130 Nm (72.5 to 94 ft-lbs)
Engine sprocket bolt (where fitted)	9 to 12 Nm (6.5 to 8.5 ft-lbs)

Katana 1100 (GSX1100F) model

General

Bore	78.00 mm (3.07 inches)
Stroke	59.00 mm (2.32 inches)
Displacement	1127 cc (68.8 cubic inches)

Camshaft and rocker arms

Lobe height (intake)	
Standard	33.378 to 33.918 mm (1.3338 to 1.3354 inch)
Minimum	33.580 mm (1.3220 inch)
Lobe height (exhaust)	
Standard	33.533 to 33.573 mm (1.3202 to 1.3218 inch)
Minimum	33.240 mm (1.3087 inch)
Bearing oil clearance	
Standard	0.032 to 0.066 mm (0.0013 to 0.0026 inch)
Maximum	0.150 mm (0.0059 inch)
Journal diameter	21.959 to 21.980 mm (0.8645 to 0.8654 inch)
Camshaft runout limit	0.10 mm (0.004 inch)
Camshaft chain 21-pin length (maximum)	158.0 mm (6.22 inches)
Rocker arm inside diameter	12.000 to 12.018 mm (0.4724 to 0.4731 inch)
Rocker shaft diameter	11.973 to 11.984 mm (0.4714 to 0.4718 inch)

Cylinder head, valves and valve springs

Cylinder head warpage limit . . . . 0.2 mm (0.008 inch)
Valve head thickness (margin) limit . . . . 0.5 mm (0.020 inch)
Valve seat width (intake and exhaust) . . . . 0.9 to 1.1 mm (0.035 to 0.043 inch)
Valve stem bend limit . . . . 0.05 mm (0.002 inch)
Valve stem length above keeper groove . . . . 2.5 mm (0.0098 inch)
Valve stem diameter
    Intake . . . . 4.965 to 4.980 mm (0.1955 to 0.1961 inch)
    Exhaust . . . . 4.945 to 4.960 mm (0.1947 to 0.1953 inch)
Valve guide inside diameter . . . . 5.000 to 5.012 mm (0.1969 to 0.1973 inch)
Valve spring free length
    Inner . . . . 35.0 mm (1.38 inch)
    Outer . . . . 37.8 mm (1.49 inch)
Valve head radial runout limit . . . . 0.03 mm (0.001 inch)

Cylinder block

Surface warp limit . . . . 0.2 mm (0.008 inch)
Bore diameter
    Standard . . . . 78.000 to 78.015 mm (3.0709 to 3.0715 inches)
    Maximum . . . . 78.080 mm (3.0740 inches)

Pistons

Piston diameter
    Standard . . . . 77.945 to 77.960 mm (3.0687 to 3.0693 inches)
    Minimum . . . . 77.880 mm (3.0661 inches)
Piston-to-cylinder clearance
    Standard . . . . 0.050 to 0.060 mm (0.0020 to 0.0024 inch)
    Maximum . . . . 0.120 mm (0.0047 inch)
Ring side clearance
    Top . . . . 0.180 mm (0.007 inch)
    Second . . . . 0.150 mm (0.006 inch)
Ring groove width
    Top and second . . . . 1.01 to 1.03 mm (0.039 to 0.040 inch)
    Oil . . . . 2.01 to 2.03 mm (0.079 to 0.080 inch)
Ring thickness (top and second) . . . . 0.97 to 0.99 mm (0.038 to 0.039 inch)
Ring free end gap
    Top
        Standard . . . . Approximately 10.0 mm (0.39 inch)
        Limit . . . . 8.0 mm (0.31 inch)
    Second
        Standard . . . . Approximately 11.5 mm (0.45 inch)
        Limit . . . . 9.2 mm (0.36 inch)
Ring end gap (installed)
    Standard
        Top . . . . 0.20 to 0.35 mm (0.008 to 0.014 inch)
        Second . . . . 0.35 to 0.50 mm (0.014 to 0.020 inch)
        Oil . . . . Not specified
    Maximum
        Top . . . . 0.7 mm (0.030 inch)
        Second . . . . 1.0 mm (0.039 inch)
        Oil . . . . Not specified

Crankshaft and bearings

Main bearing oil clearance
    Standard . . . . 0.020 to 0.044 mm (0.0008 to 0.0017 inch)
    Maximum . . . . 0.080 mm (0.0031 inch)
Main bearing journal diameter . . . . 35.976 to 36.000 mm (1.4163 to 1.4173 inch)
Crankshaft thrust clearance . . . . 0.04 to 0.08 mm (0.002 to 0.003 inch)
Right thrust bearing thickness . . . . 2.44 to 2.46 mm (0.096 to 0.097 inch)
Connecting rod side clearance
    Standard . . . . 0.010 to 0.020 mm (0.004 to 0.008 inch)
    Maximum . . . . 0.030 mm (0.010 inch)
Connecting rod big end thickness . . . . 20.95 to 21.00 mm (0.825 to 0.827 inch)
Crankpin width . . . . 21.10 to 21.15 mm (0.831 to 0.833 inch)
Connecting rod bearing oil clearance
    Standard . . . . 0.032 to 0.056 mm (0.0013 to 0.0022 inch)
    Maximum . . . . 0.080 mm (0.0031 inch)
Connecting rod journal (crankpin) diameter . . . . 37.976 to 38.000 mm (1.4951 to 1.4961 inch)
Oil pressure (60 degrees C/140 degrees F) . . . . 2.97 to 5.86 bars (43 to 85 psi)
Crankshaft runout . . . . 0.05 mm (0.002 inch)

2

Katana 1100 (GSX1100F) model (continued)

Clutch

Spring free length	38.1 mm (1.50 inch)
Friction plate thickness	
Standard	2.52 to 2.68 mm (0.100 to 0.106 inch)
Minimum	2.22 mm (0.087 inch)
Steel plate warpage limit	0.10 mm (0.004 inch)

Transmission

Shift fork gear groove width	5.0 to 5.1 mm (0.197 to 0.201 inch)
Shift fork ear thickness	4.8 to 4.9 mm (0.189 to 0.193 inch)
Shift fork to groove clearance	
Standard	0.1 to 0.3 mm (0.004 to 0.012 inch)
Maximum	0.5 mm (0.020 inch)

Torque specifications

Engine mounting bolts	
55 mm length	50 to 60 Nm (36 to 43.5 ft-lbs)
140 and 180 mm length	70 to 80 Nm (50.5 to 58 ft-lbs)
Valve cover bolts	13 to 15 Nm (9.5 to 11 ft-lbs)
Oil hose to valve cover bolts	8 to 12 Nm (6.0 to 8.5 ft-lbs)
Oil hose to cylinder block bolts	8 to 12 Nm (6.0 to 8.5 ft-lbs)
Camshaft bearing cap bolts	8 to 12 Nm (6.0 to 8.5 ft-lbs)
Camshaft sprocket bolts	24 to 26 Nm (17.4 to 18.8 ft-lbs)
Rocker arm shaft lockbolts	8 to 10 Nm (6 to 7 ft-lbs)
Camshaft chain idler	8 to 12 Nm (6.0 to 8.5 ft-lbs)
Cylinder head bolt	7 to 11 Nm (5 to 8 ft-lbs)
Cylinder head nuts	35 to 40 Nm (25.5 to 29 ft-lbs)
Cylinder block base nut	7 to 11 Nm (5 to 8 ft-lbs)
Cylinder block studs to crankcase	13 to 16 Nm (9.5 to 11.5 ft-lbs)
Cam chain tensioner bolts	6 to 8 Nm (4.5 to 6.0 ft-lbs)
Cam chain tensioner spring holder bolt	30 to 45 Nm (21.5 to 32.5 ft-lbs)
Signal generator cover bolts	12 to 16 Nm (8.5 to 11.5 ft-lbs)
Signal generator bolt	See Chapter 8
Starter clutch mounting bolt	143 to 157 Nm (103.5 to 113.5 ft-lbs)
Clutch spring bolts	11 to 13 Nm (8.0 to 9.5 ft-lbs)
Clutch sleeve hub nut	80 to 100 Nm (58 to 72.5 ft-lbs)
Oil pan bolts	12 to 16 Nm (8.5 to 11.5 ft-lbs)
Oil pump bolts	8 to 12 Nm (6.0 to 8.5 ft-lbs)
Crankcase bolts	
6 mm bolts	9 to 13 Nm (6.5 to 9.5 ft-lbs)
8 mm bolts	20 to 24 Nm 14.5 to 17.4 ft-lbs)
Connecting rod nuts	49 to 53 Nm (35.5 to 38.5 ft-lbs)
Shift cam stopper bolt	15 to 23 Nm (11 to 16.5 ft-lbs)
Engine sprocket nut	100 to 130 Nm (72.5 to 94 ft-lbs)
Engine sprocket bolt (where fitted)	9 to 12 Nm (6.5 to 8.5 ft-lbs)

GSX-R1100 model

General

Bore	
1986 through 1988	76.00 mm (2.992 inches)
1989 on	78.00 mm (3.07 inches)
Stroke	
1986 through 1988	58.00 mm (2.283 inches)
1989 on	59.00 mm (2.32 inches)
Displacement	
1986 through 1988	1052 cc (64.2 cubic inches)
1989 on	1127 cc (68.8 cubic inches)

Camshaft and rocker arms

Lobe height (intake)	
1986 through 1990	
Standard	33.378 to 33.918 mm (1.3338 to 1.3354 inch)
Minimum	33.580 mm (1.3220 inch)

Camshaft and rocker arms (continued)

Lobe height (intake)
  1991 on
    US
      Standard .... 33.922 to 33.978 mm (1.3355 to 1.3377 inch)
      Minimum .... 33.630 mm (1.3240 inch)
    UK
      Standard .... 33.892 to 33.948 mm (1.3343 to 1.3365 inch)
      Minimum .... 33.600 mm (1.3228 inch)
Lobe height (exhaust)
  1986 through 1990
    Standard .... 33.533 to 33.573 mm (1.3202 to 1.3218 inch)
    Minimum .... 33.240 mm (1.3087 inch)
  1991 on
    US and Canada
      Standard .... 33.632 to 33.688 mm (1.3241 to 1.3263 inch)
      Minimum .... 33.320 mm (1.3126 inch)
    UK
      Standard .... 33.612 to 33.668 mm (1.3233 to 1.3255 inch)
      Minimum .... 33.320 mm (1.3118 inch)
Bearing oil clearance
  Standard .... 0.032 to 0.066 mm (0.0013 to 0.0026 inch)
  Maximum .... 0.150 mm (0.0059 inch)
Journal diameter .... 21.959 to 21.980 mm (0.8645 to 0.8654 inch)
Camshaft runout limit .... 0.10 mm (0.004 inch)
Camshaft chain 21-pin length (maximum) .... 158.0 mm (6.22 inch)
Rocker arm inside diameter .... 12.000 to 12.018 mm (0.4724 to 0.4731 inch)
Rocker shaft diameter .... 11.973 to 11.984 mm (0.4714 to 0.4718 inch)

Cylinder head, valves and valve springs

Cylinder head warpage limit .... 0.2 mm (0.008 inch)
Valve head thickness (margin) limit .... 0.5 mm (0.020 inch)
Valve seat width (intake and exhaust) .... 0.9 to 1.1 mm (0.035 to 0.043 inch)
Valve stem bend limit .... 0.05 mm (0.002 inch)
Valve stem length above keeper groove .... 2.5 mm (0.0098 inch)
Valve stem diameter
  Intake .... 4.965 to 4.980 mm (0.1955 to 0.1961 inch)
  Exhaust .... 4.945 to 4.960 mm (0.1947 to 0.1953 inch)
Valve guide inside diameter .... 5.000 to 5.012 mm (0.1969 to 0.1973 inch)
Valve spring free length
  1986 through 1990
    Inner .... 35.0 mm (1.38 inch)
    Outer .... 37.8 mm (1.49 inch)
  1991 on
    Inner .... 39.4 mm (1.55 inch)
    Outer .... 41.8 mm (1.65 inch)
Valve head radial runout limit .... 0.03 mm (0.001 inch)

Cylinder block

Surface warp limit .... 0.2 mm (0.008 inch)
Bore diameter
  1986 and 1987
    Standard .... 76.000 to 76.015 mm (2.7921 to 2.9927 inches)
    Maximum .... 76.065 mm (2.9947 inches)
  1988
    Standard .... 76.000 to 76.015 mm (2.7921 to 2.9927 inches)
    Maximum .... 76.075 mm (2.9951 inches)
  1989 on
    Standard .... 78.000 to 78.015 mm (3.0709 to 3.0715 inches)
    Maximum .... 78.080 mm (3.0740 inches)

Pistons

Piston diameter
  1986 and 1987
    Standard .... 75.930 to 75.945 mm (2.9894 to 2.9899 inches)
    Minimum .... 75.880 mm (2.9874 inches)
  1988
    Standard .... 75.940 to 75.955 mm (2.9898 to 2.9903 inches)
    Minimum .... 75.880 mm (2.9874 inches)

2

GSX-R1100 model (continued)

Piston diameter
  1989 on
    Standard .... 77.945 to 77.960 mm (3.0687 to 3.0693 inches)
    Minimum .... 77.080 mm (3.0346 inches)
Piston-to-cylinder clearance
  1986 and 1987
    Standard .... 0.065 to 0.075 mm (0.0022 to 0.0026 inch)
    Maximum .... 0.120 mm (0.0047 inch)
  1988
    Standard .... 0.055 to 0.065 mm (0.0021 to 0.0025 inch)
    Maximum .... 0.120 mm (0.0047 inch)
  1989 on
    Standard .... 0.050 to 0.060 mm (0.0020 to 0.0024 inch)
    Maximum .... 0.120 mm (0.0047 inch)
Ring side clearance
  Top .... 0.180 mm (0.007 inch)
  Second .... 0.150 mm (0.006 inch)
Ring groove width
  Top and second .... 1.01 to 1.03 mm (0.040 to 0.041 inch)
  Oil .... 2.01 to 2.03 mm (0.079 to 0.080 inch)
Ring thickness (top and second) .... 0.97 to 0.99 mm (0.038 to 0.039 inch)
Ring free end gap
  1986 and 1987
    Top
      Standard .... Approximately 9.7 mm (0.38 inch)
      Limit .... 7.8 mm (0.31 inch)
    Second
      Standard .... Approximately 8.2 mm (0.32 inch)
      Limit .... 6.6 mm (0.259 inch)
  1988
    Top
      Standard .... Approximately 8.4 mm (0.33 inch)
      Limit .... 6.7 mm (0.263 inch)
    Second
      Standard .... Approximately 8.2 mm (0.32 inch)
      Limit .... 6.6 mm (0.26 inch)
  1989 on
    Top
      Standard .... Approximately 10.0 mm (0.39 inch)
      Limit .... 8.0 mm (0.31 inch)
    Second
      Standard .... Approximately 11.5 mm (0.45 inch)
      Limit .... 9.2 mm (0.36 inch)
Ring end gap (installed)
  1986 through 1988 (top and second)
    Standard .... 0.20 to 0.35 mm (0.008 to 0.014 inch)
    Maximum .... 0.7 mm (0.030 inch)
  1989 on
    Standard
      Top .... 0.20 to 0.35 mm (0.008 to 0.014 inch)
      Second; .... 0.35 to 0.50 mm (0.014 to 0.020 inch)
      Oil .... Not specified
    Maximum
      Top .... 0.7 mm (0.030 inch)
      Second .... 1.0 mm (0.039 inch)
      Oil .... Not specified

Crankshaft and bearings

Main bearing oil clearance
  Standard .... 0.020 to 0.044 mm (0.0008 to 0.0017 inch)
  Maximum .... 0.080 mm (0.0031 inch)
Main bearing journal diameter .... 35.976 to 36.000 mm (1.4163 to 1.4173 inch)
Crankshaft thrust clearance
  1986 and 1987 .... 0.04 to 0.16 mm (0.002 to 0.006 inch)
  1988 on .... 0.05 to 0.13 mm (0.002 to 0.005 inch)
Right thrust bearing thickness
  1986 and 1987 .... 2.39 to 2.45 mm (0.094 to 0.096 inch)
  1988 on .... 2.42 to 2.44 mm (0.095 to 0.096 inch)

Crankshaft and bearings (continued)

Connecting rod side clearance
  Standard . . . . 0.010 to 0.020 mm (0.004 to 0.008 inch)
  Maximum . . . . 0.030 mm (0.010 inch)
Connecting rod big end thickness . . . . 20.95 to 21.00 mm (0.825 to 0.827 inch)
Crankpin width . . . . 21.10 to 21.15 mm (0.831 to 0.833 inch)
Connecting rod bearing oil clearance
  Standard . . . . 0.032 to 0.056 mm (0.0013 to 0.0022 inch)
  Maximum . . . . 0.080 mm (0.0031 inch)
Connecting rod journal (crankpin) diameter . . . . 37.976 to 38.000 mm (1.4951 to 1.4961 inch)
Oil pressure (60 degrees C/140 degrees F) . . . . 2.97 to 5.86 bars (43 to 85 psi)
Crankshaft runout . . . . 0.05 mm (0.002 inch)

Clutch

Spring free length (coil spring, limit) . . . . 34.0 mm (1.34 inch)
Spring height (diaphragm spring, limit) . . . . 3.1 mm (0.12 inch)
Friction plate thickness
  Standard . . . . 2.52 to 2.68 mm (0.100 to 0.106 inch)
  Minimum . . . . 2.22 mm (0.087 inch)
Steel plate warpage limit . . . . 0.10 mm (0.004 inch)

Transmission

Shift fork gear groove width . . . . 5.0 to 5.1 mm (0.197 to 0.201 inch)
Shift fork ear thickness . . . . 4.8 to 4.9 mm (0.189 to 0.193 inch)
Shift fork to groove clearance
  Standard . . . . 0.1 to 0.3 mm (0.004 to 0.012 inch)
  Maximum . . . . 0.5 mm (0.020 inch)

Torque specifications

Engine mounting bolts
  55 mm length . . . . 50 to 60 Nm (36 to 43.5 ft-lbs)
  60 mm length (1991 on) . . . . 70 to 88 Nm (50.5 to 63.5 ft-lbs)
  180 and 255 mm length . . . . 70 to 88 Nm (50.5 to 63.5 ft-lbs)
  150 and 178 mm length . . . . 70 to 88 Nm (50.5 to 58 ft-lbs)
  All others . . . . 25 to 38 Nm (18.5 to 25.5 ft-lbs)
Valve cover bolts . . . . 13 to 15 Nm (9.5 to 11 ft-lbs)
Oil hose to valve cover bolts . . . . 8 to 12 Nm (6.0 to 8.5 ft-lbs)
Oil hose to cylinder block bolts . . . . 8 to 12 Nm (6.0 to 8.5 ft-lbs)
Camshaft bearing cap bolts . . . . 8 to 12 Nm (6.0 to 8.5 ft-lbs)
Camshaft sprocket bolts . . . . 24 to 26 Nm (17.4 to 18.8 ft-lbs)
Rocker arm shaft lockbolts . . . . 8 to 10 Nm (6 to 7 ft-lbs)
Camshaft chain idler
  1986 through 1988 . . . . 9 to 11 Nm (6.5 to 8 ft-lbs)
  1989 on . . . . 8 to 12 Nm (6.0 to 8.5 ft-lbs)
Camshaft chain guide . . . . 4 to 7 Nm (3 to 5 ft-lbs)
Cylinder head bolt
  1986 through 1988 . . . . 7 to 11 Nm (5 to 8 ft-lbs)
  1989 on . . . . 8 to 12 Nm (6 to 8.5 ft-lbs)
Cylinder head nuts . . . . 35 to 40 Nm (25.5 to 29 ft-lbs)
Cylinder block base nut . . . . 7 to 11 Nm (5 to 8 ft-lbs)
Cylinder block studs to crankcase . . . . 13 to 16 Nm (9.5 to 11.5 ft-lbs)
Cam chain tensioner bolts . . . . 6 to 8 Nm (4.5 to 6.0 ft-lbs)
Cam chain tensioner spring holder bolt . . . . 30 to 45 Nm (21.5 to 32.5 ft-lbs)
Signal generator cover bolts . . . . 12 to 16 Nm (8.5 to 11.5 ft-lbs)
Signal generator bolt . . . . See Chapter 8
Starter clutch mounting bolt . . . . 143 to 157 Nm (103.5 to 113.5 ft-lbs)
Clutch spring bolts (coil springs) . . . . 11 to 13 Nm (8.0 to 9.5 ft-lbs)
Clutch diaphragm spring holder nut . . . . 90 to 110 Nm (65 to 79.5 ft-lbs)
Clutch sleeve hub nut
  1986 through 1988 . . . . 50 to 70 Nm (36 to 50.5 ft-lbs)
  1989 on . . . . 140 to 160 Nm (102 to 115 ft-lbs)
Oil pan bolts . . . . 12 to 16 Nm (8.5 to 11.5 ft-lbs)
Oil pump bolts . . . . 8 to 12 Nm (6.0 to 8.5 ft-lbs)
Crankcase bolts
  6 mm bolts . . . . 9 to 13 Nm (6.5 to 9.5 ft-lbs)
  8 mm bolts . . . . 20 to 24 Nm 14.5 to 17.4 ft-lbs)
Connecting rod nuts . . . . 49 to 53 Nm (35.5 to 38.0 ft-lbs)
Shift cam stopper bolt . . . . 15 to 23 Nm (11 to 16.5 ft-lbs)
Engine sprocket nut . . . . 100 to 130 Nm (72.5 to 94 ft-lbs)
Engine sprocket bolt (where fitted) . . . . 9 to 12 Nm (6.5 to 8.5 ft-lbs)

2

1 General information

The engine/transmission unit is an air/oil-cooled in-line four. The valves are operated by double overhead camshafts which are chain driven off the crankshaft. The engine/transmission assembly is constructed from aluminum alloy. The crankcase is divided horizontally.

The crankcase incorporates a wet sump, pressure-fed lubrication system which uses a gear-driven, dual-rotor oil pump, an oil filter and by-pass valve assembly, a relief valve and an oil pressure switch.

Power from the crankshaft is routed to the transmission via the clutch, which is of the wet, multi-plate type and is gear-driven off the crankshaft. The transmission is a five-speed or six-speed, constant-mesh unit.

2 Operations possible with the engine in the frame

The components and assemblies listed below can be removed without having to remove the engine from the frame. If, however, a number of areas require attention at the same time, removal of the engine is recommended.

Gear shift mechanism external components
Engine sprocket
Starter motor and starter clutch
Alternator
Signal generator
Clutch assembly
Oil hoses, cooler, filter, pan, pickup tube and pump gears
Valve cover, camshafts and rocker arms
Cam chain tensioner
Cylinder head (GSX-R750 and 1985 through 1988 GSX-R1100 only)
Cylinder block and pistons (GSX-R750 and 1985 through 1988 GSX-R1100 only)

3 Operations requiring engine removal

It is necessary to remove the engine/transmission assembly from the frame to gain access to the following components:

Cylinder head (all except GSX-R750 and 1985 through 1988 GSX-R1100)
Cylinder block and pistons (all except GSX-R750 and 1985 through 1988 GSX-R1100)

It is necessary to remove the engine from the frame and separate the crankcase halves to gain access to the following components:

Oil pump
Crankshaft, connecting rods and bearings
Transmission shafts
Shift drum and forks
Primary chain

4 Major engine repair - general note

1 It is not always easy to determine when or if an engine should be completely overhauled, as a number of factors must be considered.

2 High mileage is not necessarily an indication that an overhaul is needed, while low mileage, on the other hand, does not preclude the need for an overhaul. Frequency of servicing is probably the single most important consideration. An engine that has regular and frequent oil and filter changes, as well as other required maintenance, will most likely give many miles of reliable service. Conversely, a neglected engine, or one which has not been broken in properly, may require an overhaul very early in its life.

3 Exhaust smoke and excessive oil consumption are both indications that piston rings and/or valve guides are in need of attention. Make sure oil leaks are not responsible before deciding that the rings and guides are bad. Refer to Chapter 1 and perform a cylinder compression check to determine for certain the nature and extent of the work required.

4 If the engine is making obvious knocking or rumbling noises, the connecting rod and/or main bearings are probably at fault.

5 Loss of power, rough running, excessive valve train noise and high fuel consumption rates may also point to the need for an overhaul, especially if they are all present at the same time. If a complete tune-up does not remedy the situation, major mechanical work is the only solution.

6 An engine overhaul generally involves restoring the internal parts to the specifications of a new engine. During an overhaul the piston rings are replaced and the cylinder walls are bored and/or honed. If a rebore is done, then new pistons are also required. The main and connecting rod bearings are generally replaced with new ones and, if necessary, the crankshaft is also replaced. Generally the valves are serviced as well, since they are usually in less than perfect condition at this point. While the engine is being overhauled, other components such as the carburetors and the starter motor can be rebuilt also. The end result should be a like-new engine that will give as many trouble-free miles as the original.

7 Before beginning the engine overhaul, read through all of the related procedures to familiarize yourself with the scope and requirements of the job. Overhauling an engine is not all that difficult, but it is time consuming. Plan on the motorcycle being tied up for a minimum of two weeks. Check on the availability of parts and make sure that any necessary special tools, equipment and supplies are obtained in advance.

8 Most work can be done with typical shop hand tools, although a number of precision measuring tools are required for inspecting parts to determine if they must be replaced. Often a dealer service department or motorcycle repair shop will handle the inspection of parts and offer advice concerning reconditioning and replacement. As a general rule, time is the primary cost of an overhaul so it doesn't pay to install worn or substandard parts.

9 As a final note, to ensure maximum life and minimum trouble from a rebuilt engine, everything must be assembled with care in a spotlessly clean environment.

5 Engine - removal and installation

Note: *Engine removal and installation should be done with the aid of an assistant to avoid damage or injury that could occur if the engine is dropped. A hydraulic floor jack should be used to support and lower the engine if possible (they can be rented at low cost).*

Removal

1 Support the bike securely so it can't be accidentally knocked over while removing the engine.

2 Remove the seat (see Chapter 7) and the fuel tank (see Chapter 3).

3 Remove the frame covers, upper fairing and lower fairing (if equipped) (see Chapter 7).

4 Drain the engine oil (see Chapter 1).

5 Remove the battery (see Chapter 1).

6 Remove the air ducts (if equipped).

7 Remove the air cleaner air box (see Chapter 3).

8 Remove the carburetors (see Chapter 3) and plug the intake openings with rags.

9 Drain the engine oil and remove the oil cooler hoses (see Chapter 1 and Section 7).

10 On the following models, remove the oil cooler (see Section 7):
a) *Katana 600 (GSX600F)*
b) *GSX-R750 (1988 and later)*
c) *Katana 750 (GSX750F)*
d) *GSX-R1100 (1988 and later)*

11 On 1985 through 1987 GSX-R750 models, remove the oil filter (see Chapter 1).

12 Mark and disconnect the wires from the oil pressure switch, neutral switch and the starter motor. Unplug the alternator, sidestand switch and signal generator electrical connectors (see Chapters 4 and 8).

13 Disconnect the spark plug wires (see Chapter 1).

14 If necessary, remove the ignition coils and brackets (see Chapter 4).

15 Remove the exhaust system (see Chapter 3).

16 Remove the engine sprocket cover, engine sprocket and drive chain (see Chapter 5).

17 Cable clutch models: Disconnect the lower end of the clutch cable from the lever and bracket (see Chapter 1).

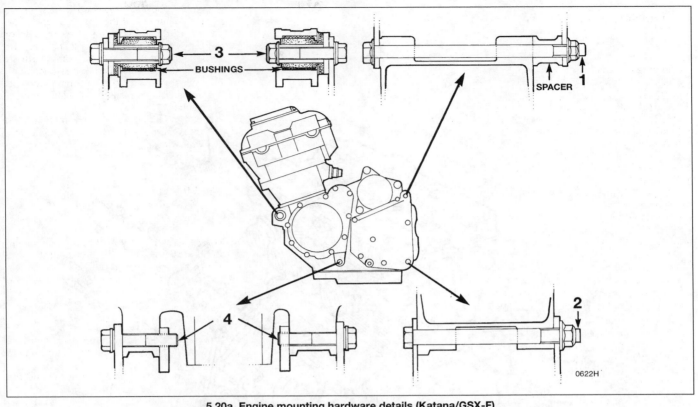

5.20a Engine mounting hardware details (Katana/GSX-F)

1 Bolt and nut   2 Bolt and nut   3 Bolt and nut   4 Bolt and nut

18 Hydraulic clutch models: Disconnect and plug the clutch fluid line (see Section 22).
19 Support the engine with a floor jack and a wood block.

 Warning: The engine is heavy. Support it securely so it won't fall off the jack during removal and cause injury.

20 Remove the mounting nuts and bolts **(see illustrations)**. **Note:** *Discard the self-locking nuts and replace them with new ones.*
21 Make sure no wires or hoses are still attached to the engine assembly.

5.20b Engine mounting hardware details (GSX-R750, 1985 through 1987)

1 Bolt
2 Bolt
3 Through-bolt
4 Through-bolt
5 Nut
6 Spacer
7 Spacer
8 Tabbed nuts
9 Spacer

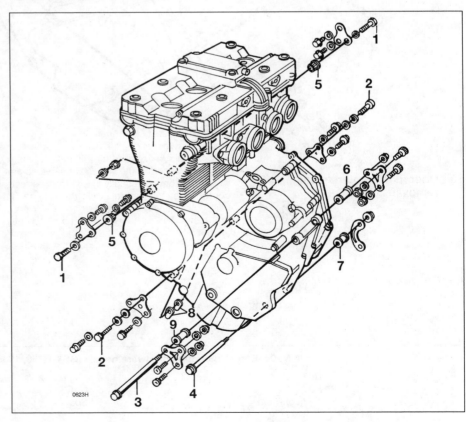

2

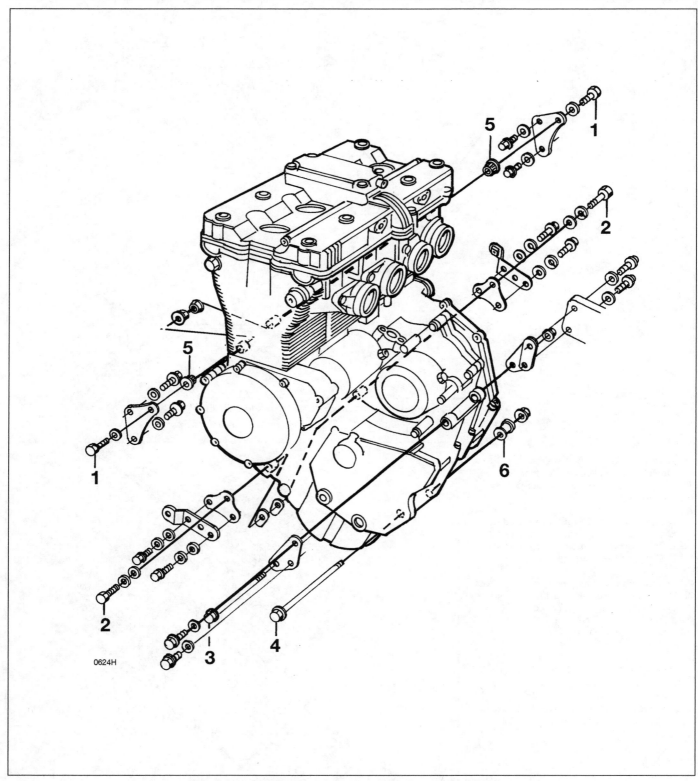

0624H

5.20c Engine mounting hardware details (GSX-R750, 1988 and later)

1 Bolt
2 Bolt
3 Through-bolt

4 Through-bolt
5 Nut
6 Spacer

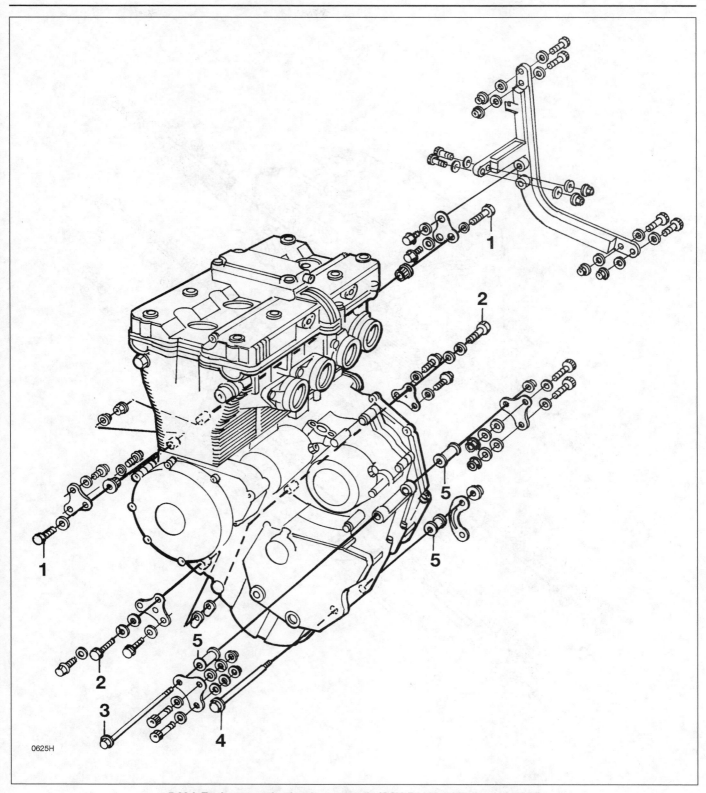

5.20d Engine mounting hardware details (GSX-R1100, 1985 through 1988)

1 Bolt
2 Bolt
3 Through-bolt

4 Through-bolt
5 Spacer

0625H

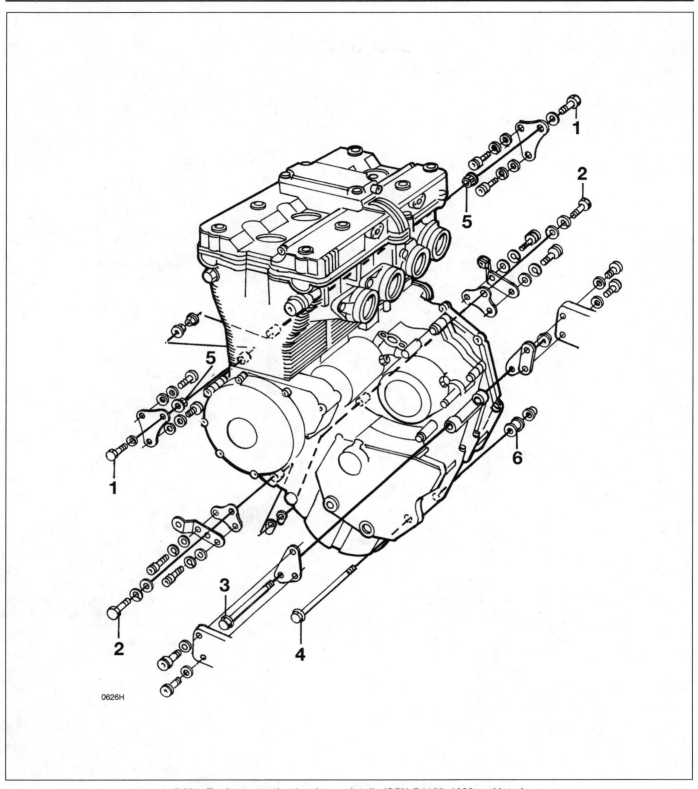

0626H

5.20e Engine mounting hardware details (GSX-R1100, 1989 and later)

1	Bolt	4	Through-bolt
2	Bolt	5	Nut
3	Through-bolt	6	Spacer

5.22a On GSX-R1100 models, remove the downtube from the right side of the frame . . .

5.22b . . . pad the frame with rags to prevent damage to the engine; with the engine supported by a floor jack, have an assistant help you lower it and guide it out of the frame

5.26 This type of nut has a tab that prevents it from turning when the bolt is tightened

GSX-R models

22 Remove the right frame downtube, then pad the frame with rags to protect the engine and frame during removal **(see illustrations)**.

23 Raise the engine to detach it from the mounts, then remove it through the right side of the frame. **Note:** *On GSX-R750 models, remove the engine breather cover if it obstructs engine removal.*

Katana (GSX-F) models

24 On Katana (GSX-F) models, unbolt the front subframe from the frame, but leave it attached to the engine.

25 Slowly and carefully lower the engine assembly to the floor.

Installation

26 Installation is the reverse of removal. Note the following points:

a) *Don't tighten any of the engine mounting bolts until they all have been installed. Some of the nuts have a tab that prevents them from turning when the bolt is tightened **(see illustration)**.*

b) *Use new gaskets at all exhaust pipe connections.*

c) *Tighten the engine mounting bolts and frame downtube bolts securely.*

d) *Adjust the drive chain, throttle cable, choke cable and clutch cable (if equipped) following the procedures In 'Daily (pre-ride) checks' at the beginning of this Manual, and Chapter 1.*

e) *Fill the engine with oil (see Chapter 1).*

6 Engine disassembly and reassembly - general information

1 Before disassembling the engine, clean the exterior with a degreaser and rinse it with water. A clean engine will make the job easier and prevent the possibility of getting dirt into the internal areas of the engine.

2 In addition to the precision measuring tools mentioned earlier, you will need a torque wrench, a valve spring compressor, oil gallery brushes, a piston ring removal and installation tool, a piston ring compressor, a pin-type spanner wrench and a clutch holder tool (which is described in Section 19). Some new, clean engine oil of the correct grade and type, some engine assembly lube (or moly-based grease), a tube of Suzuki Bond 1207B gasket liquid or equivalent, and a tube of RTV (silicone) sealant will also be required. Although it may not be considered a tool, some Plastigage (type HPG-1) should also be obtained to use for checking bearing oil clearances **(see illustrations)**.

3 An engine support stand make from short lengths of 2 x 4's bolted together will facilitate the disassembly and reassembly procedures **(see illustration)**. The perimeter of the mount should be just big enough to accommodate the engine oil pan. If you have an automotive-type engine stand, an adapter plate can be made from a piece of plate, some angle iron and some nuts and bolts.

4 When disassembling the engine, keep "mated" parts together (including gears, cylinders, pistons, etc. that have been in contact with each other during engine operation). These "mated" parts must be reused or replaced as an assembly.

5 Engine/transmission disassembly should be done in the following general order with reference to the appropriate Sections.

  Remove the valve cover
  Remove the cam chain tensioner
  Remove the camshafts
  Remove the cylinder head
  Remove the cylinder block
  Remove the pistons
  Remove the signal generator (see Chapter 4)
  Remove the clutch
  Remove the external shift mechanism
  Remove the starter clutch
  Remove the oil pan and pickup
  Separate the crankcase halves
  Remove the crankshaft and connecting rods
  Remove the cam chain
  Remove the transmission shafts/gears
  Remove the shift drum/forks

6 Reassembly is accomplished by reversing the general disassembly sequence.

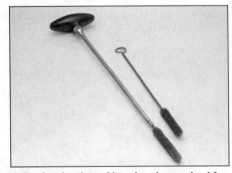

6.2a A selection of brushes is required for cleaning holes and passages in the engine components

2

6.2b Type HPG-1 Plastigage is needed to check the crankshaft, connecting rod and camshaft oil clearances

6.3 An engine stand can be made from short lengths of 2 x 4 lumber and lag bolts or nails

7.3 Remove two bolts that secure each oil hose fitting to the valve cover

7.4a If the hoses are equipped with compression fittings, hold the fittings in the oil pan with a backup wrench and loosen the hose nuts with a second wrench . . .

7.4b . . . if the hoses are secured with union bolts, remove them and detach the hoses from the oil pan

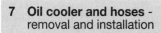

7 Oil cooler and hoses - removal and installation

1 Support the bike securely so it can't be knocked over during this procedure.
2 Drain the engine oil (see Chapter 1) and remove the fairing (see Chapter 7).
3 Unbolt the cylinder head cooling hoses from the valve cover and from the crankcase in front of the alternator (see illustration).
4 If the oil cooler hoses are connected to the oil pan with compression fittings, hold the fittings with a backup wrench and disconnect the hoses at the oil pan (see illustration). If

they're connected with union bolts, remove the bolts and disconnect the hoses from the oil pan (see illustration).
5 If the oil cooler hoses are connected to the cooler with union bolts, remove them (see illustration). Remove and discard the sealing washers. If the hoses are connected with bolt-on fittings, remove the two bolts that secure each fitting to the cooler.
6 Remove the oil cooler mounting bolts (see illustration).
7 Lift the oil cooler out of the lower brackets (see illustration).
8 Remove the rubber mounts from the lower brackets and inspect them (see illustration).

Replace the mounts if they're brittle, cracked, or compressed.
9 Installation is the reverse of the removal steps. Use new O-rings at the fittings that connect the cylinder head cooling hoses to the valve cover and crankcase (see illustration).

8 Valve cover - removal and installation

Note: The valve cover can be removed with the engine in the frame. If the engine has been removed, ignore the steps which don't apply.

Removal

1 Support the bike securely so it can't be knocked over during this procedure.
2 Remove the seat, fuel tank and fairing (see Chapters 3 and 7).
3 If necessary for removal access, remove the frame crossmember above and behind the engine.
4 Disconnect the crankcase breather hose from the valve cover (see Chapter 1). Disconnect the oil cooling hoses from the valve cover (see Section 7).
5 Remove the air suction valve (if equipped) (see Chapter 3).
6 If necessary for removal access, remove the ignition coils and their brackets, along with the spark plug wires (see Chapter 4).

7.5 Remove the union bolts or bolt-on fittings that secure the hoses to the oil cooler (union bolt shown)

7.6 The top of the oil cooler is secured by bolts . . .

7.7 . . . the bottom rests in rubber vibration mounts

7.8 Replace the rubber vibration mounts if they're cracked, worn or compressed

7.9 Use new O-rings on bolt-on hose fittings

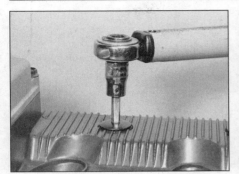

8.7a Unscrew the valve cover bolts . . .

8.7b . . . and lift them out, together with the seals

8.8 Lift the cover off the engine - if it's stuck, tap gently on the side with a soft faced hammer; don't pry the cover loose - be careful not to lose the spark plug hole gaskets

7 Remove the valve cover Allen-head and hex-head bolts **(see illustrations)**.

8 Lift the cover off the cylinder head **(see illustration)**. If it's stuck, don't attempt to pry it off - tap around the sides with a plastic hammer to dislodge it. **Note:** *Pay attention to the locating dowels as you remove the cover - if they fall into the engine, major disassembly may be required to get them out.*

Installation

9 Peel the rubber gasket from the cover. If it's cracked, hardened, has soft spots or shows signs of general deterioration, replace it with a new one.

10 Clean the mating surfaces of the cylinder head and the valve cover with lacquer thinner, acetone or brake system cleaner. Apply a thin film of RTV sealant to the half-circle cutouts on each side of the head.

11 Install the gasket to the cover. Make sure it fits completely into the cover groove **(see illustration)**. Apply a small amount of silicone sealer to the corners of the half-circle portions of the gasket.

12 Position the cover on the cylinder head, making sure the gasket doesn't slip out of place.

13 Check the seals on the valve cover bolts, replacing them if necessary. Apply a small amount of sealant (Suzuki Bond 1207B or equivalent) to the seals. Install the bolts, tightening them evenly to the torque listed in this Chapter's Specifications.

14 The remainder of installation is the reverse of removal. Use new O-rings on the oil cooling pipes.

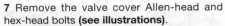

9 Camshaft chain tensioner - removal and installation

Removal

Caution: Once you start to remove the tensioner bolts, you must remove the tensioner all the way and reset it before tightening the bolts. The tensioner extends and locks in place, so if you loosen the bolts partway and then retighten them, the tensioner or cam chain will be damaged.

1 Remove the tensioner cap bolt and spring **(see illustration)**.

2 Remove the tensioner mounting bolts and take it off the engine.

Installation

3 Release the ratchet and press the tensioner piston all the way into the tensioner body **(see illustration)**.

4 Place a new gasket on the tensioner body, then install it in the engine **(see illustration)**. Tighten the bolts to the torque listed in this Chapter's Specifications.

5 Install a new sealing washer on the tensioner cap bolt. Install the spring and cap bolt and tighten the cap bolt to the torque listed in this Chapter's Specifications.

6 Check the cam chain to make sure it's tight; if it's loose, the tensioner piston didn't release.

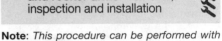

10 Camshafts, rocker arm shafts and rocker arms - removal, inspection and installation

Note: *This procedure can be performed with the engine in the frame.*

Camshafts

Removal

1 Remove the valve cover (see Section 8).

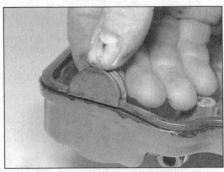

8.11 Be sure the gasket seats securely in the groove

9.1 Remove the tensioner cap bolt and spring

9.3 Release the ratchet and press the tensioner piston all the way in

9.4 Install the tensioner body in the engine with a new gasket

2

10.3a The camshafts can be identified by the EX mark (exhaust) and IN mark (intake)

10.3b The no. 1 arrow on the exhaust camshaft should point directly at the gasket mating surface

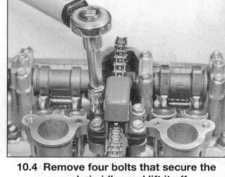

10.4 Remove four bolts that secure the cam chain idler and lift it off

2 Remove the camshaft chain tensioner (see Section 9).

3 Turn the engine in its normal direction of rotation until the num-ber 1 arrow on the exhaust camshaft points at the valve cover gasket mating surface on the cylinder head **(see illustrations)**.

4 Note which way round it is fitted, and unbolt the cam chain idler/top guide **(see illustration)**.

5 Check the positions of the marks on the exhaust and intake sprockets **(see illustration)**. This is how they should be positioned for installation later.

Caution: Pay close attention to the number of chain pins between the marks
*   21 pins on 1988 through 1995 600 models*
*   24 pins on 1996 600 models*
*   21 pins on 750 models*
*   22 pins on 1100 models*
If the sprockets are positioned incorrectly, the valves could strike the piston tops and be bent.

6 Unscrew the bearing cap bolts for one of the camshafts, a little at a time, until they are all loose, then unscrew the bearing cap bolts for the other camshaft.

Caution: If the bearing cap bolts aren't loosened evenly, the camshaft may bind. Remove the bolts and lift off the bearing caps. Note the letters on the bearing caps which correspond to those on the cylinder head (see illustration). When you reinstall the caps, be sure to install them in the correct positions.

7 Pull up on the camshaft chain and carefully guide the camshaft out. With the chain still held taut, remove the other camshaft. **Note:** *Don't remove the sprockets from the camshafts unless absolutely necessary.*

8 While the camshafts are out, don't allow the chain to go slack - the chain may fall off and bind between the crankshaft and case, which could damage these components. Wire the chain to another component to prevent it from dropping down. Also, cover the top of the cylinder head with a rag to prevent foreign objects from falling into the engine.

9 Lift out the chain guide **(see illustration)**.

10.5 With the camshafts correctly positioned, the no. 2 arrow on the exhaust camshaft should point straight up, the no. 3 arrow on the exhaust camshaft should point toward the intake camshaft, and the no. 2 arrow on the intake camshaft should point to the exhaust camshaft

Inspection

Note: *Before replacing camshafts or the cylinder head and bearing caps because of damage, check with local machine shops specializing in motorcycle engine work. In the case of the camshafts, it may be possible for cam lobes to be welded, reground and hardened, at a cost far lower than that of a new camshaft. If the bearing surfaces in the cylinder head are damaged, it may be possible for them to be bored out to accept bearing inserts. Due to the cost of a new cylinder head it is recommended that all options be explored before condemning it as trash!*

10.9 Lift the chain guide out

10.6 Each cam bearing cap has a letter inside a rectangle or triangle that indicates its position on the engine, but for easy installation, it's a good idea to label each of the caps yourself

10 Inspect the cam bearing surfaces of the head and the bearing caps. Look for score marks, deep scratches and evidence of spalling (a pitted appearance).

11 Check the camshaft lobes for heat discoloration (blue appearance), score marks, chipped areas, flat spots and spalling **(see illustration)**. Measure the height of each lobe with a micrometer **(see illustration)** and compare the results to the minimum lobe height listed in this Chapter's Specifications. If damage is noted or wear is excessive, the camshaft must be replaced. Also, be sure to

10.11a Check the lobes of the camshaft for wear - here's a good example of damage which will require replacement (or repair) of the camshaft

10.11b Measure the height of the camshaft lobes with a micrometer

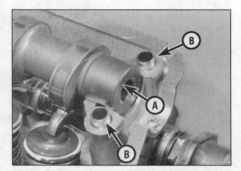

10.13 Place a piece of Plastigage parallel to the camshaft centerline along the top of the bearing journal (A); be sure the dowels (B) are in place before installing the cap

check the condition of the rocker arms, as described later in this Section.

12 Next, check the camshaft bearing oil clearances. Clean the camshafts, the bearing surfaces in the cylinder head and the bearing caps with a clean, lint-free cloth, then lay the cams in place in the cylinder head, with the sprocket marks correctly aligned **(see illustrations 10.3b and 10.5)**. Engage the cam chain with the sprockets, so the camshafts don't turn as the bearing caps are tightened.

13 Cut eight strips of Plastigage (type HPG-1) and lay one piece on each bearing journal, parallel with the camshaft centerline **(see illustration)**.

14 Make sure the bearing cap dowels are

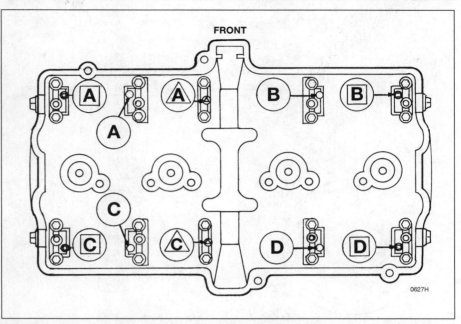

FRONT

10.14 Cam bearing cap positions - the caps must be installed in their original locations or the camshafts may seize

installed **(see illustration 10.13)**. Install the bearing caps in their proper positions **(see illustration)** and install the bolts. Tighten the bolts in three steps, in a criss-cross pattern, to the torque listed in this Chapter's Specifications. While doing this, DO NOT let the camshafts rotate!

15 Now unscrew the bolts, a little at a time, and carefully lift off the bearing caps.

16 To determine the oil clearance, compare the crushed Plastigage (at its widest point) on each journal to the scale printed on the Plastigage container **(see illustration)**. Compare the results to this Chapter's Specifications. If the oil clearance is greater than specified, measure the diameter of the cam bearing journal with a micrometer **(see illustration)**. If the journal diameter is less than the specified limit, replace the camshaft with a new one and recheck the clearance. If the clearance is still too great, replace the cylinder head and bearing caps with new parts (see the Note that precedes Step 10).

17 Except in cases of oil starvation, the camshaft chain wears very little. If the chain has stretched excessively, which makes it difficult to maintain proper tension, replace it with a new one (see Section 31).

18 Check the sprockets for wear, cracks and other damage, replacing them if necessary. If the sprockets are worn, the chain is also worn, and also the sprocket on the crankshaft (which can only be remedied by replacing the crankshaft). If wear this severe is apparent, the entire engine should be disassembled for inspection.

19 If you remove the sprockets, be sure to install them correctly; use the notches in the ends of the camshafts and the numbered arrow marks on the sprockets to position the sprockets **(see illustration)**.

20 Check the chain guide for wear or damage. If it is worn or damaged, the chain is worn out or improperly adjusted.

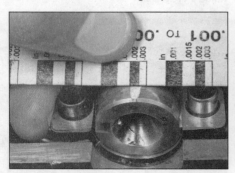

10.16a Compare the width of the crushed Plastigage to the scale on the Plastigage envelope to obtain the clearance

10.16b Measure the cam bearing journal with a micrometer

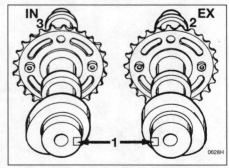

IN   EX

10.19 If the sprockets are removed from the camshaft, use the notch in the end of each camshaft and the number mark on the sprockets to position the sprockets correctly

2

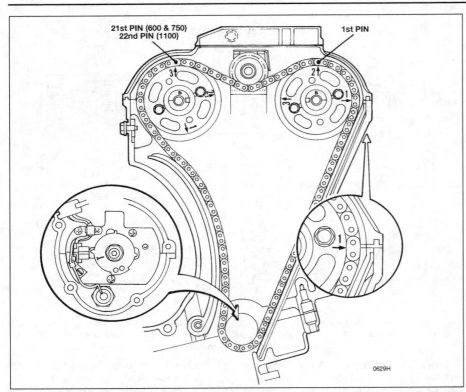

10.24a The timing marks on the signal generator and camshaft must be aligned correctly - there must be 21 pins between the exhaust and intake camshaft marks on 600 (1988 through 1995) and 750 models; there must be 22 pins between the marks on 1100 models

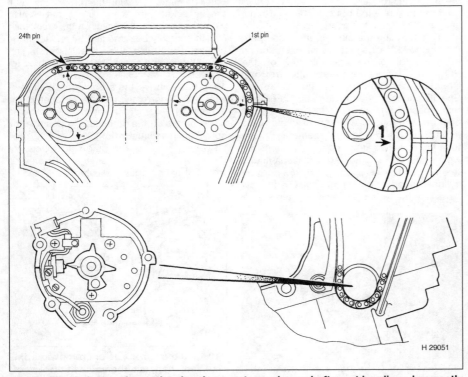

10.24b The timing marks on the signal generator and camshaft must be aligned correctly - there must be 24 pins between the exhaust and intake camshaft marks on 1996 600 models

21 Spin the sprocket in the cam chain idler with a finger. If it's loose, rough or noisy, replace the idler with a new one. If a top guide is fitted in place of the idler, check for deep grooves, cracking and other obvious damage, replacing it if necessary.

Installation

22 Make sure the bearing surfaces in the cylinder head and the bearing caps are clean, then apply a light coat of engine assembly lube or moly-based grease to each of them.

23 Apply a coat of moly-based grease to the camshaft lobes. Make sure the camshaft bearing journals are clean, then lay the camshafts in the cylinder head (do not mix them up), ensuring the marks on the cam sprockets are aligned properly **(see illustrations 10.3b and 10.5)**.

24 Make sure the timing marks are aligned as described in Steps 3 and 5, then mesh the chain with the camshaft sprockets. Count the number of chain link pins between the mark and the IN mark **(see illustrations)**. There should be no slack in the chain between the two sprockets.

25 Carefully set the bearing caps in their proper positions **(see illustration 10.14)** and install the bolts. **Note**: *The bearing cap bolts are made of a high-strength material, indicated by a 9 mark on the bolt head. Don't use any other type of bolt. Tighten them evenly, in a criss-cross pattern, to the torque listed in this Chapter's Specifications.*

26 Insert your finger or a wood dowel into the cam chain tensioner hole and apply pressure to the cam chain. Check the timing marks to make sure they are aligned (see Step 3) and there are still the correct number of link pins between the number marks on the cam sprockets. If necessary, change the position of the sprocket(s) on the chain to bring all of the marks into alignment.

Caution: If the marks are not aligned exactly as described, the valve timing will be incorrect and the valves may strike the pistons, causing extensive damage to the engine.

27 Install the cam chain idler with its arrow mark pointing to the front of the engine **(see illustration)**, or the top guide positioned as noted on removal.

10.27 The arrow mark on the cam chain idler points to the front of the engine

10.33 Remove the rocker shaft plugs and sealing washers

10.34 Remove the rocker shaft lockbolts

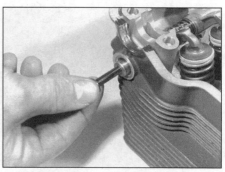

10.35 Thread an 8 mm bolt into the rocker shaft and pull it out . . .

28 Install the cam chain tensioner as described in Section 9.

29 Adjust the valve clearances (see Chapter 1).

30 Turn the engine with a socket on the signal generator hex. If you feel a sudden increase in resistance, stop turning. The valves may be hitting the pistons due to incorrect assembly. Find the problem and fix it before turning the engine any further, or serious damage may occur.

31 The remainder of installation is the reverse of removal.

Rocker arm shafts and rocker arms

Removal

32 Remove the camshafts following the procedure given above. Be sure to keep tension on the camshaft chain.

33 Unscrew one rocker shaft plug from the cylinder head and pull it out **(see illustration)**.

34 Remove the rocker shaft lockbolt **(see illustration)**.

35 Thread an 8 mm bolt into the rocker shaft and pull it out **(see illustration)**.

36 Remove the rocker arms and springs **(see illustrations)**.

37 Repeat the above Steps to remove the other rocker arm shafts and rocker arms. Keep all of the parts in order so they can be reinstalled in their original locations.

Inspection

38 Clean all of the components with solvent and dry them off. Blow through the oil passages in the rocker arms with compressed air, if available. Inspect the rocker arm faces for pits, spalling, score marks and rough spots **(see illustration)**. Check the rocker arm-to-shaft contact areas and the adjusting screws (if equipped), as well. Look for cracks in each rocker arm. If the faces of the rocker arms are damaged, the rocker arms and the camshafts should be replaced as a set.

39 Measure the diameter of the rocker arm shafts, in the area where the rocker arms ride, and compare the results with this Chapter's

Specifications. Also measure the inside diameter of the rocker arms **(see illustrations)** and compare the results with this Chapter's Specifications. If either the shaft or the rocker arms are worn beyond the specified limits, replace them as a set.

Installation

40 Position the rocker arms and springs in the cylinder head.

41 Lubricate the rocker arm shaft with engine oil and slide it into the cylinder head and through the rocker arms and springs. Tighten the rocker shaft lockbolt securely **(see illustration)**.

10.36a . . . then lift out the rocker arms (late type rocker arms shown; early type similar) . . .

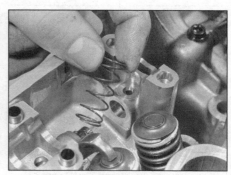

10.36b . . . and the rocker arm springs

10.38 Inspect the rocker arms, especially the faces that contact the cam lobes, for wear

10.39a Measure the inside diameter of the rocker arm - in this case a telescoping gauge is expanded against the bore of the rocker arm, then locked . . .

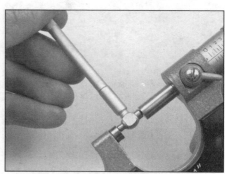

10.39b . . . and a micrometer is used to measure the gauge

2

10.41 Tighten the rocker shaft lockbolts

10.42 Install the rocker shaft plug with a new sealing washer

11.7 Remove one small bolt that threads through the cylinder block up into the cylinder head

42 Install the rocker shaft plug with a new sealing washer and tighten it to the torque listed in this Chapter's Specifications **(see illustration)**.
43 Install the camshafts following the procedure described earlier in this Section.

11 Cylinder head - removal and installation

Caution: The engine must be completely cool before beginning this procedure, or the cylinder head may become warped.
Note: *This procedure can be performed with*

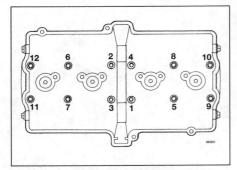

11.8a Cylinder head TIGHTENING sequence

the engine in the frame. If the engine has been removed, ignore the steps which don't apply.

Removal

1 Support the bike securely so it can't be knocked over.
2 Disconnect the oil hoses from the rear side of the cylinder head (see Section 7).
3 Remove the valve cover (see Section 8).
4 Remove the exhaust (see Chapter 3).
5 Remove the cam chain tensioner (see Section 9).

11.8b The cylinder head tightening sequence numbers are cast into the head next to the nuts; loosen from the highest number to the lowest, and tighten from the lowest number to the highest

6 Remove the camshafts (see Section 10).
7 Remove the small cylinder block-to-cylinder head bolt **(see illustration)**.
8 Loosen the cylinder head nuts, a little at a time, using the reverse order of the tightening sequence **(see illustrations)**. Remove the washers from under the nuts which use them **(see illustrations)**. **Note**: *The cylinder head nuts may be cap nuts or standard nuts, with copper washers, steel washers or no washers, depending on model and engine size. To ease assembly, label the nuts (and washers, if equipped) with the number cast next to the nut on the cylinder head.*
9 Lift off the cylinder head plate (if equipped) **(see illustration)**.
10 Pull the cylinder head off the cylinder block. Don't attempt to pry the head off by inserting a screwdriver between the head and the cylinder block - you'll damage the sealing surfaces.

HAYNES HiNT *If the head is stuck, tap upward against the rocker shaft plugs with a rubber mallet to jar it loose, or use two wooden dowels inserted into the intake or exhaust ports to lever the head off.*

11.8c Lift off the cylinder head nuts - some of the studs have cap nuts, like the one shown here . . .

11.8d . . . some of the nuts have copper washers, some have steel washers and some have no washers (depending on model); label the nuts and washers so they can be reinstalled on the correct studs

11.9 On late GSX-R 1100 models, lift off the cylinder head plate after the nuts have been removed

11.11 Lift off the cylinder head gasket and remove the O-rings from the oil drain tubes (arrows)

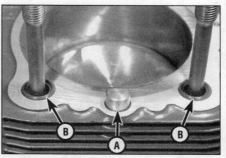

11.13 Make sure the dowels aren't lost; remove the O-rings from the four end studs and the two center studs on the front of the engine

A Dowel   B O-rings

11.16 Lay the head gasket over the dowels

11 Lift the head gasket off the cylinder block and remove the O-rings from the oil drain tubes **(see illustration)**.

12 Stuff a clean rag into the cam chain tunnel to prevent the entry of debris.

13 Locate the two dowel pins to make sure they haven't fallen into the engine. If they are in the head, put them in their holes in the cylinder block. Also remove the O-rings from the four end studs and the two center studs on the front of the engine **(see illustration)**.

14 Check the cylinder head gasket and the mating surfaces on the cylinder head and block for leakage, which could indicate warpage. Refer to Section 13 and check the flatness of the cylinder head.

15 Clean all traces of old gasket material from the cylinder head and block. Be careful not to let any of the gasket material fall into the crankcase, the cylinder bores or the oil passages.

Installation

16 Install new O-rings over the studs that use them, as well as on the oil drain tubes **(see illustrations 11.13 and 11.11)**. Lay the new gasket in place on the cylinder block **(see illustration)**. Never reuse the old gasket and don't use any type of gasket sealant.

17 Carefully lower the cylinder head over the studs and dowels. It is helpful to have an assistant support the camshaft chain with a piece of wire so it doesn't fall and become kinked or detached from the crankshaft. When the head is resting against the cylinder block, wire the cam chain to another component to keep tension on it.

18 Install the head nuts. Be sure to place the different types of nuts and washers in the correct locations **(see illustrations)**. Using the proper sequence **(see illustration)**, tighten the nuts in several steps to the torque listed in this Chapter's Specifications **(see illustration)**.

19 Install the small cylinder block-to-cylinder head bolt, tightening it to the torque listed in this Chapter's Specifications **(see illustration 11.8a)**.

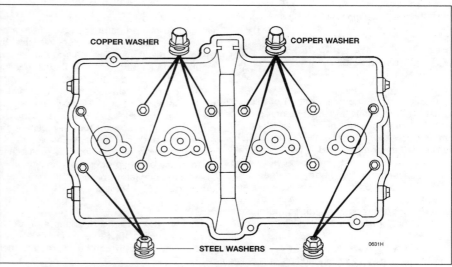

11.18a Cylinder head nuts and washers (models without cylinder head plate)

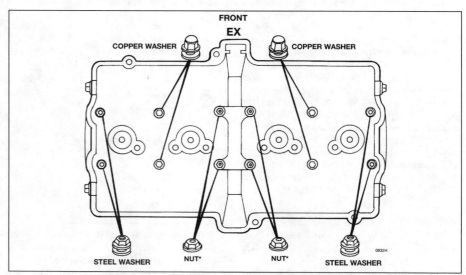

11.18b Cylinder head nuts and washers (models with cylinder head plate)

* Copper washers are also used under the center four nuts on 1990 and later GSX-R1100 models (GSX-R1100L, M, N)

2

11.18c Tighten the head nuts in sequence to the correct torque

20 Install the camshafts and the valve cover (see Sections 10 and 8).
21 Connect the oil lines to the valve cover (see Section 7).
22 Change the engine oil (see Chapter 1).

12 Valves/valve seats/valve guides - servicing

1 Because of the complex nature of this job and the special tools and equipment required, servicing of the valves, the valve seats and the valve guides (commonly known as a valve job) is best left to a professional.
2 The home mechanic can, however, remove and disassemble the head, do the initial cleaning and inspection, then reassemble and deliver the head to a dealer service department or properly equipped motorcycle repair shop for the actual valve servicing (see Section 13).
3 The dealer service department will remove the valves and springs, recondition or replace the valves and valve seats, replace the valve guides, check and replace the valve springs, spring retainers and keepers (as necessary), replace the valve seals with new ones and reassemble the valve components. **Note:** *Suzuki recommends against lapping the valves after they've been serviced. The valve seat and face must be soft in order for final seating to occur when the engine is first run.*
4 After the valve job has been performed, the head will be in like-new condition. When the head is returned, be sure to clean it again very thoroughly before installation on the engine to remove any metal particles or abrasive grit that may still be present from the valve service operations. Use compressed air, if available, to blow out all the holes and passages.

13 Cylinder head and valves - disassembly, inspection and reassembly

1 As mentioned in the previous Section, valve servicing and valve guide replacement should be left to a dealer service department or motorcycle repair shop. However,

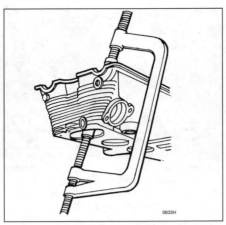

13.7a Compressing the valve springs with a valve spring compressor

disassembly, cleaning and inspection of the valves and related components can be done (if the necessary special tools are available) by the home mechanic. This way no expense is incurred if the inspection reveals that service work is not required at this time.
2 To properly disassemble the valve components without the risk of damaging them, a valve spring compressor is absolutely necessary. This special tool can usually be rented, but if it's not available, have a dealer service department or motorcycle repair shop handle the entire process of disassembly, inspection, service or repair (if required) and reassembly of the valves.

Disassembly

3 Remove the rocker arm shafts and rocker arms (see Section 10). Store the components in such a way that they can be returned to their

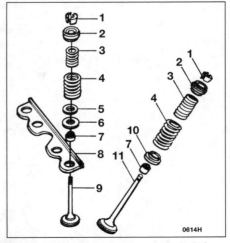

13.7c Valve components - exploded view

1 Keepers
2 Spring retainer
3 Inner spring
4 Outer spring
5 Inner spring seat
6 Outer spring seat
7 Stem oil seal
8 Metal plate
9 Exhaust valve
10 Spring seat
11 Intake valve

13.7b Remove the valve keepers with needle-nose pliers, tweezers, a magnet or a screwdriver with a dab of grease on it

original locations without getting mixed up (labeled plastic bags work well).
4 Before the valves are removed, scrape away any traces of gasket material from the head gasket sealing surface. Work slowly and do not nick or gouge the soft aluminum of the head. Gasket removing solvents, which work very well, are available at most motorcycle shops and auto parts stores.
5 Carefully scrape all carbon deposits out of the combustion chamber area. A hand held wire brush or a piece of fine emery cloth can be used once most of the deposits have been scraped away. Do not use a wire brush mounted in a drill motor, or one with extremely stiff bristles, as the head material is soft and may be eroded away or scratched by the wire brush.
6 Before proceeding, arrange to label and store the valves along with their related components so they can be kept separate and reinstalled in the same valve guides they are removed from (again, plastic bags work well for this).
7 Compress the valve spring on the first valve with a spring compressor, then remove the keepers (see illustrations) and the retainer from the valve assembly. Do not compress the springs any more than is absolutely necessary. Carefully release the valve spring compressor and remove the springs and the valve from the head (see illustration). If the valve binds in the guide (won't pull through), push it back into the head and deburr the area around the keeper groove with a very fine file or whetstone (see illustration).

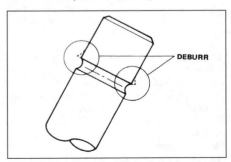

13.7d If the valve binds in the guide, deburr the area above the keeper groove

13.14 Lay a precision straightedge across the cylinder head and try to slide a feeler gauge of the specified thickness (equal to the maximum allowable warpage) under it

13.15 Measuring the valve seat width

13.16a Insert a small hole gauge into the valve guide and expand it so there's a slight drag when it's pulled out

8 Repeat the procedure for the remaining valves. Remember to keep the parts for each valve together so they can be reinstalled in the same location.

9 Once the valves have been removed and labeled, pull off the valve stem seals with pliers and discard them (the old seals should never be reused), then remove the spring seats.

10 Next, clean the cylinder head with solvent and dry it thoroughly. Compressed air will speed the drying process and ensure that all holes and recessed areas are clean.

11 Clean all of the valve springs, keepers, retainers and spring seats with solvent and dry them thoroughly. Do the parts from one valve at a time so that no mixing of parts between valves occurs.

12 Scrape off any deposits that may have formed on the valve, then use a motorized wire brush to remove deposits from the valve heads and stems. Again, make sure the valves do not get mixed up.

Inspection

13 Inspect the head very carefully for cracks and other damage. If cracks are found, a new head will be required. Check the cam bearing surfaces for wear and evidence of seizure. Check the camshafts and rocker arms for wear as well (see Section 10).

14 Using a precision straightedge and a feeler gauge, check the head gasket mating surface for warpage. Lay the straightedge lengthwise, across the head and diagonally (corner-to-corner), intersecting the head bolt holes, and try to slip a feeler gauge under it, on either side of each combustion chamber **(see illustration)**. The feeler gauge thickness should be the same as the head warpage limit listed in this Chapter's Specifications. If the feeler gauge can be inserted between the head and the straightedge, the head is warped and must either be machined or, if warpage is excessive, replaced with a new one.

15 Examine the valve seats in each of the combustion chambers. If they are pitted, cracked or burned, the head will require valve service that is beyond the scope of the home mechanic. Measure the valve seat width **(see illustration)** and compare it to this Chapter's Specifications. If it is not within the specified range, or if it varies around its circumference, valve service work is required.

16 Clean the valve guides to remove any carbon buildup, then measure the inside diameters of the guides (at both ends and the center of the guide) with a small hole gauge and a 0-to-1-inch micrometer **(see illustrations)**. Record the measurements for future reference. These measurements, along with the valve stem diameter measurements, will enable you to compute the valve stem-to-guide clearance. This clearance, when compared to the Specifications, will be one

factor that will determine the extent of the valve service work required. The guides are measured at the ends and at the center to determine if they are worn in a bell-mouth pattern (more wear at the ends). If they are, guide replacement is an absolute must.

17 Carefully inspect each valve face for cracks, pits and burned spots. Check the valve stem and the keeper groove area for cracks **(see illustration)**. Rotate the valve and check for any obvious indication that it is bent. Check the end of the stem for pitting and excessive wear and make sure the bevel is the specified width. Measure the thickness of the valve head edge and make sure it's not less than the minimum listed in this Chapter's Specifications. The presence of any of the above conditions indicates the need for valve servicing. **Note**: *The ends of the valve stems can be machined, as long as they aren't ground to less than the minimum length above the keeper groove (listed in this Chapter's Specifications) and the bevel protrudes above the keepers after installation.*

18 Measure the valve stem diameter **(see illustration)**. By subtracting the stem diameter from the valve guide diameter, the valve stem-to-guide clearance is obtained. If the stem-to-guide clearance is greater than listed in this Chapter's Specifications, the guides and valves will have to be replaced with new ones. Also check the valve stem for bending. Set the valve in a V-block with a dial

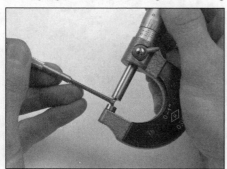

13.16b Measure the small hole gauge with a micrometer

13.17 Check the valve face, stem and keeper groove for signs of wear and damage

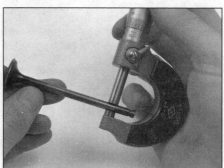

13.18a Measure the valve stem diameter with a micrometer

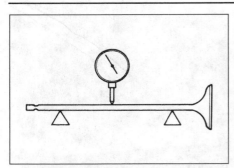

13.18b Check the valve stem for bends with a V-block (or blocks, as shown here) and a dial indicator

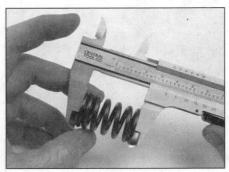

13.19a Measure the free length of the valve springs

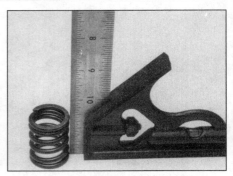

13.19b Check the valve springs for squareness

indicator touching the middle of the stem **(see illustration)**. Rotate the valve and note the reading on the gauge. If the stem runout exceeds the value listed in this Chapter's Specifications, replace the valve.

19 Check the end of each valve spring for wear and pitting. Measure the free length **(see illustration)** and compare it to this Chapter's Specifications. Any springs that are shorter than specified have sagged and should not be reused. Stand the spring on a flat surface and check it for squareness **(see illustration)**.

20 Check the spring retainers and keepers for obvious wear and cracks. Any

questionable parts should not be reused, as extensive damage will occur in the event of failure during engine operation.

21 If the inspection indicates that no service work is required, the valve components can be reinstalled in the head.

Reassembly

22 On all except Katana 750 (GSX750F) models, lay the metal plate and outer spring plate on the exhaust valve side of the head **(see illustration)**.

23 Lay the inner spring seats in place in the cylinder head, then install new valve stem seals on each of the guides **(see**

illustrations). Use an appropriate size deep socket to push the seals into place until they are properly seated. Don't twist or cock them, or they will not seal properly against the valve stems. Also, don't remove them again or they will be damaged. **Note:** *Be sure not to mix up the inner spring seat with the spring retainer. The inner spring seat has a larger hole.*

24 Coat the valve stems with assembly lube or moly-based grease, then install one of them into its guide **(see illustration)**. Next, install the springs and retainer, compress the springs and install the keepers **(see illustrations)**. **Note:** *Install the springs with*

13.22 On all except Katana 750 (GSX750F) models, a metal plate (arrow) fits over the exhaust valve stem seals next to the cylinder head and an outer spring seat goes on top of the plate

13.23a On all models, install the lower spring seat on all valves (be sure not to confuse the spring seat with the spring retainer, which goes on top of the spring)

13.23b Fit a new oil seal over each valve guide

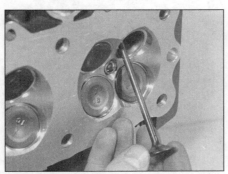

13.24a Coat the valve stem with assembly lube or molybdenum disulfide grease and install the valve in the guide

13.24b Install the inner spring with its closely wound coils at the bottom next to the head

13.24c Install the outer spring with its closely wound coils at the bottom next to the head

13.24d Install the spring retainer, then compress the springs and install the keepers . . .

13.24e . . . a small dab of grease will help hold the keepers in place on the valve while spring pressure is released

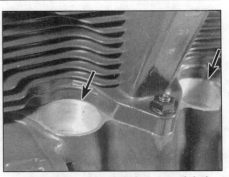

14.2 Pull the oil drain tubes out of their fittings (arrows) and remove the nut that holds the cylinder block to the crankcase

the tightly wound coils at the bottom (next to the spring seat). When compressing the springs with the valve spring compressor, depress them only as far as is absolutely necessary to slip the keepers into place. Apply a small amount of grease to the keepers **(see illustration)** to help hold them in place as the pressure is released from the springs. Make certain that the keepers are securely locked in their retaining grooves.

25 Support the cylinder head on blocks so the valves can't contact the workbench top, then very gently tap each of the valve stems with a soft-faced hammer. This will help seat the keepers in their grooves.

26 Once all of the valves have been installed in the head, check for proper valve sealing by pouring a small amount of solvent into each of the valve ports. If the solvent leaks past the valve(s) into the combustion chamber area, disassemble the valve(s) and check for foreign material on the valve faces and seats. If there isn't any, the valves require service.

---

14 Cylinder block - removal, inspection and installation

Removal

1 Following the procedure given in Section 11, remove the cylinder head. Make sure the crankshaft is positioned at Top Dead

Center (TDC) for cylinder no. 1 (see the valve adjustment procedure in Chapter 1).

2 Pull the oil drain tubes out of the fittings in the cylinder block and remove one nut that secures the block to the crankcase **(see illustration)**.

3 Hold the cam chain up and lift the cylinder block straight up to remove it **(see illustrations)**. If it's stuck, tap on the parts that don't have cooling fins with a soft-faced hammer. Don't attempt to pry between the block and the crankcase, as you will ruin the sealing surfaces. As you lift, note the location of the dowel pins. As you lift these off the studs, be careful not to let them drop into the engine.

4 Remove the oil jet **(see illustration)**.

5 Stuff clean shop towels around the pistons and remove the gasket and all traces of old gasket material from the surfaces of the cylinder block and the cylinder head.

Inspection

Caution: Don't attempt to separate the liners from the cylinder block.

6 Check the cylinder walls carefully for scratches and score marks.

7 Using the appropriate precision measuring tools, check each cylinder's diameter near the top, center and bottom of the cylinder bore, parallel to the crankshaft axis **(see illustration)**. Next, measure each cylinder's diameter at the same three locations across the crankshaft axis. Compare the results to

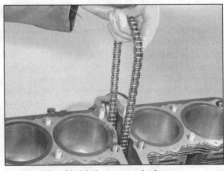

14.3a Hold the cam chain up . . .

this Chapter's Specifications. If the cylinder walls are tapered, out-of-round, worn beyond the specified limits, or badly scuffed or scored, have them rebored and honed by a dealer service department or a motorcycle repair shop. If a rebore is done, oversize pistons and rings will be required as well.

8 As an alternative, if the precision measuring tools are not available, a dealer service department or motorcycle repair shop will make the measurements and offer advice concerning servicing of the cylinders.

9 If they are in reasonably good condition and not worn to the outside of the limits, and if the piston-to-cylinder clearances can be maintained properly (see Section 15), then the cylinders do not have to be rebored; honing is all that is necessary.

2

14.3b . . . and lift the cylinder block off, then remove the gasket and dowels

14.4 Remove the oil jet; use a new O-ring during installation

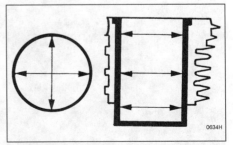

14.7 Measure the cylinder bore in the directions shown with a telescoping gauge (then measure the gauge with a micrometer)

14.14 Install the oil jet and the dowels, then install the gasket

10 To perform the honing operation you will need the proper size flexible hone with fine stones, or a "bottle brush" type hone, plenty of light oil or honing oil, some shop towels and an electric drill motor. Hold the cylinder block in a vise (cushioned with soft jaws or wood blocks) when performing the honing operation. Mount the hone in the drill motor, compress the stones and slip the hone into the cylinder. Lubricate the cylinder thoroughly, turn on the drill and move the hone up and down in the cylinder at a pace which will produce a fine crosshatch pattern on the cylinder wall with the crosshatch lines intersecting at approximately a 60-degree

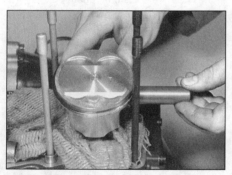

15.3a Note the arrow mark on the piston crown (pointing toward the front of the engine); mark the cylinder number on the top of the piston, then slide the piston pin out

15.3b Place a shop towel over the piston pin circlip so it won't fly out and cause injury, then pry the circlip out of the groove

angle. Be sure to use plenty of lubricant and do not take off any more material than is absolutely necessary to produce the desired effect. Do not withdraw the hone from the cylinder while it is running. Instead, shut off the drill and continue moving the hone up and down in the cylinder until it comes to a complete stop, then compress the stones and withdraw the hone. Wipe the oil out of the cylinder and repeat the procedure on the remaining cylinder. Remember, do not remove too much material from the cylinder wall. If you do not have the tools, or do not desire to perform the honing operation, a dealer service department or motorcycle repair shop will generally do it for a reasonable fee.

11 Next, the cylinders must be thoroughly washed with warm soapy water to remove all traces of the abrasive grit produced during the honing operation. Be sure to run a brush through the bolt holes and flush them with running water. After rinsing, dry the cylinders thoroughly and apply a coat of light, rust-preventative oil to all machined surfaces.

12 Make sure the oil jet is clear. Discard its O-ring and install a new one.

Installation

13 Lubricate the cylinder bores with plenty of clean engine oil. Apply a thin film of moly-based grease to the piston skirts.

14 Install the dowel pins, then place a new cylinder base gasket on the crankcase **(see illustration)**.

15 Slowly rotate the crankshaft until all of the pistons are at the same level. Slide lengths of welding rod or pieces of a straightened-out coat hanger under the pistons, on both sides of the connecting rods. This will help keep the pistons level as the cylinder block is lowered onto them.

16 Attach four piston ring compressors to the pistons and compress the piston rings. Large hose clamps can be used instead - just make sure they don't scratch the pistons, and don't tighten them too much.

17 Install the cylinder block over the pistons and carefully lower it down until the piston

crowns fit into the cylinder liners. While doing this, pull the camshaft chain up, using a hooked tool or a piece of coat hanger. Push down on the cylinder block, making sure the pistons don't get cocked sideways, until the bottoms of the cylinder liners slide down past the piston rings. A wood or plastic hammer handle can be used to gently tap the block down, but don't use too much force or the pistons will be damaged.

18 Remove the piston ring compressors or hose clamps, being careful not to scratch the pistons. Remove the rods from under the pistons.

19 The remainder of installation is the reverse of removal, with the following addition: Use new O-rings on the oil drain tubes.

15 Pistons - removal, inspection and installation

1 The pistons are attached to the connecting rods with piston pins that are a slip fit in the pistons and rods.

2 Before removing the pistons from the rods, stuff a clean shop towel into each crankcase hole, around the connecting rods. This will prevent the circlips from falling into the crankcase if they are inadvertently dropped.

Removal

3 Using a sharp scribe, scratch the number of each piston into its crown. Each piston should also have an arrow pointing toward the front of the engine **(see illustration)**. If not, scribe an arrow into the piston crown before removal. Support the first piston and pry the circlip out of the groove **(see illustration)**.

4 Push the piston pin out from the opposite end to free the piston from the rod. You may have to deburr the area around the groove to enable the pin to slide out (use a triangular file for this procedure). Repeat the procedure for the other piston. If the pin won't come out, fabricate a piston pin removal tool from threaded stock, nuts, washers and a piece of pipe **(see illustration)**.

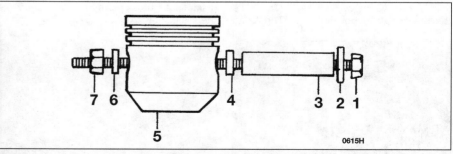

15.4 The piston pins should come out with hand pressure - if they don't, this removal tool can be fabricated from readily available parts

1	Bolt	5	Piston	A	Large enough for piston pin to fit inside
2	Washer	6	Washer (B)		
3	Pipe (A)	7	Nut (B)	B	Small enough to fit through piston pin bore
4	Padding (A)				

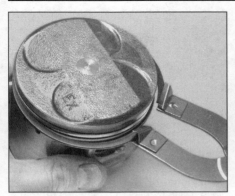

15.6 Remove the piston rings with a ring removal and installation tool

Inspection

5 Before the inspection process can be carried out, the pistons must be cleaned and the old piston rings removed.

6 Using a piston ring installation tool, carefully remove the rings from the pistons **(see illustration)**. Do not nick or gouge the pistons in the process.

7 Scrape all traces of carbon from the tops of the pistons. A hand-held wire brush or a piece of fine emery cloth can be used once most of the deposits have been scraped away. Do not, under any circumstances, use a wire brush mounted in a drill motor to remove deposits from the pistons; the piston material is soft and will be eroded away by the wire brush.

8 Use a piston ring groove cleaning tool to remove any carbon deposits from the ring grooves. Be very careful to remove only the carbon deposits. Do not remove any metal and do not nick or gouge the sides of the ring grooves.

HAYNES HiNT *If a ring groove cleaning tool is not available, a piece broken off the old ring will do the job.*

9 Once the deposits have been removed, clean the pistons with solvent and dry them thoroughly. Make sure the oil return holes below the oil ring grooves are clear.

10 If the pistons are not damaged or worn excessively and if the cylinders are not rebored, new pistons will not be necessary. Normal piston wear appears as even, vertical wear on the thrust surfaces of the piston and slight looseness of the top ring in its groove. New piston rings, on the other hand, should always be used when an engine is rebuilt.

11 Carefully inspect each piston for cracks around the skirt, at the pin bosses and at the ring lands.

12 Look for scoring and scuffing on the thrust faces of the skirt, holes in the piston crown and burned areas at the edge of the crown. If the skirt is scored or scuffed, the engine may have been suffering from

15.13 Measure the piston ring-to-groove clearance with a feeler gauge

overheating and/or abnormal combustion, which caused excessively high operating temperatures. The oil pump and oil cooling system should be checked thoroughly. A hole in the piston crown, an extreme to be sure, is an indication that abnormal combustion (pre-ignition) was occurring. Burned areas at the edge of the piston crown are usually evidence of spark knock (detonation). If any of the above problems exist, the causes must be corrected or the damage will occur again.

13 Measure the piston ring-to-groove clearance by laying a new piston ring in the ring groove and slipping a feeler gauge in beside it **(see illustration)**. Check the clearance at three or four locations around the groove. Be sure to use the correct ring for each groove; they are different. If the clearance is greater than specified, new pistons will have to be used when the engine is reassembled.

14 Check the piston-to-bore clearance by measuring the bore (see Section 14) and the piston diameter. Make sure that the pistons and cylinders are correctly matched. Measure the piston across the skirt on the thrust faces at a 90-degree angle to the piston pin, about 15 mm (5/8-inch) up from the bottom of the skirt **(see illustration)**. Subtract the piston diameter from the bore diameter to obtain the clearance. If it is greater than specified, the cylinders will have to be rebored and new oversized pistons and rings installed. If the

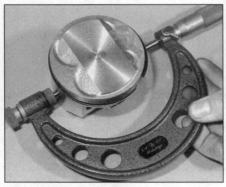

15.14 Measure the piston diameter with a micrometer

appropriate precision measuring tools are not available, the piston-to-cylinder clearances can be obtained, though not quite as accurately, using feeler gauge stock. Feeler gauge stock comes in 12-inch lengths and various thicknesses and is generally available at auto parts stores. To check the clearance, select a feeler gauge of the same thickness as the piston clearance listed in this Chapter's Specifications and slip it into the cylinder along with the appropriate piston. The piston must be positioned exactly as it normally would be. Place the feeler gauge between the piston and cylinder on one of the thrust faces (90-degrees to the piston pin bore). The piston should slip through the cylinder (with the feeler gauge in place) with moderate pressure. If it falls through, or slides through easily, the clearance is excessive and a new piston will be required. If the piston binds at the lower end of the cylinder and is loose toward the top, the cylinder is tapered, and if tight spots are encountered as the feeler gauge is placed at different points around the cylinder, the cylinder is out-of-round. Repeat the procedure for the remaining pistons and cylinders. Be sure to have the cylinders and pistons checked by a dealer service department or a motorcycle repair shop to confirm your findings before purchasing new parts.

15 Apply clean engine oil to the pin, insert it into the piston and check for freeplay by rocking the pin back-and-forth. If the pin is loose, new pistons and pins must be installed.

16 Refer to Section 16 and install the rings on the pistons.

Installation

17 Install the pistons in their original locations with the arrows pointing to the front of the engine. Lubricate the pins and the rod bores with clean engine oil. Install new circlips in the grooves in the inner sides of the pistons (don't reuse the old circlips). Push the pins into position from the opposite side and install new circlips **(see illustration)**. Compress the circlips only enough for them to fit in the piston. Make sure the circlips are properly seated in the grooves.

2

15.17 Install the circlip and make sure it's securely seated in the groove

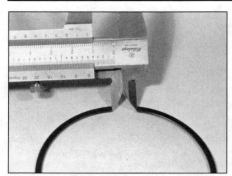

16.3 Measure the free end gap of the compression rings and replace any with excessively large gaps

16.4 Square the ring in the bore by turning the piston upside down and tapping on the ring, then check the piston ring end gap with a feeler gauge

16.6 If the end gap is too small, clamp a file in a vise and file the ring ends (from the outside in only) to enlarge the gap slightly

16 Piston rings - installation

1 Before installing the new piston rings, the ring end gaps must be checked.
2 Lay out the pistons and the new ring sets so the rings will be matched with the same piston and cylinder during the end gap

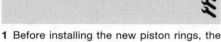

16.11a Top and second ring profiles - GSX-R750 and GSX-R1100 (1985 through 1988); Katana 600/GSX600F (all)

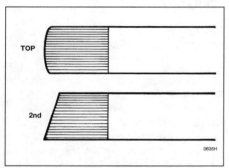

16.11b Top and second ring profiles - GSX-R750 (1989 on); Katana 750/GSX750F (all)

measurement procedure and engine assembly.
3 Measure the free end gap of each compression ring **(see illustration)**. If any are not within the range listed in this Chapter's Specifications, replace the rings as a set.
4 Insert the top (No. 1) ring into the bottom of the first cylinder and square it up with the cylinder walls by pushing it in with the top of the piston **(see illustration)**. The ring should be about one inch above the bottom edge of the cylinder. To measure the end gap, slip a feeler gauge between the ends of the ring as shown and compare the measurement to the Specifications.
5 If the gap is larger or smaller than specified, double check to make sure that you have the correct rings before proceeding.
6 If the gap is too small, it must be enlarged or the ring ends may come in contact with each other during engine operation, which can cause serious damage. The end gap can be increased by filing the ring ends very carefully with a fine file **(see illustration)**. When performing this operation, file only from the outside in.
7 Repeat the procedure for each ring that will be installed in the first cylinder and for each ring in the remaining cylinders. Remember to keep the rings, pistons and cylinders matched up.
8 Once the ring end gaps have been

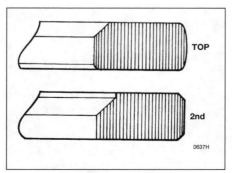

16.11c Top and second ring profiles - GSX-R1100 (1989 on); Katana 1100/GSX1100F (all)

checked/corrected, the rings can be installed on the pistons.
9 The oil control ring (lowest on the piston) is installed first. It is composed of three separate components. Slip the expander into the groove, then install the upper side rail. Do not use a piston ring installation tool on the oil ring side rails as they may be damaged. Instead, place one end of the side rail into the groove between the spacer expander and the ring land. Hold it firmly in place and slide a finger around the piston while pushing the rail into the groove. Next, install the lower side rail in the same manner.
10 After the three oil ring components have been installed, check to make sure that both the upper and lower side rails can be turned smoothly in the ring groove.
11 Install the no. 2 (middle) ring next. It can be readily distinguished from the top ring by its cross-section shape **(see illustrations)**. Do not mix the top and middle rings.
12 To avoid breaking the ring, use a piston ring installation tool and make sure that the identification mark is facing up **(see illustration)**. Fit the ring into the middle groove on the piston. Do not expand the ring any more than is necessary to slide it into place.
13 Finally, install the no. 1 (top) ring in the same manner. Make sure the identifying mark is facing up.

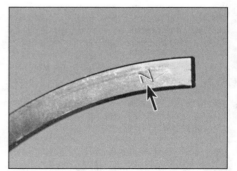

16.12 Make sure the marks on the rings (arrow) face up when the rings are installed on the pistons (late GSX-R1100 shown)

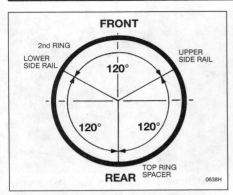

16.15 When installing the rings, stagger the end gaps as shown

17.6a Unscrew the oil gallery plugs, one on each side of the pan, while the pan is still on the engine (the relief valve and spring are behind the right-hand plug (lower arrow) - the plug in the crankcase (upper arrow) is for checking oil pressure

17.6b Remove the oil pan bolts - don't forget the one in the center of the pan (arrow)

14 Repeat the procedure for the remaining pistons and rings. Be very careful not to confuse the no. 1 and no. 2 rings.

15 Once the rings have been properly installed, stagger the end gaps, including those of the oil ring side rails **(see illustration)**.

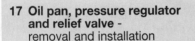

17 Oil pan, pressure regulator and relief valve - removal and installation

Note: *The oil pan can be removed with the engine in the frame.*

Removal

1 Support the bike securely so it can't be knocked over.

2 Remove body parts as necessary to provide access to the oil pan bolts (see Chapter 7).

3 Drain the engine oil and remove the oil filter (see Chapter 1).

4 Remove the exhaust system (see Chapter 3).

5 Disconnect the wire for the oil pressure switch (see Chapter 8).

6 Remove the oil gallery plugs and relief valve from the pan while it's still on the engine (the

plugs may be tight) **(see illustration)**. Remove the oil pan bolts and detach the pan from the crankcase **(see illustration)**.

7 Remove the shim and O-ring from the crankcase **(see illustrations)**.

8 Unbolt the oil pickup strainer from the pickup tube **(see illustration)**.

9 Unbolt the pickup tube from the engine **(see illustration)**. Note that one bolt is inside the pickup tube.

10 Unscrew the pressure regulator from the oil pan **(see illustration)**.

11 Remove all traces of old gasket material

17.7a Remove the O-ring protector shim from the crankcase . . .

17.7b . . . and remove the O-ring from beneath the shim - the O-ring should be replaced whenever the oil pan is removed

from the mating surfaces of the oil pan, pickup tube and crankcase.

Inspection

12 Check the hole in the relief valve for clogging. If it's clogged and you can't clear it, replace the valve.

13 Check the pressure regulator for clogging and a stuck valve. Replace it if its condition is in doubt.

Installation

14 Place a new gasket on the oil pickup tube

2

17.8 Unbolt the oil strainer from the pickup tube. . .

17.9 . . . and unbolt the pickup tube from the engine - one of the pickup bolts is inside the tube

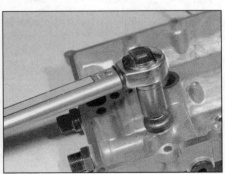

17.10 Unscrew the oil pressure regulator - use a new sealing washer during installation

17.14 Use a new gasket for the pickup tube . . .

17.17 . . . and for the oil pan

18.6 Unbolt the oil pump and lift it out of the engine

and install it on the crankcase **(see illustration)**. Tighten the bolts securely, but don't overtighten them. Install the filter screen and tighten its bolts to the Specifications.

15 Install the relief valve, spring and oil gallery plugs in the oil pan. Tighten to the torque listed in this Chapter's Specifications.

16 Install the pressure regulator in the oil pan, using a new sealing washer. Tighten to the torque listed in this Chapter's Specifications.

17 Position a new oil pan gasket on the crankcase **(see illustration)**. A thin film of RTV sealant can be used to hold the gasket in place. Install the oil pan and bolts and tighten the bolts to the torque listed in this Chapter's Specifications, using a criss-cross pattern.

18 The remainder of installation is the reverse of removal. Install a new filter and fill the

18.7a Make sure the pump dowels are in their holes; remove the small O-ring . . .

crankcase with oil (see Chapter 1), then run the engine and check for leaks.

---

18 Oil pump - pressure check, removal, inspection and installation

Note: *Oil pump removal requires that the engine be removed and the crankcase disassembled.*

Pressure check

⚠️ **Warning:** *If the oil passage plug is removed when the engine is hot, hot oil will drain out - wait until the engine is cold before beginning this check.*

1 Remove the fairing (see Chapter 7).

2 Remove the plug at the bottom of the crankcase on the right-hand side and install an oil pressure gauge **(see illustration 17.6a)**.

3 Start the engine and warm it to normal operating temperature (about 10 minutes at 3,000 rpm during warm weather or 20 minutes at 3,000 rpm during cold weather). Watch the gauge while varying the engine rpm. The pressure should stay within the range listed in this Chapter's Specifications. If the pressure is too high, the relief valve or regulator is stuck closed. To check it, see Section 17.

4 If the pressure is lower than the standard, either the relief valve or regulator is stuck open, the oil pump is faulty, or there is other engine damage. Begin diagnosis by checking the regulator and relief valve (see Section 17),

then the oil pump. If those items check out okay, chances are the bearing oil clearances are excessive and the engine needs to be overhauled.

Removal

5 Remove the engine and disassemble the crankcase (see Sections 5 and 26).

6 Remove the pump mounting bolts and lift out the pump **(see illustration)**.

7 Make sure the pump dowels are in position. If not, find them and place them in their holes. Remove the O-rings from the oil passage and pump **(see illustrations)**.

Inspection

8 The oil pump is available only as an assembly. If oil pressure was insufficient during the test and none of the other causes (defective relief valve or pressure regulator, worn bearings, clogged oil lines or passages) can be found, replace the pump. The pump should be replaced as a standard practice whenever the engine is overhauled.

Installation

9 Installation is the reverse of removal, with the following additions:

a) *Always use new O-rings.*

b) *Use non-permanent thread locking agent (Suzuki Thread Lock 1342 or equivalent) on the oil pump mounting bolts **(see illustration)**.*

c) *Tighten the bolts to the torque listed in this Chapter's Specifications **(see illustration)**.*

18.7b . . . and the large O-ring (always use new O-rings when installing the pump)

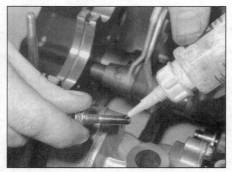

18.9a Use non-permanent thread locking agent on the bolt threads . . .

18.9b . . . and tighten the bolts to Specifications

19.5 Remove the clutch cover Allen bolts (arrows) in a criss-cross pattern

19 Clutch - removal, inspection and installation

Note: *The clutch can be removed with the engine in the frame.*

Removal

1 On all except 1989 and later GSX-R1100 models, shift the transmission into first gear. This is necessary to prevent the engine from turning when the pressure plate bolts are removed.
2 Support the bike so it can't be knocked over during the procedure.
3 Remove fairing panels as needed to gain

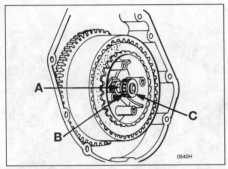

19.8a The thrust washer, bearing and push piece are mounted in the clutch sleeve . . .

A Clutch push piece   C Thrust washer
B Bearing

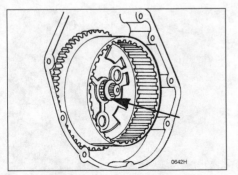

19.11a Remove the thrust washer . . .

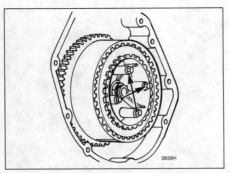

19.7 Remove the pressure plate bolts in a criss-cross pattern, then remove the springs (and spacers on 1100 models)

access to the clutch cover on the right side of the crankcase (see Chapter 7).
4 Drain the engine oil (see Chapter 1).
5 Remove the clutch cover bolts and take the cover off **(see illustration)**. If the cover is stuck, tap around its perimeter with a soft-face hammer.
6 If the clutch cover dowels came off with the cover, set them aside so they won't be lost.

All except 1989 and later GSX-R1100 models

7 Loosen the clutch spring bolts in a criss-cross pattern **(see illustration)**. Remove the springs, spacers (if equipped) and pressure plate.
8 Remove the push piece, bearing and thrust washer from the clutch hub or pressure plate

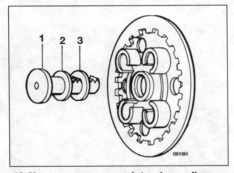

19.8b . . . or pressure plate, depending on model

1 Clutch push piece   3 Thrust washer
2 Bearing

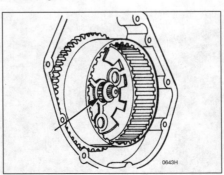

19.11b . . . then remove the bearing and spacer

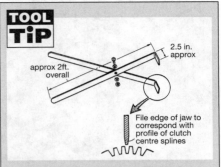

An alternative to the Suzuki clutch holding tool can be fabricated from some steel strap, bent at the ends and bolted together in the middle.

(see illustrations). Remove the clutch pushrod from the clutch hub.
9 Bend back the lockwasher and remove the clutch hub nut, using a special holding tool (Suzuki tool no. 09920-52732) to prevent the clutch housing from turning **(see illustration)**. Replace the lockwasher with a new one during installation.
10 Remove the clutch sleeve together with the friction plates and steel plates from the clutch housing.
11 Remove the thrust washer **(see illustration)**. Pull the clutch hub partway out and push it back in to expose the needle roller bearing and spacer. Remove these from the shaft **(see illustration)**, then remove the clutch hub and alternator/oil pump gears.

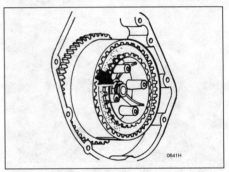

19.9 Bend back the tab on the lockwasher and remove the nut

19.12a Remove the snap ring . . .

2

19.12b . . . and pressure plate lifter

19.12c Remove the thrust washer and needle bearing . . .

19.12d . . .the push piece . . .

19.12e . . . and the pushrod

19.12f Hold the pressure plate from turning with a special tool (see Tool Tip) and loosen the diaphragm spring holder nut with a 50 mm socket . . .

19.12g . . . remove the holder nut . . .

19.12h . . . the diaphragm springs . . .

19.12i . . . the spring seat . . .

19.12j . . . and the pressure plate

19.12k Remove a friction plate. . . .

19.12l . . . then a steel plate . . .

19.12m . . . then a friction plate - continue until all the plates are removed

1989 and later GSX-R1100 models

12 These models are equipped with a diaphragm spring clutch. Refer to the accompanying illustrations for removal procedures **(see illustrations)**.
Inspection
13 Examine the splines on both the inside and the outside of the clutch sleeve and housing **(see illustration)**. If any wear is evident, replace the sleeve or housing with a new one.
14 On coil spring clutch models, measure the free length of the clutch springs **(see illustration)** and compare the results to this Chapter's Specifications. If the springs have

19.12n Remove the wave washer and the wave washer seat

19.12o Hold the clutch sleeve with a holding tool and loosen the sleeve hub nut with a socket

19.12p Unscrew the sleeve hub nut . . .

19.12q . . . and remove the thrust washer . . .

19.12r . . . the sleeve hub . . .

19.12s . . . another thrust washer . . .

19.12t . . . the clutch housing . . .

19.12u . . . the alternator and oil pump drive gears . . .

19.12v . . . the needle roller bearing . . .

19.12w . . . the bearing spacer . . .

19.12x . . . and a thrust washer

2

19.13 Check the clutch housing and sleeve hub splines for wear and damage

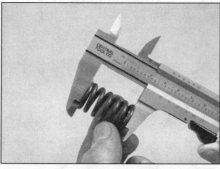

19.14 Measure the clutch spring free length (coil spring clutch)

19.15 Measure the diaphragm spring height (diaphragm spring clutch)

sagged, or if cracks are noted, replace them with new ones as a set.

15 On diaphragm spring clutch models, lay the diaphragm springs on a flat surface (such as a piece of plate glass) and measure the spring height with a vernier caliper **(see illustration)**. Replace the springs if they have sagged to less than the limit listed in this Chapter's Specifications.

16 If the lining material of the friction plates smells burnt or if it is glazed, new parts are required. If the metal clutch plates are scored or discolored, they must be replaced with new ones. Measure the thickness of each friction plate **(see illustration)** and compare the results to this Chapter's Specifications. Replace with new parts any friction plates that are near the wear limit.

17 Lay the metal plates, one at a time, on a perfectly flat surface (such as a piece of plate glass) and check for warpage by trying to slip a feeler gauge of the specified thickness (refer to this Chapter's Specifications for warpage limits) between the flat surface and the plate **(see illustration)**. Do this at several places around the plate's circumference. If the feeler gauge can be slipped under the plate, it is warped and should be replaced with a new one.

18 Check the tabs on the friction plates for excessive wear and mushroomed edges. They can be cleaned up with a file if the deformation is not severe.

19 Check the edges of the slots in the clutch housing for indentations made by the friction plate tabs. If the indentations are deep they

can prevent clutch release, so the housing should be replaced with a new one. If the indentations can be removed easily with a file, the life of the housing can be prolonged to an extent.

20 Check the clutch pressure plate for wear and damage and make sure the pushrod is not bent (roll it on a perfectly flat surface or use V-blocks and a dial indicator). Check the release bearing for wear or damage. Replace the pushrod and bearing if they're worn.

21 Clean all traces of old gasket material from the clutch cover.

Installation

22 Installation is the reverse of removal, with the following additions:

a) Use a new lockwasher on the clutch sleeve nut.

b) Tighten the sleeve nut to the torque listed in this Chapter's Specifications. Hold the housing and sleeve from turning with the tool described in Step 9 **(see illustration)**.

c) Coat the clutch friction plates with engine oil. Install the clutch plates, starting with a friction plate, then a steel plate and alternating them.

d) Lubricate the pushrod before installing it.

e) On coil spring clutch models, tighten the pressure plate bolts in a criss-cross pattern to the torque listed in this Chapter's Specifications.

f) Make sure the clutch cover dowels are in place **(see illustration)**. Install the clutch cover and bolts, using a new gasket. Tighten the bolts securely in a criss-cross pattern.

g) On GSX600F and GSX750F models, set up the release mechanism play (see Chapter 1).

h) On cable clutch models, connect the clutch cable to the release lever and adjust the freeplay (see 'Daily (pre-ride) checks' at the beginning of this manual).

i) Fill the crankcase with the recommended type and amount of engine oil (see Chapter 1).

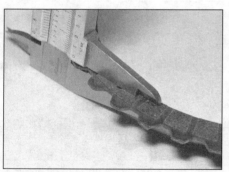

19.16 Measure the thickness of the friction plates

19.17 Check the metal plates for warpage

19.22a Hold the sleeve hub from turning and tighten the nut

19.22b Make sure the dowels are in place (arrows) and install a new gasket

21.3 The master cylinder is secured to the handlebar by two bolts (arrows)

20 Clutch cable - replacement

1 Fully back off the lockwheel on the cable adjuster at the handlebar and screw the adjuster into the clutch lever bracket to create slack in the cable. Align the slot in the adjuster and lockwheel with the slot in the bracket, then work the cable trunnion out of the bracket and slot.

2 On GSX-R750 models, back off the locknuts on the cable lower adjuster and remove the adjuster from its bracket on the clutch cover. Disconnect the cable trunnion

from the release arm. Note that access will be improved by removing the fairing right lower panel.

3 On GSX600F and GSX750F models, move the gearshift lever and the chain guard (sprocket cover) from the engine left side. Disconnect the cable trunnion from the release lever on the inside of the guard and fully unscrew the adjuster screw to separate the cable from the guard.

4 Before removing the cable from the bike, tape the lower end of the new cable to the upper end of the old cable. Slowly pull the lower end of the old cable out, guiding the new cable down into position. Using this method will ensure the cable is routed correctly.

5 Lubricate the cable (see Chapter 1). Reconnect the ends of the cable by reversing the removal procedure, then adjust the cable following the procedure given in *'Daily (pre-ride) checks'* at the beginning of this manual.

21 Clutch master cylinder - removal, overhaul and installation

Removal

1 Remove the clutch interlock switch from beneath the master cylinder.

2 Place a towel under the master cylinder to catch any spilled fluids, then remove the union bolt from the master cylinder fluid line. *Caution: Brake fluid will damage paint. Wipe up any spills immediately and wash the area with soap and water.*

3 Remove the master cylinder clamp bolts and take the cylinder body off the handlebar (see illustration). Remove the lever pivot and lever.

Overhaul

4 Remove the cap, rubber diaphragm and gasket from the reservoir (see illustration).

5 Remove the bushing, pushrod and dust seal from the master cylinder.

6 Remove the snap ring and retaining ring, then dump out the piston and primary cup, secondary cup and spring. If they won't come out, blow compressed air into the fluid line hole.

Warning: The piston may shoot out forcefully enough to cause injury. Point the piston at a block of wood or a pile of rags inside a box and apply air pressure gradually. Never point the end of the cylinder at yourself, including your fingers.

7 Thoroughly clean all of the components in clean brake fluid (don't use any type of petroleum-based solvent).

8 Check the piston and cylinder bore for

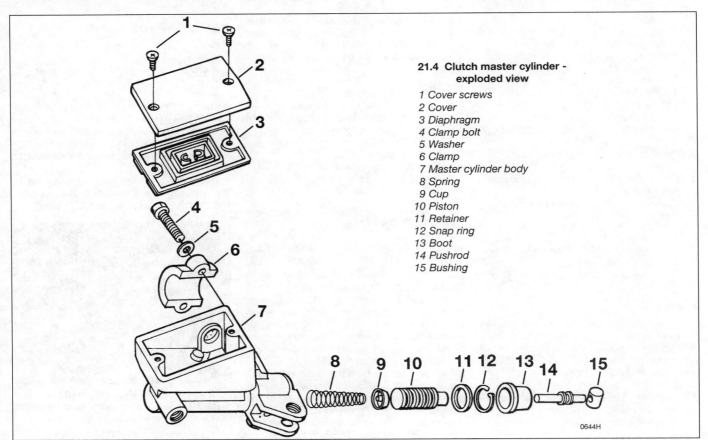

21.4 Clutch master cylinder - exploded view

1 Cover screws
2 Cover
3 Diaphragm
4 Clamp bolt
5 Washer
6 Clamp
7 Master cylinder body
8 Spring
9 Cup
10 Piston
11 Retainer
12 Snap ring
13 Boot
14 Pushrod
15 Bushing

0644H

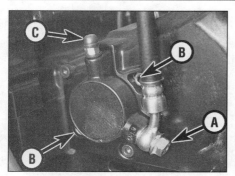

22.1 Clutch release cylinder details

A *Fluid line union bolt*
B *Cylinder mounting bolts*
C *Bleed valve and cap*

wear, scratches and rust. If the piston shows these conditions, replace it and both rubber cups as a set. If the cylinder bore has any defects, replace the entire master cylinder.

9 Install the spring in the cylinder bore, wide end first.

10 Coat a new cup with brake fluid and install it in the cylinder, wide side first.

11 Coat the piston with brake fluid and install it in the cylinder.

12 Install the retaining ring. Press the piston into the bore and install the snap ring to hold it in place.

13 Install the dust seal, pushrod and bushing.

Installation

14 Installation is the reverse of the removal steps, with the following additions:
a) *Apply molybdenum grease to both ends of the pushrod.*
b) *Align the upper mating line of the master cylinder and clamp with the punch mark on the handlebar. Tighten the upper clamp bolt first to the torque listed in this Chapter's Specifications, then tighten the lower clamp bolt. There will be a gap at the bottom between the clamp and the master cylinder body.*
c) *Fill and bleed the clutch hydraulic system (see Section 23).*
d) *Operate the clutch lever and check for fluid leaks.*

22 Clutch release cylinder - removal, overhaul and installation

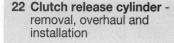

Removal

1 Place rags and a container beneath the release cylinder to catch spilled fluid, then remove the union bolt and place the end of the hose in the container to let the fluid drain **(see illustration)**.
Caution: Brake fluid will damage paint. Wipe up any spills immediately and wash the area with soap and water.

2 Remove the cylinder mounting bolts and take it off.

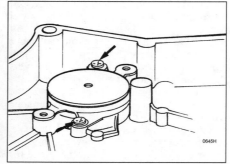

22.3 Remove the screws that secure the piston retainer to the engine

3 Remove the piston retainer from the engine **(see illustration)**.

Overhaul

4 Dump out the piston and spring **(see illustration)**. If they won't come out, blow compressed air into the fluid line hole.

 Warning: The piston may shoot out forcefully enough to cause injury. Point the piston at a block of wood or a pile of rags inside a box and apply air pressure gradually. Never point the end of the cylinder at yourself, including your fingers.

5 Thoroughly clean all of the components in clean brake fluid (don't use any type of petroleum-based solvent).

6 Check the piston and cylinder bore for wear, scratches and rust. If the piston shows these conditions, replace it and the rubber cup as a set. If the cylinder bore has any defects, replace the entire master cylinder.

Installation

7 Installation is the reverse of the removal procedure, with the following additions:
a) *Tighten the piston retainer screws, cylinder mounting bolts and fluid line union bolt securely.*
b) *Bleed the clutch (see Section 23).*
c) *Operate the clutch and check for fluid leaks.*

23 Clutch bleeding

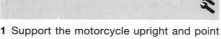

1 Support the motorcycle upright and point the front wheel straight ahead.

2 Remove the master cylinder cover, diaphragm and gasket (if equipped). Top up the master cylinder with fluid to the upper edge of the fluid level window, then set the gasket, diaphragm, and cap on the reservoir (but don't install the screws yet).

3 Remove the cap from the bleed valve **(see illustration 22.1)**. Place a box wrench over the bleed valve. Attach a rubber tube to the valve fitting and put the other end of the tube in a container. Pour enough clean brake fluid into the container to cover the end of the tube.

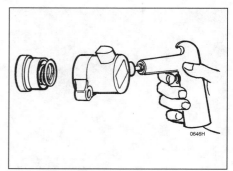

22.4 Release cylinder - exploded view

4 Rapidly squeeze the clutch lever several times, then hold it down. With the clutch lever held down, open the bleed valve 1/4-turn with the wrench, let air and fluid escape, then tighten the valve.

5 Release the clutch lever.

6 Repeat Steps 4 and 5 until there aren't any more bubbles in the fluid flowing into the container. Top up the master cylinder with fluid, then reinstall the gasket, diaphragm and cap and tighten the screws securely.

24 External shift mechanism - removal, inspection and installation

Shift lever and pedal

1 Support the bike securely so it can't be knocked over.

2 Remove fairing panels as necessary for access to the shift pedal and lever (see Chapter 7).

3 Remove the shift pedal circlip and shift pedal bolt **(see illustration)**. To ease installation, make an alignment mark on the shift lever shaft next to the gap in the shift lever **(see illustration)**. Pull the shift lever off the shaft.

4 Installation is the reverse of removal. Adjust the linkage as needed with the nuts on the linkage shaft **(see illustration 24.3a)**.

24.3a Remove the circlip and bolt to detach the linkage - use the nuts to adjust the linkage rod

A *Circlip*   B *Bolt*   C *Nuts*

24.3b Make an alignment mark next to the gap in the shift lever (arrow)

24.6a Remove the clip . . .

24.6b . . . and the washer . . .

Shift mechanism

Removal

5 Remove the shift pedal and linkage (Steps 1 through 3).

6 Remove the clip and washer from the gearshift shaft **(see illustrations)**.

7 Remove the clutch (see Section 19).

8 Remove the gearshift shaft and cam drive gear **(see illustration)**.

9 Remove the cam guide and pawl lifter **(see illustration)**.

10 Note: *During this step, don't let the pins* and springs fly out or they may be lost. Remove the cam driven gear, together with the pawls, pins and springs **(see illustrations)**.

Inspection

11 Check the shift shaft for bends and damage to the splines or drive gear. If the shaft is bent, you can attempt to straighten it, but if the splines or gear teeth are damaged it will have to be replaced.

12 Check the spring on the gearshift shaft for bending or breakage. Replace it if it has any defects.

13 Check the cam, pawls, pins and springs for wear and damage. Replace them if defects are found.

14 Check the condition of the gearshift shaft seal. If there's any doubt about its condition, pry it out **(see illustration)**. Position a new seal in the bore with its lip facing inward, then drive it in with a socket **(see illustrations)**.

Installation

15 Install the springs, pins and pawls in the cam driven gear. Be sure the wide sides of the pawls are on the same side as the driven gear teeth **(see illustration 24.10b)**.

16 Install the driven gear, then install the pawl lifter and cam guide **(see illustration 24.9)**. Use non-permanent thread locking agent

24.8 . . . then pull the gearshift shaft out of the engine

24.9 Remove the cam guide and pawl lifter - the screws have been treated with thread locking agent, so you'll probably need an impact driver

A Pawl lifter   B Cam guide

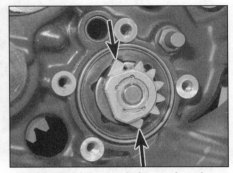

24.10a Hold the pawls (arrows) so they won't fly out . . .

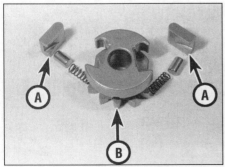

24.10b . . . and remove the cam driven gear, pawls, pins and springs - note the wide sides of the pawls; these must be on the same side as the driven gear during installation

A Wide sides of pawls   B Driven gear

24.14a Pry out the gearshift shaft seal . . .

24.14b . . . position a new one in the bore with its lip facing into the engine . . .

2

24.14c . . . and tap the seal in with a socket the same diameter as the seal

24.18 The center slot in the drive gear must align with the center tooth in the driven gear; the center of the gearshift shaft must align with the center of the cam driven gear

25.3 Remove the cover bolts (arrows) in a criss-cross pattern

(Suzuki Thread Lock 1342 or equivalent) on the screw threads.

17 Apply high-temperature grease to the lip of the gearshift shaft seal.

18 Carefully guide the gearshift shaft into place and engage the drive gear so its center aligns with the center of the driven gear **(see illustration)**.

19 Install the washer and clip in the gearshift shaft **(see illustrations 24.6b and 24.6a)**.

20 Install and adjust the shift pedal and linkage (see Steps 1 through 4).

21 Check the engine oil level and add some, if

25.4 Remove the starter idle gear and shaft

25.5 Hold the starter clutch from turning with a holding tool (you can make your own from steel strap, nuts and bolts) and loosen the starter clutch bolt

necessary (see *'Daily (pre-ride) checks'* at the beginning of this Manual).

22 The remainder of installation is the reverse of the removal steps.

25 Starter clutch - removal, inspection and installation

Removal

1 Support the bike so it can't be knocked over during this procedure.

2 Remove fairing panels as necessary for access to the starter clutch cover (see Chapter 7).

3 Remove the starter clutch cover bolts in a criss-cross pattern and remove the cover **(see illustration)**.

4 Remove the starter idle gear shaft, then remove the gear **(see illustration)**.

5 Hold the starter clutch from turning (you can make a holding tool from strap steel, bolts and nuts) and remove the bolt to make sure it's free of the thread locking agent that was used during installation **(see illustration)**.

6 Thread the bolt back in, but don't tighten it. Install a starter clutch remover (Suzuki tool 09920-34810 or equivalent) and tighten it

25.6 Position the starter clutch removal tool on the starter clutch and turn the tool bolt against the starter clutch bolt to remove the starter clutch

against the bolt head to free the starter clutch from the crankshaft **(see illustration)**.

7 Clean all old gasket and sealer from the cover and engine.

Inspection

8 Try to rotate the starter clutch in both directions on the driven gear. It should turn one way only. If it will turn in both directions or neither way, check for worn or damaged parts (see below).

9 On early GSX-R750 and 1100 models, remove the rollers, springs and pins from the starter clutch **(see illustration)**. If any of the parts are worn or damaged, replace them. Check the friction surface inside the starter clutch; if it's worn or damaged, replace the starter clutch as an assembly.

10 On later models, inspect the starter clutch

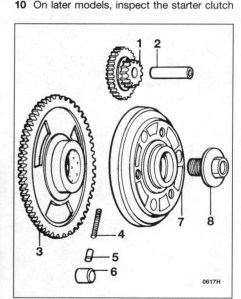

25.9 Starter clutch (early GSX-R models) - exploded view

1	Idle gear	5	Pin
2	Shaft	6	Roller
3	Driven gear	7	Housing
4	Spring	8	Bolt

25.10 Inspect the starter clutch rollers and the mounting surface (arrows)

25.11 Inspect the friction surface and the driven gear teeth (arrows)

25.14 Position the starter clutch and driven gear on the crankshaft

rollers and friction surface **(see illustration)**. If they're worn or damaged, replace the starter clutch.

11 Inspect the friction surface and the teeth on the driven gear **(see illustration)**. If they're worn or damaged, replace the starter clutch as an assembly.

12 Inspect the starter idle gear and shaft. If the teeth are chipped or if the gear fits loosely on the shaft, replace them.

Installation

13 Thoroughly clean the end of the crankshaft and the friction surface inside the starter clutch with solvent to remove all traces of oil. Blow them dry.

14 Position the starter clutch on the crankshaft **(see illustration)**.

15 Apply thread locking agent (Suzuki Thread Lock - Super 1303 for US models, Super 1305 for UK models or equivalent) to the starter clutch bolt **(see illustration)**.

16 Install the bolt, hold it with the holding tool and tighten to the torque listed in this Chapter's Specifications **(see illustration)**.

17 Install the starter idle gear and shaft. Make sure the starter clutch cover dowel is in place. Apply a thin coat of gasket sealer (Suzuki Bond 1207B or equivalent) along the seams of the crankcase halves, then position

25.17 Install the starter idle gear and shaft, make sure the dowel is in place and apply gasket sealant across the seams of the crankcase

*A Idle gear and shaft C Apply sealant here
B Dowel*

25.15 Apply thread locking agent to the threads of the starter clutch bolt . . .

a new gasket on the engine **(see illustration)**.

18 Install the cover and bolts. One upper bolt has a washer **(see illustration)**. Tighten the bolts securely in a criss-cross pattern.

26 Crankcase - disassembly and reassembly

1 To examine and repair or replace the crankshaft, connecting rods, bearings, oil pump and transmission components, the crankcase must be split into two parts.

2 Remove the alternator and starter (see Chapter 8).

3 Remove the signal generator (see Chapter 4).

25.18 Install the cover - one upper bolt uses a washer (arrow)

25.16 . . . then hold the starter clutch from turning and tighten the bolt

4 Remove the clutch (see Section 19) and the external shift mechanism (see Section 24).

5 Remove the oil pan (see Section 17).

6 Remove the neutral position indicator switch (see Chapter 8).

Disassembly

7 Remove the oil pump drive gear and pin **(see illustrations)**.

8 Remove the countershaft bearing retainer screws with an impact driver, then remove the bearing retainer **(see illustrations)**.

9 Bend back the lock tabs on the oil seal retainer bolts and remove the retainer **(see illustrations)**.

10 Remove the main oil gallery plug and O-ring **(see illustration)**.

11 Remove the threaded plug from the upper

26.7a Remove the oil pump drive gear snap ring . . .

2

26.7b . . . pull off the gear . . .

26.7c . . . and remove the drive pin from the shaft

26.8a Remove the countershaft bearing retainer screws with an impact driver . . .

26.8b . . . and lift the bearing retainer off the crankcase

26.9a Bend back the lock tabs on the oil seal retainer . . .

side of the crankcase above the starter mounting flange.

12 Remove the upper crankcase bolts and nut **(see illustrations)**. The bolt beneath the starter flange is accessible through the plug hole (the plug was removed in Step 10).

13 Remove the lower crankcase bolts and nut **(see illustrations)**.

14 Remove the crankshaft retaining bolts **(see illustration)**. Loosen the bolts in several stages, starting with no. 12 and working down to no. 1 (the bolt numbers are cast in the crankcase next to the bolt heads). Bolts 2 and 4 are Allen bolts. Note that bolt no. 1 secures an oil drain tube **(see illustrations)**.

26.9b . . . then remove the bolts and take the retainer off

26.10 Remove the main oil gallery plug and O-ring (use a new O-ring during installation)

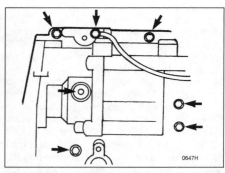

26.12a Remove the upper crankcase bolts and nut . . .

26.12b . . . one bolt secures a ground wire . . .

26.12c . . . one bolt and the nut (arrows) are located next to the starter motor flange - the bolt is accessible through the threaded plug hole

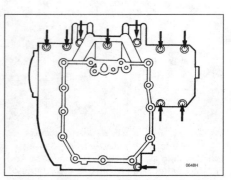

26.13a Remove the crankcase lower bolts . . .

26.13b . . . and the nut

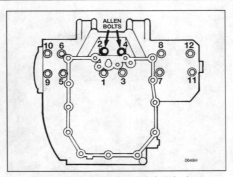

26.14a Crankshaft retaining bolts - TIGHTENING sequence

26.14b The bolt numbers are cast on the crankcase next to the heads . . .

15 Gently tap the crankcase with a rubber mallet to break the seal between the halves. Don't pry the halves apart. Once the halves separate, lift the bottom half off **(see illustration)**.

HAYNES HiNT *If the crankcases won't separate easily, recheck to make sure you've removed all of the nuts and bolts*

16 Remove the oil pump (see Section 18).

17 Refer to Sections 27 through 34 for information on the internal components of the crankcase.

Reassembly

18 Remove all traces of sealant from the crankcase mating surfaces. Be careful not to let any fall into the case as this is done.
19 Check to make sure the dowel pins are in place in their holes in the mating surface and the O-rings are in their recesses **(see illustrations)**. Pour some engine oil over the transmission gears, the crankshaft main bearings and the shift drum. Don't get any oil on the crankcase mating surface.
20 Apply a thin, even bead of Suzuki Bond 1207B to the gasket surface of the upper crankcase half.
Caution: Don't apply an excessive amount of sealant, and don't apply it next to the

bearing inserts, as it will ooze out when the case halves are assembled and may obstruct oil passages and prevent the bearings from seating.
21 Check the position of the shift drum, shift forks and transmission shafts - make sure they're in the neutral position.
22 Carefully assemble the crankcase halves. While doing this, make sure the shift forks fit into their gear grooves.
23 Install the lower crankcase half bolts and tighten them so they are just snug. Crankshaft bolts 9 and 11 have copper washers **(see illustration)**. Bolt no. 1 secure the right oil drain tube **(see illustration)**. If removed, install the left oil drain tube and secure with its bolt.

26.14c . . . bolt no. 1 secures the right oil drain tube (arrow)

26.15 With all bolts and nuts removed, lift the lower crankcase half off the upper one

26.19a Make sure the case dowels are in position (arrows) . . .

26.19b . . . as well as the O-rings (arrows)

26.23a Install copper washers on bolts 9 and 11 . . .

26.23b . . . and secure the right oil drain tube with case bolt no. 1

2

24 In two steps, tighten the crankshaft bolts in the indicated sequence, to the torque listed in this Chapter's Specifications **(see illustration)**.
25 Tighten the remaining bolts and nuts evenly to the torque listed in this Chapter's Specifications.
26 Install the oil pan (see Section 17).
27 Turn the case over and install the upper crankcase half bolts and nut. Tighten them evenly to the torque listed in this Chapter's Specifications.
28 Slip the clutch housing over the crankshaft and turn it by hand to make sure the crankshaft turns freely, then remove the clutch housing.
29 The remainder of installation is the reverse of removal, with the following additions:
a) *Use thread locking agent (Suzuki Thread Lock 1342 or equivalent) on the countershaft bearing*
b) *Once the external shift linkage is installed, shift the transmission through all the gear positions and back to Neutral.*
c) *Be sure to refill the engine oil.*

27 Crankcase components - inspection and servicing

1 After the crankcases have been separated and the crankshaft, shift drum and forks and transmission components removed, the crankcases should be cleaned thoroughly with new solvent and dried with compressed air.
2 All oil passages and pipes should be blown out with compressed air.
3 All traces of old gasket sealant should be removed from the mating surfaces. Minor damage to the surfaces can be cleaned up with a fine sharpening stone.
Caution: Be very careful not to nick or gouge the crankcase mating surfaces or leaks will result. Check both crankcase sections very carefully for cracks and other damage.
4 If any damage is found that can't be repaired, replace the crankcase halves as a set.

28 Main and connecting rod bearings - general note

1 Even though main and connecting rod bearings are generally replaced with new ones during the engine overhaul, the old bearings should be retained for close examination as they may reveal valuable information about the condition of the engine.
2 Bearing failure occurs mainly because of lack of lubrication, the presence of dirt or other foreign particles, overloading the engine and/or corrosion. Regardless of the cause of bearing failure, it must be corrected before the engine is reassembled to prevent it from happening again.

26.24 Tighten the crankshaft retaining bolts in their numbered sequence

3 When examining the bearings, remove the main bearings from the case halves and the rod bearings from the connecting rods and caps and lay them out on a clean surface in the same general position as their location on the crankshaft journals. This will enable you to match any noted bearing problems with the corresponding side of the crankshaft journal.
4 Dirt and other foreign particles get into the engine in a variety of ways. It may be left in the engine during assembly or it may pass through filters or breathers. It may get into the oil and from there into the bearings. Metal chips from machining operations and normal engine wear are often present. Abrasives are sometimes left in engine components after reconditioning operations such as cylinder honing, especially when parts are not thoroughly cleaned using the proper cleaning methods. Whatever the source, these foreign objects often end up imbedded in the soft bearing material and are easily recognized. Large particles will not imbed in the bearing and will score or gouge the bearing and journal. The best prevention for this cause of bearing failure is to clean all parts thoroughly and keep everything spotlessly clean during engine reassembly. Frequent and regular oil and filter changes are also recommended.
5 Lack of lubrication or lubrication breakdown has a number of interrelated causes. Excessive heat (which thins the oil), overloading (which squeezes the oil from the bearing face) and oil leakage or throw off (from excessive bearing clearances, worn oil pump or high engine speeds) all contribute to lubrication breakdown. Blocked oil passages will also starve a bearing and destroy it. When lack of lubrication is the cause of bearing failure, the bearing material is wiped or extruded from the steel backing of the bearing. Temperatures may increase to the point where the steel backing and the journal turn blue from overheating.
6 Riding habits can have a definite effect on bearing life. Full throttle low speed operation, or lugging the engine, puts very high loads on bearings, which tend to squeeze out the oil film. These loads cause the bearings to flex, which produces fine cracks in the bearing face (fatigue failure). Eventually the bearing material will loosen in pieces and tear away

from the steel backing. Short trip driving leads to corrosion of bearings, as insufficient engine heat is produced to drive off the condensed water and corrosive gases produced. These products collect in the engine oil, forming acid and sludge. As the oil is carried to the engine bearings, the acid attacks and corrodes the bearing material.
7 Incorrect bearing installation during engine assembly will lead to bearing failure as well. Tight fitting bearings which leave insufficient bearing oil clearances result in oil starvation. Dirt or foreign particles trapped behind a bearing insert result in high spots on the bearing which lead to failure.
8 To avoid bearing problems, clean all parts thoroughly before reassembly, double check all bearing clearance measurements and lubricate the new bearings with engine assembly lube or moly-based grease during installation.

29 Crankshaft and bearings - removal, inspection, main bearing selection and installation

Crankshaft removal

1 If you haven't already done so, remove the cylinder block and pistons (see Sections 14 and 15).
2 Before removing the crankshaft check the thrust clearance. Push the crankshaft as far as it will go toward the starter clutch end (this eliminates play). Insert a feeler gauge between the crankshaft and the left-hand thrust bearing (if equipped) or between the crankshaft and crankcase (models not equipped with thrust bearings) **(see illustration)**. Compare your findings with this Chapter's Specifications.
a) *On 1985 and some early 1986 GSX-R750 models (not equipped with thrust bearings), the crankshaft or crankcase must be replaced if the thrust clearance is excessive. Replacement crankcases are equipped with thrust bearings.*
b) *If the endplay is excessive on models equipped with thrust bearings, the thrust bearings must be replaced (see below).*
3 Lift the crankshaft out, together with the

29.2 Measure the clearance between the left-hand thrust bearing and the crankshaft

29.3 Lift the crankshaft out of the case, together with the connecting rods and cam chain

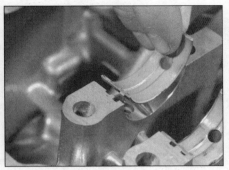

29.4a Remove the bearings from the lower case half (they can be identified by their oil holes) . . .

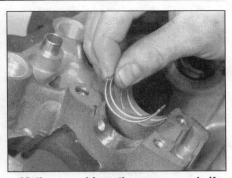

29.4b . . . and from the upper case half

connecting rods and cam chain and set them on a clean surface **(see illustration)**.

4 Lift out the thrust bearings (be sure to label them for right and left; they aren't interchangeable). The main bearing inserts can be removed from their saddles by pushing their centers to the side, then lifting them out **(see illustrations)**. Keep the bearing inserts in order. The main bearing oil clearance should be checked, however, before removing the inserts (see Step 9).

Inspection

5 Mark and remove the connecting rods from the crankshaft (see Section 30).
6 Clean the crankshaft with solvent, using a rifle-cleaning brush to scrub out the oil passages. If available, blow the crank dry with compressed air. Check the main and connecting rod journals for uneven wear, scoring and pits. Rub a copper coin across the journal several times - if a journal picks up copper from the coin, it's too rough. Replace the crankshaft.
7 Check the camshaft chain sprocket on the crankshaft for chipped teeth and other wear. If any undesirable conditions are found, replace the crankshaft. Check the chain as described in Section 31. Check the rest of the crankshaft for cracks and other damage. It should be magnafluxed to reveal hidden cracks - a dealer service department or motorcycle machine shop will handle the procedure.
8 Set the crankshaft on V-blocks and check

29.9 Lay the Plastigage strips (arrow) on the journals, parallel to the crankshaft centerline

the runout with a dial indicator touching one of the center main journals, comparing your findings with this Chapter's Specifications. If the runout exceeds the limit, replace the crank.

Main bearing selection

9 To check the main bearing oil clearance, clean off the bearing inserts (and reinstall them, if they've been removed from the case) and lower the crankshaft into the upper half of the case. Cut four pieces of Plastigage (type HPG-1) and lay them on the crankshaft main journals, parallel with the journal axis **(see illustration)**.
10 Very carefully, guide the lower case half down onto the upper case half. Install the crankshaft retaining bolts and tighten them,

29.11 Measuring the width of the crushed Plastigage (be sure to use the correct scale - standard and metric are included)

using the recommended sequence, to the torque listed in this Chapter's Specifications (see Section 26). Don't rotate the crankshaft!
11 Now, remove the bolts and carefully lift the lower case half off. Compare the width of the crushed Plastigage on each journal to the scale printed on the Plastigage envelope to obtain the main bearing oil clearance **(see illustration)**. Write down your findings, then remove all traces of Plastigage from the journals, using your fingernail or the edge of a credit card.
12 If the oil clearance falls into the specified range, no bearing replacement is required (provided they are in good shape). If the clearance is more than the standard range, but within the service limit, refer to the marks on the case and the marks on the crankshaft and select new bearing inserts **(see illustrations)**. Install the new inserts and check the oil clearance once again (the new inserts may bring bearing clearance within the specified range). Always replace all of the inserts at the same time.

2

29.12a These marks on the case are bearing size codes . . .

29.12b . . . these marks on the crankshaft are journal size codes . . .

		Crankshaft journal O.D. ②		
	Code	A	B	C
Crankcase I.D. ①	A	Green	Black	Brown
	B	Black	Brown	Yellow

0744H

29.12c . . . use them together with this chart to select the correct bearing sizes

29.13 Measure the diameter of each crankshaft journal at several points to detect taper and out-of-round conditions

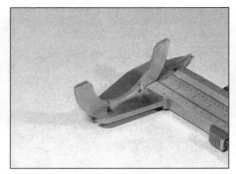

29.15 Measure the thickness of the right-hand thrust bearing

29.18 Make sure the oil jet (if equipped) is in place and not clogged

13 If the clearance is greater than the service limit listed in this Chapter's Specifications, measure the diameter of the crankshaft journals with a micrometer **(see illustration)** and compare your findings with this Chapter's Specifications. Also, by measuring the diameter at a number of points around each journal's circumference, you'll be able to determine whether or not the journal is out-of-round. Take the measurement at each end of the journal, near the crank throws, to determine if the journal is tapered.

14 If any crank journal has worn down past the service limit, replace the crankshaft.

Thrust bearing selection

15 If the thrust bearing clearance was excessive, measure the thickness of the right-hand thrust bearing and compare to the value listed in this Chapter's Specifications **(see illustration)**.

a) *If it's within the Specifications, install it in the crankcase.*

b) *If it's worn to less than the Specifications, replace it with a new one.*

16 With only the right-hand thrust bearing in place, measure the thrust clearance where the left-hand thrust bearing would go. Write down the measurement and use it to select a left-hand thrust bearing.

17 Install the new left-hand thrust bearing and recheck the left-hand thrust clearance. It should be within the range listed in this Chapter's Specifications.

Crankshaft installation

18 Clean the bearing saddles in the case halves and make sure the oil jet is in place and unobstructed (if equipped), then install the bearing inserts in their webs in the case **(see illustration)**. All of the bearing inserts have oil grooves. Those that go in the lower case half have oil holes as well **(see illustrations 29.4a and 29.4b)**. When installing the bearings, use your hands only - don't tap them into place with a hammer.

19 Lubricate the bearing inserts with engine assembly lube or moly-based grease.

20 You can install the connecting rods on the crankshaft at this point if the top end was removed from the engine (see Section 30).

21 Loop the camshaft chain over the crankshaft and lay it onto its sprocket.

22 Check to make sure the cam chain guide and its dampers are in position (see Section 31). If the connecting rods are in the engine, place pieces of hose over the studs to protect the crankshaft.

23 Carefully lower the crankshaft into place. If the connecting rods are in the engine, guide them onto the crankshaft journals.

24 Install the thrust bearings with their oil grooves toward the crankshaft **(see illustration)**.

25 Assemble the case halves (see Section 26) and check to make sure the crankshaft and the transmission shafts turn freely.

---

30 Connecting rods and bearings - removal, inspection, bearing selection and installation

Removal

1 Before removing the connecting rods from the crankshaft, measure the side clearance of each rod with a feeler gauge **(see illustration)**. If the clearance on any rod is greater than that listed in this Chapter's Specifications, that rod will have to be replaced with a new one.

2 Using a center punch, mark the position of each rod and cap, relative to its position on the crankshaft. The numbers on the rod and cap indicate bearing size grade, not cylinder number **(see illustration)**.

3 Unscrew the bearing cap nuts, separate the cap from the rod, then detach the rod from the crankshaft **(see illustration)**. If the cap is stuck, tap on the ends of the rod bolts with a soft face hammer to free them.

Caution: Don't try to remove the rod bolt from the rod. If the bolt becomes loose in the rod, the rod will have to be replaced.

29.24 Install the thrust bearings with their grooves toward the crankshaft

30.1 Slip a feeler gauge blade between the connecting rod and crankshaft throw to check connecting rod endplay

30.2 This number mark indicates the connecting rod bearing size - you'll need to make your own marks indicating cylinder number

30.3 Remove the connecting rod nuts

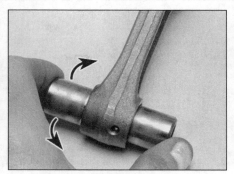

30.5 Checking the piston pin and connecting rod bore for wear

30.14a These marks indicate connecting rod journal size - use them in conjunction with the connecting rod bearing size number marks . . .

4 Separate the bearing inserts from the rods and caps, keeping them in order so they can be reinstalled in their original locations. Wash the parts in solvent and dry them with compressed air, if available.

Inspection

5 Check the connecting rods for cracks and other obvious damage. Lubricate the piston pin for each rod, install it in the proper rod and check for play **(see illustration)**. If it is loose, replace the connecting rod and/or the pin.
6 Examine the connecting rod bearing inserts. If they are scored, badly scuffed or appear to have been seized, new bearings must be installed. Always replace the bearings in the connecting rods as a set. If they are badly damaged, check the corresponding crankshaft journal. Evidence of extreme heat, such as discoloration, indicates that lubrication failure has occurred. Be sure to thoroughly check the oil pump, pressure regulator and pressure relief valve as well as all oil holes and passages before reassembling the engine.
7 Have the rods checked for twist and bending at a dealer service department or other motorcycle repair shop.

Bearing selection

8 If the bearings and journals appear to be in good condition, check the oil clearances as follows:
9 Start with the rod for the number one cylinder. Wipe the bearing inserts and the connecting rod and cap clean, using a lint-free cloth.
10 Install the bearing inserts in the connecting rod and cap. Make sure the tab on the bearing engages with the notch in the rod or cap.
11 Wipe off the connecting rod journal with a lint-free cloth. Lay a strip of Plastigage (type HPG-1) across the top of the journal, parallel with the journal axis **(see illustration 29.9)**.
12 Position the connecting rod on the bottom of the journal, then install the rod cap and nuts. Tighten the nuts to the torque listed in this Chapter's Specifications, but don't allow the connecting rod to rotate at all.
13 Unscrew the nuts and remove the connecting rod and cap from the journal, being very careful not to disturb the

Plastigage. Compare the width of the crushed Plastigage to the scale printed in the Plastigage envelope **(see illustration 29.11)** to determine the bearing oil clearance.
14 If the clearance is within the range listed in this Chapter's Specifications and the bearings are in perfect condition, they can be reused. If the clearance is beyond the service limit, replace the bearing inserts with new inserts **(see illustration 30.2 and the accompanying illustrations)**. Check the oil clearance once again (the new inserts may be thick enough to bring bearing clearance within the specified range). Always replace all of the inserts at the same time.
15 If the clearance is still greater than the service limit listed in this Chapter's Specifications, measure the diameter of the connecting rod journal with a micrometer and compare your findings with this Chapter's Specifications. Also, by measuring the diameter at a number of points around the journal's circumference, you'll be able to determine whether or not the journal is out-of-round. Take the measurement at each end of the journal to determine if the journal is tapered.
16 If any journal has worn down past the service limit, replace the crankshaft.
17 Repeat the bearing selection procedure for the remaining connecting rods.

Installation

18 Wipe off the bearing inserts, connecting rods and caps. Install the inserts into the rods and caps, using your hands only, making sure the tabs on the inserts engage with the notches in the rods and caps. When all the inserts are installed, lubricate them with engine assembly lube or moly-based grease. Don't get any lubricant on the mating surfaces of the rod or cap.
19 Assemble each connecting rod to its proper journal, making sure the previously applied matchmarks correspond to each other and the bearing grade number is toward the rear of the engine **(see illustration 30.2)**.
20 When you're sure the rods are positioned correctly, tighten the nuts to the torque listed in this Chapter's Specifications **(see illustration 30.3)**.
21 Turn the rods on the crankshaft. If any of them feel tight, tap on the bottom of the

		Journal diameter		
	Code	1	2	3
Rod code	1	Green	Black	Brown
	2	Black	Brown	Yellow

0747H

30.14b . . . and this chart to select the correct bearing size

connecting rod caps with a hammer - this should relieve stress and free them up. If it doesn't, recheck the bearing clearance.
22 As a final step, recheck the connecting rod side clearances (see Step 1). If the clearances aren't correct, find out why before proceeding with engine assembly.

31 Camshaft chain and guide - removal, inspection and installation

Removal

Cam chain

1 Remove the engine (see Section 5).
2 Separate the crankcase halves (see Section 26).
3 Remove the crankshaft (see Section 29).
4 Remove the cam chain from the crankshaft.

Chain guide

5 Remove the chain guide dampers and lift out the guide **(see illustrations)**.

31.5a The cam chain guide is held in place by two dampers . . .

31.5b . . . to remove the guide, lift out the dampers . . .

31.5c . . . then lift out the guide

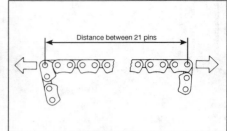

31.6 When checking the cam chain, measure the distance between 21 pins and compare to the length listed in this Chapter's Specifications

Inspection

6 Pull the chain tight to eliminate all slack and measure the length of 21 pins, pin-to-pin **(see illustration)**. Compare your findings to this Chapter's Specifications. **Note:** *1996 600 models are fitted with a different type of chain; no wear limits are specified.*

7 Also check the chains for binding and obvious damage.

8 If the 21-pin length is not as specified, or there is visible damage, replace the chain.

9 Check the guide for deep grooves, cracking and other obvious damage, replacing it if necessary.

Installation

10 Installation of these components is the

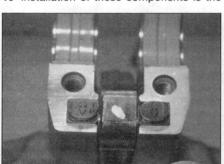

31.10 Be sure the arrow marks on the dampers point to the front and rear of the engine

reverse of the removal procedure. Be sure the arrow marks on the chain guide dampers face to front and rear of the engine, not side to side **(see illustration)**. Apply engine oil to the face of the guide and to the chain.

32 Transmission shafts - removal and installation

Removal

1 Remove the engine and clutch, then separate the case halves (see Sections 5, 19 and 26).

2 Before removing either shaft, check the

32.3a Lift out the countershaft . . .

backlash of each set of gears. To do this, mount a dial indicator with the plunger of the indicator touching a tooth on one of the gears, then move the gear back and forth within its freeplay, holding its companion gear stationary. Check each set of gears. Backlash isn't specified by Suzuki, but if it's more than about 0.25 mm (0.010 inch), check the gears closely for wear.

3 The shafts can simply be lifted out of the upper half of the case **(see illustrations)**. If they are stuck, use a soft-face hammer and gently tap on the bearings on the ends of the shafts to free them.

4 Refer to Section 33 for information pertaining to transmission shaft service and Section 34 for information pertaining to the shift cam and forks.

Installation

5 Check to make sure the dowels and C-rings are present in the upper case half, where the shaft bearings seat **(see illustrations)**.

6 Carefully lower each shaft into place. At one end of each shaft, the bearing dowel in the case must engage the hole in the bearing outer race **(see illustration)**. At the other end of each shaft, the dowel in the bearing outer race must be positioned in the case recess and the C-ring must engage the grooves in the case and bearing outer race **(see illustration)**.

7 The remainder of installation is the reverse of removal.

32.3b . . . and the driveshaft

32.5a There's a dowel at one end of each shaft - be sure it's installed in the case . . .

32.5b . . . and be sure the C-ring is installed at the other end of each shaft

32.6a Align the bearing dowel at one end of each shaft with the hole in the outer race . . .

32.6b . . . and at the other end of each shaft, position the bearing dowel in the case recess and install the C-ring in the case and bearing grooves (arrows)

33.4a Slide the spacer off the left end of the driveshaft, then remove the oil seal

33 Transmission shafts -
disassembly, inspection and reassembly

HAYNES HiNT *When disassembling the transmission shafts, place the parts on a long rod or thread a wire through them to keep them in order and facing the proper direction.*

1 Remove the shafts from the case (see Section 32).

Driveshaft - five speed transmission
Disassembly
2 All of the driveshaft parts slide off the shaft except the ball bearing, which is a press fit.
3 Use snap-ring pliers to remove the snap-rings. Be sure to keep the snap-rings in their original locations and to replace them with ones of the same size.
4 To disassemble the driveshaft, refer to the accompanying photographs (see illustrations).
Inspection
5 Wash all of the components in clean solvent and dry them off. Rotate the ball bearing on the shaft, feeling for tightness, rough spots and excessive looseness and listening for noises. If

33.4b From the right end of the driveshaft, remove the needle roller bearing . . .

33.4c . . . thrust washer . . .

33.4d . . . first driven gear . . .

33.4e . . . its bushing . . .

2

33.4f . . . and thrust washer

33.4g Slide off fourth driven gear

33.4h Remove the snap ring (look at it carefully and note which side faces the thrust washer)

33.4i Slide off the thrust washer . . .

33.4j . . . then remove third driven gear and its bushing (arrow)

33.4k Slide off the thrust washer . . .

33.4l . . . and fifth driven gear

33.4m Remove the snap ring (note which side faces the thrust washer) . . .

any of these conditions are found, replace the bearing. This will require the use of a hydraulic press or a bearing puller setup. If you don't have access to these tools, take the shaft and bearing to a Suzuki dealer or other motorcycle repair shop and have them press the old bearing off the shaft and install the new one.

6 Measure the shift fork groove in fifth driven gear. If the groove width exceeds the figure listed in this Chapter's Specifications, replace the gear, and also check the fifth gear shift fork (see Section 34).

7 Check the gear teeth for cracking and other obvious damage. Check the bushings and their surfaces in the inner diameter of the gears for scoring or heat discoloration. If the gear or bushing is damaged, replace it.

8 Inspect the dogs and the dog holes in the gears for excessive wear. Replace the paired gears as a set if necessary.

9 Check the needle bearing and outer race for wear or heat discoloration and replace them if necessary.

Reassembly

10 Reassembly is the reverse of the disassembly procedure, with the following additions:

a) Lubricate the components with engine oil before assembling them.

b) Always use new snap-rings. Install them with their sharp edge away from the thrust washer (see illustration).

33.4n . . . slide off the thrust washer . . .

33.4o . . . then slide off second driven gear and its bushing (arrow)

33.4p If the ball bearing is worn or damaged, have it replaced by a dealer service department or machine shop

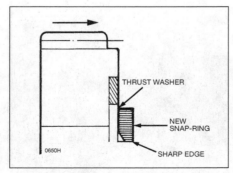

THRUST WASHER

NEW SNAP-RING

SHARP EDGE

0650H

33.10a Install the snap-rings with their sharp side facing away from the thrust washer

33.10b Align the oil hole of the second driven gear bushing with the oil hole in the shaft

33.10c Align the oil hole of the third driven gear bushing with the oil hole in the shaft . . .

33.10d . . . and fit the bushing tabs (arrow) into the thrust washer slots

c) *Align the bushing oil holes with the shaft oil holes (see illustrations). Fit the tabs of the third driven gear bushing into the slots of the thrust washer (see illustration).*

d) *Install a new O-ring under the spacer on the end of the shaft.*

e) *Check the assembled driveshaft to make sure all parts are installed correctly (see illustration 32.3b and the accompanying illustration).*

Countershaft - five speed transmission

Disassembly

11 All of the countershaft parts slide off the shaft except first gear, which is integral with the shaft, and the ball bearing, which is a

33.11b . . . and oil seal from the left end of the countershaft

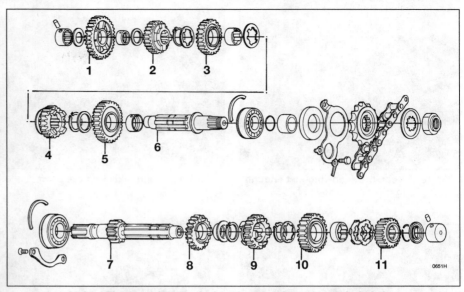

33.10e Five speed transmission shafts and gears - exploded view

1 First driven gear	5 Second driven gear	8 Fourth drive gear
2 Fourth driven gear	6 Driveshaft	9 Third drive gear
3 Third driven gear	7 Countershaft and integral	10 Fifth drive gear
4 Fifth driven gear	first drive gear	11 Second drive gear

press fit. To disassemble the countershaft, refer to the accompanying photographs **(see illustrations)**.

12 Use snap-ring pliers to remove the snap-rings. Be sure to keep the snap-rings in their original locations and to replace them with ones of the same size.

Inspection

13 Refer to Steps 5 through 9 for the inspection procedures. They are the same, except that when checking the shift fork groove width you'll be checking it on third gear and fifth gear.

Reassembly

14 Reassembly is the basically the reverse of the disassembly procedure, but take note of the following points:

a) *Always use new snap-rings. Install them with their sharp edge away from the thrust washer (see illustration 33.10a).*

33.11a Remove the needle roller bearing . . .

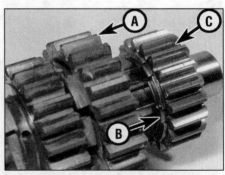

33.11d Slide fifth drive gear toward third drive gear (to the left) to expose the two thrust washers - slide them out of their groove, then slide the thrust washers and the second drive gear away from the end of the shaft (to the left) to expose its snap-ring

A *Fifth drive gear*　　C *Second drive gear*
B *Thrust washers*

33.11c Reach behind the fifth drive gear with snap-ring pliers, spread the snap-ring and slide it to the left (toward third drive gear)

2

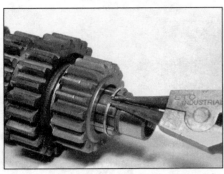

33.11e Spread the snap-ring just enough to clear the groove . . .

33.11f . . . and take it off the shaft . . .

33.11g . . . then remove second drive gear . . .

33.11h . . . the first thrust washer . . .

33.11i . . . the second thrust washer . . .

33.11j . . . fifth drive gear . . .

33.11k . . . its bushing . . .

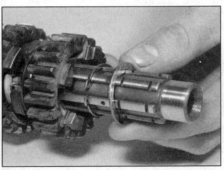

33.11l . . . and thrust washer

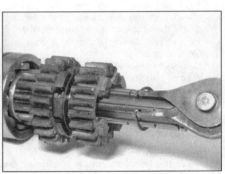

33.11m Remove the snap ring . . .

33.11n . . . and third drive gear

33.11o Remove the snap ring . . .

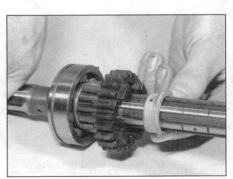

33.11p . . . the fourth drive gear bushing . . .

b) *Lubricate the components with engine oil before assembling them.*

c) *One of the second drive gear thrust washers has tabs and the other has slots. Be sure the tabs engage the slots (see illustration 33.11d).*

Driveshaft - six speed transmission

Disassembly

15 Remove the needle roller bearing and thrust washer from the right end of the shaft **(see illustration).**

16 Remove the first driven gear, its bushing, thrust washer and fifth driven gear.

33.11q . . . and fourth drive gear

33.11r If the ball bearing is worn or damaged, have it replaced by a dealer service department or machine shop

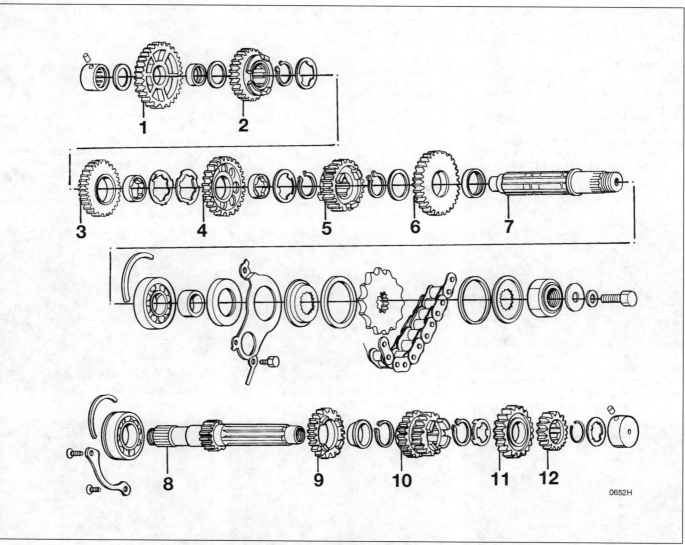

33.15 Six speed transmission shafts and gears - exploded view

1 First driven gear	5 Sixth driven gear	9 Fifth drive gear
2 Fifth driven gear	6 Second driven gear	10 Third/fourth drive gear
3 Fourth driven gear	7 Driveshaft	11 Sixth drive gear
4 Third driven gear	8 Countershaft and integral first drive gear	12 Second drive gear

2

17 Remove the snap ring.

18 Remove the thrust washer, fourth driven gear and bushing.

19 Remove the pair of interlocked thrust washers.

20 Remove third driven gear, its bushing and a thrust washer.

21 Remove the snap ring that secures sixth driven gear, then remove the gear.

22 Remove the snap ring, thrust washer, second driven gear and bushing.

23 From the other end of the shaft, remove the oil seal and spacer.

24 If the ball bearing is worn or damaged, have it replaced by a dealer service department or machine shop.

Inspection

25 Refer to Steps 5 through 9 for the inspection procedures. They are the same, except that when checking the shift fork groove width you'll be checking it on fifth gear and sixth gear.

Reassembly

26 Reassembly is the reverse of the disassembly procedure, with the following additions:

a) *Lubricate the components with engine oil before assembling them.*

b) *Always use new snap-rings. Install them with their sharp edge away from the thrust washer (see illustration 33.10a).*

34.3a It's a good idea to number the forks with a felt pen so they can be reinstalled in the correct position - note carefully which way the fork is offset, then pull the shaft out of the no. 1 fork . . .

34.4 Unhook the shift cam stopper spring from the case

c) *Align the bushing oil holes with the shaft oil holes.*

d) *One thrust washer of the interlocked pair has tabs and the other thrust washer has slots. Make sure the tabs engage the slots when the washers are in position.*

e) *Install a new O-ring under the spacer at the end of the shaft.*

f) *Check the assembled driveshaft to make sure all parts are installed correctly (see illustration 33.15).*

Countershaft - six speed transmission

Disassembly

27 Remove the needle roller bearing and oil seal from the end of the shaft (see illustration 33.15).

28 Reach behind the sixth drive gear with snap-ring pliers, spread the snap-ring and slide it toward the third-fourth drive gear.

29 Slide the sixth and second drive gears back to expose the second drive gear snap ring, then remove the snap ring. Slide the second and sixth drive gears off the shaft.

30 Remove the thrust washer and snap-ring, then slide third-fourth drive gear off the shaft.

31 Remove the snap ring and bushing, then slide fifth drive gear off the shaft.

32 If the ball bearing is worn or damaged, have it replaced by a dealer service department or machine shop.

Inspection

33 Refer to Steps 5 through 9 for the inspection procedures. They are the same,

34.3b . . . the no. 2 fork . . .

34.5a Remove the snap-ring . . .

except that when checking the shift fork groove width you'll be checking it on the third-fourth gear.

34 Reassembly is the reverse of the disassembly procedure, with the following additions:

a) *Lubricate the components with engine oil before assembling them.*

b) *Always use new snap-rings. Install them with their sharp edge away from the thrust washer (see illustration 33.10a).*

c) *Align the bushing oil holes with the shaft oil holes.*

d) *Check the assembled driveshaft to make sure all parts are installed correctly (see illustration 33.15).*

34 Shift cam and forks - removal, inspection and installation

Removal

1 Remove the engine and separate the crankcase halves (see Sections 5 and 26).

2 Remove the neutral position indicator switch (see Chapter 8).

3 Pull the shift rod out slowly, removing each shift fork as the rod clears it (see illustrations).

4 Unhook the spring from the gearshift cam stopper bolt (see illustration).

5 Remove the snap ring from the end of the gearshift cam stopper bolt inside the case, then slide the gearshift cam stopper off the bolt (see illustrations).

34.3c . . . and the no. 3 fork

34.5b . . . and slide the shift cam stopper off the bolt

34.6 Remove the bolt and washer from the case

34.7 Remove the snap-ring from the shift cam

34.8 Slide the shift cam out of the case

34.9 Remove the bearing snap-ring from the case . . .

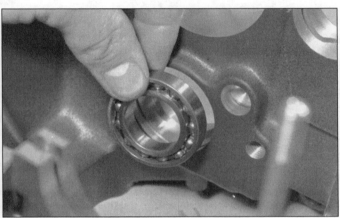

34.10 . . . and remove the bearing

6 Remove the gearshift cam stopper bolt and washer from the case (see illustration).

7 Remove the snap-ring from the gearshift cam (see illustration).

8 Slide the gearshift cam out of the case and remove it (see illustration).

9 Remove the snap-ring from the gearshift cam bearing (see illustration).

10 Slip the gearshift cam bearing out of the case (see illustration).

11 Slide the cam stopper plate off the end of the shift cam and pick out the pin (see illustrations).

Inspection

12 Check the edges of the gear grooves in the shift cam for signs of excessive wear.

Measure the widths of the gear grooves and compare your findings to this Chapter's Specifications. Check the stopper and bearing on the end of the shift drum for wear and damage. If undesirable conditions are found, replace the stopper and bearing.

13 Check the shift forks for distortion and wear, especially at the fork ears. Measure the

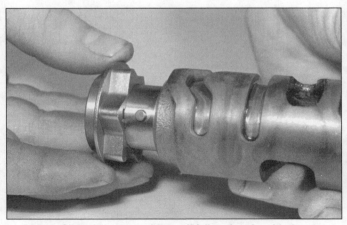

34.11a Slide the stopper plate off (align the pin with the slot during installation) . . .

34.11b . . . and remove the stopper plate pin from the shift cam

2

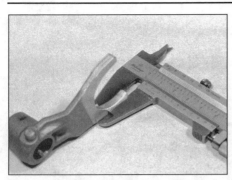

34.13 Measure the thickness of the fork ears; replace any forks that are worn excessively

thickness of the fork ears and compare your findings with this Chapter's Specifications **(see illustration)**. If they are discolored or severely worn they are probably bent. If damage or wear is evident, check the shift fork groove in the corresponding gear as well. Inspect the guide pins and the shaft bore for excessive wear and distortion and replace any defective parts with new ones.

14 Check the shift rod for evidence of wear, galling and other damage. Make sure the shift forks move smoothly on the rod. If the rod is worn or bent, replace it with a new one.

Installation

15 Installation is the reverse of removal, noting the following points:

a) *Align the slot in the cam stopper with the pin in the shaft cam* **(see illustration 34.11c)**.

b) *Be sure to use new snap-rings.*

c) *Lubricate all parts with engine oil before installing them.*

d) *Be sure the shift forks are installed in the correct positions and facing the right way* **(see illustrations 34.3a, 34.3b and 34.3c)**. *Be sure the pins on the forks engage the grooves in the shift cam.*

35 Initial start-up after overhaul

1 Make sure the engine oil level is correct, then remove the spark plugs from the engine. Place the engine STOP switch in the Off position and unplug the primary (low tension) wires from the coil.

2 Turn on the key switch and crank the engine over with the starter until the oil pressure indicator light goes off (which indicates that oil pressure exists). Reinstall the spark plugs, connect the wires and turn the switch to On.

3 Make sure there is fuel in the tank, then turn the fuel tap to the On position and operate the choke.

4 Start the engine and allow it to run at a moderately fast idle until it reaches operating temperature.

 Warning: If the oil pressure indicator light doesn't go off, or it comes on while the engine is running, stop the engine immediately.

5 Check carefully for oil leaks and make sure the transmission and controls, especially the brakes, function properly before road testing

the machine. Refer to Section 36 for the recommended break-in procedure.

6 Upon completion of the road test, and after the engine has cooled down completely, recheck the valve clearances (see Chapter 1).

36 Recommended break-in procedure

1 Any rebuilt engine needs time to break-in, even if parts have been installed in their original locations. For this reason, treat the machine gently for the first few miles to make sure oil has circulated throughout the engine and any new parts installed have started to seat.

2 Even greater care is necessary if the engine has been rebored or a new crankshaft has been installed. In the case of a rebore, the engine will have to be broken in as if the machine were new. This means greater use of the transmission and a restraining hand on the throttle until at least 500 miles (800 km) have been covered. There's no point in keeping to any set speed limit - the main idea is to keep from lugging (labouring) the engine and to gradually increase performance until the 500 mile (800 km) mark is reached. These recommendations can be lessened to an extent when only a new crankshaft is installed. Experience is the best guide, since it's easy to tell when an engine is running freely.

3 If a lubrication failure is suspected, stop the engine immediately and try to find the cause. If an engine is run without oil, even for a short period of time, severe damage will occur.

Chapter 3
Fuel and exhaust systems

Contents

Degrees of difficulty

Easy, suitable for novice with little experience	**Fairly easy,** suitable for beginner with some experience	**Fairly difficult,** suitable for competent DIY mechanic 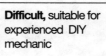	**Difficult,** suitable for experienced DIY mechanic	**Very difficult,** suitable for expert DIY or professional

Specifications

Carburetors

Synchronizing speed (all models) .... 1750 rpm

Katana 600 (GSX600F) model

1988 and 1989 US

Type	BST31SS
Main jets 1 and 4	137.5
Main jets 2 and 3	135
Main air jet	1.0 mm
Jet needle (-clip position)	
California	4CZ-5-1
Except California	4CZ-4-1
Needle jet	P-8
Pilot jet	
California	37.5
Except California	32.5
Pilot air jet	
1988	
California	155
Except California	150
1988	
California	150
Except California	155
Pilot screw setting	Preset
Starter jet	45
Float height	14.6 +/- 1 mm (0.57 +/- 0.04 inch)

1988 and 1989 UK

Type	BST31SS
Main jets 1 and 4	137.5
Main jets 2 and 3	135
Main air jet	1.0 mm
Jet needle	4CZ-3-3
Needle jet	P-9
Pilot jet	40
Pilot air jet	160
Pilot screw setting	
1988	1-7/8 turns back
1989	Preset
Starter jet	45
Float height	14.6 +/- 1 mm (0.57 +/- 0.04 inch)

3

Katana 600 (GSX600F) model (continued)

1990 on US
Type BST33SS
Main jets 112.5
Main air jet .... 0.5 mm
Jet needle
    California 5F105
    Except California 5F104
Needle jet P-2
Pilot jet 32.5
Pilot air jet
    California .... 1.45 mm
    Except California .... 1.55 mm
Pilot screw setting .... Preset
Starter jet 35
Float height .... 14.6 +/- 1 mm (0.57 +/- 0.04 inch)

1990 on UK
Type BST33SS
Main jets 110
Main air jet .... 0.5 mm
Jet needle 5FZ 102-3
Needle jet P-3
Pilot jet 32.5
Pilot air jet .... 1.3 mm
Pilot screw setting .... 1-1/2 turns back
Starter jet 35
Float height .... 14.6 +/- 1 mm (0.57 +/- 0.04 inch)

GSX-R750 model

1986 US
Type BST31SS
Main jets 117.5
Main air jet .... 1.7 mm
Jet needle 4C71
Needle jet P-8
Pilot jet 32.5
Pilot air jet 160
Pilot screw setting .... Preset
Starter jet 40
Float height .... 14.6 +/- 1 mm (0.57 +/- 0.04 inch)

1987 US
Type BST34SS
Main jets 112.5
Main air jet .... 1.8 mm
Jet needle 4C09-1
Needle jet O-6
Pilot jet 35
Pilot air jet 145
Pilot screw setting .... Preset
Starter jet 45
Float height .... 14.6 +/- 1 mm (0.57 +/- 0.04 inch)

1985 through 1987 UK
Type VM29SS
Main jets 97.5
Main air jet .... 0.5 mm
Jet needle 6DP-2-3
Needle jet P-5
Pilot jet 32.5
Pilot air jet .... 1.6 mm
Pilot screw setting .... Preset (1/2 turn back)
Starter jet 42.5
Float height .... 14.2 +/- 1 mm (0.56 +/- 0.04 inch)

1988 and 1989
Type BST36SS
Main jets 112.5
Main air jet .... 0.5 mm
Jet needle
    US 5FZ91
    UK 5FZ89-3
Needle jet Y-5
Pilot jet
    US 32.5
    UK 37.5

Pilot air jet
   California .... 1.45 mm
   US except California .... 1.55 mm
   UK .... 1.40 mm
Pilot screw setting
   US .... Preset
   UK .... Preset (1-1/2 turns back)
Starter jet 45
Float height .... 14.6 +/- 1 mm (0.57 +/- 0.04 inch)
1990 on
  Type
   California BST36SS
   Except California BST38SS
  Main jets
   California 112.5
   US except California 127.5
   UK 117.5
  Main air jet
   California .... 0.5 mm
   US except California
     Nos. 1 and 4 .... 0.9 mm
     Nos. 2 and 3 .... 1.2 mm
   UK .... 0 mm
  Jet needle
   California 5FZ91
   US except California 5ZDZ3
   UK 6ZD7-3
  Needle jet
   California Y-5
   Except California O-8
  Pilot jet
   US 37.5
   UK 32.5
  Pilot air jet
   1990 .... 1.2 mm
   1991 on .... Not specified
  Pilot screw setting
   US .... Preset
   UK .... Preset (1-1/8 turns back)
  Starter jet
   California 45
   Except California.. 40
  Float height
   California .... 14.6 +/- 1 mm (0.57 +/- 0.04 inch)
   Except California .... 14.7 +/- 1 mm (0.58 +/- 0.04 inch)

Katana 750 (GSX750F) model

Type BST36SS
Main jets
   US, cylinder no. 3 110
   All others 105
Main air jet .... 0.5 mm
Jet needle
   California 5EZ63
   US except California 5EZ62
   UK 5EZ61-3
Needle jet
   US Y-1
   UK Y-2
Pilot jet
   US 32.5
   UK 37.5
Pilot air jet
   1989 and 1990 California .... 1.25 mm
   1991 on California .... 1.2 mm
   US except California .... 1.35 mm
   UK .... 1.3 mm
Pilot screw setting
   US .... Preset
   UK .... Preset (1-5/8 turns back)
Starter jet 37.5
Float height .... 14.6 +/- 1 mm (0.57 +/- 0.04 inch)

3

GSX-R1100 model

1986 through 1988
  Type BST34SS
  Main jets 130
  Main air jet . . . . 0.6 mm
  Jet needle
    US 5D29
    UK 4D13-3
  Needle jet
    US P-2
    UK O-9
  Pilot jet
    US 32.5
    UK 42.5
  Pilot air jet
    US 135
    UK 150
  Pilot screw setting
    US . . . . Preset
    UK . . . . Preset (2 turns back)
  Starter jet 42.5
  Float height . . . . 14.6 +/- 1 mm (0.57 +/- 0.04 inch)

1989 on US
  Type BST36SS
  Main jets 122.5
  Main air jet . . . . 1.5 mm
  Jet needle
    California 5D43
    US except California 5D42
  Needle jet O-8
  Pilot jet 30
  Pilot air jet
    1989 and 1990
      California . . . . 1.35 mm
      US except California . . . . 1.2 mm
    1991 on . . . . Not specified
  Pilot screw setting . . . . Preset
  Starter jet
    1989 and 1990 45
    1991 on 42.5
  Float height . . . . 14.6 +/- 1 mm (0.57 +/- 0.04 inch)

1989 and 1990 UK
  Type BST36SS
  Main jets 122.5
  Main air jet . . . . 1.5 mm
  Jet needle 5E60-3
  Needle jet O-8
  Pilot jet 40
  Pilot air jet . . . . 1.4 mm
  Pilot screw setting . . . . Preset (2 turns back)
  Starter jet 45
  Float height . . . . 14.6 +/- 1 mm (0.57 +/- 0.04 inch)

1991 on UK
  Type BST40SS
  Main jets 125
  Main air jet . . . . 1.2 mm
  Jet needle 6ZD13-3
  Needle jet P-2
  Pilot jet 40
  Pilot air jet . . . . Not specified
  Pilot screw setting . . . . Preset (2 turns back)
  Starter jet 40
  Float height . . . . 14.7 +/- 1 mm (0.58 +/- 0.04 inch)

Katana 1100 (GSX1100F) model

Type BST34SS
Main jets
  Cylinder nos. 1 and 4 . . . . 112.5
  Cylinder nos. 2 and 3 110
Main air jet . . . . 0.6 mm

Jet needle

California	5DL16
US except California	5DL11
UK	5DL7-3

Needle jet

California and UK	P-0
All others	P-2

Pilot jet

California and UK	42.5
All others	32.5

Pilot air jet

California	155
US except California	135
UK	150

Pilot screw setting

US	Preset
1988 through 1990 UK	Preset (2-7/16 turns back)
1991 on UK	Preset (2-1/2 turns back)
Starter jet	42.5
Float height	14.6 +/- 1 mm (0.57 +/- 0.04 inch)

Fuel type

US and Canada

All except GSX-R1100

1986 through 1989	85 pump octane (89 Research octane), unleaded only
1990 on	87 pump octane (91 Research octane), unleaded only

GSX-R1100

1986 through 1988	85 pump octane (89 Research octane), unleaded only
1989 on	87 pump octane (91 Research octane), unleaded only

UK

1985 through 1988	85-95 octane or higher, unleaded or low lead recommended
1989 on	85-95 octane or higher, unleaded recommended

1 General information

The fuel system consists of the fuel tank, the fuel tap and filter, the carburetors and the connecting lines, hoses and control cables.

The carburetors used on these motorcycles are four variable venturi Mikunis with butterfly-type throttle valves. For cold starting, an enrichment circuit is actuated by a knob or a cable and the choke lever mounted on the left handlebar.

The exhaust system is a twin pipe design with a crossover pipe.

Many of the fuel system service procedures are considered routine maintenance items and for that reason are included in Chapter 1.

2 Fuel tank -
removal and installation

Warning: Gasoline (petrol) is extremely flammable, so take extra precautions when you work on any part of the fuel system. Don't smoke or allow open flames or bare light bulbs near the work area, and don't work in a garage where a natural

gas-type appliance (such as a water heater or clothes dryer) is present. If you spill any fuel on your skin, rinse it off immediately with soap and water. When you perform any kind of work on the fuel system, wear safety glasses and have a fire extinguisher suitable for a Class B type fire (flammable liquids) on hand.

1 The fuel tank is held in place at the forward end by mounts which slide over rubber dampers on the frame. The rear of the tank is fastened to a bracket by bolt and rubber insulators, which fit through a flange projecting from the tank.

2 Turn the fuel tap to the On position. On

2.2 On GSX-R1100 models, remove the fuel tap lever

GSX-R1100 models, remove the fuel tap lever **(see illustration)**.

3 Remove the following components to gain access to the tank mounting bolts:

a) *Katana 600 (GSX600F): Seat and frame covers (see Chapter 7) and fairing screws **(see illustration)**.*

b) *GSX-R750: Seat, lower and middle fairings and frame side covers (see Chapter 7).*

c) *Katana 750 (GSX750F): Remove the seat and three upper fairing screws on each side of the motorcycle (see Chapter 7).*

d) *GSX-R1100: Remove the seat and frame covers (1986 through 1988) or middle*

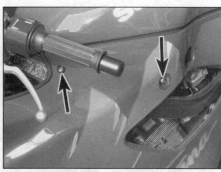

2.3a On Katana 600 (GSX600F) models, remove two fairing screws on each side of the bike (arrowed)

3

2.3b On Katana 1100 (GSX1100F) models, remove the bolts (arrowed) and lift off the fuel tank bracket

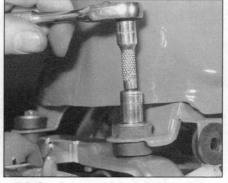

2.5 On all except Katana 1100 models, remove the mounting bolts at the rear of the tank (late GSX-R1100 shown)

2.6 Push the lines off the fuel tap fittings with a screwdriver; if you pull on them, they'll tighten on the fittings and be hard to remove

fairings (1989 and later) (see Chapter 7).
e) Katana 1100 (GSX1100F): Remove the seat (see Chapter 7) and the fuel tank bracket **(see illustration)**.

4 Disconnect the cable from the negative terminal of the battery.

5 On all except Katana 1100 (GSX1100F) models, remove the bolts securing the tank bracket **(see illustration)**.

6 Lift the rear of the tank up, slide back the hose clamps and push the fuel and vacuum lines off the fuel tap **(see illustration)**.

7 Disconnect the electrical connector for the fuel level sender.

8 Slide the tank to the rear to disengage the front of the tank from the rubber damper, then carefully lift the tank away from the machine **(see illustration)**.

9 Before installing the tank, check the condition of the rubber mounting damper and the hoses on the underside of the tank - if they're hardened, cracked, or show any other signs of deterioration, replace them.

10 When replacing the tank, reverse the above procedure. Make sure the tank seats properly and does not pinch any control cables or wires. If difficulty is encountered when trying to slide the tank onto the damper, a small amount of light oil should be used to lubricate it.

2.8 Lift the tank up and back, away from the bike

3 Fuel tank - cleaning and repair

1 All repairs to the fuel tank should be carried out by a professional who has experience in this critical and potentially dangerous work. Even after cleaning and flushing of the fuel system, explosive fumes can remain and ignite during repair of the tank.

2 If the fuel tank is removed from the vehicle, it should not be placed in an area where sparks or open flames could ignite the fumes coming out of the tank. Be especially careful inside garages where a natural gas-type appliance is located, because the pilot light could cause an explosion. It's also a good idea to place the tank where it won't be accidentally scratched or dented.

4 Idle fuel/air mixture adjustment - general information

1 Due to the increased emphasis on controlling motorcycle exhaust emissions, certain governmental regulations have been formulated which directly affect the carburetion of this machine. In order to comply with the regulations, the carburetors on some models have a metal sealing plug pressed into the hole over the pilot screw (which controls the idle fuel/air mixture) on each carburetor, so they can't be tampered with. These should not be removed. The pilot screws on other models are accessible, but the use of an exhaust gas analyzer is the only accurate way to adjust the idle fuel/air mixture and be sure the machine doesn't exceed the emissions regulations.

2 If the engine runs extremely rough at idle or continually stalls, and if a carburetor overhaul does not cure the problem, take the motorcycle to a Suzuki dealer service department or other repair shop equipped

with an exhaust gas analyzer. They will be able to properly adjust the idle fuel/air mixture to achieve a smooth idle and restore low speed performance.

5 Carburetor synchronization - check and adjustment

⚠️ **Warning: Gasoline (petrol) is extremely flammable, so take extra precautions when you work on any part of the fuel system. Don't smoke or allow open flames or bare light bulbs near the work area, and don't work in a garage where a natural gas-type appliance (such as a water heater or clothes dryer) is present. If you spill any fuel on your skin, rinse it off immediately with soap and water. When you perform any kind of work on the fuel system, wear safety glasses and have a fire extinguisher suitable for a Class B type fire (flammable liquids) on hand.**

1 Carburetor synchronization is simply the process of adjusting the carburetors so they pass the same amount of fuel/air mixture to each cylinder. This is done by measuring the vacuum produced in each cylinder. Carburetors that are out of synchronization will result in decreased fuel mileage, increased engine temperature, less than ideal throttle response and higher vibration levels.

2 To properly synchronize the carburetors, you will need some sort of vacuum gauge setup, preferably with a gauge for each cylinder, or a mercury manometer, which is a calibrated tube arrangement that utilizes columns of mercury to indicate engine vacuum.

3 A manometer can be purchased from a motorcycle dealer or accessory shop and should have the necessary rubber hoses supplied with it for hooking into the vacuum hose fittings on the carburetors.

4 A vacuum gauge setup can also be purchased

5.9a If the carburetors are equipped with vacuum inlet caps, remove the caps and connect the hoses of the test equipment to the fittings

5.9b If the carburetors are equipped with threaded vacuum fittings, remove the screw from the vacuum fitting hole on each carburetor, then thread a vacuum hose fitting into the screw hole

A Vacuum hose fitting   B Screw

5.13 Loosen the locknut on the center screw, then adjust the left screw, the right screw and the center screw to produce even vacuum readings

A Left screw - cyl 3 and 4 (adjust first)
B Right screw - cyl 1 and 2 (adjust second)
C Center screw (adjust third)

from a dealer or fabricated from commonly available hardware and automotive vacuum gauges.

5 The manometer is the more reliable and accurate instrument, and for that reason is preferred over the vacuum gauge setup; however, since the mercury used in the manometer is a liquid, and extremely toxic, extra precautions must be taken during use and storage of the instrument.

6 Because of the nature of the synchronization procedure and the need for special instruments, most owners leave the task to a dealer service department or a reputable motorcycle repair shop.

7 Start the engine and let it run until it reaches normal operating temperature, then shut it off.

8 Remove the fuel tank (see Section 2). On 1985 through 1987 GSX-R750 models (UK) only, remove the top caps from the carburetors (see Section 8).

9 If the carburetors are equipped with vacuum inlet caps **(see illustration)**, remove the caps. If not, remove the vacuum hose plugs from the carburetors and install vacuum hose fittings in place of them **(see illustration)**. Hook up the vacuum gauge set or the manometer according to the manufacturer's instructions. Make sure there are no leaks in the setup, as false readings will result. Calibrate the test setup if the manufacturer recommends it.

10 Reconnect the fuel line and vacuum line to the fuel tank (it's not necessary to hook-up the vacuum line to the fuel tap). Have an assistant hold the fuel tank out of the way, but in such a position that fuel can still be delivered and access to the carburetors is unobstructed. Place the fuel tap lever in the Prime position.

11 Start the engine and run it at the synchronizing speed listed in this Chapter's Specifications.

12 The vacuum readings for all of the cylinders should be the same. If the vacuum readings vary, adjust as necessary.

13 To perform the adjustment, loosen the locknut on the center synchronizing screw **(see illustration)**. Start by turning the screw for cylinder nos. 3 and 4 to synchronize those two carburetors, then turn the screw for cylinder nos. 1 and 2 to synchronize those two carburetors, then turn the center screw to balance the two pairs of carburetors **(see illustration)**.

14 When the adjustment is complete, recheck the vacuum readings and idle speed, then stop the engine. Tighten the locknut on the center synchronizing screw. Remove the vacuum gauge or manometer and attach the hoses to the fittings on the carburetors. Reinstall the fuel tank and seat.

6 Carburetor overhaul - general information

1 Poor engine performance, hesitation, hard starting, stalling, flooding and backfiring are all signs that major carburetor maintenance may be required.

2 Keep in mind that many so-called carburetor problems are really not carburetor problems at all, but mechanical problems within the engine or malfunctions within the ignition system. Try to establish for certain that the carburetors are in need of a major overhaul before beginning.

3 Check the fuel tap filter, the fuel lines, the fuel tank cap vent, the intake manifold hose clamps, the vacuum hoses, the air filter element, the cylinder compression, the spark plugs, the air suction system (if equipped) and the carburetor synchronization before assuming that a carburetor overhaul is required.

4 Most carburetor problems are caused by dirt particles, varnish and other deposits which build up in and block the fuel and air passages. Also, in time, gaskets and O-rings shrink or deteriorate and cause fuel and air leaks which lead to poor performance.

5 When the carburetor is overhauled, it is generally disassembled completely and the parts are cleaned thoroughly with a carburetor cleaning solvent and dried with filtered, unlubricated compressed air. The fuel and air passages are also blown through with compressed air to force out any dirt that may have been loosened but not removed by the solvent. Once the cleaning process is complete, the carburetor is reassembled using new gaskets, O-rings and, generally, a new inlet needle valve and seat.

6 Before disassembling the carburetors, make sure you have a carburetor rebuild kit (which will include all necessary O-rings and other parts), some carburetor cleaner, a supply of rags, some means of blowing out the carburetor passages and a clean place to work. It is recommended that only one carburetor be overhauled at a time to avoid mixing up parts.

7 Carburetors - removal and installation

3

 Warning: Gasoline (petrol) is extremely flammable, so take extra precautions when you work on any part of the fuel system. Don't smoke or allow open flames or bare light bulbs near the work area, and don't work in a garage where an appliance fueled by natural gas is present (such as a water heater or clothes dryer). If you spill any fuel on your skin, rinse it off immediately with soap and water. When you perform any kind of work on the fuel system, wear safety glasses and have a fire extinguisher suitable for a Class B type fire (flammable liquids) on hand.

Removal

1 Remove the fuel tank (see Section 2).
2 If you're working on a US model, remove

7.5 Loosen the clamps on the intake manifold tubes and detach the carburetors from the tubes

7.8 Pull the clips (if equipped) out of the air box

7.9 Lift the carburetor assembly and remove it to one side

the vacuum switching valve for the air suction system.

3 Disconnect the choke cable from the carburetor assembly (if equipped) (see Section 11).

4 Loosen the throttle cable adjuster at the handlebar all the way.

5 Loosen the clamp screws on the intake manifolds (the rubber tubes that connect the carburetors to the engine) **(see illustration)**.

6 Mark and disconnect the vacuum hoses from the carburetors.

7 Early GSX-R750 and 1100: Remove the air box mounting screws and pull the air box backward to detach it from the carburetors.

8 Late GSX-R750 and 1100: Pull the clips out of the air box **(see illustration)**.

9 Raise the assembly up far enough to disconnect the throttle cable(s) from the carburetor linkage, then remove the carburetors from the machine **(see illustration)**.

10 After the carburetors have been removed, stuff clean rags into the intake manifold tubes to prevent the entry of dirt or other objects.

Installation

11 Position the assembly over the intake manifold tubes. Lightly lubricate the ends of the throttle cable(s) with multi-purpose grease and attach them to the throttle pulley. Make sure the accelerator and decelerator cables (if equipped) are in their proper positions.

12 Tilt the front of the assembly down and insert the fronts of the carburetors into the intake manifold tubes. Push the assembly forward and tighten the clamps.

13 Make sure the ducts from the air cleaner housing are seated properly, then slide the spring bands into position.

14 Connect the choke cable to the assembly and adjust it (see Section 11).

15 The remainder of installation is the reverse of the removal steps, with the following additions:

a) Adjust the throttle grip freeplay (see Chapter 1).

b) Check for fuel leaks.

c) Check and, if necessary, adjust the idle speed and carburetor synchronization (see Chapter 1 and Section 5).

---

8 Carburetors - disassembly, cleaning and inspection

⚠ **Warning: Gasoline (petrol) is extremely flammable, so take extra precautions when you work on any part of the fuel system. Don't smoke or allow open flames or bare light bulbs near the work area, and don't work in a garage where an appliance fueled by natural gas is present (such as a water heater or clothes dryer). If you spill any fuel on your skin, rinse it off immediately with soap and water. When you perform any kind of work on the fuel system, wear safety glasses and have a fire extinguisher suitable for a Class B type fire (flammable liquids) on hand.**

Note: Three different carburetor designs have been used on these models. Refer to this Chapter's Specifications to determine which type is used on your machine.

VM29SS carburetors

Disassembly

1 Remove eight screws each from the upper and lower set plates and detach them from the carburetor assembly **(see illustration)**. Note: These screws have been secured with thread locking agent. Make sure the screwdriver fits correctly. You may have to use new screws during reassembly.

2 Remove four choke shaft screws, then pull out the shaft and knob.

3 Remove the spring and steel ball from the carburetors for no. 1 and no. 3 cylinders.

4 Remove the top cap from each carburetor.

5 Beneath the top cap, remove three throttle shaft screws and one bolt. Remove one more throttle shaft screw from the throttle shaft between the carburetors.

6 Squeeze the clamps on the interconnecting hoses between the carburetors and slide the clamps back along the hoses. Pull the carburetors out of the hoses to separate them. Pry the hoses off the fittings if they're stuck.

7 Slide the throttle shaft out of carburetor no. 3.

8 Unscrew the accelerator pump lever pivot bolt, then remove the lever and spring.

9 Remove and disassemble the throttle valve components.

10 If necessary, remove one screw and take off the throttle lever bracket. This screw has been secured with thread locking compound, so don't remove it unnecessarily.

11 Remove four screws and take off the float chamber body, then remove the spring, plunger and rod.

12 Pull out the float pivot pin and separate the float from the carburetor body. **Caution: Don't force the pivot pin out or the carburetor body may be damaged.**

13 Remove the needle valve and seat from the carburetor body.

14 Unscrew the main jet and pilot jet.

Cleaning

Caution: Use only a carburetor cleaning solution that is safe for use with plastic parts (be sure to read the label on the container).

15 Submerge the metal components in the carburetor cleaner for approximately thirty minutes (or longer, if the directions recommend it).

16 After the carburetor has soaked long enough for the cleaner to loosen and dissolve most of the varnish and other deposits, use a brush to remove the stubborn deposits. Rinse it again, then dry it with compressed air. Blow out all of the fuel and air passages in the main and upper body.

Caution: Never clean the jets or passages with a piece of wire or a drill bit, as they will be enlarged, causing the fuel and air metering rates to be upset.

Inspection

17 Check the operation of the choke plunger. If it doesn't move smoothly, replace it, along with the return spring.

18 Check the tapered portion of the pilot screw for wear or damage. Replace the pilot screw if necessary.

19 Check the carburetor body, float bowl and top cover for cracks, distorted sealing surfaces and other damage. If any defects are found, replace the faulty component, although

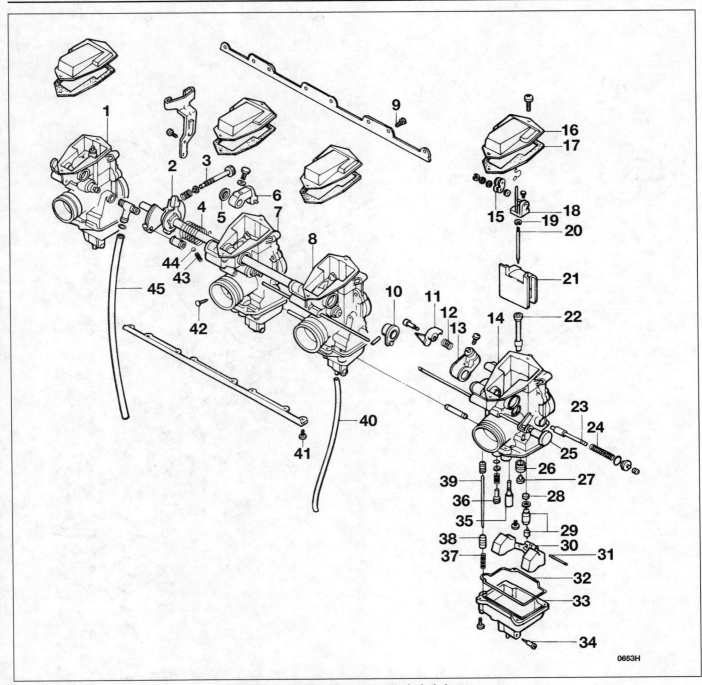

8.1 VM29SS carburetors - exploded view

1 Carburetor body
2 Throttle shaft lever
3 Throttle stop screw
4 Throttle valve return spring
5 Washer
6 Throttle lever
7 Carburetor body
8 Carburetor body
9 Screw (use thread locking
  agent on threads)
10 Throttle shaft assembly
11 Accelerator lever

12 Spring
13 Throttle lever assembly
14 Carburetor body
15 Plate
16 Top cap
17 Gasket
18 Connector
19 Clip
20 Jet needle
21 Throttle valve
22 Needle jet
23 Choke plunger

24 Spring
25 Choke shaft
26 Main jet holder
27 Main jet
28 Filter
29 Needle valve
30 Float
31 Float pivot pin
32 Float chamber O-ring
33 Float chamber
34 Float chamber drain screw
35 Pilot jet

36 Pilot screw
37 Spring
38 Accelerator plunger
39 Accelerator rod
40 Overflow tube
41 Screw (use thread locking
  agent on threads)
42 Screw
43 Spring
44 Steel ball
45 Air vent hose

3

0653H

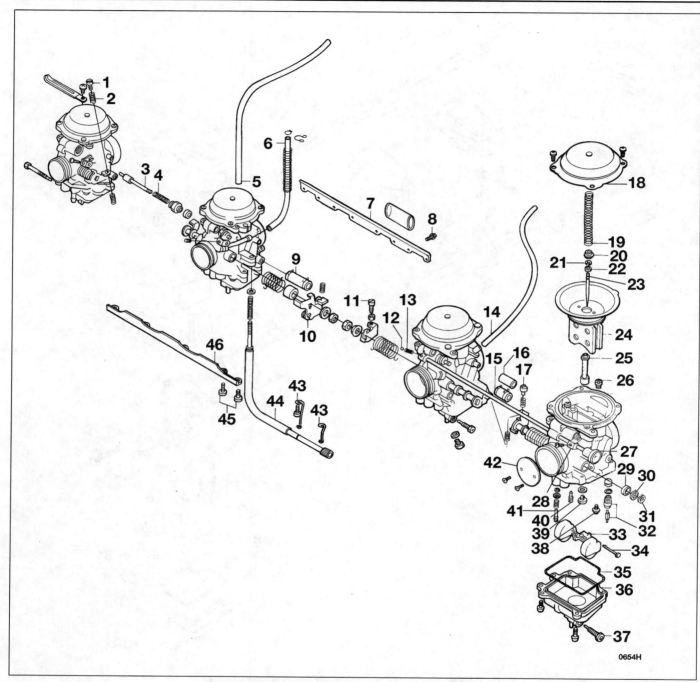

8.27 BST31SS and BST34SS carburetors - exploded view

1 Synchronizer screw
2 Spring
3 Choke plunger
4 Spring
5 Vent tube
6 Fuel tap vacuum line
7 Set plate
8 Screw (use thread locking agent)
9 Fuel line connector
10 Throttle lever
11 Synchronizer screw

12 Steel ball
13 Spring
14 Vent tube
15 Fuel line connector
16 Vent connector
17 Synchronizer screw
18 Top cap
19 Spring
20 Spring seat
21 Jet needle clip
22 Washer
23 Jet needle

24 Throttle slide
25 Needle jet
26 Pilot air jet
27 Choke shaft
28 Choke shaft bracket
29 Seal
30 Washer
31 Clip
32 Needle valve
33 Float
34 Float pivot pin
35 Float chamber O-ring

36 Float chamber
37 Float chamber drain screw
38 Retainer screw
39 Main jet
40 Pilot jet
41 Pilot screw
42 Throttle valve
43 Clip
44 Throttle stop screw
45 Screws (use thread locking agent)
46 Set plate

replacement of the entire carburetor will probably be necessary (check with your parts supplier for the availability of separate components).

20 Insert the throttle valve in the carburetor body and see that it moves up-and-down smoothly. Check the surface of the valve for wear. If it's worn excessively or doesn't move smoothly in the bore, replace the carburetor.

21 Check the jet needle for straightness by rolling it on a flat surface (such as a piece of glass). Replace it if it's bent or if the tip is worn.

22 Check the tip of the fuel inlet valve needle. If it has grooves or scratches in it, it must be replaced. Check the needle valve filter for clogging and the O-ring for damage or deterioration. Replace if necessary.

23 Check the O-rings on the float bowl and the drain plug (in the float bowl). Replace them if they're damaged.

24 Operate the throttle shaft to make sure the throttle butterfly valve opens and closes smoothly. If it doesn't, replace the carburetor.

25 Check the floats for damage. This will usually be apparent by the presence of fuel inside one of the floats. If the floats are damaged, they must be replaced.

BST31SS and BST34SS carburetors

Disassembly

26 Remove the carburetors from the machine as described in Section 7. Set the assembly on a clean working surface. **Note:** *Work on one carburetor at a time to avoid getting parts mixed up.*

27 Remove four choke shaft securing screws **(see illustration)**. **Note:** *These screws have been secured with thread locking agent and will be damaged during removal. Replace them with new ones during assembly.*

28 Remove the clip from the end of the choke shaft, then slide it out. **Note:** *There are steel balls and springs for the choke shaft in the center two carburetors. Note the locations of these so they won't be lost.*

29 GSX-R models: Remove four screws each from the upper and lower set plates and

detach them from the carburetors. Remove the connection plates from the tops of the carburetors. You'll probably need an impact driver to remove the screws. If they're damaged, use new ones during assembly.

30 Katana (GSX-F) models: Remove eight screws each from the upper and lower set plates and detach them from the carburetors **(see illustration)**. You'll probably need an impact driver to remove the screws. If they're damaged, use new ones during assembly.

31 Squeeze the connecting hose clips and slide them back along the hoses. Pull the carburetors apart. Pry the hoses off the fittings if necessary.

32 Remove four screws and take off the top cap.

33 Remove the return spring and valve from the top of the carburetor.

34 Remove four screws and take off the float chamber. You'll probably need an impact driver to remove the screws. If they're damaged, use new ones during assembly.

35 Carefully pull the float pivot pin out of the carburetor body, then remove the float.

36 Remove the needle valve retaining screw and take out the needle valve.

37 Unscrew the main jet and pilot jet. Lift the needle jet into the throttle bore and remove it.

38 Turn the carburetor over and remove the pilot air jet.

39 Remove the choke plunger nut and pull out the plunger.

8.30 The set plate screws (arrowed) are secured with thread locking agent - you'll need an impact driver to remove them

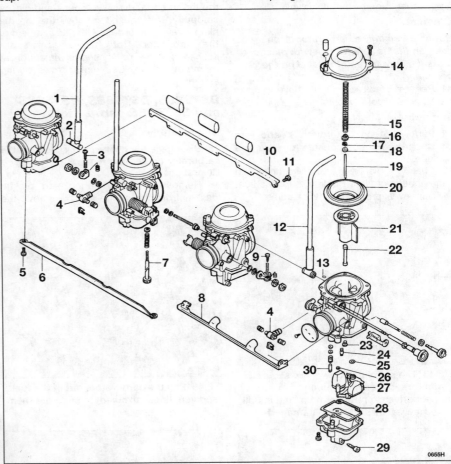

8.45a BST33SS, BST36SS, BST38SS and BST40SS carburetors - exploded view

1 Vent tube	11 Set plate screw (use thread locking agent)	21 Throttle slide
2 Vent tube fitting		22 Needle jet
3 Synchronizer screw	12 Vent tube	23 Main jet
4 Fuel line fitting	13 O-ring	24 Pilot jet
5 Set plate screw (use thread locking agent)	14 Top cap	25 O-ring
	15 Spring	26 O-ring
6 Set plate	16 Spring seat	27 Float
7 Throttle stop screw	17 Jet needle clip	28 Float chamber O-ring
8 Choke shaft bracket	18 Washer	29 Float chamber drain screw
9 Synchronizer screw	19 Jet needle	
10 Set plate	20 Diaphragm	30 Pilot screw

3

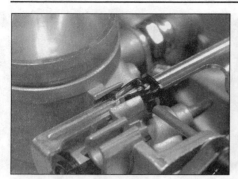

8.45b Slide the clips out of the carburetor body . . .

8.45c . . . then remove the choke shaft lever

8.47 Compress the synchronizer screw springs and remove them

40 Remove the clip, jet needle, spring seat and washer from the throttle valve.

Cleaning

Caution: Use only a carburetor cleaning solution that is safe for use with plastic parts (be sure to read the label on the container).

41 Perform Steps 15 and 16 above to clean the carburetor components.

Inspection

42 Perform Steps 17 through 25 above to check carburetor components for wear and damage.

43 Check the diaphragm for splits, holes and general deterioration. Holding it up to a light will help reveal problems of this nature.

44 Operate the throttle shaft to make sure the throttle butterfly valve opens and closes smoothly. If it doesn't, remove the throttle plate screws and slide the throttle shaft out of the carburetor. **Note**: *These screws are peened in place. You'll need an impact driver to remove them. Use new screws during assembly.*

BST33SS, BST36SS, BST38SS and BST40SS carburetors

Disassembly

45 Disengage the choke lever clips from the carburetor body, then remove the lever (**see illustrations**).

46 Remove the clip, spring and plastic washer from the choke shaft. Remove the

choke shaft pin and pull the shaft out.

47 Remove the springs from the synchronizer screws (**see illustration**).

48 Remove eight screws each that attach the upper and lower set plates to the carburetors (**see illustration**). **Note**: *These screws have been secured by thread locking agent. You'll need an impact driver to remove them. If the screws are damaged during removal, use new ones during assembly.*

49 Pull the carburetors apart, separating each from the fuel line and air vent tube (**see illustration**).

50 Remove the choke plunger retainer, spring and plunger (**see illustrations**).

51 Remove the top cap screws and lift off the cap (**see illustration**).

8.48 The set plate screws are secured with thread locking compound - use an impact driver to remove them, and install new screws if they're damaged

8.49 Pull the carburetors out of the fuel and vent lines (arrowed) to separate them

8.50a Remove the choke plunger retainer . . .

8.50b . . . its spring . . .

8.50c . . . and the plunger

8.51 Remove the top cap screws and lift off the cap

8.52 Lift out the diaphragm spring and spring seat

8.53 Carefully separate the diaphragm from the carburetor body and lift it out; also remove the O-ring (arrowed)

8.54 Lift out the throttle slide and jet needle

52 Lift out the spring and spring seat **(see illustration)**.

53 Lift out the diaphragm and remove the O-ring **(see illustration)**.

54 Lift out the throttle slide **(see illustration)**.

55 Lift out the jet needle **(see illustration)**.

56 Carefully note which groove the clip fits in (fuel mixture is affected by the position of the clip), then remove the clip and washer from the jet needle **(see illustration)**.

57 Unscrew the float chamber drain plug, then lift it out together with the O-ring **(see illustration)**.

58 Squeeze the fuel line clips and slide them back along the lines. Disconnect the lines from the fittings on the float chambers **(see illustration)**.

59 Remove the float chamber screws and lift off the float chamber body and O-ring **(see illustration)**. **Note:** *These screws have been secured with thread locking agent. You'll need an impact driver to remove them. If they're damaged during removal, use new ones during assembly.*

60 Lift out the floats **(see illustration)**.

61 Unhook the needle valve from the floats **(see illustration)**.

62 Remove the needle valve seat from the carburetor body **(see illustration)**.

63 On UK models only, remove the pilot

8.55 Separate the jet needle from the throttle slide

8.56 Write down which groove the clip is in, then take the clip and washer off the jet needle

8.57 Remove the float chamber drain plug and its O-ring

8.58 Disconnect the fuel lines from the carburetors

3

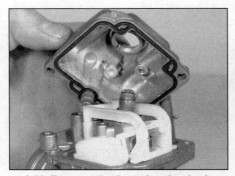

8.59 Remove the float chamber body screws (they're secured with thread locking agent, so you'll need an impact driver and may have to replace them), then lift off the float chamber body and O-ring

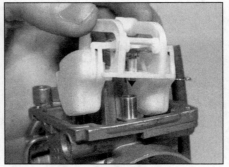

8.60 Lift out the floats

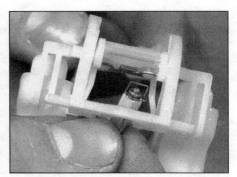

8.61 Unhook the needle valve from the floats

8.62 Lift out the needle valve seat and O-ring

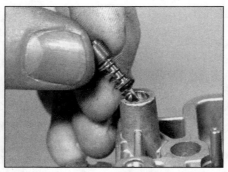

8.63 On UK models only, unscrew the pilot screw (on US models, it's preset at the factory and shouldn't be disturbed)

8.64 Unscrew the pilot jet

8.65 Unscrew the main jet

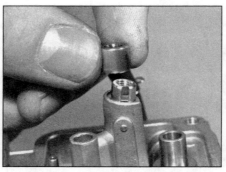

8.66 Lift out the needle jet retainer

8.67 Lift the needle jet into the throttle bore and take it out

screw **(see illustration)**. If you're working on a US model, don't remove the pilot screw. It's preset at the factory and no adjustment specifications are provided.

64 Remove the pilot jet **(see illustration)**.

65 Remove the main jet **(see illustration)**.

66 Remove the needle jet retainer **(see illustration)**.

67 Lift the needle jet up into the throttle bore and take it out **(see illustration)**.

Cleaning

Caution: Use only a carburetor cleaning solution that is safe for use with plastic parts (be sure to read the label on the container).

68 Perform Steps 15 and 16 above to clean the carburetor components.

Inspection

69 Perform Steps 17 through 25 above to check carburetor components for wear and damage.

70 Check the diaphragm for splits, holes and general deterioration. Holding it up to a light will help reveal problems of this nature.

71 Operate the throttle shaft to make sure the throttle butterfly valve opens and closes smoothly. If it doesn't, remove the throttle plate screws and slide the throttle shaft out of the carburetor. **Note**: *These screws are peened in place. You'll need an impact driver to remove them. Use new screws during assembly.*

9   Carburetors - reassembly and float height adjustment

> *Warning: Gasoline (petrol) is extremely flammable, so take extra precautions when you work on any part of the fuel system. Don't smoke or allow open flames or bare light bulbs near the work area, and don't work in a garage where a natural gas-type appliance (such as a water heater or clothes dryer) is present. If you spill any fuel on your skin, rinse it off immediately with soap and water. When you perform any kind of work on the fuel system, wear safety glasses and have a fire extinguisher suitable for a Class B type fire (flammable liquids) on hand.*

Caution: When installing the jets, be careful not to over-tighten them - they're made of soft material and can strip or shear easily.

Note: *When reassembling the carburetors, be sure to use the new O-rings, gaskets and other parts supplied in the rebuild kit.*

Reassembly

1 Reassembly is the reverse of disassembly, with the following additions.

VM29SS carburetors

2 If the throttle lever bracket was removed, use thread locking agent on the threads of the screw.

3 Install the plastic washer when installing the throttle shaft in the no. 3 carburetor **(see illustration)**.

BST31SS and BST34SS carburetors

4 If you replace the throttle valve seals, install the new ones with their grooves facing outward (away from the carburetor).

5 Engage the protrusion in the diaphragm

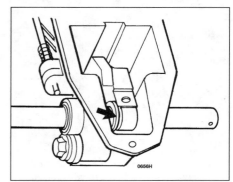

9.3 When assembling VM29SS carburetors, don't forget the plastic washer on the throttle shaft

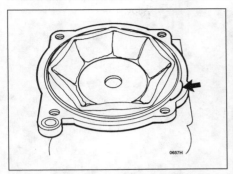

9.5 When assembling BST31SS or BST34SS carburetors, place the diaphragm protrusion in the correct spot on the rim of the carburetor body

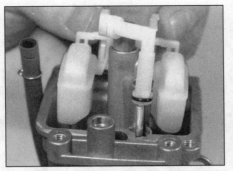

9.7 When installing the floats on BST33SS, BST36SS, BST38SS or BST40SS carburetors, slide the tube and O-ring into the body passage

9.8 Align the slot in the needle jet with the pin in the passage (arrowed)

9.9 Position the synchronizing screw and springs as shown

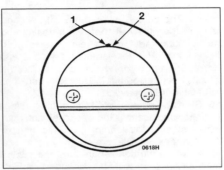

9.10 Turn the throttle stop screw and synchronizing screw to position each throttle valve (2) just inside of the forward bypass hole (1)

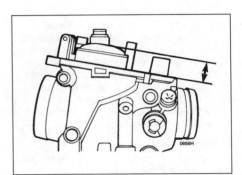

9.12 Measure float height from the gasket surface to the top of the float

with the notch in the carburetor body **(see illustration)**.

6 Line up the choke shaft screws with the indentations in the choke shaft before tightening them.

BST33SS, BST36SS, BST38SS and BST40SS carburetors

7 When installing the floats, slide the tube and O-ring into the passage in the carburetor body **(see illustration)**.

All models

8 Align the slot in the needle jet with the pin in the carburetor body **(see illustration)**.

9 Be sure the synchronizer springs and screws are installed correctly **(see illustration)**. Hook one end of the throttle spring to the spring boss on the carburetor, then rotate the other end one full turn to place tension on it before hooking the other end to the throttle lever.

10 Position the throttle valves by turning the throttle stop screws and synchronizing screws so the upper edge of the valve aligns with the forward bypass passage **(see illustration)**.

11 Use thread locking agent on the upper and lower set plate screws.

Float height adjustment

12 With the float chamber body off the carburetor, hold the carburetor upside down and measure float height from the carburetor body **(see illustration)**.

13 If the float height is not at the level listed in this Chapter's Specifications, bend the float arm to adjust it.

14 After the fuel level for each carburetor has been adjusted, assemble and install the carburetors.

---

10 Throttle cables - removal, installation and adjustment

Removal

1 Remove the seat. Remove fairing panels as necessary for access to the cable (see Chapter 7).

2 Remove the fuel tank (see Section 2).

3 Cut any tie wrap that secures the cables.

4 Loosen the accelerator cable locknut at the handlebar and loosen the adjuster all the way **(see illustration)**.

5 Remove the cable/switch housing screws and detach the housing from the handlebar. Disengage the cable from the handlebar.

6 Detach the cable(s) from the adjuster

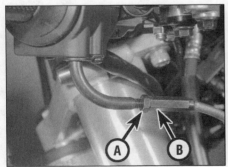

10.4 Loosen the cable locknut and slacken the cable adjuster all the way

A Locknut   B Cable adjuster

10.6a Lift the cable and slide the inner cable out of the slot in the bracket

3

10.6b Disconnect the cable from the throttle lever

11.2 Separate the choke cable housing from the bracket at the carburetor (arrowed)

bracket and from the throttle lever at the carburetor assembly (see illustrations). If necessary, detach the carburetor assembly from the bike for access to the cable(s).

7 Tie a piece of string to one end of the cable, then pull the cable out from the opposite end. The string will follow the path of the cable through the frame, so you can route it correctly during installation.

Installation

8 Route the cable(s) into place. Make sure they don't interfere with any other components and aren't kinked or bent sharply.

9 Lubricate the end of the accelerator cable with multi-purpose grease and connect it to the throttle pulley at the carburetor. Pass the inner cable through the slot in the bracket, then seat the cable housing in the bracket.

10 Repeat the previous step to connect the decelerator cable (if equipped).

11 Replace any tie wraps that were cut.

Adjustment

12 Follow the procedure outlined in Chapter 1, *Throttle operation/grip freeplay*, to adjust the cables.

13 Turn the handlebars back and forth to make sure the cables don't cause the steering to bind.

14 Operate the throttle and check the cable

12.7 Note the location of wiring harness clips (arrowed) when you remove the air box screws

action. The cable(s) should move freely and the throttle pulley at the carburetor should move back and forth in response to both acceleration and deceleration. If the cable(s) don't operate properly, find and fix the problem before you put the fuel tank back on.

15 Install the fuel tank.

16 Start the engine. With the engine idling, turn the handlebars all the way to left and right while listening and watching the tachometer for changes in idle speed. If idle speed increases as the handlebars turn, the cables are improperly routed. This is dangerous. Find the problem and fix it before riding the bike.

11 Choke cable (if equipped) - removal, installation and adjustment

Removal

1 Perform Steps 1 through 3 of Section 10.

2 Pull the choke cable casing away from its mounting bracket at the carburetor and pass the inner cable through the opening in the bracket (see illustration). Detach the cable end from the choke lever by the right-hand carburetor.

3 Tie a piece of string to one end of the cable, then pull the cable out from the opposite end. The string will follow the path of the cable through the frame, so you can route it correctly during installation.

Installation

4 Route the cable into position. Connect the upper end of the cable to the choke lever.

5 Connect the lower end of the cable to the choke lever. Pull back on the cable casing and connect it to the bracket on the right-hand carburetor (see illustration 11.2).

Adjustment

6 Suzuki doesn't provide adjustment procedures or specifications for the choke cable. If the cable on your bike has an adjuster at the handlebar, adjust it so the choke releases fully.

7 Install the fuel tank and all of the other

components that were previously removed. Replace any cut tie wraps with new ones.

12 Air filter housing - removal and installation

1 Remove the seat and fuel tank.

2 Remove fairing panels as necessary for access to the air box fasteners (see Chapter 7).

3 Disconnect the breather hose from the air filter housing.

4 Remove the clamps that secure the air box air tubes to the carburetors.

5 All except late GSX-R750 and 1100: Remove the air box mounting screws and pull the air box backward to detach it from the carburetors.

6 Late GSX-R750 and 1100: Pull the clips out of the air box (see illustration 7.8).

7 Remove the air box mounting screws. Note that some screws secure wiring harnesses (see illustration).

8 Lift the air filter housing up and out of the frame.

9 Installation is the reverse of removal.

13 Exhaust system - removal and installation

1 Remove the lower fairing (if equipped) (see Chapter 7).

2 If you plan to remove the mufflers (silencers) from the exhaust pipes, loosen the clamps (see illustration).

3 Unbolt the support bracket and loosen the crossover clamp (see illustration).

4 Unbolt the exhaust bracket from the footpeg bracket (see illustration).

5 Remove the Allen bolts that secure the exhaust pipes to the cylinder head (see illustration).

6 Grasp the exhaust system and separate it from the cylinder head (see illustration).

7 Installation is the reverse of removal, with the following addition: Install new gaskets at the cylinder head (see illustration).

13.2 Loosen the muffler clamps if you plan to separate the mufflers from the pipes

13.3 Unbolt the support bracket under the frame and loosen the crossover clamp (arrowed)

13.4 Remove the muffler mounting bolts at the rear foot pegs

13.5 Unbolt the exhaust pipes from the cylinder head

13.6 Pull the exhaust pipes free of the cylinder head

13.7 The gaskets at the cylinder head should be replaced whenever the pipes are removed

3

14.7 The evaporative emission canister is mounted on the left side of the motorcycle

14.10 The purge control valves are mounted in the evaporative control system lines

14.13 The air suction valves are mounted within the forward section of the frame

14 Emission controls

1 US models incorporate several emission control systems. These include carburetors with pilot screws sealed to prevent adjustment and close-tolerance jets.

2 California models use an evaporative emission control system, which stores vapor from the fuel tank in a carbon-filled canister so it can be pulled into the engine and burned.

3 California models also use an air suction system which uses exhaust gas pulses to pull air into the exhaust ports in the cylinder head. This air allows exhaust gases to continue oxidizing as they leave the cylinder, reducing unburned hydrocarbons and carbon monoxide in the exhaust.

4 None of the systems require maintenance, other than occasional checks for damaged or loose components.

Evaporative emission canister - removal and installation

5 The canister is mounted on the left side of the motorcycle.

6 Remove fairing panels as necessary for access to the canister (see Chapter 7).

7 Label and disconnect the hoses, remove the mounting screws and take the canister out **(see illustration)**.

8 Installation is the reverse of the removal steps. Replace hoses if they are cracked or deteriorated.

Purge control (one way) valves - removal and installation

9 Remove fairing panels as necessary for access to the purge control valves (see Chapter 7).

10 Label and disconnect the hoses, remove the mounting screws and take the valve out **(see illustration)**.

11 Installation is the reverse of the removal steps. Replace hoses if they are cracked or deteriorated.

Air suction valves - removal and installation

12 Remove the fuel tank (see Section 2).

13 Remove the air suction valve bracket **(see illustration)**. Disconnect the hoses and take the valves out.

14 Installation is the reverse of the removal

14.16 The air switching valve is mounted beneath the air suction valves

steps. Replace hoses if they are cracked or deteriorated.

Air switching valve - removal and installation

15 Remove the air suction valves (see Step 13).

16 Disconnect the hoses and remove the valve from the clip **(see illustration)**.

17 Installation is the reverse of the removal steps. Replace hoses if they are cracked or deteriorated

Chapter 4
Ignition system

Contents

Degrees of difficulty

| Easy, suitable for novice with little experience | Fairly easy, suitable for beginner with some experience | Fairly difficult, suitable for competent DIY mechanic | Difficult, suitable for experienced DIY mechanic 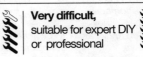 | Very difficult, suitable for expert DIY or professional |

Specifications

Ignition coil

Katana 600 and 750 (GSX600F and GSX750F)
  Primary resistance .... 2 to 4 ohms
  Secondary resistance .... 30,000 to 40,000 ohms
  Arcing distance .... 8 mm (5/16 inch) or more

GSX-R750
  1985 through 1987
    Primary resistance .... 3 to 5 ohms
    Secondary resistance .... 25,000 to 45,000 ohms
    Arcing distance .... 8 mm (5/16 inch) or more
  1988 on
    Primary resistance .... 2.4 to 3.2 ohms
    Secondary resistance .... 30,000 to 40,000 ohms
    Arcing distance .... 8 mm (5/16 inch) or more

GSX-R1100
  1986 through 1988
    Primary resistance .... 3 to 5 ohms
    Secondary resistance .... 25,000 to 45,000 ohms
    Arcing distance .... 8 mm (5/16 inch) or more
  1989 on
    Primary resistance .... 2.4 to 3.2 ohms
    Secondary resistance .... 30,000 to 40,000 ohms
    Arcing distance .... 8 mm (5/16 inch) or more

Katana 1100 (GSX1100F)
  Primary resistance .... 3 to 5 ohms
  Secondary resistance .... 25,000 to 45,000 ohms
  Arcing distance .... 8 mm (5/16 inch) or more

Signal generator resistance

  Katana 600 and 750 (GSX600F and GSX750F) .... 135 to 200 ohms
  GSX-R750
    1985 through 1987 .... 130 to 180 ohms
    1988 on .... 135 to 200 ohms
  GSX-R1100 and Katana 1100 (GSX1100F)
    1986 through 1988 .... 130 to 180 ohms
    1989 on .... 135 to 200 ohms

Ignition timing .... Not adjustable

4

Signal generator bolt torque

GSX-R750

1985 through 1987	25 to 35 Nm (18.0 to 25.5 ft-lbs)
1988 on	17 to 23 Nm (12.5 to 16.5 ft-lbs)
GSX-R1100, Katana 600 (GSX600F) and Katana 1100 (GSX1100F) . . .	25 to 35 Nm (18.0 to 25.5 ft-lbs)
Katana 750 (GSX750F)	17 to 23 Nm (12.5 to 16.5 ft-lbs)

1 General information

This motorcycle is equipped with a battery operated, fully transistorized, breakerless ignition system. The system consists of the following components:

Signal generator
IC igniter unit
Battery and fuse
Ignition coils
Spark plugs
Stop and main (key) switches
Primary and secondary circuit wiring

The transistorized ignition system functions on the same principle as a contact breaker point DC ignition system with the pickup unit and igniter performing the tasks previously associated with the contact breaker points and mechanical advance system (on some models, ignition timing is controlled by a microprocessor). As a result, adjustment and maintenance of ignition components is eliminated (with the exception of spark plug replacement).

Because of their nature, the individual ignition system components can be checked but not repaired. If ignition system troubles occur, and the faulty component can be isolated, the only cure for the problem is to replace the part with a new one. Keep in mind that most electrical parts, once purchased, can't be returned. To avoid unnecessary expense, make very sure the faulty component has been positively identified before buying a replacement part.

2 Ignition system - check

 Warning: Because of the very high voltage generated by the ignition system, extreme care should be taken to avoid electrical shock when these checks are performed.

1 If the ignition system is the suspected cause of poor engine performance or failure to start, a number of checks can be made to isolate the problem.
2 Make sure the ignition stop switch is in the Run or On position.

Engine will not start

3 Remove the fuel tank (see Chapter 3). Disconnect one of the spark plug wires, connect the wire to a spare spark plug and lay the plug on the engine with the threads contacting the engine. If it's necessary to hold the spark plug, use an insulated tool. Crank the engine over and make sure a well-defined, blue spark occurs between the spark plug electrodes.

 Warning: DO NOT remove one of the spark plugs from the engine to perform this check - atomized fuel being pumped out of the open spark plug hole could ignite, causing severe injury!

4 If no spark occurs, the following checks should be made:
5 Unscrew a spark plug cap from a plug wire and check the cap resistance with an ohmmeter **(see illustration)**. If the resistance is infinite, replace it with a new one. Repeat this check on the other plug caps.
6 Make sure all electrical connectors are clean and tight. Refer to the wiring diagrams at the end of this book and check all wires for shorts, opens and correct installation.
7 Check the battery voltage with a voltmeter and the specific gravity with a hydrometer (see Chapter 1). If the voltage is less than 12-volts or if the specific gravity is low, recharge the battery.
8 Check the ignition fuse and the fuse connections. If the fuse is blown, replace it with a new one; if the connections are loose or corroded, clean or repair them.
9 Refer to Section 3 and check the ignition coil primary and secondary resistance.

10 Refer to Section 4 and check the pickup coil resistance.
11 If the preceding checks produce positive results but there is still no spark at the plug, have the signal generator and IC igniter checked by a Suzuki dealer service department or other repair shop equipped with the special tester required. **Note**: *The igniter on models equipped with a microprocessor can be tested off the bike as well as on. If the bike is not running, it may be more convenient to remove the igniter and take it to the dealer for testing. Check this with the dealer first; they may want to test the entire system.*

Engine starts but misfires

12 If the engine starts but misfires, make the following checks before deciding that the ignition system is at fault.
13 The ignition system must be able to produce a spark across an 8 mm (5/16-inch) gap (minimum). A simple test fixture **(see illustration)** can be constructed to make sure the minimum spark gap can be jumped. Make sure the fixture electrodes are positioned eight millimeters apart.
14 Connect one of the spark plug wires to the protruding test fixture electrode, then attach the fixture's alligator clip to a good engine ground.
15 Crank the engine over (it may start and run on the remaining cylinders) and see if well-defined, blue sparks occur between the test fixture electrodes. If the minimum spark gap test is positive, the ignition coil for that cylinder is functioning properly. Repeat the check on one of the spark plug wires that is

2.5 Unscrew the spark plug caps from the plug wires and measure their resistance with an ohmmeter

2.13 A simple spark gap testing fixture can be made from a block of wood, a large alligator clip, two nails, a screw and a piece of wire

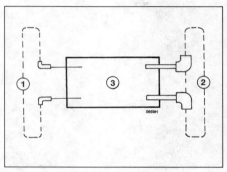

3.4 Ignition coil test

1 Measure primary winding resistance
2 Measure secondary winding resistance
3 Ignition coil

3.10a The coils are mounted inside the front portion of the frame (late GSX-R1100 shown) . . .

3.10b . . . or to the frame crossmember as on this Katana (GSX-F) (on US models, you'll need to remove the air suction valves for access) . . .

connected to the other coil. If the spark will not jump the gap during either test, or if it is weak (orange colored), refer to Steps 5 through 11 of this Section and perform the component checks described.

3 Ignition coils - check, removal and installation

Check

1 In order to determine conclusively that the ignition coils are defective, they should be tested by an authorized Suzuki dealer service department which is equipped with the special electrical tester required for this check.

2 However, the coils can be checked visually (for cracks and other damage) and the primary and secondary coil resistances can be measured with an ohmmeter. If the coils are undamaged, and if the resistances are as specified, they are probably capable of proper operation.

3 To check the coils for physical damage, they must be removed (see Step 9). To check the resistances, simply remove the fuel tank (see Chapter 3), unplug the primary circuit electrical connectors from the coil(s) and remove the spark plug wire from the plug

that's connected to the coil being checked. Mark the locations of all wires before disconnecting them.

4 To check the coil primary resistance, attach one ohmmeter lead to one of the primary terminals and the other ohmmeter lead to the other primary terminal **(see illustration)**.

5 Place the ohmmeter selector switch in the Rx1 position and compare the measured resistance to the value listed in this Chapter's Specifications.

6 If the coil primary resistance is as specified, check the coil secondary resistance by disconnecting the meter leads from the primary terminals and attaching them to the spark plug wire terminals **(see illustration 3.4)**.

7 Place the ohmmeter selector switch in the Rx1000 position and compare the measured resistance to the values listed in this Chapter's Specifications.

8 If the resistances are not as specified, unscrew the spark plug wire retainers from the coil, detach the wires and check the resistance again. If it is now within specifications, one or both of the wires are bad. If it's still not as specified, the coil is probably defective and should be replaced with a new one.

Removal and installation

9 To remove the coils, refer to Chapter 3 and

remove the fuel tank, then disconnect the spark plug wires from the plugs. After labeling them with tape to aid in reinstallation, unplug the coil primary circuit electrical connectors.

10 Support the coil with one hand and remove the coil mounting screws or bolts **(see illustrations)**, then withdraw the coil from its bracket. If necessary, detach the bracket from the frame.

11 Installation is the reverse of removal. If a new coil is being installed, disconnect the spark plug wire terminals from the coil, disconnect the wires and transfer them to the new coil. Make sure the primary circuit electrical connectors are attached to the proper terminals.

4 Signal generator - check, removal and installation

Check

1 Remove the cover bolts and take off the signal generator cover **(see illustration)**. Follow the pickup coil wiring harness from the coil to the electrical connector, then disconnect the connector.

2 Probe each pair of terminals in the signal generator connector with an ohmmeter and compare the resistance reading with the value listed in this Chapter's Specifications.

3 Set the ohmmeter on the highest resistance range. Measure the resistance between a good ground and each terminal in the electrical connector. The meter should read infinity.

4 If the signal generator fails either of the above tests, one or both of the pickup coils is defective. The pickup coils can't be replaced separately; the signal generator must be replaced.

Removal

5 Remove the signal generator cover **(see illustration 4.1)**.

6 Hold the signal generator hex with a box

3.10c . . . or to the outside of the frame as on this Katana (GSX-F)

4.1 The signal generator is beneath a cover on the right side of the engine

4

4.6 Hold the hex with a box wrench (ring spanner) when turning the Allen bolt - DO NOT turn the Allen bolt by itself or it may snap off

4.7 Take off the rotor

4.8 Remove the screw that attaches the wire to the oil pressure sender

wrench (ring spanner) and remove the bolt with an Allen wrench **(see illustration)**.

7 Lift off the signal generator rotor **(see illustration)**.

8 Remove the screw and disconnect the wire from the oil pressure sender **(see illustration)**.

9 Remove the signal generator mounting screws, detach the wiring harness from the grommet and remove the signal generator **(see illustration)**.

Installation

10 Installation is the reverse of the removal steps, with the following additions:

a) *Align the rotor slot with the protrusion on the crankshaft. Tighten the signal*

generator bolt to the torque listed in this Chapter's Specifications.

b) *Use a new gasket on the signal generator cover.*

5 IC igniter - removal, check and installation

Removal

1 Remove the seat and left frame cover (see Chapter 7).

2 On later GSX-R750 and 1100 models, remove the right frame cover, then remove the

mounting screws from the battery undercover and lower the cover out of the way.

3 Remove the mounting screws or nuts and disconnect the electrical connectors **(see illustrations)**.

Check

4 A special tester is required to accurately measure the resistance values across the various terminals of the IC igniter. Take the unit to a Suzuki dealer service department or other repair shop equipped with this tester.

Installation

5 Installation is the reverse of the removal steps.

4.9 Remove the mounting screws, pull the wiring harness grommet out of its notch and remove the signal generator

5.3a On most models, the igniter is mounted beneath the left frame cover (Katana 600/GSX600F shown)

5.3b On late GSX-R models, the battery undercover must be removed and lowered for access to the igniter unit

Chapter 5
Frame, suspension and final drive

Contents

Degrees of difficulty

| **Easy,** suitable for novice with little experience | | **Fairly easy,** suitable for beginner with some experience | | **Fairly difficult,** suitable for competent DIY mechanic | | **Difficult,** suitable for experienced DIY mechanic | | **Very difficult,** suitable for expert DIY or professional | |

Specifications

Steering damper protrusion (1)
1986 through 1988 GSX-R1100	8 mm (0.3 inch)
1989 and 1990 GSX-R1100	2 mm (0.078 inch)
1991 on GSX-R750 and 1100	4 mm (0.157 inch)

Fork spring free length (limit)
GSX-R750
1985 through 1987	377 mm (14.8 inches)
1988	299.5 mm (11.79 inches)
1989	306.5 mm (12.1 inches)
1990	
US	308.5 mm (12.14 inches)
UK	267 mm (10.5 inches)
1991 on	
US and Canada	341 mm (13.4 inches)
UK	267 mm (10.5 inches)

GSX-R1100
1986	459 mm (13.4 inches)
1987 and 1988	463 mm (18.2 inches)
1989	347 mm (13.7 inches)
1990	
US	347 mm (13.7 inches)
UK	277 mm (10.9 inches)
1991 on	277 mm (10.9 inches)

Katana 600 (GSX600F)
1988	411.9 mm (16.2 inches)
1989 on	229.4 mm (11.7 inches)
Katana 750 (GSX750F)	310 mm (12.2 inches)

Katana 1100 (GSX1100F)
1988	342 mm (13.5 inches)
1989 on	366 mm (14.4 inches)

5

Front fork installed position

GSX-R750
1985 through 1987	Inner tube flush with fork bracket
1988 through 1990	Line on fork tube flush with bracket
1991 on	10 mm (0.254 inch) above fork bracket

GSX-R1100
1986 through 1988	Flush with fork bracket
1989	42.5 mm (1.67 inch) above
1990 on	37.5 mm (1.48 inch) above
Katana 600 (GSX600F)	Flush with handlebar bracket
Katana 750 (GSX750F)	Flush with handlebar bracket

Katana 1100 (GSX1100F)
1988	3 mm (0.118 inch) below the upper surface of the triple clamp
1989 on	Not specified

Suspension settings (2)

GSX-R750 (1985 through 1987)
  Front
    Spring preload
Soft	1
Standard	2
Hard	3
With passenger	3

    Damping force
Soft	1
Standard	1
Hard	2
With passenger	2

  Rear
    Spring preload
Soft	180 mm (7.09 inches)
Standard	175 mm (6.89 inches)
Hard	170 mm (6.69 inches)

    Damping force
Soft	2
Standard	3
Hard	4

GSX-R750 (1988)
  Front
    Spring preload
Single rider	4
With passenger	5

    Rebound damping force
Single rider	5
With passenger	2

    Compression damping force
Single rider	6
With passenger	3

  Rear
    Spring preload
Single rider	187 mm (7.4 inches)
With passenger	182 mm (7.2 inches)

    Damping force
Single rider	2
With passenger	4

GSX-R750 (1989)
  Front
    Spring preload
Soft	5
Standard	4
Hard	3
With passenger	3

    Rebound damping force
Soft	8
Standard	5
Hard	2
With passenger	2

Compression damping force
    Soft 9
    Standard 6
    Hard 3
    With passenger 3
  Rear
    Spring preload
      Soft . . . . 190 mm (7.48 inches)
      Standard . . . . 187 mm (7.36 inches)
      Hard . . . . 182 mm (7.16 inches)
    Damping force
      Soft 1
      Standard 2
      Hard 4
      With passenger 4

GSX-R750 (1990)
  Front
    Spring preload
      Soft 5
      Standard 4
      Hard 3
      With passenger 4
    Rebound damping force (US)
      Soft 5
      Standard 4
      Hard 3
      With passenger 4
    Rebound damping force (UK)
      Soft 6
      Standard 5
      Hard 4
      With passenger 5
    Compression damping force (US)
      Soft 9
      Standard 8
      Hard 7
      With passenger 8
    Compression damping force (UK)
      Soft 6
      Standard 5
      Hard 4
      With passenger 5
  Rear
    Spring preload (standard) . . . . 196 mm (7.7 inches)
    Rebound damping force
      Soft 1
      Standard 2
      Hard 3
      With passenger 2
    Compression damping force
      Soft 7
      Standard 6
      Hard 5
      With passenger 6

GSX-R750 (1991 on)
  Front
    Spring preload
      Minimum 7
      Standard 4
      Maximum 1
      With passenger 4
    Rebound damping force (US and Canada)
      Softer . . . . Turn clockwise
      Standard 3
      Harder . . . . Turn counterclockwise (anticlockwise)
      With passenger 3
    Rebound damping force (UK)
      Softer . . . . Turn clockwise
      Standard 5
      Harder . . . . Turn counterclockwise (anticlockwise)
      With passenger 5

5

Suspension settings (2) continued

	GSX-R750 (1991 on)
Compression damping force	
Softer	Turn counterclockwise (anticlockwise)
Standard	5
Harder	Turn clockwise
With passenger	5
Rear	
Spring preload	196 mm (7.7 inch)
Rebound damping force	
Soft	1
Standard	2 to 4
Hard	4
With passenger	2 to 4
Compression damping force	
Soft	Turn counterclockwise (anticlockwise)
Standard	6
Hard	Turn clockwise
With passenger	6
GSX-R1100 (1986 through 1988)	
Front	
Spring preload	
Soft	1
Standard	2
Hard	3
With passenger	2
NEAS setting (US and Canada)	
Soft	1
Standard	2
Hard	3
With passenger	2
NEAS setting (UK)	
Soft	1
Standard	1
Hard	2
With passenger	2
Rear	
Spring preload (1986)	
Soft	191.5 mm (7.54 inches)
Standard	190 mm (7.48 inches)
Hard	188.5 mm (7.42 inches)
With passenger	187 mm (7.36 inches)
Spring preload (1987)	
Soft	180.5 mm (7.11 inches)
Standard	179 mm (7.05 inches)
Hard	177.5 mm (6.99 inches)
With passenger	176 mm (6.93 inches)
Spring preload (1988)	
Soft	179 mm (7.05 inches)
Standard	177.5 mm (6.99 inches)
Hard	176 mm (6.93 inches)
With passenger	174.5 mm (6.87 inches)
Damping force (US and Canada)	
Soft	3
Standard	4
Hard	4
With passenger	4
Damping force (UK)	
Soft	1
Standard	2
Hard	3
With passenger	3
GSX-R1100 (1989)	
Front	
Spring preload	
Soft	6
Standard	5
Hard	4
With passenger	4 or 5

Rebound damping force
  Soft 6
  Standard 4
  Hard 2
  With passenger . . . . 3 or 4
Compression damping force
  Soft 8
  Standard 5
  Hard 3
  With passenger . . . . 4 or 5
Rear
  Spring preload
    Permissible range . . . . 187.2 to 197.2 mm (7.37 to 7.76 inches)
    Standard . . . . 192.2 mm (7.57 inches)
  Damping force
    Soft 1
    Standard 2
    Hard 3
    With passenger . . . . 2 or 3
GSX-R1100 (1990)
  Front
    Spring preload (US)
      Soft 6
      Standard 5
      Hard 4
      With passenger 5
    Spring preload (UK and Canada)
      Soft 5
      Standard 4
      Hard 3
      With passenger 4
    Rebound damping force (US)
      Soft 5
      Standard 4
      Hard 3
      With passenger 4
    Rebound damping force (UK and Canada)
      Soft 4
      Standard 3
      Hard 2
      With passenger 3
    Compression damping force (US)
      Soft 3
      Standard 2
      Hard 1
      With passenger 3
    Compression damping force (UK and Canada)
      Soft 6
      Standard 5
      Hard 4
      With passenger 5
  Rear
    Spring preload (US)
      Soft 2
      Standard 3
      Hard 4
      With passenger 3
    Spring preload (UK and Canada)
      Soft 4
      Standard 5
      Hard 6
      With passenger 5
    Rebound and compression damping force
      Soft . . . . Standard plus one click counterclockwise (anticlockwise)
      Standard . . . . Stamped in shock absorber body
      Hard . . . . Standard plus one click clockwise
      With passenger . . . . Standard setting

5

Suspension settings (2) continued

GSX-R1100 (1991 on)
  Front
    Spring preload (US and Canada)
      Soft   4
      Standard   3
      Hard   2
      With passenger   3
    Spring preload (UK)
      Soft   5
      Standard   4
      Hard   3
      With passenger   4
    Rebound damping force
      Soft   4
      Standard   3
      Hard   2
      With passenger   3
    Compression damping force (US and Canada)
      Soft   6
      Standard   5
      Hard   4
      With passenger   5
    Compression damping force (UK)
      Soft   5
      Standard   4
      Hard   3
      With passenger   4
  Rear
    Spring preload
      Soft   3
      Standard   4
      Hard   5
      With passenger   4
    Rebound and compression damping force
      Soft . . . .   Standard plus one click counterclockwise (anticlockwise)
      Standard . . . .   Stamped in shock absorber body
      Hard . . . .   Standard plus one click clockwise
      With passenger . . . .   Standard setting
Katana 600/GSX600F (1988)
  Front . . . .   Not adjustable
  Rear
    Spring preload
      Limits . . . .   172.3 to 182.3 mm (6.78 to 7.18 inches)
      Standard setting . . . .   177.3 mm (6.98 inches)
Katana 600/GSX600F (1989 on)
  Front
    Damping force
      Soft   1
      Standard   2
      Hard   3
      With passenger . . . .   2 to 3
  Rear
    Spring preload
      Single rider   4
      With passenger . . . .   4 to 6
    Damping force
      Soft   2
      Standard   3
      Hard . . . .   3 to 4
      With passenger . . . .   3 to 4
Katana 750/GSX750F
  Front (all US; all Canada; UK Type I) (3)
    Damping force
      Soft   1
      Standard   2
      Hard   3
      With passenger . . . .   2 or 3

Rear (all US; all Canada; UK Type I) (3)
  Spring preload
    Single rider 4
    With passenger .... 4 to 6
  Damping force
    Soft 1
    Standard 2
    Hard 3
    With passenger .... 2 or 3
Front (UK Type II) (3)
  Damping force
    Soft .... 1 or 2
    Standard 2
    Hard .... 2 or 3
    With passenger or load 3
Rear (UK Type II) (3)
  Spring preload
    Soft .... 182 to 184 mm (7.24 to 7.17 inches)
    Standard .... 182 mm (7.17 inches)
    Hard .... 180 to 182 mm (7.17 to 7.09 inches)
    With passenger or load .... 182 mm (7.17 inches)
  Rebound damping force
    Soft .... 1 or 2
    Standard 2
    Hard .... 2 or 3
    With passenger or load 2
  Compression damping force
    Soft .... Standard to standard plus 5 clicks out
    Standard .... 10+/-2 clicks out from full clockwise (4)
    Hard .... Standard to standard minus 5 clicks
    With passenger .... Standard minus 5 clicks
    With single rider and 30 kg (66 lb) load .... Standard minus 5 clicks
    With passenger and 30 kg (66 lb) load .... Zero (full clockwise)
Katana 1100/GSX1100F (1988)
  Front .... Not adjustable
  Rear
    Spring preload
      Soft 1
      Standard .... 2 to 5
      Hard 5
      With passenger or load .... 4 to 5
    Damping force
      Soft 1
      Standard .... 2 to 4
      Hard 4
      Single rider with 30 kg (66 lb) load .... 3 to 4
      With passenger and 30 kg (66 lb) load .... 4 to 4
Katana 1100/GSX1100F (1989 on)
  Front
    Spring preload 4
  Rear
    Spring preload
      Single rider 2
      With passenger 4
    Rebound damping force
      Soft 1
      Standard 2
      Hard .... 2 or 3
    Compression damping force
      Soft and standard .... Minimum
      Hard 10
      With passenger 5

1. Change the adjustment by turning the damper bracket. Don't turn the nut and locknut on the damper shaft.
2. Don't leave any suspension adjuster between settings; in most cases this will give the equivalent of the stiffest setting.
3. Type I suspension uses a rear shock without remote reservoir; Type II suspension uses a rear shock with remote reservoir.
4. The standard position is indicated by a paint mark on the adjuster knob that aligns with an indicator on the adjuster body.

5

Torque specifications

GSX-R750 (1985 through 1987)

Handlebar holder bolts	15 to 25 Nm (11 to 18 ft-lbs)
Handlebar holder set bolts	6 to 10 Nm (4.5 to 7.0 ft-lbs)
Front fork cap bolt	15 to 30 Nm (11.0 to 21.5 ft-lbs)
Triple clamp bolts	20 to 30 Nm (14.5 to 21.5 ft-lbs)
Front fork damper rod bolt	54 to 70 Nm (39.5 to 50.5 ft-lbs)
Front fork damping force adjuster mounting bolt	6 to 8 Nm (4.5 to 6.0 ft-lbs)
Steering bearing nut initial torque	40 to 50 to Nm (29 to 36 ft-lbs)
Steering stem top nut	30 to 40 Nm (21.5 to 29.0 ft-lbs)
Swingarm pivot nut	50 to 80 Nm (36 to 58 ft-lbs)
Rear shock absorber mounting nuts	40 to 60 Nm (29.0 to 43.5 ft-lbs)
Cushion lever pivot bolt nuts	70 to 100 Nm (50.5 to 72.5 ft-lbs)
Rear sprocket nuts	48 to 72 Nm (35 to 52 ft-lbs)

GSX-R750 (1988 and 1989)

Handlebar holder bolts	15 to 25 Nm (11 to 18 ft-lbs)
Handlebar holder set bolts	7 to 11 Nm (5 to 8 ft-lbs)
Front fork cap bolt	15 to 30 Nm (11.0 to 21.5 ft-lbs)
Upper triple clamp bolts	35 to 55 Nm (25.5 to 40.0 ft-lbs)
Lower triple clamp bolts	25 to 40 Nm (18 to 29 ft-lbs)
Front fork damper rod bolt	30 to 40 Nm (21.5 to 29.0 ft-lbs)
Front fork damping force adjuster mounting bolt	15 to 20 Nm (11.0 to 14.5 ft-lbs)
Front fork spring adjuster locknut	25 to 30 Nm (18.0 to 21.5 ft-lbs)
Steering bearing nut initial torque	40 to 60 Nm (29.0 to 43.5 ft-lbs)
Steering stem top nut	30 to 40 Nm (21.5 to 29.0 ft-lbs)
Swingarm pivot nut	85 to 115 Nm (61.5 to 83.0 ft-lbs)
Rear shock absorber mounting nuts	40 to 60 Nm (29.0 to 43.5 ft-lbs)
Cushion lever pivot bolt nuts	110 to 160 Nm (79.5 to 115.5 ft-lbs)
Rear sprocket nuts	48 to 72 Nm (35 to 52 ft-lbs)

GSX-R750 (1990)

Handlebar holder bolts	15 to 25 Nm (11 to 18 ft-lbs)
Handlebar holder set bolts	7 to 11 Nm (5 to 8 ft-lbs)
Front fork cap bolt	
US	15 to 30 Nm (11.0 to 21.5 ft-lbs)
UK	30 to 40 Nm (21.5 to 29.0 ft-lbs)
Triple clamp bolts (US)	22 to 35 Nm (16.0 to 25.5 ft-lbs)
Triple clamp bolts (UK)	
Upper	35 to 55 Nm (25.5 to 40.0 ft-lbs)
Lower	25 to 40 Nm (18 to 29 ft-lbs)
Front fork damper rod bolt	30 to 40 Nm (21.5 to 29.0 ft-lbs)
Front fork damping force adjuster mounting bolt	15 to 20 Nm (11.0 to 14.5 ft-lbs)
Front fork spring adjuster locknut (US)	25 to 30 Nm (18.0 to 21.5 ft-lbs)
Front fork damping adjuster locknut (UK)	18 to 22 Nm (13 to 16 ft-lbs)
Front fork cap bolt stopper screw (UK)	1 Nm (0.7 ft-lb)
Steering bearing nut initial torque	40 to 60 Nm (29.0 to 43.5 ft-lbs)
Steering stem top nut	
US	50 to 80 Nm (36 to 58 ft-lbs)
UK	30 to 40 Nm (21.5 to 29.0 ft-lbs)
Swingarm pivot nut	85 to 115 Nm (61.5 to 83.0 ft-lbs)
Swingarm pivot adjuster locknut	60 to 70 Nm (43.5 to 50.5 ft-lbs)
Rear shock absorber mounting nuts	40 to 60 Nm (29.0 to 43.5 ft-lbs)
Cushion lever pivot bolt nuts	110 to 160 Nm (79.5 to 115.5 ft-lbs)
Rear sprocket nuts	48 to 72 Nm (35 to 52 ft-lbs)

GSX-R750 (1991 on)

Handlebar holder bolts	15 to 25 Nm (11 to 18 ft-lbs)
Handlebar holder set bolts	7 to 11 Nm (5 to 8 ft-lbs)
Front fork cap bolt	30 to 40 Nm (21.5 to 29.0 ft-lbs)
Triple clamp bolts	22 to 35 Nm (16.0 to 25.5 ft-lbs)
Front fork damper rod bolt	30 to 40 Nm (21.5 to 29.0 ft-lbs)
Front fork compression damping adjuster	15 to 20 Nm (11.0 to 14.5 ft-lbs)
Front fork rebound damping adjuster locknut	18 to 22 Nm (13 to 16 ft-lbs)
Steering bearing nut initial torque	40 to 60 Nm (29.0 to 43.5 ft-lbs)
Steering stem top nut	50 to 80 Nm (36 to 58 ft-lbs)
Swingarm pivot nut	85 to 115 Nm (61.5 to 83.0 ft-lbs)
Swingarm pivot adjuster locknut	60 to 70 Nm (43.5 to 50.5 ft-lbs)
Rear shock absorber mounting nuts	40 to 60 Nm (29.0 to 43.5 ft-lbs)
Cushion lever pivot bolt nuts	110 to 160 Nm (79.5 to 115.5 ft-lbs)
Rear sprocket nuts	48 to 72 Nm (35 to 52 ft-lbs)

GSX-R1100 (1986 through 1988)

Handlebar holder bolts	15 to 25 Nm (11 to 18 ft-lbs)
Handlebar holder set bolts	6 to 10 Nm (4.5 to 7.0 ft-lbs)
Front fork cap bolt	15 to 30 Nm (11.0 to 21.5 ft-lbs)
Triple clamp bolts	
Upper	20 to 30 Nm (14.5 to 21.5 ft-lbs)
Lower (1986)	15 to 25 Nm (11 to 18 ft-lbs)
Lower (1987 and 1988)	20 to 25 Nm (14.5 to 18.0 ft-lbs)
Front fork damper rod bolt	54 to 70 Nm (39.5 to 50.5 ft-lbs)
NEAS unit mounting bolts	6 to 8 Nm (4.5 to 6.0 ft-lbs)
Steering bearing nut initial torque	40 to 50 Nm (29 to 36 ft-lbs)
Steering stem top nut	30 to 40 Nm (21.5 to 29.0 ft-lbs)
Steering damper inner and outer nuts	15 to 20 Nm (11 to 14 ft-lbs)
Steering damper bracket bolt	20 to 25 Nm (14 to 18 ft-lbs)
Swingarm pivot nut	55 to 85 Nm (40.0 to 61.5 ft-lbs)
Rear shock absorber mounting nuts	40 to 60 Nm (29.0 to 43.5 ft-lbs)
Cushion lever pivot bolt nuts	70 to 100 Nm (50.5 to 72.5 ft-lbs)
Rear sprocket nuts	48 to 72 Nm (35 to 52 ft-lbs)

GSX-R1100 (1989 on)

Handlebar holder mounting bolts	
1989	50 to 60 Nm (36.0 to 43.5 ft-lbs)
1990	18 to 28 Nm (13 to 20 ft-lbs)
1991 on	10 to 16 Nm (7.0 to 11.5 ft-lbs)
Handlebar holder mounting nuts	
1989	22 to 35 Nm (16.0 to 25.5 ft-lbs)
1990 on	10 to 16 Nm (7.0 to 11.5 ft-lbs)
Front fork cap bolt	15 to 30 Nm (11.0 to 21.5 ft-lbs)
Triple clamp bolts	22 to 35 Nm (16.0 to 25.5 ft-lbs)
Front fork damper rod bolt	34 to 46 Nm (24.5 to 33.5 ft-lbs)
Steering bearing nut initial torque	40 to 50 Nm (29 to 36 ft-lbs)
Steering stem top nut	50 to 80 Nm (36 to 58 ft-lbs)
Swingarm pivot nut	85 to 115 Nm (61.5 to 83.0 ft-lbs)
Swingarm pivot adjuster locknut (1990 on)	60 to 70 Nm (43.5 to 50.5 ft-lbs)
Rear shock absorber mounting nuts	40 to 60 Nm (29.0 to 43.5 ft-lbs)
Cushion lever pivot bolt nuts	110 to 160 Nm (79.5 to 115.5 ft-lbs)
Rear sprocket nuts	48 to 72 Nm (35 to 52 ft-lbs)

Katana 600/GSX600F

Handlebar holder mounting bolt	50 to 60 Nm (36.0 to 43.5 ft-lbs)
Handlebar holder mounting nut	20 to 30 Nm (14.5 to 21.5 ft-lbs)
Handlebar set bolt	6 to 10 Nm (4.5 to 7.0 ft-lbs)
Triple clamp bolts	
Upper	15 to 25 Nm (11 to 18 ft-lbs)
Lower	25 to 40 Nm (18 to 29 ft-lbs)
Front fork damper rod bolt	15 to 25 Nm (11 to 18 ft-lbs)
Steering bearing nut initial torque	40 to 50 Nm (29 to 36 ft-lbs)
Steering stem bolt	35 to 55 Nm (25.5 to 40.0 ft-lbs)
Swingarm pivot nut	55 to 88 Nm (40.0 to 63.5 ft-lbs)
Rear shock absorber mounting nuts	48 to 72 Nm (35 to 52 ft-lbs)
Cushion lever rod nuts	84 to 120 Nm (60.5 to 87.0 ft-lbs)
Cushion lever mounting nut	132 to 192 Nm (95.5 to 139.0 ft-lbs)
Rear sprocket nuts	48 to 72 Nm (35 to 52 ft-lbs)

Katana 750/GSX750F

Handlebar holder mounting nut	27 to 42 Nm (19.5 to 30.5 ft-lbs)
Handlebar holder set bolt	
US	15 to 25 Nm (11 to 18 ft-lbs)
UK	6 to 10 Nm (4.5 to 7.0 ft-lbs)
Triple clamp bolts	
Upper	15 to 25 Nm (11 to 18 ft-lbs)
Lower	25 to 40 Nm (18 to 29 ft-lbs)
Front fork damper rod bolt	15 to 25 Nm (11 to 18 ft-lbs)
Steering bearing nut initial torque	40 to 50 Nm (29 to 36 ft-lbs)
Steering stem bolt	35 to 55 Nm (25.5 to 40.0 ft-lbs)
Swingarm pivot nut	55 to 88 Nm (40.0 to 63.5 ft-lbs)
Rear shock absorber mounting nuts	48 to 72 Nm (35 to 52 ft-lbs)
Cushion lever rod nuts	84 to 120 Nm (60.5 to 87.0 ft-lbs)
Cushion lever mounting nut	132 to 192 Nm (95.5 to 139.0 ft-lbs)
Rear sprocket nuts	48 to 72 Nm (35 to 52 ft-lbs)

5

Torque specifications (continued)

Katana 1100/GSX1100F

Handlebar mounting bolt	25 to 35 Nm (18.0 to 25.5 ft-lbs)
Triple clamp bolts	
Upper	20 to 30 Nm (14.5 to 21.5 ft-lbs)
Lower	15 to 25 Nm (11 to 18 ft-lbs)
Front fork damper rod bolt	15 to 25 Nm (11 to 18 ft-lbs)
Steering bearing nut initial torque	40 to 50 Nm (29 to 36 ft-lbs)
Steering stem bolt	35 to 55 Nm (25.5 to 40.0 ft-lbs)
Swingarm pivot nut	55 to 88 Nm (40.0 to 63.5 ft-lbs)
Rear shock absorber mounting nuts	40 to 60 Nm (29.0 to 43.5 ft-lbs)
Cushion lever nuts	70 to 100 Nm (50.5 to 72.5 ft-lbs)
Rear sprocket nuts	48 to 72 Nm (35 to 52 ft-lbs)

1 General information

The machines covered by this manual use a full cradle frame. The right downtube on GSX-R models is detachable, which allows for easy engine removal. The front subframe is detachable on Katana (GSX-F) models.

Front forks of the conventional coil spring, hydraulically-damped telescopic type are used on the following models:

a) GSX-R750, 1985 through 1987
b) GSX-R1100, 1986 through 1988
c) Katana 600 (GSX600F), all years
d) Katana 750 (GSX750F), all years
e) Katana 1100 (GSX1100F), 1988

Cartridge type front forks are used on the following models:

a) GSX-R750, 1988 and later
b) GSX-R1100, 1989 and later
c) Katana 1100 (GSX1100F), 1989 and later

The cartridge type forks used on 1991 and later GSX-R models are of the inverted type (inner fork tube on the bottom of the fork, rather than on the top).

The rear suspension is Suzuki's Full Floater design, which consists of a single shock absorber, a rocker arm, two tie-rods and a swingarm.

The final drive uses an endless chain (which means it doesn't have a master link). A rubber damper is installed between the rear wheel coupling and the wheel.

2 Frame - inspection and repair

1 The frame should not require attention unless accident damage has occurred. In most cases, frame replacement is the only satisfactory remedy for such damage. A few frame specialists have the jigs and other equipment necessary for straightening the frame to the required standard of accuracy, but even then there is no simple way of assessing to what extent the frame may have been over stressed.

2 After the machine has accumulated a lot of miles, the frame should be examined closely for signs of cracking or splitting at the welded joints. Rust can also cause weakness at these joints. Loose engine mount bolts can cause ovaling or fracturing of the mounting tabs. Minor damage can often be repaired by welding, depending on the extent and nature of the damage.

3 Remember that a frame which is out of alignment will cause handling problems. If misalignment is suspected as the result of an accident, it will be necessary to strip the machine completely so the frame can be thoroughly checked.

3 Footpegs and brackets - removal and installation

1 If it's only necessary to detach the footpeg from the bracket, pry the C-clip off the pivot pin (see illustrations), slide out the pin and detach the footpeg from the bracket. Be careful not to lose the spring.

2 Installation is the reverse of removal, but be sure to install the spring correctly.

3 If it's necessary to remove the entire bracket from the frame, remove the bolts that secure the bracket to the frame, then detach the footpeg and bracket.

4 Installation is the reverse of removal.

4 Side and centerstand - maintenance

1 The centerstand (if equipped) pivots on two bolts attached to the frame (see illustration). Periodically, remove the pivot bolts and grease them thoroughly to avoid excessive wear.

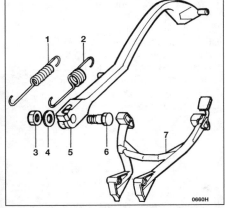

4.1 Centerstand and sidestand details (Katana 600/GSX600F shown)

1 Spring
2 Spring
3 Nut
4 Washer
5 Sidestand
6 Pivot bolt
7 Centerstand

3.1a To detach a footpeg from the bracket, remove the C-clip and push out the pivot pin (arrowed) (Katana 1100/GSX1100F shown)

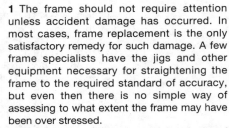

3.1b The footpeg brackets are bolted to the frame (Katana 1100/GSX1100F shown)

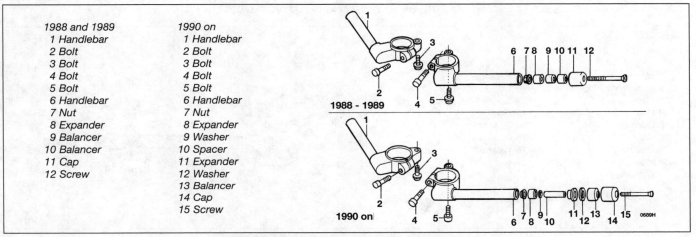

1 Trim plug
2 Bolt
3 Bolt
4 Handlebar
5 Handlebar

6 Spacer
7 Balancer
8 Cap
9 Screw

0661H

5.1a Handlebar details - 1985 through 1987 GSX-R750

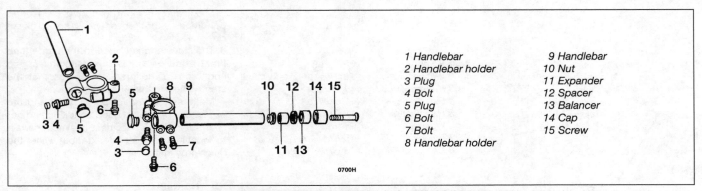

1988 and 1989
1 Handlebar
2 Bolt
3 Bolt
4 Bolt
5 Bolt
6 Handlebar
7 Nut
8 Expander
9 Balancer
10 Balancer
11 Cap
12 Screw

1990 on
1 Handlebar
2 Bolt
3 Bolt
4 Bolt
5 Bolt
6 Handlebar
7 Nut
8 Expander
9 Washer
10 Spacer
11 Expander
12 Washer
13 Balancer
14 Cap
15 Screw

1988 - 1989

1990 on

0689H

5.1b Handlebar details - 1988 and later GSX-R750

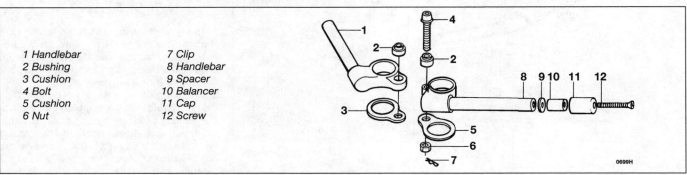

1 Handlebar
2 Handlebar holder
3 Plug
4 Bolt
5 Plug
6 Bolt
7 Bolt
8 Handlebar holder

9 Handlebar
10 Nut
11 Expander
12 Spacer
13 Balancer
14 Cap
15 Screw

0700H

5.1c Handlebar details - 1986 through 1988 GSX-R1100

1 Handlebar
2 Bushing
3 Cushion
4 Bolt
5 Cushion
6 Nut

7 Clip
8 Handlebar
9 Spacer
10 Balancer
11 Cap
12 Screw

0699H

5.1d Handlebar details - 1989 and later GSX-R1100

5

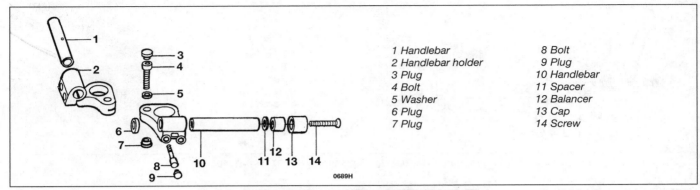

1 Handlebar
2 Handlebar holder
3 Plug
4 Bolt
5 Washer
6 Plug
7 Plug

8 Bolt
9 Plug
10 Handlebar
11 Spacer
12 Balancer
13 Cap
14 Screw

0689H

5.1e Handlebar details - Katana 600/GSX600F

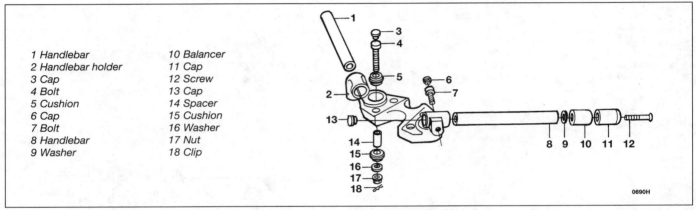

1 Handlebar
2 Handlebar holder
3 Cap
4 Bolt
5 Cushion
6 Cap
7 Bolt
8 Handlebar
9 Washer

10 Balancer
11 Cap
12 Screw
13 Cap
14 Spacer
15 Cushion
16 Washer
17 Nut
18 Clip

0690H

5.2a Handlebar details - Katana 750/GSX750F

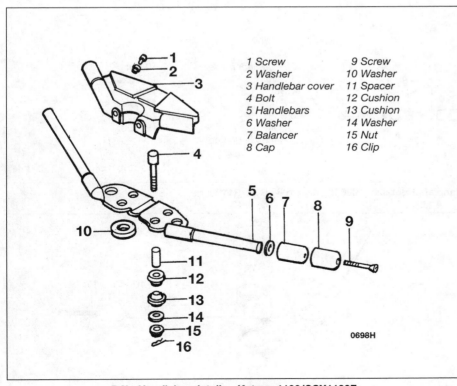

1 Screw
2 Washer
3 Handlebar cover
4 Bolt
5 Handlebars
6 Washer
7 Balancer
8 Cap

9 Screw
10 Washer
11 Spacer
12 Cushion
13 Cushion
14 Washer
15 Nut
16 Clip

0698H

5.2b Handlebar details - Katana 1100/GSX1100F

2 Make sure the return spring is in good condition. A broken or weak spring is an obvious safety hazard.

3 The sidestand is bolted to the frame **(see illustration 4.1)**. An extension spring anchored to the bracket ensures that the stand is held in the retracted position.

4 Make sure the pivot bolt is tight and the extension spring is in good condition and not over stretched. An accident is almost certain to occur if the stand extends while the machine is in motion.

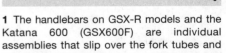

5   Handlebars -
     removal and installation

1 The handlebars on GSX-R models and the Katana 600 (GSX600F) are individual assemblies that slip over the fork tubes and are secured by clamping and positioning bolts **(see illustrations)**.

2 The handlebars on Katana 750 (GSX750F) models are individual assemblies that slip into the steering head, each being retained with a pinch bolt **(see illustration)**. The handlebars on Katana 1100 (GSX1100F) models are combined into one assembly that bolts to the steering stem and has a cover on top **(see illustration)**.

3 If the handlebars must be removed for access to other components, such as the forks or the steering head, simply detach the handlebar(s) and move them out of the way. It's not necessary to disconnect the cables, wires or hoses, but it is a good idea to support the assembly with a piece of wire or rope, to avoid unnecessary strain on the cables, wires and (on the right side) the brake hose.

4 To remove the grip portion of the handlebar, refer to Chapter 6 for the *master cylinder removal procedure* (right handlebar and left handlebar on hydraulic clutch models) and Chapter 8 for the throttle cable/switch housing and choke cable/switch housing removal procedures. Remove the screw from the end of the grip **(see illustration)**, then detach the grip components from the handlebar.

5 Check the handlebars for cracks and distortion and replace them if any undesirable conditions are found.

6 Installation is the reverse of the removal steps. Tighten the bolts to the torques listed in this Chapter's Specifications.

6 Forks -
removal and installation

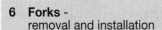

Removal

1 Support the bike securely so it can't be knocked over during this procedure.

2 Remove the fairing panels as needed for removal access (see Chapter 7).

3 1986 through 1988 GSX-R1100 models: Disconnect the electrical connectors for the NEAS units.

4 Remove the front brake calipers and front wheel (see Chapter 6).

5 Remove the front fender (see Chapter 7).

6 Remove the handlebars (see Section 5). Support them so the cables, wires and brake hose aren't strained or kinked.

5.4 Remove the screw from the end of the grip to separate the handlebar components

7 Remove any wiring harness clamps or straps from the fork tubes. On late GSX-R750 and GSX-R1100 models, detach the steering damper from the right front fork (see Section 10).

8 If you're planning to disassemble the forks, loosen the cap bolt at the top of each fork (all except Katana 1100/GSX1100F) or press down on the fork cap and remove the retaining ring (Katana 1100/GSX1100F). Don't remove the cap bolts yet.

9 Loosen the fork upper and lower triple clamp bolts **(see illustrations)**, then twist the fork tubes and slide them downward and out of the triple clamps **(see illustration)**.

Installation

10 Slide each fork leg into the lower triple clamp.

11 Slide the fork legs up, installing the tops of the tubes into the upper triple clamp.

12 The remainder of installation is the reverse of the removal procedure, with the following additions:

a) Position the fork in the triple clamp at the level listed in this Chapter's Specifications.

b) Be sure to tighten the triple clamp bolts to

6.9a Remove the upper triple clamp bolts (late GSX-R1100 shown) . . .

the torque listed in this Chapter's Specifications.

c) Tighten the caliper mounting bolts to the torque listed in the Chapter 6 Specifications.

d) Fill the fork with oil to the correct level (see Chapter 1). Be sure to pump the fork until all air bubbles are removed. It's a good idea to fill the fork to the top temporarily so you can see the bubbles better, then draw off fluid to the specified level after all the bubbles are removed.

e) Pump the front brake lever several times to bring the pads into contact with the discs.

7 Conventional forks -
disassembly, inspection and reassembly

Disassembly

1 Remove the forks following the procedure in Section 6. Work on one fork leg at a time to avoid mixing up the parts.

2 On GSX-R models, remove the damping force adjuster or NEAS unit from the bottom of the fork.

6.9b . . . and the lower triple clamp bolts (late GSX-R1100 shown) . . .

6.9c . . . and lower the fork away from the machine

5

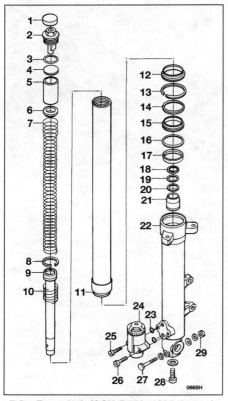

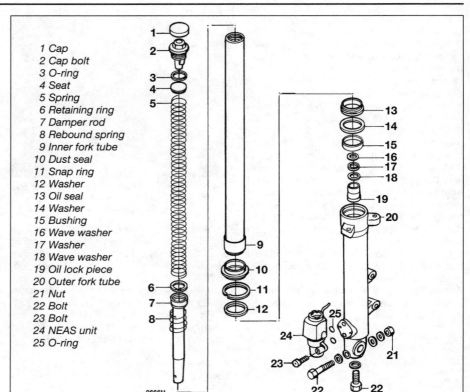

7.3a Front fork (GSX-R750, 1985 through 1987) - exploded view

1 Fork cap	*16 Washer*
2 Cap bolt	*17 Bushing*
3 O-ring	*18 Wave washer*
4 Seat	*19 Washer*
5 Spacer	*20 Wave washer*
6 Spring guide	*21 Oil lock piece*
7 Spring	*22 Outer fork tube*
8 Circlip	*23 O-ring*
9 Damper rod	*24 Damping force*
10 Rebound spring	*adjuster*
11 Inner fork tube	*25 Bolt*
12 Dust seal	*26 Bolt*
13 Snap ring	*27 Bolt*
14 Washer	*28 Bolt*
15 Oil seal	*29 Nut*

7.3b Front fork (GSX-R1100, 1986 to 1988) - exploded view

1 Cap	
2 Cap bolt	
3 O-ring	
4 Seat	
5 Spring	
6 Retaining ring	
7 Damper rod	
8 Rebound spring	
9 Inner fork tube	
10 Dust seal	
11 Snap ring	
12 Washer	
13 Oil seal	
14 Washer	
15 Bushing	
16 Wave washer	
17 Washer	
18 Wave washer	
19 Oil lock piece	
20 Outer fork tube	
21 Nut	
22 Bolt	
23 Bolt	
24 NEAS unit	
25 O-ring	

7.3c Front fork (Katana 600/GSX600F and Katana 1100/GSX1100F, 1988) - exploded view

1 Cap	*11 Dust seal*
2 Stopper ring	*12 Retainer*
3 Cap	*13 Oil seal*
4 O-ring	*14 Washer*
5 Spacer	*15 Bushing*
6 Washer	*16 Oil lock piece*
7 Seat	*17 Outer fork tube*
8 Damper rod and	*18 Nut*
rebound spring	*19 Bolt*
9 Inner fork tube	*20 Bolt*
10 Bushing	

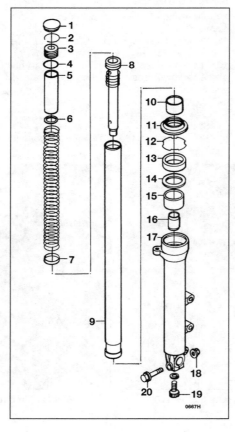

3 Remove the fork cap bolt and take out the upper internal components **(see illustrations)**.

4 Invert the fork assembly over a container. Pump the fork in-and-out several times to pump out the oil, then allow the remaining oil to drain for several minutes.

5 Prevent the damper rod from turning using a holding handle and adapter **(see illustration)**. Unscrew the Allen bolt at the bottom of the outer tube and retrieve the copper washer **(see illustration)**. **Note**: *If you don't have access to these special tools, you can fabricate your own by grinding a taper on the end of a suitable piece of square stock welded to a socket.*

6 Pull out the damper rod and the rebound spring. Don't remove the Teflon ring from the damper rod; the damper rod is sold as an assembly, so if the ring is worn, you'll need a new damper rod.

7 Pry the dust seal from the outer tube **(see illustration)**.

8 Pry the retaining ring from its groove in the outer tube **(see illustrations)**. Remove the ring from the fork tube.

9 Hold the outer tube and yank the inner tube upward, repeatedly (like a slide hammer), until the seal and outer tube guide bushing pop loose.

10 GSX-R models: remove the wave washer, plain washer and wave washer.

11 Slide the oil seal, washer and guide bushings from the inner tube.

12 Remove the oil lock piece.

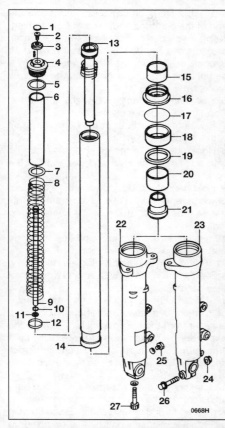

7.3d Front fork (Katana 600/GSX600F and Katana 750/GSX750F, 1989 on) - exploded view

1 Cap	16 Dust seal
2 Screw	17 Oil seal stopper
3 Damping force	ring
adjuster	18 Oil seal
4 Cap bolt	19 Oil seal retainer
5 O-ring	20 Bushing
6 Spacer	21 Oil lock piece
7 Spring seat	22 Right outer fork
8 Spring	tube
9 Inner rod	23 Left outer fork
10 O-ring	tube
11 Washer	24 Nut
12 Seat	25 Oil lock piece
13 Damper rod	stopper bolt
14 Damper rod ring	26 Bolt
15 Bushing	27 Bolt

Inspection

13 Clean all parts in solvent and blow them dry with compressed air, if available. Check the inner and outer fork tubes, the guide bushings and the damper rod for score marks, scratches, flaking of the chrome and excessive or abnormal wear. Look for dents in the tubes and replace them if any are found. Check the fork seal seat for nicks, gouges and scratches. If damage is evident, leaks will occur around the seal-to-outer tube junction. Replace worn or defective parts with new ones.

7.5a This is the tool that keeps the damper rod from turning - the corners of the tapered section bite into the round hole in the damper to hold it

7.7 Pry the dust seal out of the outer tube with a small screwdriver

7.8b . . . and slide it off the inner fork tube

14 Have the fork inner tube checked for runout at a dealer service department or other repair shop.

> ⚠ **Warning: If it is bent, it should not be straightened; replace it with a new one.**

15 Measure the overall length of the long spring and check it for cracks and other damage. Compare the length to the minimum length listed in this Chapter's Specifications. If it's defective or sagged, replace both fork springs with new ones. Never replace only one spring.

Reassembly

16 Assembly is the reverse of the disassembly steps, with the following additions:
a) Use thread locking agent on the threads of the damper rod bolt.

7.5b Hold the damper rod and remove the screw with an Allen wrench

7.8a Pry the retaining ring (arrowed) out of its groove . . .

7.16 Install the guide bushing and seal with a driver like this one

b) Be careful not to scratch the Teflon coating on the guide bushings.
c) Use thread locking agent on the NEAS unit mounting bolts (GSX-R1100 only).
d) Install the guide bushing and oil seal in the outer tube with a seal driver (Suzuki tool no. 09940-50012) **(see illustration)**. If you don't have access to one of these, it is recommended that you take the assembly to a Suzuki dealer service department or other motorcycle repair shop to have the seal driven in. If you are very careful, the seal can be driven in with a hammer and a drift punch. Work around the circumference of the seal, tapping gently on the outer edge of the seal until it's seated. Be careful if you distort the

5

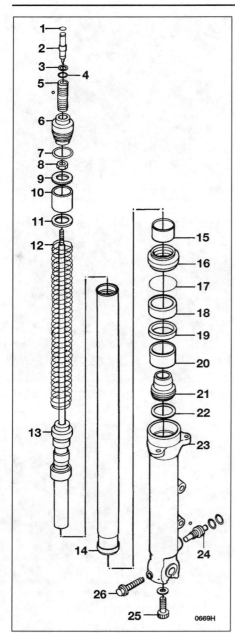

8.1 Front fork (1988 through 1990 US GSX-R750 models; 1988 and 1989 UK GSX-R750 models) - exploded view (1989 and later Katana 1100/GSX1100F similar)

1 O-ring	14 Inner fork tube
2 Adjuster	15 Bushing
3 O-ring	16 Dust seal
4 Expander	17 Stopper ring
5 Adjuster	18 Oil seal
6 Cap bolt	19 Seal spacer
7 O-ring	20 Bushing
8 Nut	21 Oil lock piece
9 Upper spring seat	22 O-ring
10 Spacer	23 Outer fork tube
11 Lower spring seat	24 Adjuster
12 Spring	25 Bolt
13 Cartridge	26 Bolt

seal, you'll have to disassemble the fork again and end up taking it to a dealer anyway!

e) If the oil lock piece has a notch for a bolt, align the notch with the bolt hole. If it has a flat, align it with the flat in the end of the damper rod.

f) Compress the fork fully and add the recommended type and quantity of fork oil (see Chapter 1).

g) Install the fork spring with the closely wound coils at the top.

8 Cartridge forks - disassembly, inspection and reassembly

GSX-R750 (1988 through 1990 US models; 1988 and 1989 UK models) and Katana 1100/GSX1100F (1989 and later)

Disassembly

1 Unscrew the fork cap until it separates from the fork **(see illustration)**.

2 Slip the inner fork tube down to provide access to the spring adjuster locknut. Hold the adjuster with a wrench and loosen the locknut (turn it away from the adjuster) with another wrench **(see illustration)**.

3 Unscrew the cap bolt from the fork rod, then remove the spring retainer, spacer and spring seat. Pull the spring out of the fork tube.

4 Hold the fork upside down and pump the fork rod several times to force out the oil. Leave the fork rod upside down over a container for several minutes to let the remaining oil drain out.

5 Hold the cartridge from turning with Suzuki tool 09940-31710 or equivalent while you remove the damper rod bolt from the bottom of the fork with an Allen wrench. The tool consists of a hollow tube that fits over the fork

rod with a fitting on one end that fits into the end of the cartridge and keeps it from turning. **Note**: *If you don't have access to the special tool, remove the damper rod bolt with an air wrench. If you don't have an air wrench, a dealer can do this when you go to buy replacement parts.*

6 Take the cartridge out of the fork tube. Don't try to disassemble it.

7 Pry the dust seal out of the outer fork tube with a small screwdriver.

8 Hook one end of the oil seal retaining ring with a small screwdriver and pry it out of the bore.

9 Hold the outer tube and yank the inner tube upward, repeatedly (like a slide hammer), until the seal and outer tube guide bushing pop loose.

10 Remove the oil lock piece from the bottom of the outer tube.

11 Remove the guide bushings. If necessary, spread them slightly with a screwdriver so they can be slipped off.

12 Unscrew the spring adjuster from the cap bolt, then unscrew the rebound damping adjuster from the spring adjuster. Remove the expander, O-ring and steel ball **(see illustration 8.1)**. **Note**: *These parts are small and easily lost. It's a good idea to keep them in a container.*

13 Unscrew the compression damping adjuster from the outer fork tube. Remove the expander, O-ring and steel ball. Place them in a container so they won't be lost or mixed up with the rebound damping adjuster parts. **Note**: *Don't try to disassemble the compression damping adjuster.*

Inspection

14 Perform Steps 13 through 15 of Section 7 to inspect the fork.

15 Check the cartridge for wear or damage. Don't try to disassemble it; install a new one if any defects are found.

16 Replace the oil seal, dust seal and both guide bushings whenever the fork is disassembled.

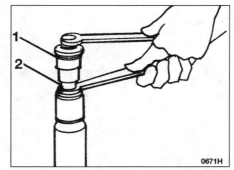

8.2 Hold the adjuster with one wrench and loosen the damper rod locknut with another wrench

1 Adjuster   2 Damper rod locknut

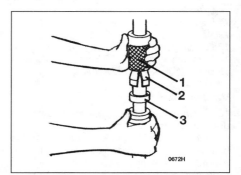

8.18a Position the Suzuki special tool or equivalent against the seal, then use the driver portion of the tool to tap the seal into position

1 Seal driver   3 Fork seal
2 Seal driver adapter

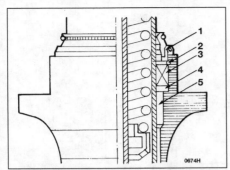

8.18b Fork seal details - 1988 through 1990 US GSX-R750 models; 1988 and 1989 UK GSX-R750 models; 1989 and later Katana 1100/GSX1100F models

1 Dust seal
2 Oil seal stopper ring
3 Oil seal
4 Oil seal retainer
5 Bushing

17 Replace the O-rings for the compression damping adjuster and rebound damping adjuster whenever the fork is disassembled.

Reassembly

18 Assembly is the reverse of the disassembly steps, with the following additions:
a) Drive in a new outer tube guide bushing, retainer and new oil seal with Suzuki tool no. 09940-501112 or equivalent **(see illustration)**. Assemble the seals and bushings in the correct order, with the seals facing in the proper direction **(see illustration)**.
b) Use thread locking agent on the damper rod bolt.

GSX-R750 (1990 and later UK models)

Disassembly

19 Remove the stop ring from the spring adjuster at the top of the fork, then remove the adjuster bolt and adjuster **(see illustration)**.
20 Remove the damper rod bolt from the bottom of the fork with an Allen wrench. The tension of the fork spring should keep the damper rod from turning, but if it doesn't, remove the bolt with an air wrench. If you don't have an air wrench, a dealer can remove the bolt for you when you go to buy replacement parts.
21 Unscrew the fork cap bolt from the fork, then remove the stop screw from the cap with a 2 mm Allen wrench.
22 Press down on the spacer with Suzuki special tool 09940-94910 or equivalent **(see illustration)**. Slip the plate of the special tool between the fork cap locknut and the spacer seat (on top of the spacer).
23 Hold the fork cap with a wrench and turn the locknut away from the fork cap with another wrench. Unscrew the fork cap from the fork rod.
24 Remove the spacer seat, the spacer, the

1 Adjuster bolt
2 O-ring
3 Cap bolt and adjuster
4 O-ring
5 Rubber seat
6 O-ring
7 Expander
8 Stopper ring
9 O-ring
10 Upper adjuster
11 Spring spacer, guide and joint
12 Nut
13 Stop screw
14 Spring
15 Cartridge
16 Centering plate
17 Outer fork tube
18 O-ring
19 Oil seal case
20 Snap ring
21 Bushing
22 Seal spacer
23 Oil seal
24 Stopper ring
25 Dust seal
26 Bushing
27 Inner fork tube
28 Expander
29 O-ring
30 Compression damping adjuster
31 Gasket
32 Bolt

8.19 Front fork (1990 and later UK GSX-R750 models) - exploded view

spring seat and the rubber seat from the fork rod. Pull the spring out of the fork tube.
25 Loosen the locknut on the rebound damping adjuster, then unscrew the adjuster from the fork rod.
26 Hold the fork upside down over a pan and

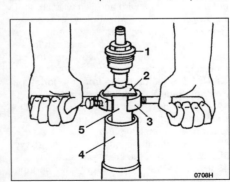

8.22 Press down on the spring spacer to compress the spring, then slip the plate between the spacer and the damper rod locknut

1 Fork cap bolt
2 Tool plate
3 Tool handle
4 Fork tube
5 Spacer

pump it several times to drain the oil. Leave the fork upside down over the pan for several minutes to let the remaining oil drain out.
27 Remove the cartridge and bottom plate from the fork. Don't try to disassemble the cartridge.
28 Pry the dust seal out of its bore with a small screwdriver. Pry one end of the oil seal retaining ring out of its groove, then slide the dust seal and retaining ring up the fork tube.
29 Hold the outer tube and yank the inner tube upward, repeatedly (like a slide hammer), until the seal and outer tube guide bushing pop loose.
30 Remove the stop ring and take off the oil seal case **(see illustration)**. Remove the O-ring from the oil seal case.

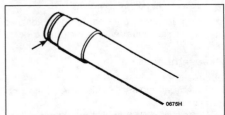

8.30 Remove the stopper ring (arrowed), then take off the oil seal case

5

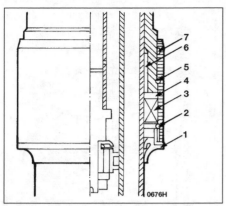

8.36a Fork seal details (1990 and later UK GSX-R750 models)

1 Dust seal
2 Oil seal stopper ring
3 Oil seal
4 Oil seal retainer
5 Oil seal case stopper ring
6 Bushing
7 O-ring

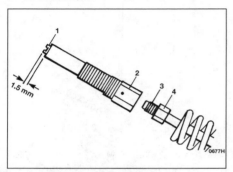

8.36b Set the damping adjuster height, then thread the adjuster onto the damper rod and secure it with the locknut

1 Damping adjuster
2 Adjuster housing
3 Damper rod
4 Locknut

31 Unscrew the compression damping adjuster from the bottom of the fork.

Inspection

32 Perform Steps 13 through 15 of Section 7 to inspect the fork.

33 Check the cartridge for wear or damage. Don't try to disassemble it; install a new one if any defects are found.

34 Replace the oil seal, dust seal and both guide bushings whenever the fork is disassembled.

35 Replace the O-rings for the compression damping adjuster, rebound damping adjuster and oil seal case whenever the fork is disassembled.

Reassembly

36 Assembly is the reverse of the disassembly steps, with the following additions:

a) Install the dust seal, the stop ring and the oil seal on the inner fork tube before installing the guide bushing.

b) Be careful not to damage the Teflon coating on the guide bushings when installing them.

c) Support the fork tube in an upright position and drive in the oil seal and retainer with Suzuki tool 09940-52820 or equivalent **(see illustration 8.18a)**. Be sure the seals and related parts are installed in the correct order, with the seals facing in the proper directions **(see illustration)**.

d) Use thread locking agent on the threads of the damper rod bolt. If the cartridge spins while you're trying to tighten the bolt, install the spring and related parts, then tighten the bolt.

e) Adjust the height of the rebound damping adjuster **(see illustration)**. Thread the locknut all the way onto the shaft, tighten the damping adjuster against the locknut by hand, then tighten the locknut against the damping adjuster to the torque listed in this Chapter's Specifications.

GSX-R750 (1991 and later US and Canadian models)

Disassembly

37 Unscrew the fork cap until it separates from the fork **(see illustration)**.

38 Compress the spacer against the spring and slip Suzuki special tool 09940-94920 or equivalent between the spacer and the fork cap locknut **(see illustration 8.22)**.

39 Hold the fork cap with a socket and turn the locknut downward, away from the fork cap. Then unscrew the fork cap from the damper rod.

40 Remove the locknut from the end of the cartridge rod, then remove the spacer and spring.

41 Hold the fork over a drain pan with its rod pointed downward. Work the rod back and forth several times to pump out the oil, then let the fork continue to drain for several minutes.

42 Remove the damper rod bolt from the bottom of the fork with an Allen wrench. If the cartridge spins and the bolt won't loosen, remove the bolt with an air wrench. If you don't have an air wrench, a dealer can loosen the bolt for you when you go to buy replacement parts.

43 Remove the cartridge from the fork tube. Don't try to disassemble the cartridge.

44 Pry the dust seal out of its bore with a small screwdriver and slide it up the fork tube to expose the retaining ring.

45 Pry the retaining ring out of its groove, then slide it along the inner fork tube.

46 Hold the outer tube and yank the inner tube upward, repeatedly (like a slide hammer), until the seal and guide bushing pop loose. **Caution: Don't scratch the surface of the inner tube, or the fork will leak oil after it's assembled.**

47 Remove the stopper ring and take off the oil seal case **(see illustration 8.30)**. Remove the O-ring from the oil seal case.

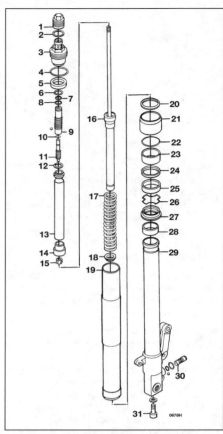

8.37 Front fork (1991 and later US and Canada GSX-R750 models) - exploded view

1 Spring adjuster
2 O-ring
3 Cap bolt
4 O-ring
5 Rubber seat
6 O-ring
7 Expander
8 Stopper ring
9 Adjuster case
10 O-ring
11 Upper adjuster
12 Spring upper joint
13 Spacer
14 Spring lower joint
15 Damper rod nut
16 Cartridge
17 Spring
18 Centering plate
19 Outer fork tube
20 Case O-ring
21 Oil seal case
22 Snap ring
23 Bushing
24 Seal spacer
25 Oil seal
26 Stopper ring
27 Dust seal
28 Bushing
29 Inner fork tube
30 Compression damping adjuster
31 Damper rod bolt

48 Unscrew the compression damping adjuster from the bottom of the fork.

Inspection

49 Perform Steps 13 through 15 of Section 7 to inspect the fork.

50 Check the cartridge for wear or damage. Don't try to disassemble it; install a new one if any defects are found.

51 Replace the oil seal, dust seal and both guide bushings whenever the fork is disassembled.

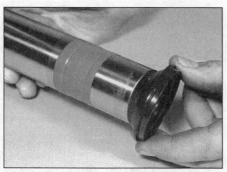

8.53a Wrap the guide bushing on the inner fork tube with vinyl tape so the bushing won't scratch the seal lips during installation (don't forget to remove the tape after the seals are installed)

52 Replace the O-rings for the compression damping adjuster, rebound damping adjuster and oil seal case whenever the fork is disassembled.

Reassembly

53 Assembly is the reverse of the disassembly steps, with the following additions:

a) Install the spring with its closely wound coils at the bottom.

b) Be careful not to damage the Teflon coating on the guide bushings when installing them.

c) Before installing the seals, wrap vinyl tape around the guide bushing on the inner tube to protect the seal lips **(see illustration)**.

d) Support the fork tube in an upright position and drive in the oil seal and retainer with Suzuki tool 09940-52820 or equivalent. Be sure the seals and related parts are installed in the correct order, with the seals facing in the proper directions **(see illustration)**.

e) Use thread locking agent on the threads of the damper rod bolt. If the cartridge spins while you're trying to tighten the bolt, install the spring and related parts, then tighten the bolt.

f) Adjust the height of the rebound damping adjuster. Thread the locknut all the way onto the shaft, tighten the damping adjuster against the locknut by hand, then tighten the locknut against the damping adjuster to the torque listed in this Chapter's Specifications.

GSX-R1100 (all 1989 models and 1990 US models)

Disassembly

54 Unscrew the fork cap from the inner fork tube **(see illustration)**.

55 Slide the inner fork tube down to provide access to the fork cap locknut. Loosen the locknut and unscrew the fork cap from the damper rod.

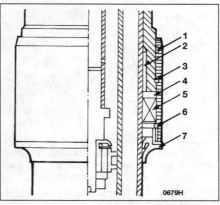

8.53b Fork seal details (1991 and later US and Canada GSX-R750 models)

1 O-ring
2 Bushing
3 Oil seal case stopper ring
4 Oil seal retainer
5 Oil seal
6 Oil seal stopper ring
7 Dust seal

56 Remove the spring retainer and pull the spring out of the fork tube.

57 Hold the fork over a drain pan with its rod pointed downward. Work the rod back and forth several times to pump out the oil, then let the fork continue to drain for several minutes.

58 Hold the cartridge from turning with Suzuki tool 09940-54820 or equivalent while you remove the damper rod bolt from the bottom of the fork with an Allen wrench. The tool consists of a hollow tube that fits over the fork rod with a fitting on one end that fits into the end of the cartridge and keeps it from turning. **Note:** If you don't have access to the special tool, remove the damper rod bolt with an air wrench. If you don't have an air wrench, a dealer can remove the Allen bolt when you go to buy replacement parts.

59 Remove the cartridge from the fork tube. Don't try to disassemble the cartridge.

60 Hold the outer tube and yank the inner tube upward, repeatedly (like a slide hammer), until the seal and guide bushing pop loose.

Caution: Don't scratch the surface of the inner tube, or the fork will leak oil after it's assembled.

61 Unscrew the spring adjuster from the fork cap. Remove the O-ring from the spring adjuster and discard it.

Inspection

62 Perform Steps 13 through 15 of Section 7 to inspect the fork.

63 Check the cartridge for wear or damage. Don't try to disassemble it; install a new one if any defects are found.

64 Replace the oil seal, dust seal and both guide bushings whenever the fork is disassembled.

65 Replace the spring adjuster O-ring whenever the fork is disassembled.

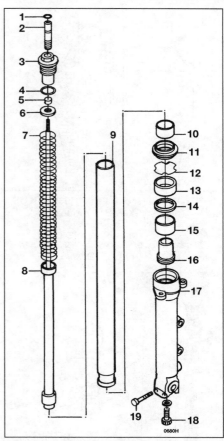

8.54 Front fork (all 1989 and US 1990 GSX-R1100 models) - exploded view

1 O-ring
2 Upper adjuster
3 Cap bolt
4 O-ring
5 Damper rod nut
6 Spring seat
7 Spring
8 Cartridge
9 Inner fork tube
10 Bushing
11 Dust seal
12 Stopper ring
13 Bushing
14 Washer
15 Bushing
16 Oil lock piece
17 Outer fork tube
18 Damper rod bolt
19 Bolt

Reassembly

66 Assembly is the reverse of the disassembly steps, with the following additions:

a) Be careful not to damage the Teflon coating on the guide bushings when installing them.

b) Before installing the seals, wrap vinyl tape around the guide bushing on the inner tube to protect the seal lips **(see illustration 8.53a)**.

c) Support the fork tube in an upright position and drive in the oil seal and retainer with Suzuki tool 09940-50112 or equivalent **(see illustration 8.18a)**. Be sure the seals and related parts are installed in the correct order, with the seals facing in the proper directions **(see illustration)**.

d) Use thread locking agent on the threads of the damper rod Allen bolt. Tighten the

5

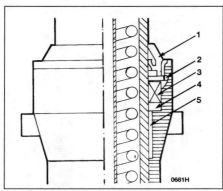

8.66a Fork seal details (all 1989 and US 1990 GSX-R1100 models)

1	Dust seal	3	Oil seal
2	Oil seal stopper ring	4	Oil seal retainer
		5	Bushing

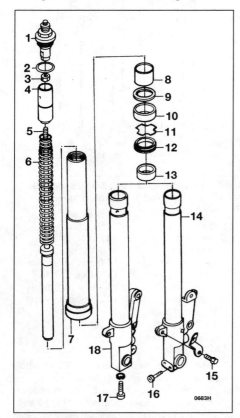

8.67 Front fork (GSX-R1100 models, 1991 and later US and 1990 and later UK) - exploded view

1	Fork cap	11	Stopper ring
2	O-ring	12	Dust seal
3	Nut	13	Bushing
4	Spacer	14	Left inner fork tube
5	Damper rod		
6	Spring	15	Bolt
7	Outer fork tube	16	Bolt
8	Bushing	17	Damper rod bolt
9	Washer	18	Right inner fork tube
10	Oil seal		

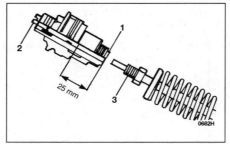

8.66b Set the damping adjuster height, then thread the adjuster onto the damper rod and secure it with the locknut

1 Bottom end of spring adjuster
2 Rebound damping force adjuster
3 Damper rod

bolt to the torque listed in this Chapter's Specifications. If the cartridge spins when you try to tighten the bolt, have it torqued by a dealer service department.

e) *Adjust the height of the rebound damping adjuster (see illustration). Thread the locknut all the way onto the shaft, tighten the spring adjuster against the locknut by hand, then tighten the locknut against the*

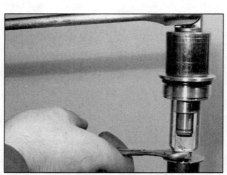

8.68 Compress the fork spring, slip the Suzuki special tool between the spacer and locknut, then turn the locknut away from the fork cap - if you don't have the special tool, you can use a washer with a slot cut in it

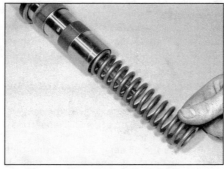

8.69b . . . and pull the spring out of the fork tube

spring adjuster to the torque listed in this Chapter's Specifications. Then install the fork cap on the spring adjuster.

GSX-R1100 (1991 and later US models; 1990 and later UK models)

Disassembly

67 Unscrew the fork cap until it separates from the fork (**see illustration**).

68 Compress the spacer against the spring and slip Suzuki special tool 09940-94910 or equivalent between the spacer and the fork cap locknut (**see illustration**). Hold the fork cap with a socket and turn the locknut downward, away from the fork cap. Then unscrew the fork cap from the cartridge rod.

69 Remove the locknut from the end of the cartridge rod, then remove the spring (**see illustrations**).

70 Hold the fork over a drain pan with its rod pointed downward. Work the rod back and forth several times to pump out the oil, then let the fork continue to drain for several minutes.

71 Pry the dust seal out of its bore with a small screwdriver and slide it up the fork tube to expose the retaining ring (**see illustration**).

8.69a After you've unscrewed the fork cap, loosen the locknut, then remove the special tool or washer . . .

8.71 Pry the dust seal out of its bore with a small screwdriver (be careful not to scratch the fork tube)

8.72a Pry one end of the retaining ring out of its slot . . .

8.72b . . . and slip the retaining ring up the fork tube

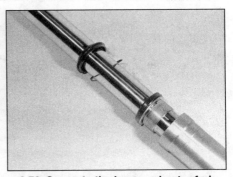

8.73 Separate the inner and outer fork tubes to expose the oil seal and guide bushing

72 Pry the retaining ring out of its groove, then work it free of the fork tube (see illustrations).

73 Hold the outer tube and yank the inner tube upward, repeatedly (like a slide hammer), until the seal and guide bushing pop loose (see illustration).
Caution: Don't scratch the surface of the inner tube, or the fork will leak oil after it's assembled.

74 Carefully spread the guide bushings just enough so they can be slipped off the fork tube, then remove the washer, oil seal, retaining ring and dust seal (see illustrations).

75 Hold the cartridge from turning with a special tool inserted into the hex fitting on the cartridge (see illustration). The tool can be fabricated by welding a nut to the end of a piece of steel tubing or pipe. Remove the damper rod bolt with an Allen wrench, then slip the cartridge out of the inner tube (see illustrations).

Inspection

76 Perform Steps 13 through 15 of Section 7 to inspect the fork.

77 Check the cartridge for wear or damage (see illustration). Don't try to disassemble it; install a new one if any defects are found.

Reassembly

78 Assembly is the reverse of the disassembly steps, with the following additions:
a) *After you've installed the guide bushing on the inner fork tube, wrap electrical*

8.74a Carefully spread the guide bushing just enough to slip it off the fork tube

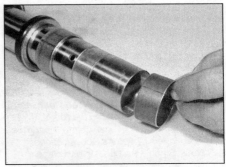

8.74b Slide the bushing off; install a new one during assembly

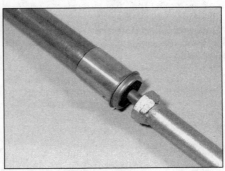

8.75a The damper rod holding tool fits in the hex on top of the cartridge and keeps it from spinning when the damper rod bolt is loosened

8.75b While you hold the cartridge, remove the damper rod bolt with an Allen wrench . . .

8.75c . . . then pull the cartridge out of the fork tube

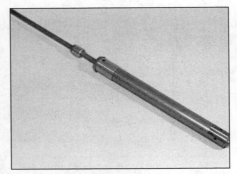

8.77 Check the cartridge for wear or damage; don't try to disassemble it

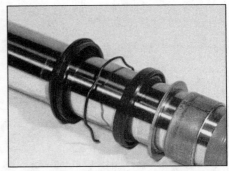

8.78a Arrange the guide bushing, washer, oil seal, stopper ring and dust seal in this order

5

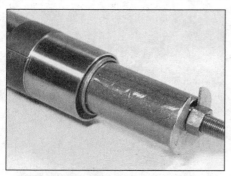

8.78b Use the Suzuki special tool or a washer with a slot cut in it to compress the spring

tape around it to protect the seals during installation **(see illustration 8.53a)**.
b) Assemble the dust seal, stopper ring, oil seal, washer and outer tube guide bushing on the inner tube in the correct order and with the seals facing in the proper direction **(see illustration)**.
c) Use a Suzuki special tool or equivalent to compress the fork spring **(see illustration)**. Thread the fork cap onto the rod, then tighten the locknut against it to the torque listed in this Chapter's Specifications. **Note:** Since it isn't possible to place a socket over the locknut, use a crow's foot socket on the torque wrench.

9 Steering head bearings - replacement

1 If the steering head bearing check/adjustment (see Chapter 1) does not remedy excessive play or roughness in the steering head bearings, the entire front end must be disassembled and the bearings and races replaced with new ones.
2 Refer to Chapter 7 and remove the front fairing.
3 Refer to Chapter 6 and remove the front wheel.
4 Katana 1100/GSX1100F: Refer to Chapter 7

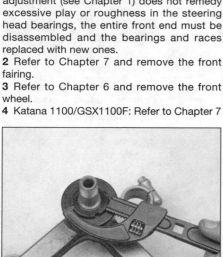

9.13 Unscrew the locknut with an adjustable spanner wrench (use a hammer and punch if you don't have the special tool)

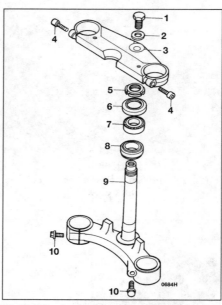

9.12 Steering stem and bearings (Katana 600/GSX600F shown, others similar)

1 Steering stem bolt	6 Dust cover
2 Washer	7 Upper bearing
3 Upper triple clamp	8 Lower bearing
4 Allen bolts	9 Steering stem
5 Steering stem nut	10 Bolts

and remove the front fender and fork stabilizer.
5 Refer to Section 6 and remove the front forks.
6 Refer to Section 5 and remove the handlebars.
7 GSX-R models, Katana 750/GSX750F, Katana 1100/GSX1100F: Unbolt the brake hose assembly from the underside of the steering head. It isn't necessary to disconnect any brake hoses.
8 GSX-R750 (1988 and later), GSX-R1100 (1989 and later): Refer to Chapter 8 and remove the speedometer and tachometer.
9 Katana 750/GSX750F, Katana 1100/GSX1100F: Disconnect the ignition switch electrical connector.
10 GSX-R750 (1988 and later), Katana

600/GSX600F, Katana 750/GSX750F: Refer to Chapter 8 and unbolt the horn.
11 GSX-R1100 (1986 through 1988): Remove the windshield brace.
12 Remove the steering stem nut or bolt **(see illustration)**, then lift off the upper triple clamp (sometimes called the fork bridge, yoke or crown).
13 Using an adjustable spanner wrench, remove the stem locknut **(see illustration)** while supporting the steering head from the bottom. Lift off the locknut and dust cover.
14 Remove the steering stem and lower triple clamp assembly. If it's stuck, gently tap on the top of the steering stem with a plastic mallet or hammer and a wood block.
15 Remove the upper bearing.
16 Clean all the parts with solvent and dry them thoroughly, using compressed air, if available. If you do use compressed air, don't let the bearings spin as they're dried it could ruin them. Wipe the old grease out of the frame steering head and bearing races.
17 Examine the races in the steering head for cracks, dents, and pits. If even the slightest amount of wear or damage is evident, the races should be replaced with new ones.
18 To remove the races, drive them out of the steering head with a brass drift **(see illustration)**. A slide hammer with the proper internal-jaw puller will also work. When installing the races, tap them gently into place with a hammer and punch or a large socket. Do not strike the bearing surface or the race will be damaged.

> **HAYNES HiNT** *Since the races are an interference fit in the frame, installation will be easier if the new races are left overnight in a refrigerator. This will cause them to contract and slip into place in the frame with very little effort.*

19 Check the bearings for wear. Look for cracks, dents, and pits in the races and flat spots on the bearings. Replace any defective parts with new ones. If a new bearing is required, replace both of them as a set.
20 To remove the lower bearing from the steering stem, use a bearing puller **(see illustration)**. Don't

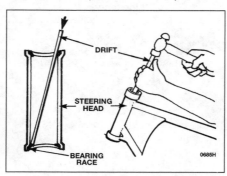

9.18 Drive the bearing races out of the steering head with a brass drift only if they need to be replaced - don't reuse the races once they have been removed

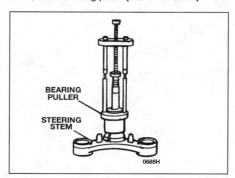

9.20 Remove the lower bearing from the steering stem with a puller (or have a dealer service department do it when you go to buy new bearings)

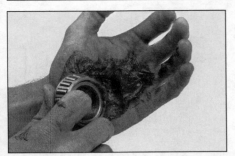

9.23 Work the grease completely into the rollers

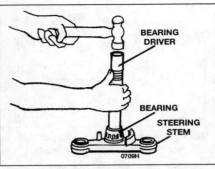

9.24 Protect the bearing with a washer, then tap the new bearing on with a bearing driver or length of pipe that bears against the inner race (not against the rollers or cage)

10.2 Measure the damper protrusion and compare with this Chapter's Specifications

remove this bearing unless it, or the grease seal underneath, must be replaced. **Note:** *Bearing pullers can be rented, but it may be cheaper and more convenient to have a dealer service department do this for you when you go to buy replacement parts.*

21 Check the grease seal under the lower bearing and replace it with a new one if necessary.

22 Inspect the steering stem/lower triple clamp for cracks and other damage. Do not attempt to repair any steering components. Replace them with new parts if defects are found.

23 Pack the bearings with high-quality grease (preferably a moly-based grease) **(see illustration).** Coat the outer races with grease also.

24 Install the lower bearing onto the steering stem. Drive the lower bearing onto the steering stem with an appropriate bearing driver **(see illustration).** If you don't have access to this tool, a section of pipe with a diameter the same as the inner race of the bearing can be used. Drive the bearing on until it is fully seated.

25 Insert the steering stem/lower triple clamp into the frame head. Install the upper bearing stem locknut. Using the adjustable spanner, tighten the locknut while moving the lower triple clamp back and forth from lock to lock. Continue to tighten the nut to the initial torque listed in this Chapter's Specifications, then back off 1/4 to 1/2 turn. Make sure the steering head turns smoothly.

26 The remainder of installation is the reverse of the removal steps.

27 Refer to Chapter 1 and check the steering tension adjustment.

10 Steering damper - adjustment, removal and installation

Adjustment

1 Remove fairing panels as necessary for access to the damper (see Chapter 7).

2 Turn the handlebars all the way to the left and measure damper protrusion **(see illustration).** If it's not at the setting listed in this Chapter's Specifications, loosen the

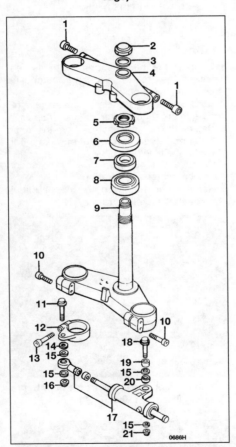

10.3a Steering damper and stem (early models)

1 Bolt	12 Steering damper
2 Nut	bracket
3 Washer	13 Bolt
4 Upper triple clamp	14 Washer
5 Steering stem nut	15 Dust seal
6 Dust seal	16 Nut
7 Upper bearing	17 Steering damper
8 Lower bearing	18 Bolt
9 Steering stem	19 Spacer
10 Bolts	20 Bearing
11 Bolt	21 Nut

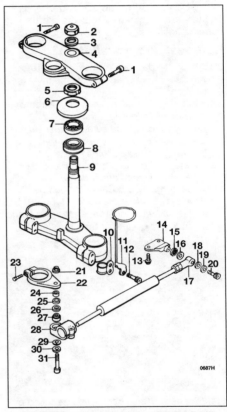

10.3b Steering damper and stem (later models)

1 Bolts	17 Steering damper
2 Nut	18 Shim
3 Washer	19 Dust seal
4 Upper triple clamp	20 Bolt
5 Steering stem nut	21 Nut
6 Dust seal	22 Bracket
7 Upper bearing	23 Bolt
8 Lower bearing	24 Spacer
9 Steering stem	25 Dust seal
10 Clip	26 Shim
11 Holder	27 Bearing
12 Bolt	28 Damper end
13 Bolt	29 Shim
14 Bracket	30 Dust seal
15 Dust Seal	31 Bolt
16 Shim	

5

10.3c The damper is secured to the fork tube by a clamp

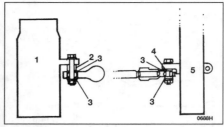

10.4a On early models, be sure the dust seals are positioned correctly

1 Steering stem   4 Washer
2 Spacer   5 Front fork
3 Dust seal

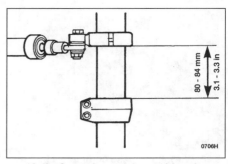

10.4b On early models, position the damper clamp the specified distance above the lower triple clamp

locknut and turn the adjuster to change it. Tighten the locknut once the setting is correct.

Removal and installation

3 Unbolt the damper from the bracket and the fork tube, then take it off the machine **(see illustrations)**.

4 Installation is the reverse of the removal steps, with the following additions:

a) On early models, be sure the dust seals are correctly installed. Position the steering damper 80 to 84 mm (3.1 to 3.3 inch) up the fork tube from the lower triple clamp **(see illustrations)**.

b) On later models, position the damper against the holder on the fork tube.

c) Tighten all fasteners to the torque settings listed in this Chapter's Specifications.

11 Rear shock absorber - removal and installation

Removal

1 Support the bike securely with its rear wheel off the ground so it can't be knocked over during this procedure.

2 Remove fairing panels as necessary for access to the shock absorber (see Chapter 7).

3 Detach the remote reservoir from the frame (if equipped) **(see illustrations)**. Leave it in place for the time being.

4 Remove the nut from the lower shock absorber bolt **(see illustration)**.

5 Remove the nut from the upper shock absorber bolt **(see illustration)**.

6 Raise the swingarm with a jack just enough to remove the tension from the shock absorber bolts, then remove them.

⚠️ **Warning: Don't raise the bike enough so it can fall over.**

7 Take the shock absorber out **(see illustration)**.

Installation

8 Installation is the reverse of the removal procedure. Tighten the shock absorber bolts and nuts to the torque values listed in this Chapter's Specifications.

12 Swingarm bearings - check

1 Refer to Chapter 6 and remove the rear wheel, then refer to Section 11 and remove the rear shock absorber.

2 Grasp the rear of the swingarm with one hand and place your other hand at the junction of the swingarm and the frame. Try to move the rear of the swingarm from side-to-side. Any wear (play) in the bearings should be felt as movement between the swingarm and the frame at the front. The swingarm will actually be felt to move forward and backward at the front (not from side-to-side). If any play is noted, the bearings should be replaced with new ones (see Section 14).

11.3a The remote reservoir is secured by hose clamps below the frame member (GSX-R1100) . . .

11.3b . . . or above the frame member (Katana 1100/GSX1100F)

11.4 Remove the nut from the shock absorber upper bolt . . .

11.5 . . . and from the lower bolt, then support the swingarm and remove the bolts

11.7 Lift the shock absorber out of the frame; guide the remote reservoir (if equipped) out at the same time

13.10 Remove the Allen bolts to detach the adjuster from the frame (Katana 1100/GSX1100F)

3 Next, move the swingarm up and down through its full travel. It should move freely, without any binding or rough spots. If it does not move freely, refer to Section 13 for servicing procedures.

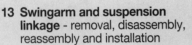

13 Swingarm and suspension linkage - removal, disassembly, reassembly and installation

Removal

1 Support the bike securely so it can't be knocked over during this procedure.
2 Remove the frame covers from both sides of the bike (see Chapter 7).
3 Remove the rear wheel (see Chapter 6).
4 Detach the brake torque link from the swingarm (see Chapter 6).

GSX-R750 and 1100

5 1989 and later GSX-R1100: Remove the seat and rear lower fender (see Chapter 7).
6 Unbolt the shock absorber reservoir (if equipped) from the frame (see Section 11).
7 Disconnect the brake line from the caliper. Cap the caliper fitting and brake line to prevent fluid loss, then slip the brake line out of the fitting on the swingarm.

Katana 750/GSX750F

8 Detach the rear suspension adjuster cable from its clamp on the frame (see Section 15).

Katana 1100/GSX1100F

9 Detach the left muffler from the motorcycle (see Chapter 3).
10 Unbolt the spring preload adjuster from the frame (see illustration). Detach the shock reservoir (1989 on).
11 Detach the brake hose from the clips on the swingarm (see Chapter 6).

All models

12 Remove the shock absorber upper bolt and nut (see Section 11).
13 Remove the swingarm pivot nut and bolt (see illustrations).
14 Remove the pivot bolt and nut that secure the cushion lever to the frame.
15 Remove the swingarm, together with the

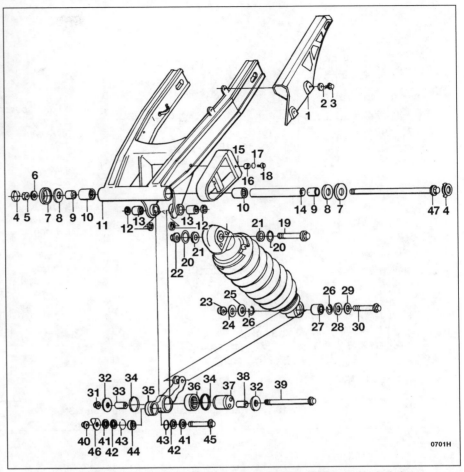

13.13a Rear suspension (1985 through 1987 GSX-R750) - exploded view

1 Chain guard	17 Washer	33 Spacer
2 Washer	18 Screw	34 Dust seal
3 Screw	19 Bolt	35 Cushion lever
4 Cap	20 Rubber washer	36 Bearing
5 Nut	21 Dust seal	37 Spacer
6 Washer	22 Nut	38 Spacer
7 Dust cover	23 Nut	39 Bolt
8 Washer	24 Spacer	40 Nut
9 Spacer	25 Dust seal	41 Shim
10 Bearing	26 Snap-ring	42 Spacer
11 Swingarm	27 Bearing	43 Dust seal
12 Dust seal	28 Dust seal	44 Bearing
13 Bearing	29 Washer	45 Bolt
14 Spacer	30 Bolt	46 Shim
15 Chain buffer	31 Nut	47 Swingarm pivot bolt
16 Spacer	32 Washer	

cushion lever, its linkage and the shock absorber.

Disassembly

16 Remove the pivot bolts from the lower end of the shock absorber, the cushion lever, and the cushion lever rods. Separate the cushion lever rods from the cushion lever and swingarm.
17 Rotate the pivot bearing sleeves with a finger and check for noise and roughness that indicate bearing dryness or deterioration. If

they're in need of lubrication or replacement, refer to Section 14.

Reassembly and installation

18 Assembly and installation are the reverse of the removal and disassembly steps, with the following additions:
a) Be sure the bearing seals are in position before installing the pivot bolts.
b) Tighten all fasteners to the torque values listed in this Chapter's Specifications.
c) 1990 and later GSX-R750 and 1100

5

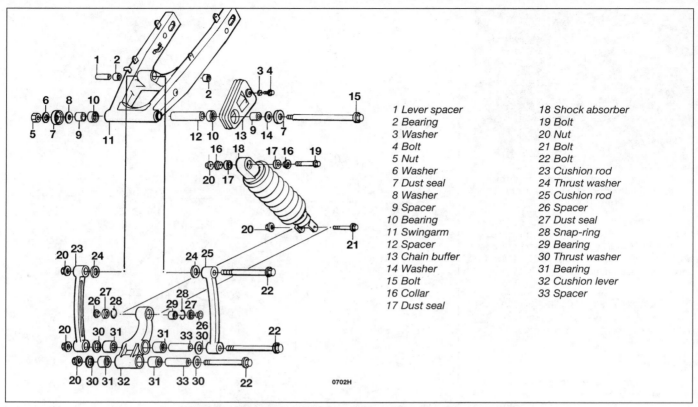

1 Lever spacer
2 Bearing
3 Washer
4 Bolt
5 Nut
6 Washer
7 Dust seal
8 Washer
9 Spacer
10 Bearing
11 Swingarm
12 Spacer
13 Chain buffer
14 Washer
15 Bolt
16 Collar
17 Dust seal
18 Shock absorber
19 Bolt
20 Nut
21 Bolt
22 Bolt
23 Cushion rod
24 Thrust washer
25 Cushion rod
26 Spacer
27 Dust seal
28 Snap-ring
29 Bearing
30 Thrust washer
31 Bearing
32 Cushion lever
33 Spacer

0702H

13.13b Rear suspension (1988 and later GSX-R750) - exploded view

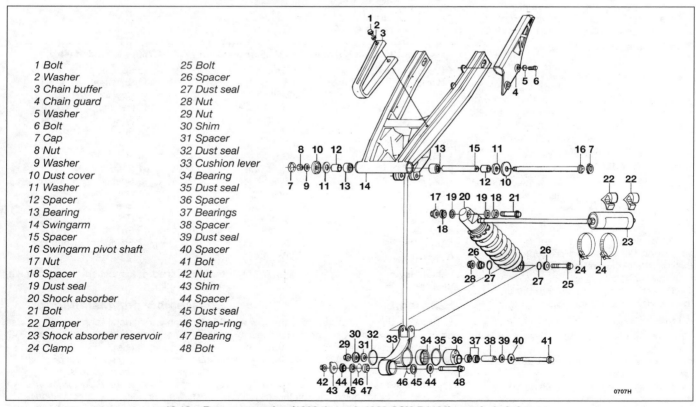

1 Bolt
2 Washer
3 Chain buffer
4 Chain guard
5 Washer
6 Bolt
7 Cap
8 Nut
9 Washer
10 Dust cover
11 Washer
12 Spacer
13 Bearing
14 Swingarm
15 Spacer
16 Swingarm pivot shaft
17 Nut
18 Spacer
19 Dust seal
20 Shock absorber
21 Bolt
22 Damper
23 Shock absorber reservoir
24 Clamp
25 Bolt
26 Spacer
27 Dust seal
28 Nut
29 Nut
30 Shim
31 Spacer
32 Dust seal
33 Cushion lever
34 Bearing
35 Dust seal
36 Spacer
37 Bearings
38 Spacer
39 Dust seal
40 Spacer
41 Bolt
42 Nut
43 Shim
44 Spacer
45 Dust seal
46 Snap-ring
47 Bearing
48 Bolt

0707H

13.13c Rear suspension (1986 through 1988 GSX-R1100) - exploded view

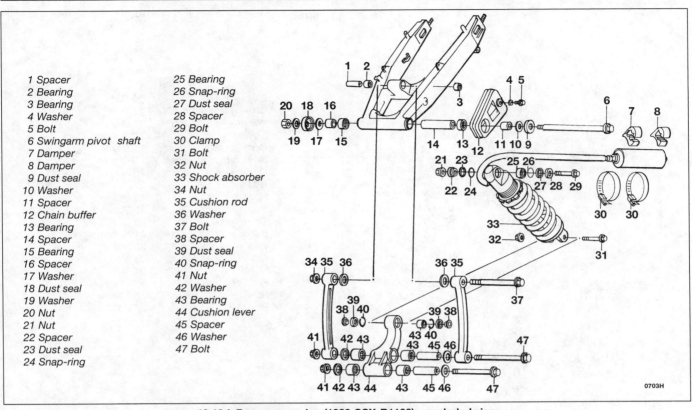

1 Spacer
2 Bearing
3 Bearing
4 Washer
5 Bolt
6 Swingarm pivot shaft
7 Damper
8 Damper
9 Dust seal
10 Washer
11 Spacer
12 Chain buffer
13 Bearing
14 Spacer
15 Bearing
16 Spacer
17 Washer
18 Dust seal
19 Washer
20 Nut
21 Nut
22 Spacer
23 Dust seal
24 Snap-ring

25 Bearing
26 Snap-ring
27 Dust seal
28 Spacer
29 Bolt
30 Clamp
31 Bolt
32 Nut
33 Shock absorber
34 Nut
35 Cushion rod
36 Washer
37 Bolt
38 Spacer
39 Dust seal
40 Snap-ring
41 Nut
42 Washer
43 Bearing
44 Cushion lever
45 Spacer
46 Washer
47 Bolt

13.13d Rear suspension (1989 GSX-R1100) - exploded view

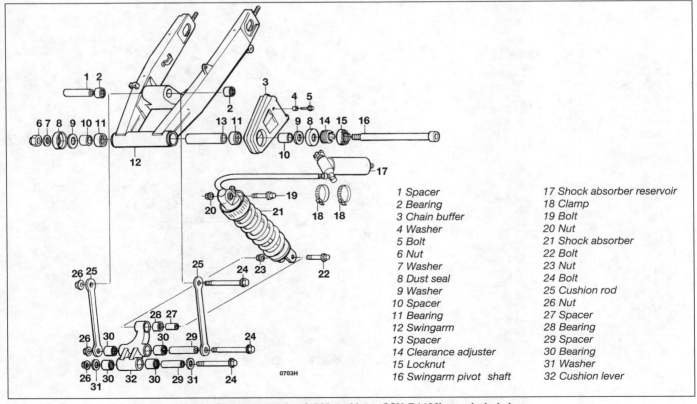

1 Spacer
2 Bearing
3 Chain buffer
4 Washer
5 Bolt
6 Nut
7 Washer
8 Dust seal
9 Washer
10 Spacer
11 Bearing
12 Swingarm
13 Spacer
14 Clearance adjuster
15 Locknut
16 Swingarm pivot shaft

17 Shock absorber reservoir
18 Clamp
19 Bolt
20 Nut
21 Shock absorber
22 Bolt
23 Nut
24 Bolt
25 Cushion rod
26 Nut
27 Spacer
28 Bearing
29 Spacer
30 Bearing
31 Washer
32 Cushion lever

13.13e Rear suspension (1990 and later GSX-R1100) - exploded view

5

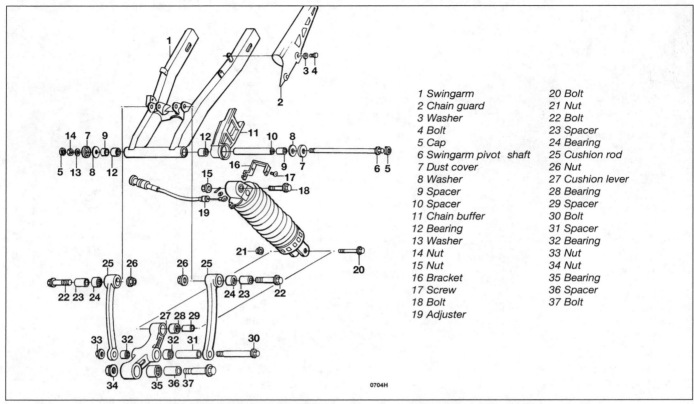

1 Swingarm
2 Chain guard
3 Washer
4 Bolt
5 Cap
6 Swingarm pivot shaft
7 Dust cover
8 Washer
9 Spacer
10 Spacer
11 Chain buffer
12 Bearing
13 Washer
14 Nut
15 Nut
16 Bracket
17 Screw
18 Bolt
19 Adjuster

20 Bolt
21 Nut
22 Bolt
23 Spacer
24 Bearing
25 Cushion rod
26 Nut
27 Cushion lever
28 Bearing
29 Spacer
30 Bolt
31 Spacer
32 Bearing
33 Nut
34 Nut
35 Bearing
36 Spacer
37 Bolt

0704H

13.13f Rear suspension (Katana 600 and 750, GSX600F and 750F) - exploded view

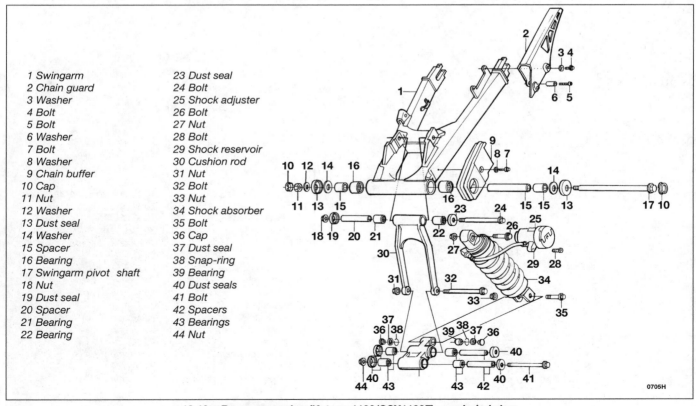

1 Swingarm
2 Chain guard
3 Washer
4 Bolt
5 Bolt
6 Washer
7 Bolt
8 Washer
9 Chain buffer
10 Cap
11 Nut
12 Washer
13 Dust seal
14 Washer
15 Spacer
16 Bearing
17 Swingarm pivot shaft
18 Nut
19 Dust seal
20 Spacer
21 Bearing
22 Bearing

23 Dust seal
24 Bolt
25 Shock adjuster
26 Bolt
27 Nut
28 Bolt
29 Shock reservoir
30 Cushion rod
31 Nut
32 Bolt
33 Nut
34 Shock absorber
35 Bolt
36 Cap
37 Dust seal
38 Snap-ring
39 Bearing
40 Dust seals
41 Bolt
42 Spacers
43 Bearings
44 Nut

0705H

13.13g Rear suspension (Katana 1100/GSX1100F) - exploded view

13.18a Tighten the clearance adjuster (arrowed) until it bottoms against the bearing seal cover . . .

models: Tighten the swingarm clearance adjuster against the bearing seal cover, then tighten the pivot shaft nut and clearance adjuster locknut to the torques listed in this Chapter's Specifications **(see illustrations).**

d) Adjust the chain as described in Chapter 1.
e) If the brake line was disconnected, bleed the brakes (see Chapter 6).

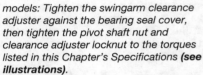

14 Swingarm bearings - replacement

1 Bearing replacement isn't complicated, but it requires a blind hole (expanding) puller, a slide hammer and a hydraulic press. The puller and slide hammer can be rented if you don't have them, but compare the cost of having the bearings replaced by a Suzuki dealer to that of renting the equipment before you proceed. It may be cheaper, and it will probably be easier, to have the bearings replaced by the dealer. You can save money by removing the swingarm from the bike yourself. **Note**: Don't reinstall the bearings once they have been removed. Replace them with new ones.
2 Remove the swingarm (see Section 13).
3 Pry out the seals and remove the washers **(see illustration)**.
4 Slide the sleeve out **(see illustration)**.

14.3 Pry the seals out with a screwdriver and remove the washer behind each seal

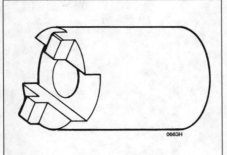

13.18b . . . with a tool like this one

5 Remove the bearings with a blind hole (expanding) puller and slide hammer.
6 Press new bearings into the swingarm.
7 Pack the bearings with Suzuki Super Grease A or equivalent.
8 Install the sleeve.
9 Install the washer and tap in a new seal.

15 Suspension adjustments

1 Suspension settings for various riding conditions are listed in this Chapter's Specifications.

Warning: To prevent erratic handling which could result in loss of control of the motorcycle, the suspension settings must be balanced between front and rear and the settings for both front forks must be the same.

GSX-R750 (1985 through 1987)

2 To adjust the front fork spring preload, loosen the locknut and turn the adjuster on top of the fork (see Section 7).
3 To adjust the damping force of the front forks, turn the knob on the adjuster at the bottom of each fork.
4 To adjust the spring preload of the rear shock, turn the adjuster ring at the bottom of the shock.

14.4 Slide the sleeve out of the bearing

13.18c After tightening the pivot bolt, hold the pivot bolt with an Allen wrench and tighten the adjuster locknut (arrowed) . . .

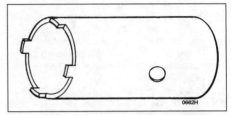

13.18d . . . with a tool like this one

5 To adjust the damping force of the rear shock, turn the adjuster at the top of the shock.

GSX-R1100 (1986 and 1987)

6 To adjust the front fork spring preload, loosen the locknut and turn the adjuster on top of the fork (see Section 7).
7 To adjust the damping force of the front forks, turn the knob on the NEAS (anti-dive) unit at the bottom of each fork.
8 To adjust the spring preload of the rear shock, turn the adjuster ring at the top of the shock.
9 To adjust the damping force of the rear shock, turn the adjuster at the bottom of the shock.

GSX-R750 (1988 and 1989) and GSX-R1100 (1988)

10 To set the spring preload of the front forks, turn the adjuster at the top of each fork with a wrench to raise or lower it **(see illustration)**. The preload setting is indicated

15.10a Turn the preload adjuster with a wrench to change spring preload

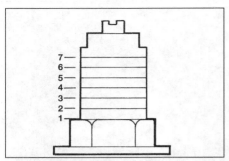

15.10b The number of exposed adjuster grooves indicates the setting (1 is the softest and 7 is the hardest)

by the number of adjuster grooves that are exposed (see illustration).

11 To set the rebound damping force of the front forks, turn the adjuster at the top of each fork with a screwdriver (see illustration).

12 To set the compression damping of the front forks, turn the adjuster at the base of the fork (see illustration).

13 To adjust the spring preload of the rear shock, turn the toothed adjuster ring at the bottom of the shock (GSX-R750) or top of the shock (GSX-R1100).

14 To adjust the damping force of the rear shock, turn the adjuster knob at the top of the shock (GSX-R750) or bottom of the shock (GSX-R1100).

15.18 Turn the adjuster and count the clicks to set rebound damping force; standard settings for rebound (R) and compression (C) are stamped in the shock (arrowed)

GSX-R750 (1990 and later) and GSX-R1100 (1989 and later)

15 To set the spring preload of the front forks, turn the adjuster at the top of each fork with a wrench to raise or lower it (see illustration 15.10a). The preload setting is indicated by the number of adjuster grooves that are exposed (see illustration 15.10b).

16 To set the rebound damping force of the front forks, turn the adjuster at the top of each fork with a screwdriver (see illustration 15.11).

17 To set the compression damping of the front forks, turn the adjuster at the base of the fork (see illustration 15.12).

18 To set the rebound damping of the rear shock, turn the adjuster on the shock absorber and count the clicks outward from the fully turned-in position (see illustration). **Note**: *The standard rebound and compression settings vary from one bike to another. On some models, the standard settings are stamped in the base of the shock absorber.*

19 To set the compression damping of the rear shock, turn the adjuster on the remote reservoir and count the clicks (see illustration).

20 To set the spring preload of the rear shock, turn the adjuster ring on top of the shock.

Katana 600 (GSX600F)

21 Front fork spring preload is not adjustable on 1988 models. On 1989-on models, adjust preload by turning the knob at the top of each fork.

22 On 1988 models the rear shock is adjustable for spring preload only. Use the nut

15.11 Turn the adjuster with a screwdriver to set rebound damping force

at the bottom of the shock spring to alter the spring length and secure it with the locknut.

23 On 1989-on models turn the adjuster ring at the base of the shock (see illustration 15.25a). Rear shock damping is adjusted by turning the knob at the top of the shock.

Katana 750 (GSX750F)

24 To adjust the front fork spring preload, turn the knob on top of each fork.

All US models; UK models with Type I rear suspension

25 To adjust the rear spring preload, turn the adjuster on the shock absorber (see illustration). To adjust the rear damping force, push or pull the adjusting knob (see illustration).

UK models with Type II rear suspension

26 Rear spring preload is set by turning the locknut and adjusting nut on top of the shock absorber. Rebound damping force is set by turning the adjuster on the bottom of the shock. Compression damping force is set by turning the knob on the remote reservoir.

Katana 1100 (GSX1100F)

1988 models

27 The front forks are not adjustable.

28 To adjust the rear spring preload, flip open the handle on the adjuster and turn it to change the setting. The setting is indicated by numbers on the adjuster body (1 is the softest; 5 is the hardest).

15.12 Turn the adjuster at the bottom of the fork to set compression damping force

15.19 Turn the adjuster on the remote reservoir to set compression damping force

15.25a Turn the adjuster ring on the shock absorber to set spring preload

15.25b Pull or push the adjuster handle to set damping force

16.2a Remove the chain guard; the clutch release cylinder (if equipped) can be left attached . . .

16.2b . . . but make sure the clutch pushrod isn't pulled out of position

17.8 With the chain adjuster removed, remove the nuts (arrowed) to separate the sprocket from the hub (one nut is hidden behind the chain adjuster)

1989 and later models

29 Remove the cover from the handlebar assembly to expose the adjuster on top of each fork. Turn the adjuster clockwise to increase the spring preload or counterclockwise (anticlockwise) to decrease it. The preload setting is indicated by the number of adjuster grooves that are exposed **(see illustration 15.10b)**.

30 The rear spring preload is adjusted in the same manner as for 1988 models (see Step 25).

31 To adjust extension damping force, turn the adjuster on the bottom of the shock. **Note:** *Don't leave the adjuster between settings. This will give the equivalent of the hardest setting.*

32 To adjust compression damping force, turn the adjuster on the remote reservoir clockwise to increase damping force and counterclockwise (anticlockwise) to decrease it **(see illustration 13.10)**.

16 Drive chain - removal, cleaning and installation

Removal

1 Remove the shift lever (see Chapter 2).
2 Remove the chain guard **(see illustrations)**.
3 Remove the rear wheel (see Chapter 6).
4 Lift the chain off the engine sprocket.
5 Remove the swingarm (see Section 13).

Pass the chain between the swingarm and frame and take it out.

Cleaning

6 Soak the chain in kerosene (paraffin) or diesel fuel for approximately five or six minutes. **Caution: Don't use gasoline (petrol) or other cleaning fluids. Remove the chain, wipe it off then blow dry it with compressed air immediately. The entire process shouldn't take longer than ten minutes if it does, the O-rings in the chain rollers could be damaged.**

Installation

7 Installation is the reverse of the removal procedure, with the following additions:
a) *Tighten the suspension fasteners to the torque values listed in this Chapter's Specifications.*
b) *Tighten the rear axle nut to the torque listed in the Chapter 6 Specifications.*
c) *Adjust and lubricate the chain following the procedure described in Chapter 1.*

17 Sprockets - check and replacement

1 Support the bike securely so it can't be knocked over during this procedure.

2 Whenever the drive chain is inspected, the sprockets should be inspected also. If you are replacing the chain, replace the sprockets as well. Likewise, if the sprockets are in need of replacement, install a new chain also.

3 Remove the engine sprocket cover following the procedure outlined in the previous Section.

4 Check the wear pattern on the sprockets (see the section on *drive train and sprockets* in Chapter 1). If the sprocket teeth are worn excessively, replace the chain and sprockets.

5 To remove the engine sprocket, bend back the lockwasher that secures the sprocket nut. Have an assistant apply the rear brake. Remove the engine sprocket bolt (if equipped), nut and lockwasher.

6 Remove the rear wheel (see Chapter 6).

7 Slip the engine sprocket off the shaft (if the nut was removed in Step 5).

8 To replace the rear sprocket, unscrew the nuts holding it to the wheel coupling and lift the sprocket off **(see illustration)**. When installing the sprocket, use new self-locking nuts. Tighten the nuts to the torque listed in this Chapter's Specifications. Also, check the condition of the rubber damper under the rear wheel coupling (see Section 18).

9 When installing the engine sprocket, engage it with the chain and slip it onto the shaft **(see illustration)**. Install the lockwasher, apply a non-hardening thread locking

17.9a Engage the chain with the sprocket and slip the sprocket onto the shaft . . .

17.9b . . . install the lockwasher . . .

17.9c . . . apply thread locking agent to the shaft threads . . .

5

17.9d ... tighten the nut to the correct torque ...

17.9e ... and bend over the lockwasher to secure it

compound to the shaft threads, tighten the nut to the torque listed in the Chapter 2 Specifications and bend over the lockwasher to secure the nut **(see illustrations)**.

10 Install the sprocket bolt (if equipped) and tighten it to the torque listed in the Chapter 2 Specifications.

11 The remainder of installation is the reverse of the removal steps.

18 Rear wheel coupling/rubber damper - check and replacement

1 Remove the rear wheel (see Chapter 6).
2 Lift the rear sprocket/rear wheel coupling from the wheel **(see illustration)**.
3 Lift the rubber damper segments from the

wheel **(see illustration)** and check them for cracks, hardening and general deterioration. Replace them with new ones if necessary.
4 Checking and replacement procedures for the coupling bearing are similar to those described for the wheel bearings. Refer to Chapter 6.
5 Installation is the reverse of the removal procedure.

18.2 Lift the sprocket and hub from the rear wheel

18.3 Pull the damper segments out of the recesses

Chapter 6
Brakes, wheels and tires

Contents

Degrees of difficulty

Easy, suitable for novice with little experience	**Fairly easy,** suitable for beginner with some experience	**Fairly difficult,** suitable for competent DIY mechanic	**Difficult,** suitable for experienced DIY mechanic	**Very difficult,** suitable for expert DIY or professional

Specifications

General
Brake fluid type	See Chapter 1
Brake pad minimum thickness	See Chapter 1
Tire pressures	See Chapter 1

GSX-R750 and GSX-R1100
Disc thickness (front)
  1985 through 1989
    Standard . . . . 4.5 +/- 0.2 mm (0.177 +/- 0.008 inch)
    Minimum . . . . 4.0 mm (0.150 inch)*
  1990 on
    Standard . . . . 5.0 +/- 0.2 mm (0.197 +/- 0.008 inch)
    Minimum . . . . 4.5 mm (0.180 inch)*
Disc thickness (rear)
  Standard . . . . 6.0 +/- 0.2 mm (0.236 +/- 0.008 inch)
  Minimum . . . . 5.5 mm (0.220 inch)*
Disc runout maximum . . . . 0.30 mm (0.012 inch)
Wheel runout (limit) . . . . 2.0 mm (0.080 inch)
Axle runout (limit) . . . . 0.25 mm (0.010 inch)

Katana 600 (GSX600F) and Katana 750 (GSX750F)
Disc thickness (front)
  Standard . . . . 4.5 +/- 0.2 mm (0.177 +/- 0.008 inch)
  Minimum . . . . 4.0 mm (0.150 inch)*
Disc thickness (rear)
  Standard . . . . 6.0 +/- 0.2 mm (0.236 +/- 0.008 inch)
  Minimum . . . . 5.5 mm (0.220 inch)*
Disc runout (maximum) . . . . 0.30 mm (0.012 inch)
Wheel runout (limit) . . . . 2.0 mm (0.080 inch)
Axle runout (limit) . . . . 0.25 mm (0.010 inch)

6

Katana 1100 (GSX1100F)

Disc thickness (front)	
Standard	5.0 +/- 0.2 mm (0.197 +/- 0.008 inch)
Minimum	4.5 mm (0.150 inch)*
Disc thickness (rear)	
Standard	6.7 +/- 0.2 mm (0.264 +/- 0.008 inch)
Minimum	5.5 mm (0.220 inch)*
Disc runout (maximum)	0.30 mm (0.012 inch)
Wheel runout (limit)	2.0 mm (0.080 inch)
Axle runout (limit)	0.25 mm (0.010 inch)

Refer to information stamped in the disc; it supersedes information listed here.

Tightening torques

GSX-R750 (1985 through 1987)

Caliper mounting bolts	15 to 25 Nm (11 to 18 ft-lbs)
Caliper housing bolts	30 to 36 Nm (21.5 to 26.0 ft-lbs)
Brake disc mounting bolts	15 to 25 Nm (11 to 18 ft-lbs)
Front master cylinder bolts	5 to 8 Nm (3.5 to 6.0 ft-lbs)
Rear master cylinder bolts	6 to 10 Nm (4.5 to 7.0 ft-lbs)
Bleed valves	6 to 9 Nm (4.5 to 6.5 ft-lbs)
Front brake lever nut	8 to 12 Nm (6.0 to 8.5 ft-lbs)
Rear brake pedal bolt	
1985 and 1986	6 to 10 Nm (4.5 to 7.0 ft-lbs)
1987	8 to 12 Nm (6.0 to 8.5 ft-lbs)
Brake hose union bolts	20 to 25 Nm (14.5 to 18 ft-lbs)
Front axle nut	
1985 and 1986	
With cotter pin	36 to 52 Nm (26.0 to 37.5 ft-lbs)
Self-locking nut	40 to 58 Nm (29 to 41 ft-lbs)
1987	
With cotter pin	50 to 80 Nm (36 to 58 ft-lbs)
Self-locking nut	55 to 85 Nm (40 to 61 ft-lbs)
Front axle pinch nut or bolt	15 to 25 Nm (11 to 18 ft-lbs)
Rear axle nut	
With cotter pin	85 to 115 Nm (61.5 to 83.0 ft-lbs)
Self-locking nut	94 to 127 Nm (68 to 91 ft-lbs)

GSX-R750 (1988 and 1989)

Front caliper mounting bolts	28 to 44 Nm (20 to 32 ft-lbs)
Front brake pad retaining bolt	15 to 20 Nm (11.0 to 14.5 ft-lbs)
Front caliper housing bolts	20 to 25 Nm (14.5 to 18.0 ft-lbs)
Rear caliper mounting bolts	17 to 28 Nm (12.5 to 20.5 ft-lbs)
Brake torque link nuts	18 to 28 Nm (13 to 20 ft-lbs)
Rear caliper housing bolts	30 to 36 Nm (21.5 to 26.0 ft-lbs)
Brake disc mounting bolts	15 to 25 Nm (11 to 18 ft-lbs)
Front master cylinder bolts	5 to 8 Nm (3.5 to 6.0 ft-lbs)
Rear master cylinder bolts	15 to 25 Nm (11 to 18 ft-lbs)
Bleed valves	6 to 9 Nm (4.5 to 6.5 ft-lbs)
Front brake lever nut	8 to 12 Nm (6.0 to 8.5 ft-lbs)
Rear brake rod locknut	15 to 25 Nm (11 to 18 ft-lbs)
Brake hose union bolts	20 to 25 Nm (14.5 to 18.0 ft-lbs)
Front axle nut	85 to 115 Nm (61.5 to 83.0 ft-lbs)
Front axle pinch bolt	15 to 25 Nm (11 to 18 ft-lbs)
Rear axle nut	85 to 115 Nm (61.5 to 83.0 ft-lbs)

GSX-R750 (1990 on)

Front caliper mounting bolts	28 to 44 Nm (20 to 32 ft-lbs)
Front brake pad retaining bolt	15 to 20 Nm (11.0 to 14.5 ft-lbs)
Front caliper housing bolts	20 to 25 Nm (14.5 to 18.0 ft-lbs)
Rear caliper mounting bolts	17 to 28 Nm (12.5 to 20.5 ft-lbs)
Brake torque link nuts	
1990 (all) and 1991 on UK	22 to 34 Nm (16.0 to 24.5 ft-lbs)
1991 on US and Canada	18 to 28 Nm (13 to 20 ft-lbs)
Rear caliper housing bolts	30 to 36 Nm (21.5 to 26.0 ft-lbs)
Brake disc mounting bolts	15 to 25 Nm (11 to 18 ft-lbs)
Front master cylinder bolts	5 to 8 Nm (3.5 to 6.0 ft-lbs)
Rear master cylinder bolts	15 to 25 Nm (11 to 18 ft-lbs)

Bleed valves	6 to 9 Nm (4.5 to 6.5 ft-lbs)
Front brake lever nut	8 to 12 Nm (6.0 to 8.5 ft-lbs)
Rear brake rod locknut	15 to 20 Nm (11.0 to 14.5 ft-lbs)
Brake hose union bolts	15 to 20 Nm (11.0 to 14.5 ft-lbs)
Front axle shaft	85 to 115 Nm (61.5 to 83.0 ft-lbs)
Front axle pinch bolt	15 to 25 Nm (11 to 18 ft-lbs)
Rear axle nut	85 to 115 Nm (61.5 to 83.0 ft-lbs)

GSX-R1100 (1986 through 1988)

Caliper mounting bolts	15 to 25 Nm (11 to 18 ft-lbs)
Caliper housing bolts	30 to 36 Nm (21.5 to 26.0 ft-lbs)
Brake disc mounting bolts	15 to 25 Nm (11 to 18 ft-lbs)
Front master cylinder bolts	5 to 8 Nm (3.5 to 6.0 ft-lbs)
Rear master cylinder bolts	6 to 10 Nm (4.5 to 7.0 ft-lbs)
Bleed valves	6 to 9 Nm (4.5 to 6.5 ft-lbs)
Front brake lever nut	8 to 12 Nm (6.0 to 8.5 ft-lbs)
Rear brake pedal bolt	
1986	6 to 10 Nm (4.5 to 7.0 ft-lbs)
1987 and 1988	8 to 12 Nm (6.0 to 8.5 ft-lbs)
Brake hose union bolts	20 to 25 Nm (14.5 to 18.0 ft-lbs)
Front axle nut	
1986	
US and Canada	36 to 52 Nm (26.0 to 37.5 ft-lbs)
UK	40 to 58 Nm (29 to 41 ft-lbs)
1987 and 1988	
US and Canada	50 to 80 Nm (36 to 58 ft-lbs)
UK	55 to 88 Nm (40.0 to 63.7 ft-lbs)
Front axle pinch nut	20 to 40 Nm (14 to 29 ft-lbs)
Rear axle nut	
US and Canada	85 to 115 Nm (61.5 to 83.0 ft-lbs)
UK	94 to 127 Nm (68 to 91 ft-lbs)

GSX-R1100 (1989 on)

Front caliper mounting bolts	27 to 43 Nm (19.5 to 31.0 ft-lbs)
Front brake pad retaining bolt	15 to 20 Nm (11.0 to 14.5 ft-lbs)
Front caliper housing bolts	20 to 25 Nm (14.5 to 18.0 ft-lbs)
Rear caliper mounting bolts	18 to 28 Nm (13 to 20 ft-lbs)
Brake torque link nuts	
US and Canada	18 to 28 Nm (13 to 20 ft-lbs)
UK	22 to 34 Nm (16.0 to 24.5 ft-lbs)
Rear caliper housing bolts	30 to 36 Nm (21.5 to 26.0 ft-lbs)
Brake disc mounting bolts	15 to 25 Nm (11 to 18 ft-lbs)
Front master cylinder bolts	5 to 8 Nm (3.5 to 6.0 ft-lbs)
Rear master cylinder bolts	18 to 28 Nm (13 to 20 ft-lbs)
Bleed valves	6 to 9 Nm (4.5 to 6.5 ft-lbs)
Front brake lever nut	Not specified
Rear brake pedal bolt	Not specified
Rear brake rod locknut	
1989	18 to 28 Nm (13 to 20 ft-lbs)
1990 on	15 to 20 Nm (11.0 to 14.5 ft-lbs)
Brake hose union bolts	
1989	20 to 25 Nm (14.5 to 18 ft-lbs)
1990 on	15 to 20 Nm (11.0 to 14.5 ft-lbs)
Front axle nut	85 to 115 Nm (61.5 to 83.0 ft-lbs)
Front axle pinch bolt	18 to 28 Nm (13 to 20 ft-lbs)
Rear axle nut	85 to 115 Nm (61.5 to 83.0 ft-lbs)

Katana 600 (GSX600F)

Caliper mounting bolts	15 to 25 Nm (11 to 18 ft-lbs)
Caliper housing bolts	30 to 36 Nm (21.5 to 26.0 ft-lbs)
Brake torque link nuts	20 to 30 Nm (14.5 to 21.5 ft-lbs)
Brake disc mounting bolts	15 to 25 Nm (11 to 18 ft-lbs)
Front master cylinder bolts	5 to 8 Nm (3.5 to 6.0 ft-lbs)
Rear master cylinder bolts	8 to 12 Nm (6.0 to 8.5 ft-lbs)
Bleed valves	6 to 9 Nm (4.5 to 6.5 ft-lbs)
Front brake lever nut	8 to 12 Nm (6.0 to 8.5 ft-lbs)
Rear brake pedal bolt	8 to 12 Nm (6.0 to 8.5 ft-lbs)
Brake hose union bolts	15 to 20 Nm (11.0 to 14.5 ft-lbs)
Front brake hose bolt and nut (1989 on)	20 to 25 Nm (14.5 to 18.0 ft-lbs)

6

Tightening torques (continued)

Katana 600 (GSX600F)

Front axle nut
  With cotter pin .... 36 to 52 Nm (26.0 to 37.5 ft-lbs)
  Self-locking nut
    1988 .... 39 to 57 Nm (28 to 41 ft-lbs)
    1989 on .... 44 to 63 Nm (32.0 to 45.5 ft-lbs)
Front axle pinch nut .... 15 to 25 Nm (11 to 18 ft-lbs)
Rear axle nut
  With cotter pin .... 50 to 80 Nm (36 to 58 ft-lbs)
  Self-locking nut .... 55 to 88 Nm (40.0 to 63.5 ft-lbs)

Katana 750 (GSX750F)

Caliper mounting bolts .... 18 to 30 Nm (13.0 to 21.5 ft-lbs)
Front caliper housing bolts .... 30 to 36 Nm (21.5 to 26.0 ft-lbs)
Rear caliper housing bolts .... 28 to 32 Nm (20 to 23 ft-lbs)
Brake torque link nuts .... 20 to 30 Nm (14.5 to 21.5 ft-lbs)
Brake disc mounting bolts .... 18 to 30 Nm (13.0 to 21.5 ft-lbs)
Front master cylinder bolts .... 5 to 8 Nm (3.5 to 6.0 ft-lbs)
Rear master cylinder bolts .... 8 to 12 Nm (6.0 to 8.5 ft-lbs)
Bleed valves .... 6 to 9 Nm (4.5 to 6.5 ft-lbs)
Front brake lever nut .... 8 to 12 Nm (6.0 to 8.5 ft-lbs)
Rear brake pedal bolt .... 8 to 12 Nm (6.0 to 8.5 ft-lbs)
Brake hose union bolts .... 15 to 20 Nm (11.0 to 14.5 ft-lbs)
Front axle nut
  With cotter pin .... 36 to 52 Nm (26.0 to 37.5 ft-lbs)
  Self-locking nut .... 44 to 63 Nm (32.0 to 45.5 ft-lbs)
Front axle pinch nut .... 15 to 25 Nm (11 to 18 ft-lbs)
Rear axle nut
  With cotter pin .... 50 to 80 Nm (36 to 58 ft-lbs)
  Self-locking nut .... 55 to 88 Nm (40.0 to 63.5 ft-lbs)

Katana 1100 (GSX1100F)

Caliper mounting bolts .... 25 to 40 Nm (18 to 29 ft-lbs)
Caliper housing bolts .... 18 to 23 Nm (13.0 to 16.5 ft-lbs)
Brake torque link nuts .... 22 to 33 Nm (16 to 24 ft-lbs)
Brake disc mounting bolts .... 15 to 25 Nm (11 to 18 ft-lbs)
Front master cylinder bolts .... 8 to 12 Nm (6.0 to 8.5 ft-lbs)
Rear master cylinder bolts .... 15 to 25 Nm (11 to 18 ft-lbs)
Bleed valves .... 6 to 9 Nm (4.5 to 6.5 ft-lbs)
Front brake lever nut .... 8 to 12 Nm (6.0 to 8.5 ft-lbs)
Rear brake pedal bolt .... 15 to 25 Nm (11 to 18 ft-lbs)
Brake hose union bolts .... 20 to 25 Nm (14.5 to 18.0 ft-lbs)
Front axle nut
  With cotter pin .... 55 to 88 Nm (40.0 to 63.5 ft-lbs)
  Self-locking nut .... 60 to 96 Nm (43.5 to 69.5 ft-lbs)
Front axle pinch nut .... 15 to 25 Nm (11 to 18 ft-lbs)
Rear axle nut
  With cotter pin .... 94 to 127 Nm (68 to 91 ft-lbs)
  Self-locking nut .... 102 to 138 Nm (74 to 100 ft-lbs)

---

1 General information

The models covered by this manual are equipped with hydraulic disc brakes on both wheels. All models use dual calipers at the front and a single caliper at the rear. The front brakes on all except the Katana 1100 (GSX1100F) use four-piston calipers. Katana 1100 (GSX1100F) front brakes and all rear brakes use dual-piston calipers.

All models are equipped with cast aluminum wheels, which require very little maintenance and allow tubeless tires to be used.

Caution: Disc brake components rarely require disassembly. Do not disassemble components unless absolutely necessary. If any hydraulic brake line connection in the system is loosened, the entire system should be disassembled, drained, cleaned and then properly filled and bled upon reassembly. Do not use solvents on internal brake components. Solvents will cause seals to swell and distort. Use only clean brake fluid or alcohol for cleaning. Use care when working with brake fluid as it can injure your eyes and it will damage painted surfaces and plastic parts.

2 Front brake pads - replacement

Warning: The dust created by the brake system may contain asbestos, which is harmful to your health. Never blow it out with compressed air and don't inhale any of it. An approved filtering mask should be worn when working on the brakes.

1 Support the bike securely so it can't be knocked over during this procedure.

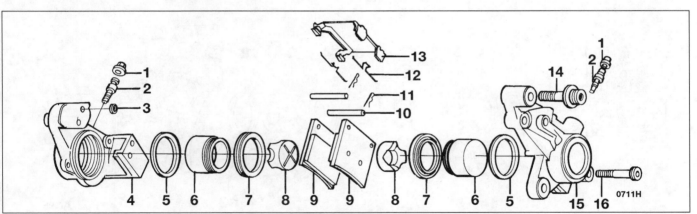

2.2a Front brake caliper (early GSX-R750/1100, Katana 600/GSX600F, Katana 750/GSX750F) - exploded view

1 Bolt	5 O-ring	9 Piston inserts	13 Retaining pin clips
2 Caliper half	6 Piston seals	10 Anti-rattle springs	14 Pads
3 Bleed valve cap	7 Dust seals	11 Pad retaining pins	15 Caliper half
4 Bleed valve	8 Pistons	12 Pad cover	16 Bolt

2.2b Front brake caliper (Katana 1100/GSX1100F) - exploded view

1 Bleed valve cap	6 Piston	9 Pads	13 Pad cover
2 Bleed valve	7 Dust seal	10 Pad retaining pins	14 Bolt
3 O-ring	8 Piston insert	11 Pad retaining pin clips	15 Caliper half
4 Caliper half	*(1988/J models only)*	12 Anti-rattle springs	16 Bolt
5 Piston seal			

2.3 Pull the clips (arrowed) out of the pad retaining pins

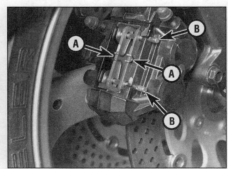

2.4 Disengage the anti-rattle springs from the pad retaining pin and pull the pins out

A Anti-rattle springs   *B Pad retaining pins*

2.6 Straighten the cotter pin (arrowed) and remove it from the pad retaining bolt - use a new cotter pin during installation

6

GSX-R750 (1985 through 1987); GSX-R1100 (1986 through 1988); all Katana/GSX-F models

2 Remove the brake pad cover (see illustrations).

3 Pull the clips out of the pad retaining pins (see illustration).

4 Pull the anti-rattle spring out of one pad retaining pin, then pull out the pin. Slide the spring out of the remaining pin and pull the pin out (see illustration).

5 Pull the pads out of the caliper.

GSX-R750 (1988 and later); GSX-R1100 (1989 and later)

6 Remove the cotter pin from the pad securing bolt (see illustration).

7 Unscrew the pad securing bolt and pull it out far enough to clear the pads (see illustrations).

8 Remove the anti-rattle spring (see illustration).

9 Remove the brake pads from the caliper (see illustration).

All models

10 Inspect the pad cavity for signs of fluid leakage past the piston seals (see illustration). If fluid has been leaking, the calipers must be removed for overhaul.

11 Check the condition of the brake disc (see Section 5). If it is in need of machining or replacement, follow the procedure in that Section to remove it. If it is okay, deglaze it with sandpaper or emery cloth, using a swirling motion.

12 Remove the cap from the master cylinder reservoir and siphon out some fluid. Push the pistons into the caliper as far as possible, while checking the master cylinder reservoir to make sure it doesn't overflow. If you can't depress the pistons with thumb pressure, try using a C-clamp (G-clamp). If any of the pistons stick, remove the caliper and overhaul it as described in Section 4.

13 Install both pads in the caliper.

14 The remainder of installation is the reverse of the removal steps, with the following addition: On late GSX-R750/1100 calipers, tighten the pad retaining bolt to the torque

2.7a Unscrew the pad retaining bolt with an Allen wrench

listed in this Chapter's Specifications and secure it with a new cotter pin.

15 Refill the master cylinder reservoir (see 'Daily (pre-ride) checks' at the beginning of this Manual) and install the diaphragm and cap.

16 Operate the brake lever several times to bring the pads into contact with the disc. Check the operation of the brakes carefully before riding the motorcycle.

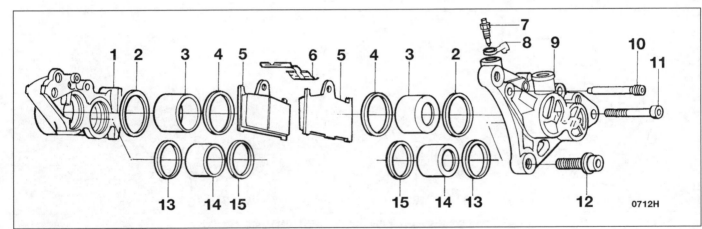

2.7b Front brake caliper (late GSX-R750/1100) - exploded view

1 Caliper half	4 Dust seal	7 Bleed valve	10 Bolt	13 Piston seals
2 Piston seal	5 Pads	8 Bleed valve cap	11 Bolt	14 Pistons
3 Piston	6 Anti-rattle spring	9 Caliper half	12 Bolt	15 Dust seals

2.8 Pull the pad retaining bolt out and remove the anti-rattle spring

2.9 Pull the pads out of the caliper

2.10 Inspect the brake pad cavity for signs of fluid leakage past the seals - if fluid has been leaking, overhaul the calipers

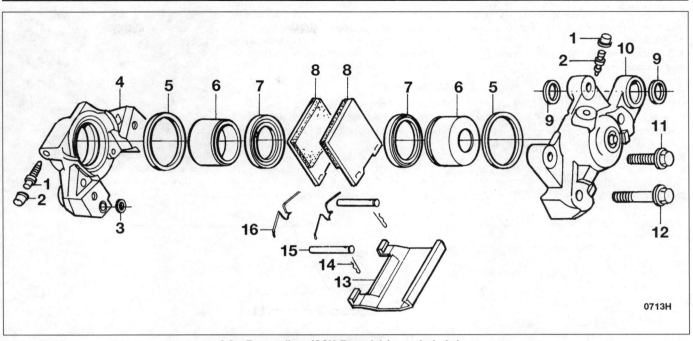

3.2a Rear caliper (GSX-R models) - exploded view

1 Bleed valve	5 Piston seal	9 Bushing	13 Pad cover
2 Bleed valve cap	6 Piston	10 Caliper half	14 Pad retaining pin clips
3 O-ring	7 Dust seal	11 Bolt	15 Pad retaining pins
4 Caliper half	8 Pads	12 Bolt	16 Anti-rattle springs

3 Rear brake pads - replacement

1 Support the bike securely so it can't be knocked over during this procedure.

GSX-R models

2 Remove the pad cover from the caliper **(see illustrations)**.
3 Pull the clips out of the pad retaining pins **(see illustration)**.
4 Pull the anti-rattle spring out of one pad retaining pin and pull out the pin **(see illustration)**.

3.2b The pads are removed from beneath the caliper - start by removing the pad cover

3.3 Pull the clips out of the pad retaining pins

3.4 Pull the anti-rattle spring out of one retaining pin and slide that pin out

3.5a Pull the anti-rattle spring out of the remaining pin . . .

3.5b . . . and pull the pin out to free the pads

6

5 Pull the anti-rattle spring out of the other retaining pin and pull out the pin **(see illustrations)**.

6 Pull the pads and shims out of the caliper **(see illustration)**.

Katana (GSX-F) models

7 Remove the pad cover from the caliper **(see illustrations)**.

8 Pull the clips out of the pad retaining pins **(see illustration)**.

9 Pull the anti-rattle springs out of one pad retaining pin, then pull out the pin **(see illustration)**.

10 Slide the spring out of the remaining pin and pull the pin out **(see illustration)**.

11 Pull the pads and shims out of the caliper **(see illustration)**. Note the installed position of the shims **(see illustration)**.

All models

12 Inspect the pad cavity for signs of fluid leakage past the piston seals. If fluid has been leaking, the calipers must be removed for overhaul.

13 Check the condition of the brake disc (see Section 5). If it is in need of machining or replacement, follow the procedure in that Section to remove it. If it is okay, deglaze it

3.6 Lower the pads and shims out of the caliper

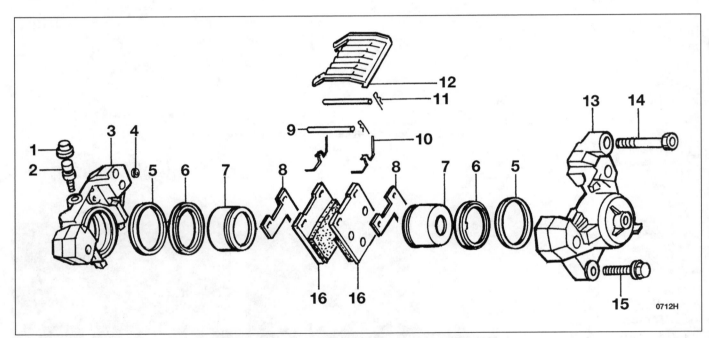

3.7a Rear caliper (Katana/GSX-F models) - exploded view

1 Bleed valve cap	5 Piston seal	9 Pad retaining pins	13 Caliper half
2 Bleed valve	6 Dust seal	10 Anti-rattle springs	14 Bolt
3 Caliper half	7 Piston	11 Retaining pin clips	15 Bolt
4 O-ring	8 Pad shims	12 Pad cover	16 Pads

3.7b Lift the pad cover off the caliper

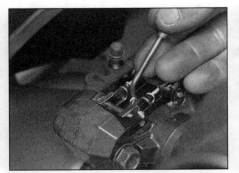

3.8 Pull out the pad retaining pin clips

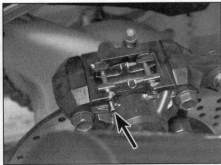

3.9 Pull the anti-rattle spring out of one pad retaining pin and withdraw the pin (arrowed)

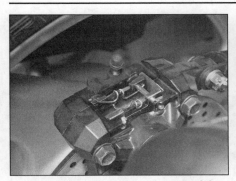

3.10 Pull the anti-rattle spring out of the remaining pin and withdraw the pin

3.11a Pull out the pads, together with the shims . . .

3.11b . . . and note the installed position of the shims for reassembly

with sandpaper or emery cloth, using a swirling motion.

14 Remove the cap from the master cylinder reservoir and siphon out some fluid. Push the pistons into the caliper as far as possible, while checking the master cylinder reservoir to make sure it doesn't overflow. If you can't depress the pistons with thumb pressure, try using a C-clamp (G-clamp). If any of the pistons stick, remove the caliper and overhaul it as described in Section 4.

15 Install the pads and shims in the caliper.

16 The remainder of installation is the reverse of the removal steps.

17 Operate the brake pedal several times to bring the pads into contact with the disc. Check the operation of the brakes carefully before riding the motorcycle.

---

4 Brake caliper - removal, overhaul and installation

⚠️ *Warning: If a caliper indicates the need for an overhaul (usually due to leaking fluid or sticky operation), all old brake fluid should be flushed from the system. Also, the dust created by the brake system may contain asbestos, which is harmful to your health. Never blow it out with compressed air and don't inhale any of it. An approved filtering mask should be worn when*

working on the brakes. Do not, under any circumstances, use petroleum-based solvents to clean brake parts. Use clean brake fluid, brake cleaner or denatured alcohol only!

Note: *If you are removing the caliper only to replace or inspect the brake pads, don't disconnect the hose from the caliper.*

Removal

1 Support the bike securely so it can't be knocked over during this procedure. **Note:** *If you're planning to overhaul the caliper and don't have a source of compressed air to blow out the*

pistons, use the bike's hydraulic system instead. To do this, remove the pads (see Section 2 or 3) and squeeze the brake lever or push the pedal to force the pistons out of the cylinder.

2 Detach the brake hose from the caliper **(see illustrations)**. Discard the sealing washers (if equipped). Plug the end of the hose or wrap a plastic bag tightly around it to prevent excessive fluid loss and contamination.

3 On rear calipers, unbolt the brake torque rod from the caliper **(see illustrations 4.2b and 4.2c)**.

4 Remove the caliper mounting bolts and lift the caliper off **(see illustrations)**.

4.2a If the brake line uses a compression fitting, hold the fitting with a backup wrench and undo the line with another wrench

4.2b If the brake line uses a union bolt, remove it - on rear calipers, remove the cotter pin and nut from the torque rod bolt (arrowed) (this is a Katana/GSX-F caliper) . . .

4.2c . . . and withdraw the bolt to separate the torque rod from the caliper (this is a GSX-R caliper)

4.4a Remove the caliper mounting bolts . . .

4.4b . . . and lift the caliper off (late GSX-R1100 shown)

6

Overhaul

5 Remove the brake pads (see Section 2 or Section 3, if necessary).

6 Remove the caliper piston inserts (if equipped) **(see illustrations 2.2a or 2.2b).**

7 Clean the exterior of the caliper with denatured alcohol or brake system cleaner.

8 Unbolt the caliper halves from each other. Separate the caliper halves and remove the O-rings **(see illustration 2.2a, 2.2b, 2.7b, 3.2a or 3.7a).** Throw these away; they must be replaced each time the caliper halves are separated.

9 If you didn't blow out the pistons with the bike's hydraulic system in Step 1, place a few rags against the piston(s) to act as a cushion, then use compressed air, directed into the fluid inlet, to remove the pistons. Use only enough air pressure to ease the pistons out of the bore. If a piston is blown out, even with the cushion in place, it may be damaged.

> ⚠ **Warning: Never place your fingers in front of the piston in an attempt to catch or protect it when applying compressed air, as serious injury could occur.**

10 Using a wood or plastic tool, remove the dust seals. Metal tools may cause bore damage.

11 Using a wood or plastic tool, remove the piston seal from the groove in each caliper bore.

12 Clean the pistons and the bores with denatured alcohol, clean brake fluid or brake system cleaner and blow them dry with filtered, unlubricated compressed air. Inspect the surfaces of the pistons for nicks and burrs and loss of plating. Check the caliper bores, too. If surface defects are present, the caliper must be replaced. If the caliper is in bad shape, the master cylinder should also be checked.

13 Lubricate the piston seals with clean brake fluid and install them in their grooves in the caliper bore. Make sure they seat completely and aren't twisted.

14 Lubricate the dust seals with clean brake fluid and install them in their grooves, making sure they seat correctly.

15 Lubricate the pistons with clean brake fluid and install them into the caliper bores. Using your thumbs, push the pistons all the way in, making sure they don't get cocked in the bore.

16 Install the piston inserts (if equipped).

Installation

17 Install the caliper, tightening the mounting bolts to the torque listed in this Chapter's Specifications.

18 Install the pads (see Section 2 or 3).

19 Connect the brake hose to the caliper, using new sealing washers. Tighten the banjo fitting bolt or brake hose to the torque listed in this Chapter's Specifications.

20 Fill the master cylinder with the recommended brake fluid (see 'Daily (pre-ride) checks' at the beginning of this Manual) and bleed the system (see Section 10). Check for leaks.

21 Check the operation of the brakes carefully before riding the motorcycle.

---

5 Brake disc(s) - inspection, removal and installation

Inspection

1 Support the bike so it can't be knocked over during this procedure.

2 Visually inspect the surface of the disc(s) for score marks and other damage. Light scratches are normal after use and won't affect brake operation, but deep grooves and heavy score marks will reduce braking efficiency and accelerate pad wear. If the discs are badly grooved they must be machined or replaced.

3 To check disc runout, mount a dial indicator to a fork leg with the plunger on the indicator touching the surface of the disc about 1/2-inch from the outer edge. Slowly turn the wheel (have an assistant sit on the seat to raise the front wheel off the ground) and watch the indicator needle, comparing your reading with the limit listed in this Chapter's Specifications. If the runout is greater than allowed, check the hub bearings for play (see Chapter 1). If the bearings are worn, replace them and repeat this check. If the disc runout is still excessive, it will have to be replaced.

4 The disc must not be machined or allowed to wear down to a thickness less than the minimum allowable thickness, listed in this Chapter's Specifications. The thickness of the disc can be checked with a micrometer. If the thickness of the disc is less than the minimum allowable, it must be replaced.

Removal

5 Remove the wheel (see Section 13 or 14). *Caution: Don't lay the wheel down and allow it to rest on the disc - the disc could become warped. Set the wheel on wood blocks so the disc doesn't support the weight of the wheel.*

5.6 Loosen the disc retaining bolts a little at a time to prevent distortion

6 Mark the relationship of the disc to the wheel, so it can be installed in the same position. Remove the Allen bolts that retain the disc to the wheel **(see illustration).** Loosen the bolts a little at a time, in a criss-cross pattern, to avoid distorting the disc.

7 Take note of any shims that may be present where the disc mates to the wheel. If there are any, mark their position and be sure to include them when installing the disc.

Installation

8 Position the disc on the wheel, aligning the previously applied match marks (if you're reinstalling the original disc). Make sure the arrow (stamped on the disc) marking the direction of rotation is pointing in the proper direction.

9 Apply a non-hardening thread locking compound (Suzuki Thread Lock 1360 or equivalent) to the threads of the bolts. Install the bolts, tightening them a little at a time, in a criss-cross pattern, until the torque listed in this Chapter's Specifications is reached. Clean off all grease from the brake disc using acetone or brake system cleaner.

10 Install the wheel.

11 Operate the brake lever several times to bring the pads into contact with the disc. Check the operation of the brakes carefully before riding the motorcycle.

---

6 Front brake master cylinder (all except late GSX-R750) - removal, overhaul and installation

1 If the master cylinder is leaking fluid, or if the lever does not produce a firm feel when the brake is applied, and bleeding the brakes does not help, master cylinder overhaul is recommended.

2 Before disassembling the master cylinder, read through the entire procedure and make sure that you have the correct rebuild kit. Also, you will need some new, clean brake fluid of the recommended type, some clean rags and internal snap-ring pliers. **Note:** *To prevent damage to the paint from spilled*

6.3 If you're going to remove the master cylinder cover, loosen the cover screws (it's easier to do this when the master cylinder is still bolted to the handlebar)

6.4 Remove the master cylinder banjo fitting bolt - use a six-point box wrench (ring spanner), and expect some leakage

brake fluid, always cover the fuel tank when working on the master cylinder.
Caution: Disassembly, overhaul and reassembly of the brake master cylinder must be done in a spotlessly clean work area to avoid contamination and possible failure of the brake hydraulic system components.

Removal

3 Loosen, but do not remove, the screws holding the reservoir cover in place **(see illustration)**.

4 Loosen the banjo fitting bolt or disconnect the reservoir hose **(see illustration)** and separate the brake hose from the master cylinder. Wrap the end of the hose in a clean rag and suspend the hose in an upright position or bend it down carefully and place the open end in a clean container. The objective is to prevent excess loss of brake fluid, fluid spills and system contamination.

5 Remove the locknut from the underside of the lever pivot bolt, then unscrew the bolt.

6 Remove the master cylinder mounting bolts and separate the master cylinder from the handlebar.
Caution: Do not tip the master cylinder upside down or brake fluid will run out.

7 Disconnect the electrical connectors from the brake light switch.

Overhaul

8 Detach the top cover, gasket (if equipped) and rubber diaphragm **(see illustration)**, then drain the brake fluid into a suitable container. Wipe any remaining fluid out of the reservoir with a clean rag.

9 Carefully remove the rubber dust boot from the end of the piston.

10 Using snap-ring pliers, remove the snap-ring and slide out the piston, the cup seals and the spring. Lay the parts out in the proper order to prevent confusion during reassembly.

11 Clean all of the parts with brake system cleaner (available at auto parts stores), isopropyl alcohol or clean brake fluid.
Caution: Do not, under any circumstances, use a petroleum-based solvent to clean brake parts. If compressed air is available,

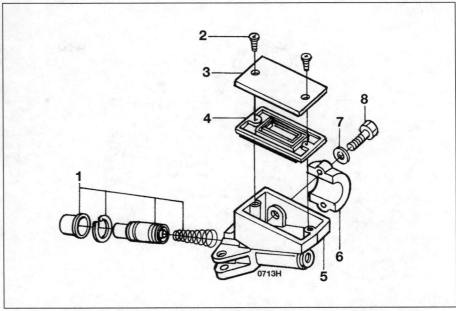

6.8 Exploded view of the master cylinder (all except late GSX-R750 models)

1 Piston assembly	*4 Diaphragm*	*7 Washer*
2 Cover screws	*5 Master cylinder body*	*8 Bolt*
3 Cover	*6 Master cylinder clamp*	

use it to dry the parts thoroughly (make sure it's filtered and unlubricated). Check the master cylinder bore for corrosion, scratches, nicks and score marks. If damage is evident, the master cylinder must be replaced with a new one. If the master cylinder is in poor condition, then the caliper should be checked as well.

12 Pistons and cups are supplied by Suzuki as a complete set. Replace them as a set whenever the master cylinder is overhauled.

13 Before reassembling the master cylinder, soak the piston and the rubber cup seals in clean brake fluid for ten to fifteen minutes. Lubricate the master cylinder bore with clean brake fluid, then carefully insert the piston and related parts in the reverse order of disassembly. Make sure the lips on the cup seals do not turn inside out when they are slipped into the bore.

14 Depress the piston, then install the snap-ring (make sure the snap-ring is properly seated in the groove). Install the rubber dust boot (make sure the lip is seated properly).

Installation

15 Attach the master cylinder to the handlebar with the master cylinder clamp next to the punch mark on the handlebar. Tighten the bolts to the torque listed in this Chapter's Specifications. **Note**: *Tighten the upper bolt first, then the lower bolt. There will be a gap at the bottom between the clamp and master cylinder body.*

16 Install the brake lever and tighten the pivot bolt locknut. Connect the brake light switch wires.

17 Connect the brake hose to the master

cylinder, using new sealing washers. Tighten the banjo fitting bolt to the torque listed in this Chapter's Specifications. Refer to Section 10 and bleed the air from the system.

---

7   Front brake master cylinder (late GSX-R750) - removal, overhaul and installation

Removal

1 Disconnect the wires from the front brake light switch at the master cylinder.

2 Place a rag beneath the master cylinder union bolt to protect the paint and remove the bolt with a six-point box wrench (ring spanner).

3 Remove the master cylinder and fluid reservoir mounting bolts, then remove the master cylinder together with the reservoir **(see illustration)**.

Overhaul

4 Disconnect the reservoir hose from the master cylinder **(see illustration 7.3)**.

5 Remove the pivot bolt and take off the brake lever.

6 Carefully remove the rubber dust boot from the end of the piston.

7 Using snap-ring pliers, remove the snap-ring and slide out the piston, the cup seals and the spring. Lay the parts out in the proper order to prevent confusion during reassembly.

8 Remove the cover from the reservoir hose fitting, then remove the snap-ring, fitting and O-ring from the master cylinder.

9 Clean all of the parts with brake system

6

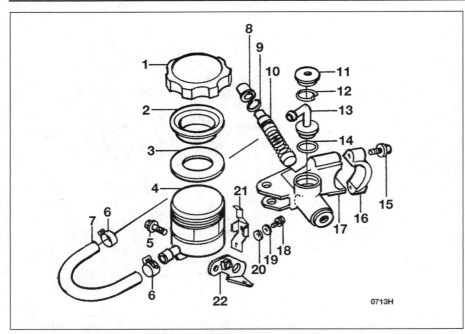

7.3 Master cylinder (late GSX-R750 models) - exploded view

1 Cap	9 Snap-ring	16 Master cylinder clamp
2 Diaphragm	10 Piston, cups and spring	17 Master cylinder body
3 Seal	11 Retainer	18 Screw
4 Reservoir	12 Snap-ring	19 Lockwasher
5 Bolt	13 Hose fitting	20 Washer
6 Hose clamps	14 O-ring	21 Retainer
7 Hose	15 Bolt	22 Bracket
8 Dust boot		

cleaner (available at auto parts stores), isopropyl alcohol or clean brake fluid. *Caution: Do not, under any circumstances, use a petroleum-based solvent to clean brake parts. If compressed air is available, use it to dry the parts thoroughly (make sure it's filtered and unlubricated). Check the master cylinder bore for corrosion, scratches, nicks and score marks. If damage is evident, the master cylinder must be replaced with a new one. If the master cylinder is in poor condition, then the caliper should be checked as well.*

10 Pistons and cups are supplied by Suzuki as a complete set. Replace them as a set whenever the master cylinder is overhauled.

11 Before reassembling the master cylinder, soak the piston and the rubber cup seals in clean brake fluid for ten to fifteen minutes. Lubricate the master cylinder bore with clean brake fluid, then carefully insert the piston and related parts in the reverse order of disassembly. Make sure the lips on the cup seals do not turn inside out when they are slipped into the bore.

12 Depress the piston, then install the snap-ring (make sure the snap-ring is properly seated in the groove). Install the rubber dust boot (make sure the lip is seated properly).

13 Install the reservoir hose fitting with a new O-ring and secure it with the snap ring. Install the cover on the fitting.

14 Install the brake lever and connect the reservoir hose to the master cylinder body.

Installation

15 Installation is the reverse of the removal steps, with the following additions:

a) Tighten the fluid hose union bolt to the torque listed in this Chapter's Specifications.

b) Tighten the upper mounting bolt first, then the lower bolt to the torque listed in this Chapter's Specifications. There will be a gap at the bottom between the

8.3 Disconnect the master cylinder fluid line and immediately direct it into a container to catch the fluid - diagonally mounted master cylinders are secured to the frame by two bolts (arrowed)

clamp and master cylinder body.

c) Connect the fluid hose to the master cylinder, using new sealing washers. Tighten the banjo fitting bolt to the torque listed in this Chapter's Specifications.

d) Refer to Section 10 and bleed air from the system.

8 Rear master cylinder - removal, overhaul and installation

1 If the master cylinder is leaking fluid, or if the lever does not produce a firm feel when the brake is applied, and bleeding the brakes does not help, master cylinder overhaul is recommended.

2 Before disassembling the master cylinder, read through the entire procedure and make sure that you have the correct rebuild kit. Also, you will need some new, clean brake fluid of the recommended type, some clean rags and internal snap-ring pliers. **Note:** *To prevent damage to the paint from spilled brake fluid, always protect surrounding plastic and painted components when working on the master cylinder.*

Caution: Disassembly, overhaul and reassembly of the brake master cylinder must be done in a spotlessly clean work area to avoid contamination and possible failure of the brake hydraulic system components.

Removal

3 Place a rag beneath the master cylinder to catch brake fluid spills. With a container handy, disconnect the fluid line from the master cylinder and direct it into the container to catch the brake fluid **(see illustration)**.

Caution: Brake fluid will damage paint. Wipe up any spilled fluid immediately and clean the area with soap and water.

4 Remove the cotter pin and disconnect the master cylinder pushrod from the brake pedal **(see illustration)**. Remove the mounting bolts and take the master cylinder out.

8.4 Remove the cotter pin and clevis pin to detach the pushrod from the brake pedal (lower arrow) - vertically mounted master cylinders are secured to the pedal bracket by two bolts (upper arrows)

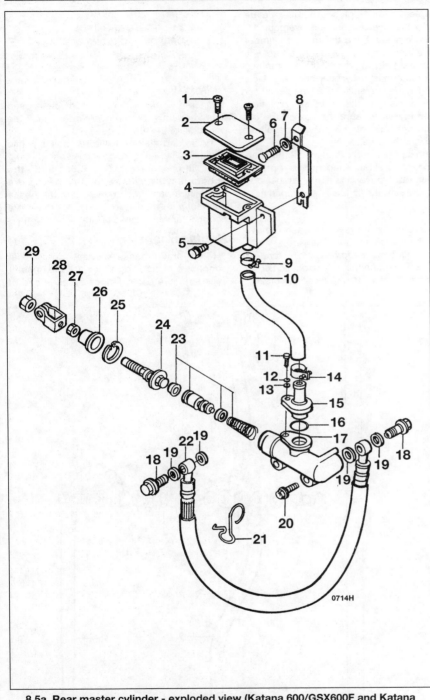

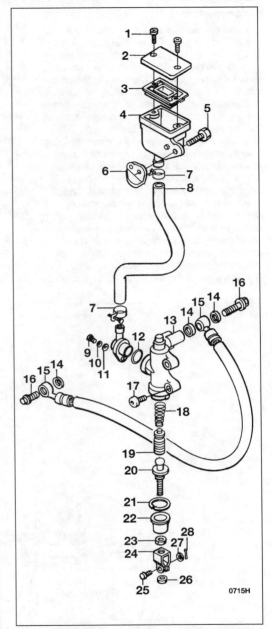

8.5a Rear master cylinder - exploded view (Katana 600/GSX600F and Katana 750/GSX750F shown; early GSX-R750 and GSX-R1100 similar)

1 Screws	11 Screw	21 Clip
2 Cover	12 Washer	22 Hose
3 Diaphragm	13 Washer	23 Piston assembly
4 Cylinder body	14 Hose clamp	24 Pushrod
5 Bolt	15 Hose fitting	25 Snap-ring
6 Bolt	16 O-ring	26 Dust boot
7 Washer	17 Cylinder body	27 Nut
8 Bracket	18 Union bolt	28 Pushrod clevis
9 Hose clamp	19 Sealing washer	29 Nut
10 Hose	20 Mounting bolt	

8.5b Rear master cylinder - exploded view (late GSX-R750 and GSX-R1100 shown; Katana 1100/GSX1100F similar)

1 Cover screws	15 Hose
2 Cover	16 Bolt
3 Diaphragm	17 Bolt
4 Reservoir	18 Spring
5 Bolt	19 Piston
6 Bracket	20 Pushrod
7 Hose clamp	21 Snap-ring
8 Reservoir hose	22 Dust boot
9 Screw	23 Nut
10 Washer	24 Pushrod clevis
11 Washer	25 Clevis pin
12 O-ring	26 Nut
13 Cylinder body	27 Washer
14 Sealing washer	28 Cotter pin

6

Overhaul

5 Carefully remove the rubber dust boot from the end of the piston **(see illustrations)**.

6 Using snap-ring pliers, remove the snap-ring and slide out the piston, the cup seals and the spring. Lay the parts out in the proper order to prevent confusion during reassembly.

7 Clean all of the parts with brake system cleaner (available at auto parts stores), isopropyl alcohol or clean brake fluid. *Caution: Do not, under any circumstances, use a petroleum-based solvent to clean brake parts. If compressed air is available, use it to dry the parts thoroughly (make sure it's filtered and unlubricated). Check the master cylinder bore for corrosion, scratches, nicks and score marks. If damage is evident, the master cylinder must be replaced with a new one. If the master cylinder is in poor condition, then the caliper should be checked as well.*

8 Pistons and cups are supplied by Suzuki as a complete set. Replace them as a set whenever the master cylinder is overhauled.

9 Before reassembling the master cylinder, soak the piston and the rubber cup seals in clean brake fluid for ten to fifteen minutes. Lubricate the master cylinder bore with clean brake fluid, then carefully insert the piston and related parts in the reverse order of disassembly. Make sure the lips on the cup seals do not turn inside out when they are slipped into the bore.

10 Depress the piston, then install the snap-ring (make sure the snap-ring is properly seated in the groove). Install the rubber dust boot (make sure the lip is seated properly).

Installation

11 Installation is the reverse of the removal steps, with the following additions:

a) Tighten the mounting bolts to the torque listed in this Chapter's Specifications.

b) Refer to Section 10 and bleed the brakes.

9 Brake hoses and lines - inspection and replacement

Inspection

1 Once a week, or if the motorcycle is used less frequently, before every ride, check the condition of the brake hoses.

2 Twist and flex the rubber hoses while looking for cracks, bulges and seeping fluid **(see illustrations 8.5a, 8.5b and the accompanying illustrations)**. Check extra carefully around the areas where the hoses connect with the banjo fittings, as these are common areas for hose failure.

Replacement

3 Most brake hoses (except hoses that connect the fluid reservoir to the master cylinder) have banjo fittings on each end of

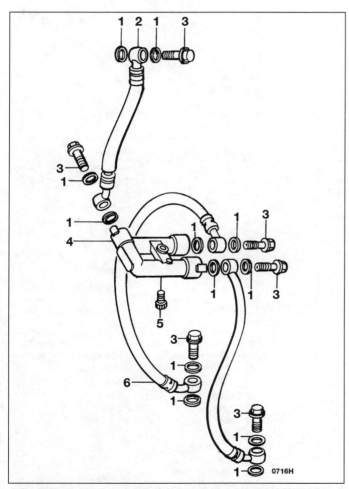

9.2a Front brake line details (all except Katana 600/GSX600F and Katana 750/GSX750F)

1	Sealing washers	4	Brake line joint fitting
2	Hose	5	Bolt
3	Union bolt	6	Hose

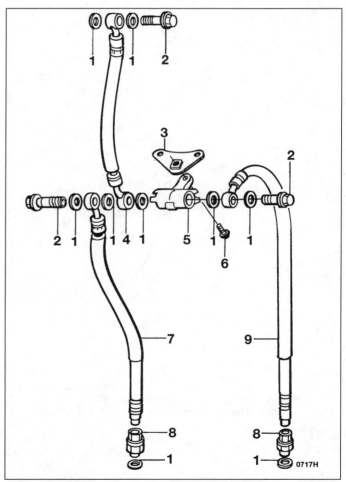

9.2b Front brake line details (Katana 600/GSX600F and Katana 750/GSX750F)

1	Sealing washers	4	Hose	7	Hose
2	Union bolt	5	Hose joint fitting	8	Fitting
3	Bracket	6	Bolt	9	Hose

9.3a The front brake lines meet at a fitting under the steering stem (this type is used on all except Katana 600/GSX600F and Katana 750/GSX750F models) . . .

9.3b . . . and this type is used on Katana 600/GSX600F and Katana 750/GSX750F models - use a six-point box wrench (ring spanner) on the banjo bolts and be prepared for some leakage

9.3c For threaded fittings like this one, hold the fitting with a backup wrench and use another wrench to undo the brake line

the hose **(see illustrations)**. Cover the surrounding area with plenty of rags and unscrew the banjo bolts on either end of the hose. If a threaded fitting is used instead of a banjo bolt **(see illustration)**, hold the fitting from turning with a backup wrench and use another wrench to loosen the hose. Detach the hose from any clips that may be present and remove the hose.

4 Position the new hose, making sure it isn't twisted or otherwise strained, between the two components. Make sure the metal tube portion of the banjo fitting is located between the casting protrusions on the component it's connected to, if equipped. Install the banjo bolts, using new sealing washers on both sides of the fittings, and tighten them to the torque listed in this Chapter's Specifications. If a threaded fitting is used instead of a banjo bolt, tighten it securely, again using a backup wrench to keep the fitting from turning.

5 Flush the old brake fluid from the system, refill the system with the recommended fluid (see 'Daily (pre-ride) checks' at the beginning of this Manual) and bleed the air from the system (see Section 10). Check the operation of the brakes carefully before riding the motorcycle.

10 Brake system bleeding

1 Bleeding the brake is simply the process of removing all the air bubbles from the brake fluid reservoir, the lines and the brake caliper. Bleeding is necessary whenever a brake system hydraulic connection is loosened, when a component or hose is replaced, or when the master cylinder or caliper is overhauled. Leaks in the system may also allow air to enter, but leaking brake fluid will reveal their presence and warn you of the need for repair.

2 To bleed the brake, you will need some new, clean brake fluid of the recommended type (see Chapter 1), a length of clear vinyl or

plastic tubing, a small container partially filled with clean brake fluid, some rags and a wrench to fit the brake caliper bleeder valve.

3 Cover the fuel tank and other painted components to prevent damage in the event that brake fluid is spilled.

4 Remove the reservoir cap or cover and slowly pump the brake lever or pedal a few times, until no air bubbles can be seen floating up from the holes at the bottom of reservoir. Doing this bleeds the air from the master cylinder end of the line. Reinstall the reservoir cap or cover.

5 Remove the rubber cap from the bleed valve (from both valves on calipers so equipped) **(see illustration)**.

10.5 Remove the rubber cap from the bleed valve (arrowed) . . .

10.6b . . . place the other end of the tube in a clean container

6 Attach one end of the clear vinyl or plastic tubing to the brake caliper bleed valve and submerge the other end in the brake fluid in the container **(see illustrations)**. **Note**: On calipers with two bleed valves, start bleeding at the inner valve (nearest the wheel).

7 Remove the reservoir cap or cover and check the fluid level. Do not allow the fluid level to drop below the lower mark during the bleeding process.

8 Carefully pump the brake lever or pedal three or four times and hold it while opening the caliper bleeder valve. When the valve is opened, brake fluid will flow out of the caliper into the clear tubing and the lever will move toward the handlebar or the pedal will move down.

10.6a . . . and place a box wrench (ring spanner) and vinyl tube on the valve (Katana/GSX-F rear caliper shown; GSX-R rear caliper similar) . . .

10.6c If the caliper has two bleed valves, start with the one closest to the wheel

6

9 Retighten the bleed valve, then release the brake lever or pedal gradually. Repeat the process until no air bubbles are visible in the brake fluid leaving the caliper and the lever or pedal is firm when applied. **Note**: *On models with two bleed valves, air must be bled from both, one after the other. Remember to add fluid to the reservoir as the level drops. Use only new, clean brake fluid of the recommended type. Never reuse the fluid lost during bleeding.*

10 If you're bleeding the front brakes, repeat this procedure on the other caliper. Be sure to check the fluid level in the master cylinder reservoir frequently.

11 Replace the reservoir cover, wipe up any spilled brake fluid and check the entire system for leaks.

> **HAYNES HINT** *If it's not possible to produce a firm feel to the lever or pedal the fluid may be aerated. Let the brake fluid in the system stabilise for a few hours and then repeat the procedure when the tiny bubbles in the system have settled out.*

11 Wheels - inspection and repair

1 Place the motorcycle on the centerstand (if equipped) or support it securely, then clean the wheels thoroughly to remove mud and dirt that may interfere with the inspection procedure or mask defects. Make a general check of the wheels and tires as described in *'Daily (pre-ride) checks'* at the beginning of this Manual.

2 With the motorcycle securely supported and the wheel in the air, attach a dial indicator to the fork slider or the swingarm and position the stem against the side of the rim. Spin the wheel slowly and check the side-to-side (axial) runout of the rim, then compare your readings with the value listed in this Chapter's Specifications. In order to accurately check radial runout with the dial indicator, the wheel would have to be removed from the machine and the tire removed from the wheel. With the axle clamped in a vise, the wheel can be rotated to check the runout.

3 An easier, though slightly less accurate, method is to attach a stiff wire pointer to the fork slider or the swingarm and position the end a fraction of an inch from the wheel (where the wheel and tire join). If the wheel is true, the distance from the pointer to the rim will be constant as the wheel is rotated. Repeat the procedure to check the runout of the rear wheel. **Note**: *If wheel runout is excessive, refer to the appropriate Section in this Chapter and check the wheel bearings very carefully before replacing the wheel.*

4 The wheels should also be visually

inspected for cracks, flat spots on the rim and other damage. Since tubeless tires are involved, look very closely for dents in the area where the tire bead contacts the rim. Dents in this area may prevent complete sealing of the tire against the rim, which leads to deflation of the tire over a period of time.

5 If damage is evident, or if runout in either direction is excessive, the wheel will have to be replaced with a new one. Never attempt to repair a damaged cast aluminum wheel.

12 Wheels - alignment check

1 Misalignment of the wheels, which may be due to a cocked rear wheel or a bent frame or triple clamps, can cause strange and possibly serious handling problems. If the frame or triple clamps are at fault, repair by a frame specialist or replacement with new parts are the only alternatives.

2 To check the alignment you will need an assistant, a length of string or a perfectly straight piece of wood and a ruler graduated in 1/64 inch increments. A plumb bob or other suitable weight will also be required.

3 Place the motorcycle on the centerstand, then measure the width of both tires at their widest points. Subtract the smaller measurement from the larger measurement, then divide the difference by two. The result is the amount of offset that should exist between the front and rear tires on both sides.

4 If a string is used, have your assistant hold one end of it about half way between the floor and the rear axle, touching the rear sidewall of the tire.

5 Run the other end of the string forward and pull it tight so that it is roughly parallel to the floor. Slowly bring the string into contact with the front sidewall of the rear tire, then turn the front wheel until it is parallel with the string. Measure the distance from the front tire sidewall to the string.

6 Repeat the procedure on the other side of the motorcycle. The distance from the front tire sidewall to the string should be equal on both sides.

7 As was previously pointed out, a perfectly straight length of wood may be substituted for the string. The procedure is the same.

8 If the distance between the string and tire is greater on one side, or if the rear wheel appears to be cocked, refer to Chapter 5, *Swingarm bearings - check*, and make sure the swingarm is tight.

9 If the front-to-back alignment is correct, the wheels still may be out of alignment vertically.

10 Using the plumb bob, or other suitable weight, and a length of string, check the rear wheel to make sure it is vertical. To do this, hold the string against the tire upper sidewall and allow the weight to settle just off the floor. When the string touches both the upper and lower tire sidewalls and is perfectly straight,

the wheel is vertical. If it is not, place thin spacers under one leg of the centerstand.

11 Once the rear wheel is vertical, check the front wheel in the same manner. If both wheels are not perfectly vertical, the frame and/or major suspension components are bent.

13 Front wheel - removal and installation

Removal

1 On late GSX-R750 and 1100 models, remove the lower fairing (see Chapter 7).

2 Support the motorcycle securely so it can't be knocked over during this procedure.

3 Raise the front wheel off the ground by placing a floor jack, with a wood block on the jack head, under the engine.

4 On 1985 through 1987 UK GSX-R750 models, disconnect the speedometer cable from the drive unit.

5 Remove the brake calipers and support them with pieces of wire. Don't disconnect the brake hoses from the calipers.

6 Remove the cotter pin from the axle nut (if equipped).

All except late GSX-R750 and GSX-R1100 models

7 Katana 1100/GSX1100F: Remove the pinch bolt from the front side of the right-hand fork.

8 Katana 600/GSX600F, Katana 750/GSX750F, GSX-R750, GSX-R1100: Remove the clamp nut on the rear side of the front fork.

9 If the axle nut has a cotter pin, remove it. Unscrew the axle nut.

10 Support the wheel and remove the axle shaft from the front wheel and forks **(see illustrations)**. Lower the front wheel away from the bike.

Late GSX-R750 and GSX-R1100 models

11 Loosen the right side axle clamp bolts **(see illustration)**.

12 Support the wheel, unscrew the axle and pull it out **(see illustrations)**. Lower the wheel away from the bike.

All models

Caution: Don't lay the wheel down and allow it to rest on one of the discs - the disc could become warped. Set the wheel on wood blocks so the disc doesn't support the weight of the wheel. If the axle is corroded, remove the corrosion with fine emery cloth.

Note: *Do not operate the front brake lever with the wheel removed.*

13 Check the condition of the wheel bearings (see Section 15).

Installation

14 Installation is the reverse of removal, with the following additions:

a) *Apply a thin coat of grease to the seal lip,*

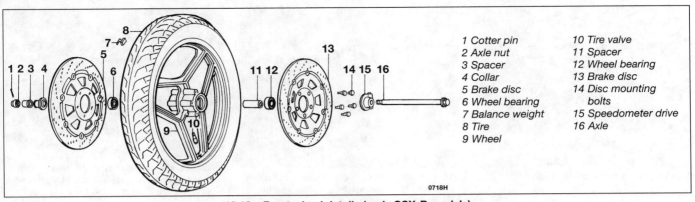

1 Cotter pin
2 Axle nut
3 Spacer
4 Collar
5 Brake disc
6 Wheel bearing
7 Balance weight
8 Tire
9 Wheel
10 Tire valve
11 Spacer
12 Wheel bearing
13 Brake disc
14 Disc mounting bolts
15 Speedometer drive
16 Axle

13.10a Front wheel details (early GSX-R models)

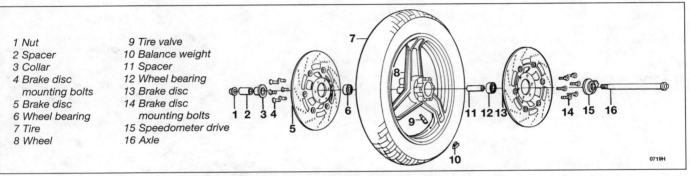

1 Nut
2 Spacer
3 Collar
4 Brake disc mounting bolts
5 Brake disc
6 Wheel bearing
7 Tire
8 Wheel
9 Tire valve
10 Balance weight
11 Spacer
12 Wheel bearing
13 Brake disc
14 Brake disc mounting bolts
15 Speedometer drive
16 Axle

13.10b Front wheel details (Katana/GSX-F models)

13.11 Loosen the fork pinch bolts . . .

13.12a . . . unscrew the axle . . .

13.12b . . . support the wheel and pull the axle out

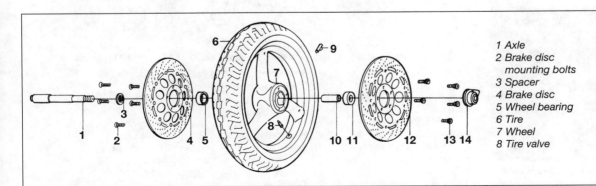

1 Axle
2 Brake disc mounting bolts
3 Spacer
4 Brake disc
5 Wheel bearing
6 Tire
7 Wheel
8 Tire valve
9 Balance weight
10 Spacer
11 Wheel bearing
12 Brake disc
13 Brake disc mounting bolts
14 Speedometer drive

13.12c Front wheel details (late GSX-R models)

6

13.15a Position the collar on the right side

13.15b Align the speedometer gear drive lugs with the notches in the wheel

13.15c Be sure the speedometer drive gear is properly positioned between the wheel and the fork

then place the collar (if equipped) in the right side of the hub **(see illustration)**.

b) Position the speedometer drive unit in place in the left side of the hub, then slide the wheel into place.

c) Refer to the exploded view for your model and make sure any spacers are in place.

d) Make sure the notches in the speedometer drive housing line up with the lugs in the wheel **(see illustration)**. Make sure the speedometer drive housing is properly positioned after the wheel is installed **(see illustration)**.

e) Slip the axle into place, then tighten the axle or the axle nut to the torque listed in this Chapter's Specifications. Tighten the side axle clamp bolts or nut to the torque listed in this Chapter's Specifications.

14 Rear wheel - removal and installation

Removal

1 Support the bike securely so it can't be knocked over during this procedure.

All except Katana 1100 (GSX1100F)

2 Remove the caliper mounting bolts (see

Section 4). Lower the caliper away from the disc (it isn't necessary to disconnect the torque rod or the brake hose).

Katana 1100 (GSX1100F)

3 Remove the caliper (see Section 4).
4 Loosen the axle pinch bolts **(see illustration)**.

All models

5 If the axle nut has a cotter pin, remove it **(see illustration)**. Remove the axle nut **(see illustrations)**.

14.4 On Katana 1100 (GSX1100F) models, loosen the nut (arrowed) on the axle pinch bolt at each side of the swingarm

14.5a If the axle nut is equipped with a cotter pin (arrowed), remove it - use a new cotter pin during installation

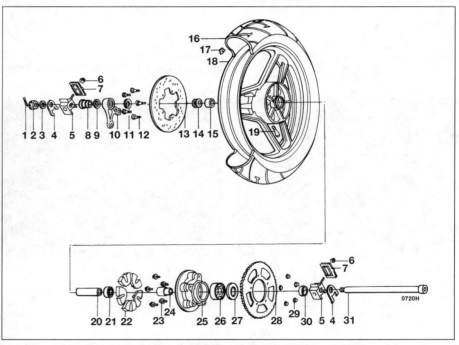

14.5b Rear wheel and axle details - early GSX-R750 and 1100 models

1 Cotter pin	12 Brake disc mounting bolts	22 Damper
2 Nut	13 Brake disc	23 Bolts
3 Washer	14 Spacer	24 Spacer
4 Chain adjuster washer	15 Wheel bearing	25 Coupling
5 Chain adjuster bolt	16 Tire	26 Bearing
6 Chain adjuster nut	17 Balance weight	27 Oil seal
7 Chain adjuster cover	18 Wheel	28 Sprocket
8 Spacer	19 Tire valve	29 Nuts
9 Oil seal	20 Spacer	30 Spacer
10 Caliper bracket	21 Wheel bearing	31 Axle
11 Oil seal		

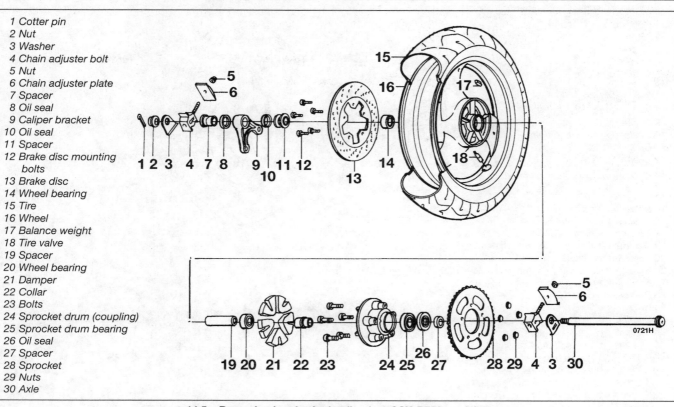

1 Cotter pin
2 Nut
3 Washer
4 Chain adjuster bolt
5 Nut
6 Chain adjuster plate
7 Spacer
8 Oil seal
9 Caliper bracket
10 Oil seal
11 Spacer
12 Brake disc mounting
    bolts
13 Brake disc
14 Wheel bearing
15 Tire
16 Wheel
17 Balance weight
18 Tire valve
19 Spacer
20 Wheel bearing
21 Damper
22 Collar
23 Bolts
24 Sprocket drum (coupling)
25 Sprocket drum bearing
26 Oil seal
27 Spacer
28 Sprocket
29 Nuts
30 Axle

14.5c Rear wheel and axle details - late GSX-R750 models

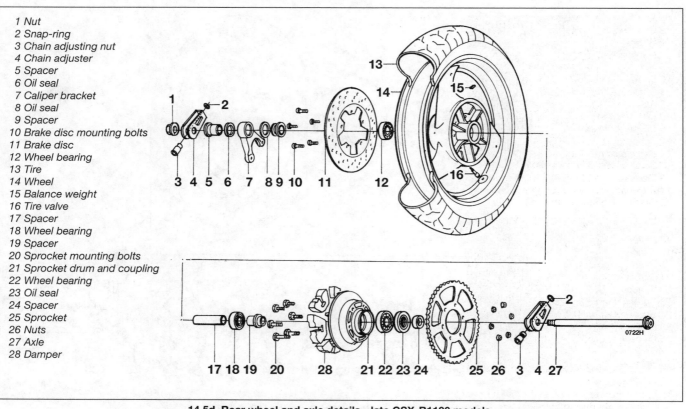

1 Nut
2 Snap-ring
3 Chain adjusting nut
4 Chain adjuster
5 Spacer
6 Oil seal
7 Caliper bracket
8 Oil seal
9 Spacer
10 Brake disc mounting bolts
11 Brake disc
12 Wheel bearing
13 Tire
14 Wheel
15 Balance weight
16 Tire valve
17 Spacer
18 Wheel bearing
19 Spacer
20 Sprocket mounting bolts
21 Sprocket drum and coupling
22 Wheel bearing
23 Oil seal
24 Spacer
25 Sprocket
26 Nuts
27 Axle
28 Damper

14.5d Rear wheel and axle details - late GSX-R1100 models

6

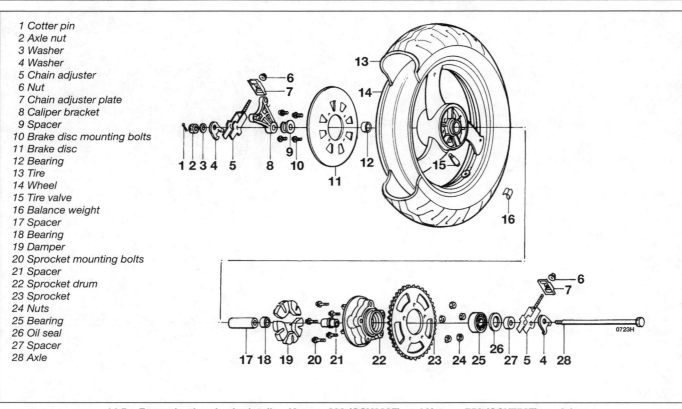

1 Cotter pin
2 Axle nut
3 Washer
4 Washer
5 Chain adjuster
6 Nut
7 Chain adjuster plate
8 Caliper bracket
9 Spacer
10 Brake disc mounting bolts
11 Brake disc
12 Bearing
13 Tire
14 Wheel
15 Tire valve
16 Balance weight
17 Spacer
18 Bearing
19 Damper
20 Sprocket mounting bolts
21 Spacer
22 Sprocket drum
23 Sprocket
24 Nuts
25 Bearing
26 Oil seal
27 Spacer
28 Axle

14.5e Rear wheel and axle details - Katana 600 (GSX600F) and Katana 750 (GSX750F) models

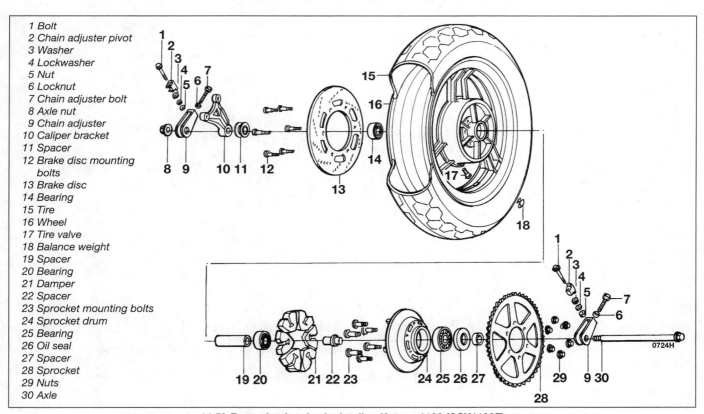

1 Bolt
2 Chain adjuster pivot
3 Washer
4 Lockwasher
5 Nut
6 Locknut
7 Chain adjuster bolt
8 Axle nut
9 Chain adjuster
10 Caliper bracket
11 Spacer
12 Brake disc mounting
    bolts
13 Brake disc
14 Bearing
15 Tire
16 Wheel
17 Tire valve
18 Balance weight
19 Spacer
20 Bearing
21 Damper
22 Spacer
23 Sprocket mounting bolts
24 Sprocket drum
25 Bearing
26 Oil seal
27 Spacer
28 Sprocket
29 Nuts
30 Axle

14.5f Rear wheel and axle details - Katana 1100 (GSX1100F)

14.7 With the rear wheel as far forward as possible, disengage the chain from the sprocket - don't let your fingers get caught between the sprocket and chain

14.8a Pull the wheel rearward away from the swingarm

14.8b Note the position of the spacers so they can be reinstalled correctly

6 Loosen the chain adjusters (see Chapter 1).

7 Disengage the chain from the sprocket (see illustration).

 Warning: Don't let your fingers slip between the chain and the sprocket.

8 Support the wheel and slide the axle out. Lower the wheel and remove it from the swingarm, being careful not to lose the spacers on either side of the hub (see illustrations).

Caution: Don't lay the wheel down and allow it to rest on the disc or the sprocket - they could become warped. Set the wheel on wood blocks so the disc or the sprocket doesn't support the weight of the wheel. Do not operate the brake pedal with the wheel removed.

9 Before installing the wheel, check the axle for straightness. If the axle is corroded, first remove the corrosion with fine emery cloth. Set the axle on V-blocks and check it for runout using a dial indicator (see illustration). If the axle exceeds the maximum allowable runout limit listed in this Chapter's Specifications, it must be replaced.

10 Check the condition of the wheel bearings (see Section 15).

Installation

11 Apply a thin coat of grease to the seal lips, then slide the spacers into their proper positions on the sides of the hub (see illustration 14.8b).

12 Slide the wheel into place.

13 Pull the chain up over the sprocket, raise the wheel and install the axle and axle nut. Don't tighten the axle nut at this time.

14 Adjust the chain slack (see Chapter 1) and tighten the adjuster locknuts.

15 Tighten the axle nut to the torque listed in this Chapter's Specifications. Install a new cotter pin (if equipped), tightening the axle nut an additional amount, if necessary, to align the hole in the axle with the castellations on the nut.

16 On Katana 1100 (GSX1100F) models, tighten the axle pinch bolts securely.

17 The remainder of installation is the reverse of the removal steps.

18 Check the operation of the brakes carefully before riding the motorcycle.

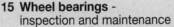
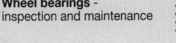

15 Wheel bearings - inspection and maintenance

1 Support the bike so it can't be knocked over during this procedure.

2 Remove the wheel. Refer to Section 13 (front wheel) or 14 (rear wheel).

3 Set the wheel on blocks so as not to allow the weight of the wheel rest on the brake disc or sprocket.

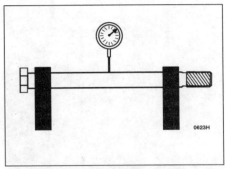

14.9 Check the axle for runout using a dial indicator and V-blocks

4 If you're removing the front wheel bearings, remove the speedometer drive (see illustration 13.15b). Remove the speedometer drive from the hub.

5 If you're removing the rear wheel bearings, lift off the sprocket and coupling (see Chapter 5).

6 Lift out the spacer and pry out the grease seal (see illustration).

7 Lift the spacer out of the other side of the coupling (see illustration).

8 Using a metal rod (preferably a brass drift punch) inserted through the center of the hub bearing, tap evenly around the inner race of the opposite bearing to drive it from the hub (see illustration). The bearing spacer will also come out.

9 Lay the wheel on its other side and remove

15.6 Lift off the spacer and pry out the grease seal

15.7 Remove the spacer from the other side of the coupling

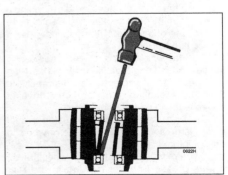

15.8 Drive the bearings from the hub with a metal rod and hammer

6

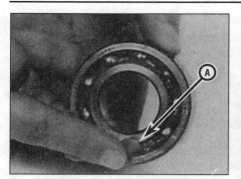

15.11 Pack grease (A) into the bearing until it's full

15.12 Drive the bearing in with a bearing driver or socket the same diameter as the outer race

15.13a Into the other side of the hub, install the spacer . . .

15.13b . . . then install the remaining bearing

the remaining bearing using the same technique.

10 Clean the bearings with a high flash-point solvent (one which won't leave any residue) and blow them dry with compressed air (don't let the bearings spin as you dry them). Apply a few drops of oil to the bearing. Hold the outer race of the bearing and rotate the inner race - if the bearing doesn't turn smoothly, has rough spots or is noisy, replace it with a new one.

11 If the bearing checks out okay and will be reused, wash it in solvent once again and dry it, then pack the bearing from the open side with high-quality bearing grease (see illustration).

12 Thoroughly clean the hub area of the wheel. Install the bearing into the recess in the hub, with the shielded side facing out. Using a bearing driver or a socket large enough to contact the outer race of the bearing, drive it in (see illustration).

13 Turn the wheel over and install the bearing spacer and bearing (see illustrations), driving the bearing into place as described in Step 12. Install the speedometer drive (if you're working on the front wheel).

14 Install a new grease seal, using a seal driver, large socket or a flat piece of wood to drive it into place.

15 If you're working on the rear wheel, press a little grease into the bearing in the rear wheel coupling. Install the coupling to the wheel, making sure the coupling spacer is

located in the inside of the inner race (between the wheel and the coupling).

16 Clean off all grease from the brake disc(s) using acetone or brake system cleaner. Install the wheel.

16 Tubeless tires - general information and fitting

General information

1 The wheels fitted to all models are designed to take tubeless tires only.

2 Refer to Daily (pre-ride) checks at the beginning of this manual, and to the scheduled checks in Chapter 1 for tire and wheel maintenance.

Fitting new tires

3 When selecting new tires, refer to the tire information label on the swingarm and the tire options listed in the owners manual. Ensure that front and rear tire types are compatible, the correct size and correct speed rating; if necessary seek advice from a Suzuki dealer or tire fitting specialist (see illustration).

4 It is recommended that tires are fitted by a motorcycle tire specialist rather than attempted in the home workshop. The force required to break the seal between the wheel rim and tire bead is substantial, and is usually beyond the capabilities of an individual working with normal tire levers. Additionally, the specialist will be able to balance the wheels after tire fitting.

5 Only certain types of puncture repair are suitable for tubeless motorcycle tires. Refer to a tire fitting specialist for advice and to your owners manual for details of the reduced speeds advised for a repaired tire.

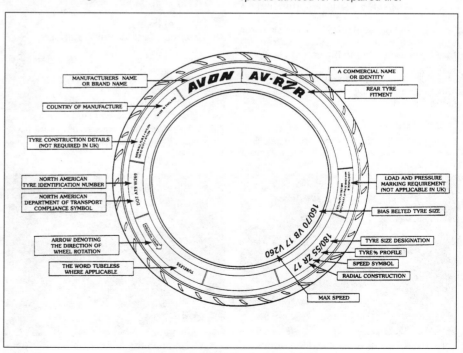

16.3 Comon tyre sidewall markings

Chapter 7
Fairing and bodywork

Contents

Degrees of difficulty

Easy, suitable for novice with little experience	**Fairly easy,** suitable for beginner with some experience	**Fairly difficult,** suitable for competent DIY mechanic	**Difficult,** suitable for experienced DIY mechanic	**Very difficult,** suitable for expert DIY or professional

1 General information

This Chapter covers the procedures necessary to remove and install the fairing and other body parts. Since many service and repair operations on these motorcycles require removal of the fairing and/or other body parts, the procedures are grouped here and referred to from other Chapters.

In the case of damage to the fairing or other body part, it is usually necessary to remove the broken component and replace it with a new (or used) one. The material that the fairing and other body parts is composed of doesn't lend itself to conventional repair techniques. There are, however, some shops that specialize in "plastic welding", so it would be advantageous to check around first before throwing the damaged part away.

2.1 The seat lock is operated by the ignition key

2 Seat and lock - removal and installation

Seat removal

1 To remove the seat, insert the ignition key into the seat lock and turn it clockwise (see illustration). Lift the seat up and detach it from the motorcycle.

2 On models with a separate rear seat, undo the fasteners and lift the rear seat off (on some models the fasteners also secure the seat lock).

Lock removal

3 Remove the screws and detach the lock from the motorcycle (see illustration).
4 Remove the screws at the rear and detach the latch assembly (see illustration).

Installation

5 Installation is the reverse of the removal steps. Tighten the fasteners securely.

3 Fairing - removal and installation

1 Support the bike securely so it can't be knocked over during this procedure. Refer to Chapter 3 and remove the fuel tank.
2 Remove the screws and detach the front piece (if equipped) from the fairing (see illustration).

2.3 To detach the lock assembly from the motorcycle, remove the lock cylinder screws . . .

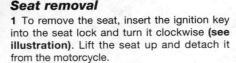

2.4 . . . and the latch screws, then undo any tie wraps that secure the lock cable

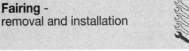
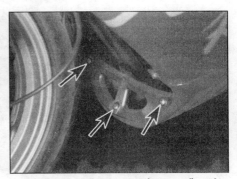

3.2 Remove the screws (arrowed) and detach the front piece from the lower fairing

7

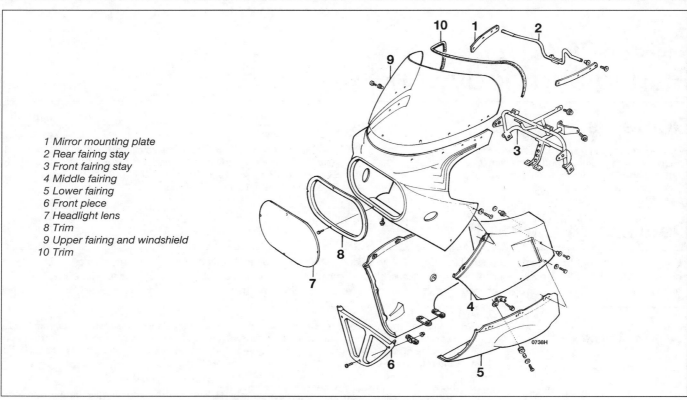

1 Mirror mounting plate
2 Rear fairing stay
3 Front fairing stay
4 Middle fairing
5 Lower fairing
6 Front piece
7 Headlight lens
8 Trim
9 Upper fairing and windshield
10 Trim

3.3a Fairing details - GSX-R750, 1986 and 1987 (1985 similar)

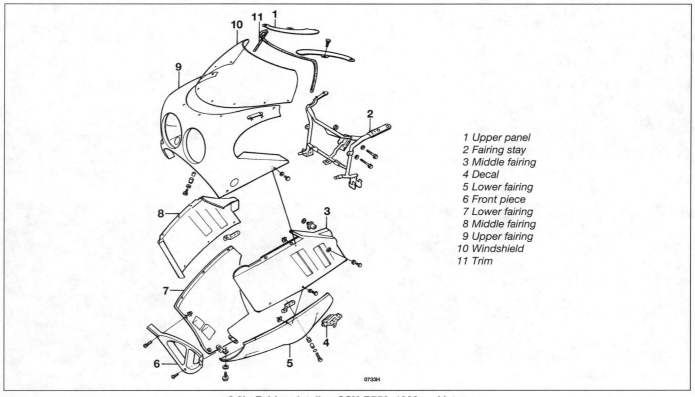

1 Upper panel
2 Fairing stay
3 Middle fairing
4 Decal
5 Lower fairing
6 Front piece
7 Lower fairing
8 Middle fairing
9 Upper fairing
10 Windshield
11 Trim

3.3b Fairing details - GSX-R750, 1988 and later

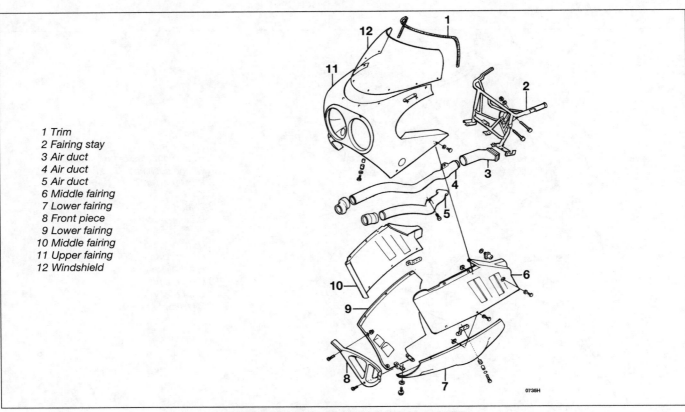

1 Mirror mounting plate
2 Rear fairing stay
3 Mirror mounting plate
4 Fairing stay brace
5 Fairing stay
6 Middle fairing
7 Lower fairing
8 Front piece
9 Lower fairing
10 Headlight trim
11 Screw
12 Windshield
13 Trim
14 Upper fairing

0734H

3.3c Fairing details - GSX-R1100, 1986 through 1988

1 Trim
2 Fairing stay
3 Air duct
4 Air duct
5 Air duct
6 Middle fairing
7 Lower fairing
8 Front piece
9 Lower fairing
10 Middle fairing
11 Upper fairing
12 Windshield

0735H

3.3d Fairing details - GSX-R1100, 1989 and 1990

7

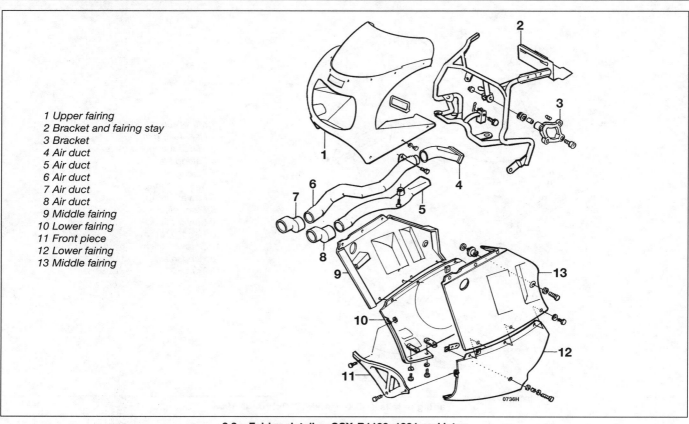

1 Upper fairing
2 Bracket and fairing stay
3 Bracket
4 Air duct
5 Air duct
6 Air duct
7 Air duct
8 Air duct
9 Middle fairing
10 Lower fairing
11 Front piece
12 Lower fairing
13 Middle fairing

3.3e Fairing details - GSX-R1100, 1991 and later

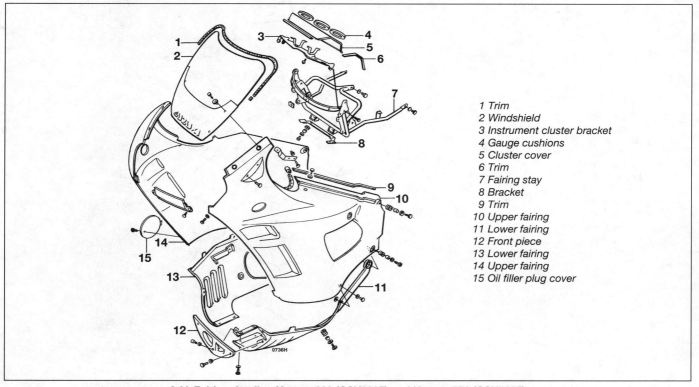

1 Trim
2 Windshield
3 Instrument cluster bracket
4 Gauge cushions
5 Cluster cover
6 Trim
7 Fairing stay
8 Bracket
9 Trim
10 Upper fairing
11 Lower fairing
12 Front piece
13 Lower fairing
14 Upper fairing
15 Oil filler plug cover

3.3f Fairing details - Katana 600 (GSX600F) and Katana 750 (GSX750F)

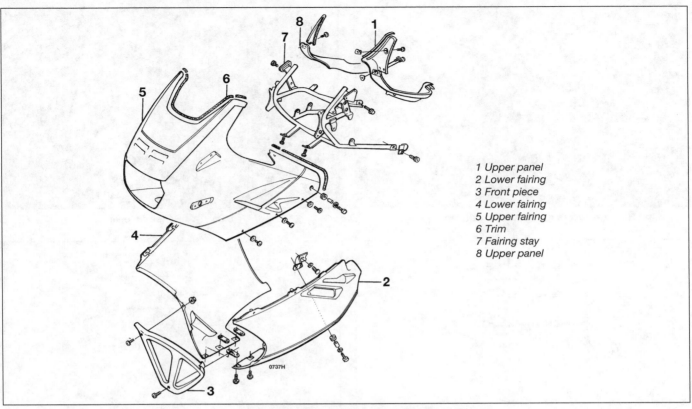

1 Upper panel
2 Lower fairing
3 Front piece
4 Lower fairing
5 Upper fairing
6 Trim
7 Fairing stay
8 Upper panel

0737H

3.3g Fairing details - Katana 1100 (GSX1100F)

3 Remove the fasteners and detach the lower fairing **(see illustrations)**.

4 Remove the turn signals.

5 Remove the rearview mirrors **(see illustrations)**.

6 Katana 600 (GSX600F) and Katana 750 (GSX750F): Remove the windshield (see Section 4).

7 Remove the upper fairing mounting fasteners and take the fairing off **(see illustration)**.

8 If necessary, remove the fairing brace mounting fasteners and take the brace off the motorcycle.

9 Installation is the reverse of removal.

4 Fixed windshield - removal and installation

1 Remove the screws securing the windshield to the fairing **(see illustration)**.

2 Carefully separate the windshield from the fairing. If it sticks, don't attempt to pry it off - just keep applying steady pressure with your fingers.

3 Installation is the reverse of the removal procedure. Be sure each screw has a plastic washer under its head. Tighten the screws

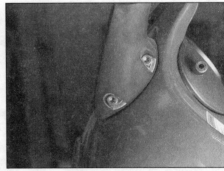

3.5a The mirrors are secured by Allen bolts - on some models, they're exposed . . .

3.5b . . . and on other models you'll need to pull back the cover for access

3.7 Be sure you've removed all the fairing fasteners, including those below the headlight housing

4.1 Windshield mounting screws (typical fixed windshield)

7

6.2a The side covers are secured by Phillips screws . . .

6.2b . . . or Allen screws

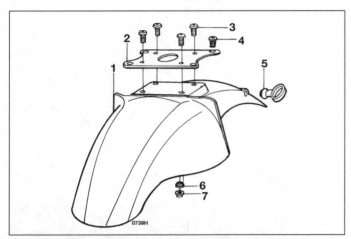

7.2a Front fender/mudguard details - GSX-R750 (1985 through 1987) and GSX-R1100 (1986 through 1988)

1 Fender/mudguard	4 Screw	6 Washer
2 Plate	5 Speedometer	7 Nut
3 Screws	cable holder	

7.2b Front fender/mudguard details - GSX-R750 (1988 through 1990) and GSX-R1100 (1989 and 1990); Katana 600/GSX600F and Katana 750/GSX750F similar

1 Fender/mudguard	3 Screws	5 Plate
2 Plate	4 Screw	

7.2c Front fender/mudguard details - GSX-R750 and GSX-R1100 (1991 and later)

1 Fender/	2 Bolt	4 Bolt
mudguard	3 Washer	

7.2d Front fender/mudguard details - Katana 1100/GSX1100F

1 Fender	5 Washer	9 Screw
2 Plate	6 Plug	10 Cushion
3 Screw	7 Rear section	11 Screw
4 Nut	8 Washer	12 Washer

7.2e Make sure all of the fasteners have been removed and lift the fender/mudguard off

securely, but be careful not to overtighten them, as the windshield might crack.

5 Rear view mirrors - removal and installation

Refer to Section 3, Step 5 - removing the rear view mirrors is part of the upper fairing removal procedure.

8.3 The rear fender/mudguard on late GSX-R models is attached to the swingarm

6 Side covers - removal and installation

1 Remove the seat.
2 Remove the side cover mounting screw from each side of the motorcycle **(see illustrations)**.
3 On models where the side covers are secured by the grab rail bolts, remove the bolt covers (if equipped) and remove the bolts.

4 Installation is the reverse of the removal procedure.

7 Front fender/mudguard - removal and installation

1 Support the bike securely so it can't be knocked over during this procedure.
2 Remove the fender/mudguard fasteners **(see illustrations)**. Take the fender/mudguard off the motorcycle.
3 Installation is the reverse of removal.

8 Rear fender/mudguard - removal and installation

1 On late GSX-R models with the fender/mudguard attached to the swingarm, remove the rear wheel (see Chapter 6).
2 Remove the seat and other components as necessary for access to the fender/mudguard fasteners .
3 Detach the fender/mudguard and take it off of the motorcycle **(see illustration)**.
4 Installation is the reverse of the removal steps.

Notes

Chapter 8
Electrical system

Contents

Degrees of difficulty

Easy, suitable for novice with little experience	Fairly easy, suitable for beginner with some experience	Fairly difficult, suitable for competent DIY mechanic	Difficult, suitable for experienced DIY mechanic	Very difficult, suitable for expert DIY or professional

Specifications

Battery

Type	12 volt, 14Ah (amp hours)
Specific gravity	see Chapter 1

Charging system

Charging system output	13.5 or more volts at 5000 rpm
Alternator brush length limit	4.5 mm (0.18 inch)

Starter motor

Brush length limit

GSX-R750	
1985 through 1987	6 mm (0.2 inch)
1988 on	9 mm (0.35 inch)
GSX-R1100	6 mm (0.2 inch)
Katana 600/GSX600F	6 mm (0.2 inch)
Katana 750/GSX750F	9 mm (0.35 inch)
Katana 1100/GSX1100F	6 mm (0.2 inch)
Commutator undercut, maximum	0.2 mm (0.008 inch)
Starter relay resistance	3 to 5 ohms

Circuit fuse ratings

All except main fuse	10 amps
Main fuse	25 amps
Circuit breaker	30 amps

Fuel sender resistance

Full position	Approximately 3 ohms
Half full position	Approximately 32.5 ohms
Empty position	Approximately 110 ohms

8

Bulb specifications

Headlight
  High beam . . . . 60 watts
  Low beam . . . . 55 watts
  Combined high/low beam . . . . 60/55 watts
Tail/brake lights
  1986 and 1987 US . . . . 8/23 watts
  All others . . . . 5/21 watts
Separate taillights
  1986 and 1987 US . . . . 23 watts
  All others . . . . 21 watts
Separate brake lights . . . . 5 watts
Separate turn signals
  1986 and 1987 US . . . . 23 watts
  All others . . . . 21 watts
Turn signal/running lights . . . . 5/21 watts
License plate light
  1986 and 1987 US . . . . 8 watts
  Katana 1100 (all US) . . . . 8 watts
  All others . . . . 5 watts
Parking or position light
  GSX-R
    1985 . . . . 3.4 watts
    1986 through 1990 . . . . 4 watts
    1991 on . . . . 5 watts
  GSX600F . . . . 3.4 watts
  GSX750F, GSX1100F . . . . 4 watts
Tachometer and speedometer lights . . . . 3 watts

1 General information

The machines covered by this manual are equipped with a 12-volt electrical system. The components include a three-phase alternator with an integrated circuit regulator built in.

The regulator maintains the charging system output within the specified range to prevent overcharging. The alternator diodes convert the AC (alternating current) output of the alternator to DC (direct current) to power the lights and other components and to charge the battery.

The alternator is similar to an automotive alternator, with the field current being produced electromagnetically, rather than by permanent magnets.

An electric starter mounted to the engine case behind the cylinders is standard equipment. The starting system includes the motor, the battery, the solenoid and the various wires and switches. On models equipped with a sidestand switch and clutch switch, if the engine stop switch and the main key switch are both in the On position, the circuit relay allows the starter motor to operate only if the transmission is in Neutral (Neutral switch on) and the clutch lever is pulled to the handlebar (clutch switch on) and the sidestand is up (sidestand switch on).

Note: *Keep in mind that electrical parts, once purchased, can't be returned. To avoid unnecessary expense, make very sure the faulty component has been positively identified before buying a replacement part.*

2 Electrical fault finding

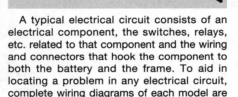

A typical electrical circuit consists of an electrical component, the switches, relays, etc. related to that component and the wiring and connectors that hook the component to both the battery and the frame. To aid in locating a problem in any electrical circuit, complete wiring diagrams of each model are included at the end of this Chapter.

Before tackling any troublesome electrical circuit, first study the appropriate diagrams thoroughly to get a complete picture of what makes up that individual circuit. Trouble spots, for instance, can often be narrowed down by noting if other components related to that circuit are operating properly or not. If several components or circuits fail at one time, chances are the fault lies in the fuse or ground connection, as several circuits often are routed through the same fuse and ground connections.

Electrical problems often stem from simple causes, such as loose or corroded connections or a blown fuse. Prior to any electrical Fault Finding, always visually check the condition of the fuse, wires and connections in the problem circuit.

If testing instruments are going to be utilized, use the diagrams to plan where you will make the necessary connections in order to accurately pinpoint the trouble spot.

The basic tools needed for electrical fault finding include a test light or voltmeter, a continuity tester (which includes a bulb, battery and set of test leads) and a jumper wire, preferably with a circuit breaker incorporated, which can be used to bypass electrical components. Specific checks described later in this Chapter may also require an ohmmeter.

Voltage checks should be performed if a circuit is not functioning properly. Connect one lead of a test light or voltmeter to either the negative battery terminal or a known good ground. Connect the other lead to a connector in the circuit being tested, preferably nearest to the battery or fuse. If the bulb lights, voltage is reaching that point, which means the part of the circuit between that connector and the battery is problem-free. Continue checking the remainder of the circuit in the same manner. When you reach a point where no voltage is present, the problem lies between there and the last good test point. Most of the time the problem is due to a loose connection. Keep in mind that some circuits only receive voltage when the ignition key is in the On position.

One method of finding short circuits is to remove the fuse and connect a test light or voltmeter in its place to the fuse terminals. There should be no load in the circuit. Move the wiring harness from side-to-side while watching the test light. If the bulb lights, there is a short to ground (earth) somewhere in that area, probably where insulation has rubbed off a wire. The same test can be performed on other components in the circuit, including the switch.

A ground (earth) check should be done to see if a component is grounded (earthed) properly. Disconnect the battery and connect one lead of a self-powered test light (continuity tester) to a known good ground. Connect the other lead to the wire or ground connection being tested. If the bulb lights, the ground is good. If the bulb does not light, the ground is not good.

A continuity check is performed to see if a circuit, section of circuit or individual component is capable of passing electricity through it. Disconnect the battery and connect one lead of a self-powered test light (continuity tester) to one end of the circuit being tested and the other lead to the other end of the circuit. If the bulb lights, there is continuity, which means the circuit is passing electricity through it properly. Switches can be checked in the same way.

Remember that all electrical circuits are designed to conduct electricity from the battery, through the wires, switches, relays, etc. to the electrical component (light bulb, motor, etc.). From there it is directed to the frame (ground) where it is passed back to the battery. Electrical problems are basically an interruption in the flow of electricity from the battery or back to it.

3 Battery - inspection and maintenance

1 Most battery damage is caused by heat, vibration, and/or low electrolyte levels, so keep the battery securely mounted, check the electrolyte level frequently and make sure the charging system is functioning properly.
2 Refer to Chapter 1 for electrolyte level and specific gravity checking procedures.
3 Check around the base inside of the battery for sediment, which is the result of sulfation caused by low electrolyte levels. These deposits will cause internal short circuits, which can quickly discharge the battery. Look for cracks in the case and replace the battery if either of these conditions is found.
4 Check the battery terminals and cable ends for tightness and corrosion. If corrosion is evident, remove the cables from the battery and clean the terminals and cable ends with a wire brush or knife and emery paper. Reconnect the cables, connecting the positive (+) cable first.

 Battery corrosion can be kept to a minimum by applying a layer of petroleum jelly to the terminals after the cables have been connected.

5 The battery case should be kept clean to prevent current leakage, which can discharge the battery over a period of time (especially when it sits unused). Wash the outside of the case with a solution of baking soda and water. Do not get any baking soda solution in the battery cells. Rinse the battery thoroughly, then dry it.
6 If acid has been spilled on the frame or battery box, neutralize it with the baking soda and water solution, dry it thoroughly, then touch up any damaged paint. Make sure the battery vent tube is directed away from the frame and is not kinked or pinched.
7 If the motorcycle sits unused for long periods of time, disconnect the cables from the battery terminals. Refer to Section 4 and charge the battery approximately once every month.

4 Battery - charging

1 If the machine sits idle for extended periods or if the charging system malfunctions, the battery can be charged from an external source.
2 To properly charge the battery, you will need a charger of the correct rating, a hydrometer, a clean rag and a syringe for adding distilled water to the battery cells.
3 The maximum charging rate for any battery is 1/10 of the rated amp/hour capacity. As an example, the maximum charging rate for a 14 amp/hour battery would be 1.4 amps. If the battery is charged at a higher rate, it could be damaged.
4 Do not allow the battery to be subjected to a so-called quick charge (high rate of charge over a short period of time) unless you are prepared to buy a new battery.

5 When charging the battery, always remove it from the machine and be sure to check the electrolyte level before hooking up the charger. Add distilled water to any cells that are low.
6 Loosen the cell caps, hook up the battery charger leads (red to positive, black to negative), cover the top of the battery with a clean rag, then, and only then, plug in the battery charger.

⚠ *Warning: Remember, the gas escaping from a charging battery is explosive, so keep open flames and sparks well away from the area. If the gas ignites, the entire battery can explode and spray acid. Also, the electrolyte is extremely corrosive and will damage anything it comes in contact with.*

7 Allow the battery to charge until the specific gravity is as specified (refer to Chapter 1 for specific gravity checking procedures). The charger must be unplugged and disconnected from the battery when making specific gravity checks. If the battery overheats or gases excessively, the charging rate is too high. Either disconnect the charger or lower the charging rate to prevent damage to the battery.
8 If one or more of the cells do not show an increase in specific gravity after a long slow charge, or if the battery as a whole does not seem to want to take a charge, it is time for a new battery.
9 When the battery is fully charged, unplug the charger first, then disconnect the leads from the battery. Install the cell caps and wipe any electrolyte off the outside of the battery case.

5 Fuses and circuit breaker - check and replacement

Fuses

1 The fuses are located behind the right frame cover or under the seat **(see illustrations)**. The fuses are protected by a plastic cover, which clips on or is secured by a screw. The fuse block contains fuses (and spares) which protect the main, headlight, taillight and accessory circuit wiring and components from damage caused by short

5.1a The fuse block is under the seat on some models (this is a 750 Katana/GSX750F) . . .

5.1b . . . and behind the right frame cover on others (this is a 600 Katana/GSX600F)

5.1c Unclip the cover to expose the fuses . . .

5.1d ... or remove the cover securing screw

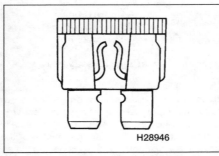

5.3 A blown fuse can be identified by a broken element - be sure to replace a blown fuse with one of the same amperage rating

circuits. The fuse block on most models also contains accessory output terminals (positive and negative).

Caution: Before connecting an accessory to the output terminals, check with a dealer service department to make sure the accessory is compatible with the motorcycle's electrical system.

2 If you have a test light, the fuses can be checked without removing them. Turn the ignition to the On position, connect one end of the test light to a good ground (earth), then probe each terminal on top of the fuse. If the fuse is good, there will be voltage available at both terminals. If the fuse is blown, there will only be voltage present at one of the terminals.

3 The fuses can be removed and checked visually. If you can't pull the fuse out with your fingertips, use a pair of needle-nose pliers. A blown fuse is easily identified by a break in the element **(see illustration)**.

4 If a fuse blows, be sure to check the wiring harnesses very carefully for evidence of a short circuit. Look for bare wires and chafed, melted or burned insulation. If a fuse is replaced before the cause is located, the new fuse will blow immediately.

5 Never, under any circumstances, use a higher rated fuse or bridge the fuse block terminals, as damage to the electrical system - including melted wires, ruined components, and fire - could result.

6 Occasionally a fuse will blow or cause an

open circuit for no obvious reason. Corrosion of the fuse ends and fuse block terminals may occur and cause poor fuse contact. If this happens, remove the corrosion with a wire brush or emery paper, then spray the fuse end and terminals with electrical contact cleaner.

Circuit breaker

7 A circuit breaker (where fitted) is mounted behind the right frame cover or under the seat **(see illustrations)**. If an overload occurs in the main circuit, the red button on the circuit breaker will pop out approximately 1 to 2 mm (0.040 to 0.080 inch).

8 If the button pops out, let the circuit breaker cool for about ten minutes, then push the button back in.

9 If the circuit breaker continues to pop out, check the wiring harnesses for a short. Never, under any circumstances, bypass the circuit breaker or replace it with a breaker of higher capacity - the overload could damage electrical components, melt wires or start a fire.

---

6 Lighting system - check

1 The battery provides power for operation of the headlight, taillight, brake light, license plate light and instrument cluster lights. If

none of the lights operate, always check battery voltage before proceeding. Low battery voltage indicates either a faulty battery, low battery electrolyte level or a defective charging system. Refer to Chapter 1 for battery checks and Section 26 for charging system tests. Also, check the condition of the fuses (and circuit breaker, if equipped). Replace any blown fuses with new ones or reset the circuit breaker if its red button has popped out.

Headlight

2 If the headlight is out when the engine is running (US and Canadian models) or won't come on (UK models), check the fuse first with the key On (see Section 5), then unplug the electrical connector for the headlight and use jumper wires to connect the bulb directly to the battery terminals. If the light comes on, the problem lies in the wiring or one of the switches in the circuit. Refer to Section 17 for the switch testing procedures, and also the wiring diagrams at the end of this Chapter.

Taillight/license plate light

3 If the taillight fails to work, check the bulbs and the bulb terminals first, then check for battery voltage at the taillight electrical connector. If voltage is present, check the ground circuit for an open or poor connection.

4 If no voltage is indicated, check the wiring between the taillight and the main (key) switch, then check the switch.

Brake light

5 See Section 11 for the brake light circuit checking procedure.

Neutral indicator light

6 If the neutral light fails to operate when the transmission is in Neutral, check the fuses and the bulb (see Section 14 for bulb removal procedures). If the bulb and fuses are in good condition, check for battery voltage at the neutral switch electrical connector. If battery voltage is present, refer to Section 19 for the neutral switch check and replacement procedures.

7 If no voltage is indicated, refer to the wiring diagrams at the end of the book and check the wiring and the bulb for open circuits and poor connections.

Oil pressure warning light

8 See Section 15 for the oil pressure warning light circuit check.

---

7 Headlight bulb - replacement

1 Reach behind the headlight assembly and disconnect the electrical connector **(see illustration)**.

2 Pull up the tab and remove the dust cover **(see illustration)**.

5.7a A circuit breaker is mounted under the seat (this is a Katana 1100/GSX1100F) ...

5.7b ... or behind the right frame cover (this is a late GSX-R1100)

7.1 Disconnect the electrical connector

7.2 Pull up on the tab and remove the rubber dust cover

7.4 Pull out the bulb holder, being careful not to touch the glass

 3 Lift up the retaining clip and swing it out of the way. *Warning: If the headlight has just been on, let the bulb cool before you continue. It will be hot enough to cause burns.*

4 Remove the bulb holder **(see illustration)**.

5 When installing the new bulb, reverse the removal procedure. Be sure not to touch the

 HAYNES HiNT *If you do touch the headlight bulb, wipe it off with a clean rag dampened with rubbing alcohol.*

bulb with your fingers - oil from your skin will cause the bulb to overheat and fail prematurely.

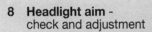 **8 Headlight aim -** check and adjustment

1 An improperly adjusted headlight may cause problems for oncoming traffic or provide poor, unsafe illumination of the road ahead. Before adjusting the headlight, be sure to consult with local traffic laws and regulations.

2 The headlight beam can be adjusted both vertically and horizontally. Before performing the adjustment, make sure the fuel tank is at least half full, and have an assistant sit on the seat.

3 Insert a Phillips screwdriver into the horizontal adjuster guide **(see illustration)**, then turn the adjuster as necessary to center the beam. **Note:** *Models with dual headlights have two sets of adjusters, one for each headlight.*

4 To adjust the vertical position of the beam, insert the screwdriver into the vertical adjuster guide and turn the adjuster as necessary to raise or lower the beam **(see illustration)**.

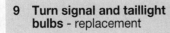 **9 Turn signal and taillight bulbs** - replacement

Turn signal bulbs

1 Bulb replacement for the turn signals is the

8.3 Turn the horizontal adjuster to move the beam from side to side

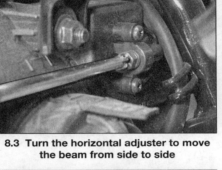

8.4 Turn the vertical adjuster to move the beam up or down

9.2a On some turn signals, the lens is incorporated into the cover (this is a Katana 1100/GSX1100F) - remove the screw and take the lens/cover off . . .

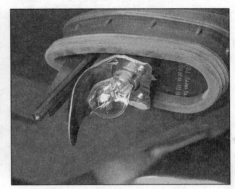

9.2b . . . to expose the bulb

9.2c On other models, the lens securing screws are on the back side of the housing (this is a late GSX-R1100) - remove the screws and lift off the lens

9.2d On all models, press the bulb into the socket and turn it counterclockwise (anticlockwise) to remove

8

9.6a To reach the tail/brake light bulb, twist the bulb holder counterclockwise (anticlockwise) and pull it out of the mounting hole . . .

9.6b . . . to remove the bulb, press it into the socket, turn counterclockwise (anticlockwise) and pull out

same for the front and rear.

2 Remove the screws securing the lens to the reflector **(see illustrations)**.

3 Push the bulb in and turn it counterclockwise (anticlockwise) to remove it. Check the socket terminals for corrosion and clean them if necessary. Line up the pins on the new bulb with the slots in the socket, push in and turn the bulb clockwise until it locks in place. **Note**: *The pins on the bulb are offset so it can only be installed one way. It is a good idea to use a paper towel or dry cloth when handling the new bulb to prevent injury if the bulb should break and to increase bulb life.*

4 Position the lens on the housing and install the screws. Be careful not to overtighten them.

Tail/brake light bulb

5 To remove the bulb, remove the seat.

6 Turn the bulb holder counterclockwise (anticlockwise) until it stops, then pull straight out to remove it from the taillight housing **(see illustration)**. The bulb can be removed from the holder by pressing it in, turning it counterclockwise (anticlockwise) and pulling it straight out **(see illustration)**.

7 Check the socket terminals for corrosion and clean them if necessary. Line up the pins on the new bulb with the slots in the socket, push in and turn the bulb clockwise until it locks in place. **Note**: *The pins on the bulb are*

offset so it can only be installed one way. It is a good idea to use a paper towel or dry cloth when handling the new bulb to prevent injury if the bulb should break and to increase bulb life.

8 Make sure the rubber gaskets are in place and in good condition, then line up the tabs on the holder with the slots in the housing and push the holder into the mounting hole. Turn it clockwise until it stops to lock it in place. **Note**: *The tabs and slots are two different sizes so the holders can only be installed one way.*

9 Reinstall the seat.

10 Turn signal circuit - check

1 The battery provides power for operation of the signal lights, so if they do not operate, always check the battery voltage and specific gravity first. Low battery voltage indicates either a faulty battery, low electrolyte level or a defective charging system. Refer to Chapter 1 for battery checks and Section 26 for charging system tests. Also, check the fuses (see Section 5).

2 Most turn signal problems are the result of a burned out bulb or corroded socket. This is especially true when the turn signals function

properly in one direction, but fail to flash in the other direction. Check the bulbs and the sockets (see Section 9).

3 If the bulbs and sockets check out okay, refer to the wiring diagrams at the end of this Chapter and check for power at the turn signal flasher **(see illustrations)** with the ignition On. If there's no power at the flasher, check the switch (see Section 17).

4 If switch is okay, check the wiring between the turn signal flasher and the turn signal lights (see the wiring diagrams at the end of this Chapter).

5 If the wiring checks out okay, replace the turn signal flasher.

11 Brake light switches - check and replacement

Circuit check

1 Before checking any electrical circuit, check the fuses (see Section 5).

2 Using a test light connected to a good ground (earth), check for voltage at the electrical connector at the brake light switch. If there's no voltage present, check the wiring between the switch and the battery (see the wiring diagrams at the end of this Chapter).

3 If voltage is available, touch the probe of the test light to the other terminal of the switch, then pull the brake lever or depress the brake pedal - if the test light doesn't light up, replace the switch.

4 If the test light does light, check the wiring between the switch and the brake lights (see the wiring diagrams at the end of this Chapter).

Switch replacement

Brake lever switch

5 Unplug the electrical connectors from the switch.

6 Remove the mounting screw or screws **(see illustration)** and detach the switch from the brake lever bracket/front master cylinder.

10.3a The turn signal flasher (arrowed) is mounted under the seat - this is a Katana 1100/GSX1100F flasher

10.3b . . . and this is a late GSX-R1100 flasher

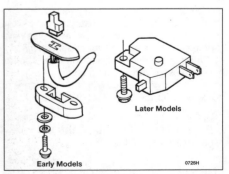

11.6 The brake light switch mounted on the brake lever is retained by two screws (early models) or a single screw (later models)

11.9 Loosen the adjusting nut (arrowed) to remove the rear brake light switch

7 Installation is the reverse of the removal procedure. On early models, the brake lever switch can be adjusted (see Chapter 1). On later models, the brake lever switch isn't adjustable.

Brake pedal switch

8 Unplug the electrical connector from the switch.

9 Loosen the adjuster nut **(see illustration)** and unscrew the switch.

10 Install the switch by reversing the removal procedure.

11 Adjust the switch by following the procedure described in Chapter 1.

12 Instrument cluster - removal and installation

1 Late GSX-R750: Remove the fairings and windshield (see Chapter 7). Remove the headlight assembly.

2 Late GSX-R1100, all Katana 750/GSX750F: Remove the upper fairing and windshield (see Chapter 7).

3 Katana 600/GSX600F: Remove the upper and lower fairings (see Chapter 7).

4 Katana 1100/GSX1100F: Remove the upper and lower fairings (see Chapter 7). Remove the headlight assembly.

5 Disconnect the electrical connectors from the cluster harness **(see illustrations)**.

6 Disconnect the speedometer cable (see Section 13).

7 Remove the instrument cluster mounting screws or nuts, then detach the cluster from the bike.

Caution: Keep the cluster in an upright position while it's off the motorcycle or the gauges will be ruined.

8 Installation is the reverse of the removal procedure.

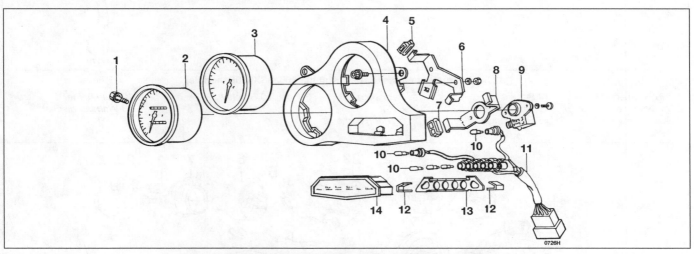

12.5a Instrument cluster details (early GSX-R models)

1 Trip odometer knob	4 Cluster housing	7 Cushion	10 Bulbs	13 Bulb holder
2 Speedometer	5 Cushion	8 Bracket	11 Wiring harness	14 Warning display
3 Tachometer	6 Bracket	9 Speedometer head	12 Clip	

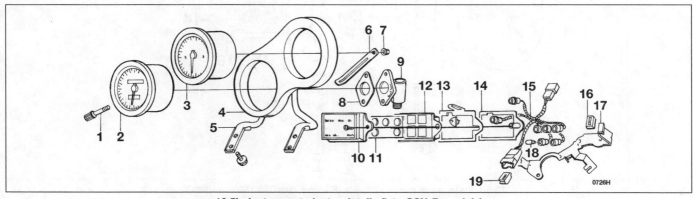

12.5b Instrument cluster details (late GSX-R models)

1 Trip odometer knob	5 Bracket	9 Speedometer head	13 Case	17 Bracket
2 Speedometer	6 Bracket	10 Warning display	14 Case	18 Bulb
3 Tachometer	7 Nut	11 Case	15 Wiring harness	19 Cushion
4 Cluster housing	8 Gasket	12 Case	16 Cushion	

8

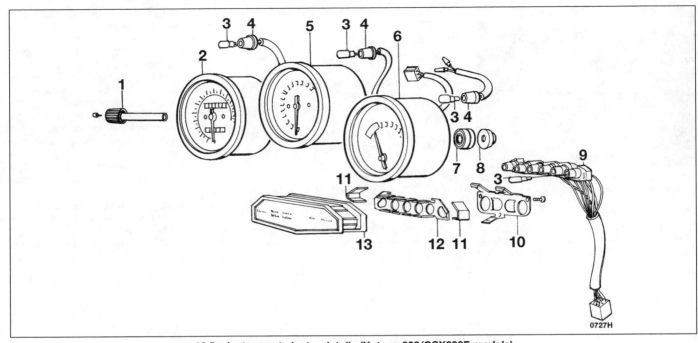

12.5c Instrument cluster details (Katana 600/GSX600F models)

1 Trip odometer knob
2 Speedometer
3 Bulb

4 Socket
5 Tachometer
6 Fuel gauge

7 Bushing
8 Nut
9 Wiring harness

10 Bracket
11 Clip

12 Bulb holder
13 Warning display

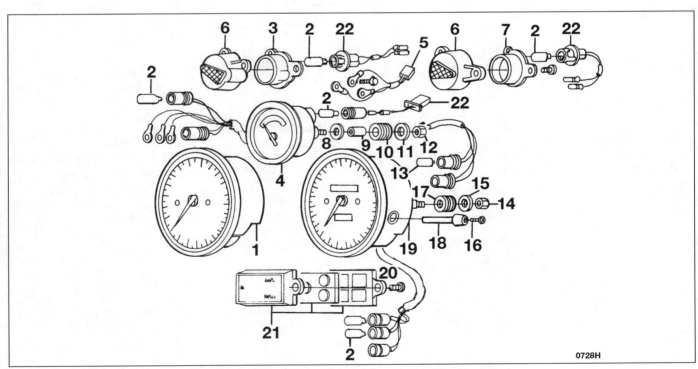

12.5d Instrument cluster details (Katana 750/GSX750F models)

1 Tachometer
2 Bulbs
3 Bulb housing
4 Fuel gauge
5 Wiring harness

6 Lens
7 Bulb housing
8 Washer
9 Spacer
10 Cushion

11 Washer
12 Nut
13 Bulb
14 Nut

15 Washer
16 Screw
17 Cushion
18 Trip odometer knob

19 Speedometer
20 Case
21 Warning display
22 Socket

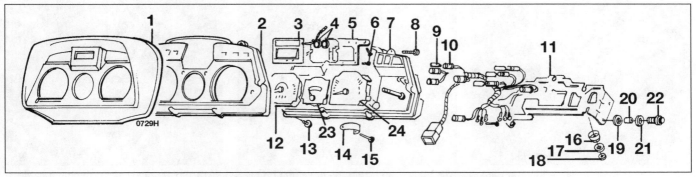

12.5e Instrument cluster details (Katana 1100/GSX1100F models)

1 Cluster cover	6 Screws	11 Bracket	16 Cushion	21 Cushion
2 Cluster face	7 Cluster housing	12 Speedometer	17 Washer	22 Screw
3 Clock	8 Screw	13 Screw	18 Nut	23 Fuel gauge
4 Clock batteries	9 Bulb	14 Clip	19 Washer	24 Tachometer
5 Clock back	10 Socket	15 Screw	20 Spacer	

13 Meters and gauges - replacement

Check

Tachometer and speedometer

1 Special instruments are required to properly check the operation of these meters. Take the instrument cluster to a Suzuki dealer service department or other qualified repair shop for diagnosis.

Fuel warning light (GSX-R models)

2 Some models have a warning light that warns of low fuel level.
3 Locate the fuel level sensor in the tank and disconnect its electrical connector.
4 Connect the two terminals in the harness side of the connector to each other with a short piece of wire.
5 Turn the key to the On position. The fuel warning light should come on. If it doesn't, the bulb is probably burned out. If replacing the bulb doesn't solve the problem, check the wiring for a break or bad connection.

6 If the light goes on in Step 4 but not when the bike is low on fuel, the switch may be defective. To test, unscrew the switch from the tank (disconnect the electrical connector if you haven't already done so) **(see illustration)**.
7 Check the switch for obvious damage, such as a broken connection, and replace it if necessary **(see illustration)**.
8 Connect the positive terminal of a 12-volt battery (the bike's battery will work) to one of the switch terminals with a length of wire. Connect the other terminal to ground (earth) through a 3.4-watt, 12-volt bulb **(see illustration)**. The bulb should light after several seconds.
9 Repeat the test in Step 8 with the in-tank portion of the switch immersed in water. The bulb should go out.
10 If the switch doesn't perform as described, replace it with a new one.

Fuel gauge

11 Remove the seat and the right frame cover. Find the black/white and yellow/black wires that run to the fuel level sender and disconnect them.
12 Connect the wires in the harness side of the connector to each other with a short

length of wire and turn on the key. The gauge should move to the Full position. If the gauge doesn't indicate Full, check the wiring to the gauge for a break or bad connection. If the wiring is good, the gauge is probably defective.

13 To test the gauge for accuracy, connect a 110-ohm resistor between the wire terminals in place of the short length of wire used in Step 12. The gauge should indicate Empty. It should indicate Full when a 3-ohm resistor is connected in place of the 110-ohm resistor.
14 To test the sender, remove it from the tank. Connect an ohmmeter between the sender terminals and move the float through its range. Compare the readings to those listed in this Chapter's Specifications. If the ohmmeter readings aren't correct, replace the sender.

13.6 Disconnect the electrical connector and unscrew the switch from the tank

13.7 Check the switch for visible damage (such as a broken solder joint) in the area between the threads and the end of the switch

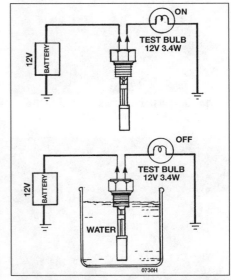

13.8 The switch should conduct electricity when it's dry, but not when it's immersed in water

8

13.18 Disconnect the speedometer cable from the speedometer

13.19a ... and from the drive unit on the front fork

13.19b If necessary, detach the cable support from the fork

Gauge replacement

15 Katana 1100/GSX1100F models: Remove the screws that secure the instrument cluster cover **(see illustration 12.5e)**. Detach the cover.
Caution: Always store the cluster with the gauges facing up or the gauges will be ruined.
16 Remove the attaching hardware and remove the gauge to be replaced.
17 Installation is the reverse of the removal procedure.

Speedometer cable replacement

18 Disconnect the speedometer cable from the speedometer **(see illustration)**.
19 Disconnect the lower end of the speedometer cable from the drive **(see**

14.1a Pull the bulb socket out of the cluster . . .

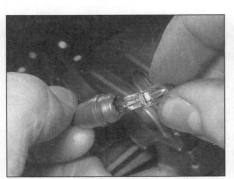

14.1b . . . then pull the bulb out of the socket

illustration). Note carefully how the cable is routed, then remove it. If necessary, detach the cable support from the front fork **(see illustration)**.
20 Installation is the reverse of the removal steps.

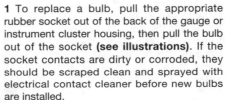

14 Instrument and warning light bulbs - replacement

1 To replace a bulb, pull the appropriate rubber socket out of the back of the gauge or instrument cluster housing, then pull the bulb out of the socket **(see illustrations)**. If the socket contacts are dirty or corroded, they should be scraped clean and sprayed with electrical contact cleaner before new bulbs are installed.
2 Carefully push the new bulb into position, then push the socket into the gauge or cluster housing.

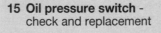

15 Oil pressure switch - check and replacement

1 If the oil pressure warning light fails to operate properly, check the oil level and make sure it is correct.
2 If the oil level is correct, disconnect the wire from the oil pressure switch, which is located

15.4 Location of the oil pressure switch

on the right side of the engine. Turn the ignition key On and ground (earth) the end of the wire. If the light comes on, the oil pressure switch is defective and must be replaced with a new one (only after draining the engine oil).
3 If the light does not come on, check the oil pressure warning light bulb, the wiring between the oil pressure switch and the light, and between the light and its power source (see the wiring diagrams at the end of this Chapter).
4 To replace the switch, drain the engine oil (see Chapter 1) and remove the signal generator cover (see Chapter 4). Unscrew the switch from the case. Coat the threads of the new switch with sealant (Suzuki Bond 1207B or equivalent), then screw the unit into its hole, tightening it securely **(see illustration)**.
5 Fill the crankcase with the recommended type and amount of oil (see Chapter 1) and check for leaks.

16 Ignition main (key) switch - check and replacement

Check

1 Disconnect the switch electrical connector (remove the upper fairing if necessary for access).
2 Using an ohmmeter, check the continuity of the terminal pairs indicated in the accompanying table **(see illustration)**.

IGNITION SWITCH

	R/W	O	Gr	Br
OFF				
ON	O——O		O——O	
P	O——O			O

0745H

16.2 Check the continuity of the ignition switch in the different switch positions across the indicated terminals

See wiring diagrams for color codes

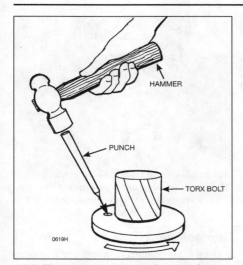

16.6 The shear-head bolts (arrowed) must be carefully drilled and removed with a screw extractor or knocked in a counterclockwise direction with a hammer and punch

0619H

ENGINE STOP AND START SWITCH

	O/Bl	O/W	Y/G
OFF			
RUN	O——————O		
START (Push)		O——————O

LIGHTING SWITCH (UK only)

	Gr	O/Bl *	O/R	Y/W
OFF				
S	O——————O			
ON	O——————O	O——————O	

* O/Lg on Katana 1100/GSX1100F models

TURN SIGNAL SWITCH

	B	Lbl	LG
R		O——————O	
•			
L	O——————O	

IGNITION SWITCH

	R*	O	Gr	Br
OFF				
ON	O——————O	O——————O	
P	O——————————————————O

* RW on Katana 1100/GSX1100F models

0746H

DIMMER SWITCH

	W	Y	Y/W
HI		O——————O	
LO	O——————————————O

17.4 Continuity tables for the handlebar switches
See wiring diagrams for color codes

Continuity should exist between the terminals connected by a solid line when the switch is in the indicated position.

3 If the switch fails any of the tests, replace it.

Replacement

4 Remove the instrument cluster (see Section 12).

5 Unplug the switch electrical connector.

6 The switch is held to the upper clamp with two shear-head bolts **(see illustration)**. Using a hammer and a sharp punch, knock the shear-head bolts in a counterclockwise (anticlockwise) direction to unscrew them. If they're too tight and won't turn, carefully drill holes through the centers of the bolts and unscrew them using a screw extractor (E-Z Out). If necessary, remove the fairing mount for better access to the bolts. Detach the switch from the upper clamp.

7 Hold the new switch in position and install the new shear-head bolts. Tighten the bolts until the heads break off or the Torx socket rounds them off.

8 The remainder of installation is the reverse of the removal steps.

17 Handlebar switches - check

1 Generally speaking, the switches are reliable and trouble-free. Most troubles, when they do occur, are caused by dirty or corroded contacts, but wear and breakage of internal parts is a possibility that should not be overlooked. If breakage does occur, the entire switch and related wiring harness will have to be replaced with a new one, since individual parts are not usually available.

2 The switches can be checked for continuity with an ohmmeter or a continuity test light. Always disconnect the battery ground (earth) cable, which will prevent the possibility of a short circuit, before making the checks.

3 Trace the wiring harness of the switch in question and unplug the electrical connectors.

4 Using the ohmmeter or test light, check for continuity between the terminals of the switch harness with the switch in the various positions **(see illustration)**. Continuity should exist between the terminals connected by a solid line when the switch is in the indicated position.

5 If the continuity check indicates a problem exists, disassemble the switch and spray the switch contacts with electrical contact cleaner. If they are accessible, the contacts can be scraped clean with a knife or polished with crocus cloth. If switch components are damaged or broken, it will be obvious when the switch is disassembled.

18 Handlebar switches - removal and installation

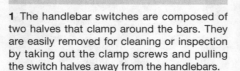

1 The handlebar switches are composed of two halves that clamp around the bars. They are easily removed for cleaning or inspection by taking out the clamp screws and pulling the switch halves away from the handlebars.

2 To completely remove the switches, the electrical connectors in the wiring harness should be unplugged. The right side switch must be separated from the throttle cables, also.

3 When installing the switches, make sure the wiring harnesses are properly routed to avoid pinching or stretching the wires.

19 Neutral switch - check and replacement

Check

1 Locate the neutral switch (it's mounted behind the engine sprocket on the left side of the engine) and follow its wire to the connector. Disconnect the wire from the neutral switch. Connect one lead of an ohmmeter to a good ground (earth) and the other lead to the post on the switch.

2 When the transmission is in neutral, the ohmmeter should read 0 ohms - in any other gear, the meter should read infinite resistance.

3 If the switch doesn't check out as described, replace it.

Replacement

4 Remove the engine sprocket and drive chain (see Chapter 5).

5 Unplug the neutral switch electrical connector. Remove the neutral switch screws and lift it from the engine **(see illustrations)**.

19.5a Remove the screws . . .

8

19.5b . . . and remove the switch and its O-ring - use a new O-ring during installation

19.6a Remove the switch pin . . .

19.6b . . . and the spring - replace the pin if it's worn and replace the spring if it's weak

6 Remove the switch pin and spring (use a magnet if necessary) **(see illustrations)**.

7 Installation is the reverse of the removal steps. Use a new O-ring and tighten the screws securely.

20 Sidestand switch - check and replacement

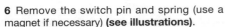

Check

1 Support the bike so the sidestand can be raised and lowered (put it on the centerstand if equipped).

2 Follow the wiring harness from the switch

to the connector, then disconnect the connector.

3 Connect the leads of an ohmmeter to the wire terminals.

4 With the sidestand in the up position, there should be continuity through the switch (0 ohms). With the sidestand down, there should be no continuity (infinite resistance).

5 If the switch fails either of these tests, replace it.

Replacement

6 With the sidestand down, remove the switch screws and remove the switch **(see illustrations)**.

7 Installation is the reverse of the removal procedure.

21 Horn - check and replacement

Check

1 Unplug the electrical connectors from the horn **(see illustration)**. Using two jumper wires, apply battery voltage directly to the terminals on the horn. If the horn sounds, check the switch and the wiring between the switch and the horn (see the wiring diagrams at the end of this Chapter).

2 If the horn doesn't sound, replace it.

Replacement

3 Detach the electrical connectors. If access to the horn mounting nut is restricted, unbolt the horn bracket from the frame.

4 Remove the mounting nut and detach the horn from the bracket **(see illustration 21.1)**.

5 Installation is the reverse of removal.

22 Starter relay - check and replacement

Check

1 Lift the rubber cover off the starter relay **(see illustration)**. Disconnect the battery positive cable and the starter wire from the terminals on the relay.

Caution: Don't let the battery positive cable make contact with anything, as it would be a direct short to ground (earth).

2 Connect the leads of an ohmmeter to the large terminals of the starter relay.

3 Turn the ignition switch to On and the engine stop switch to Run. Place the transmission in Neutral.

4 Press the starter button - the relay should click and the ohmmeter should indicate 0 ohms.

5 If the meter doesn't read 0 ohms or the relay doesn't click, replace it.

20.6a The sidestand switch is secured by two screws - this is a late GSX-R1100 switch . . .

20.6b . . . and this is a Katana 600/GSX600F switch

21.1 Disconnect the wires and remove the mounting nut (arrowed) to detach the horn from the bracket

22.1 The starter relay wires are beneath this rubber cover

23.4 Pull back the rubber cover, remove the nut and disconnect the cable from the starter

6 Disconnect the cable from the negative terminal of the battery.
7 Connect the ohmmeter between the small terminals on the relay. It should indicate the value listed in this Chapter's Specifications. If not, replace the relay.

Replacement

8 Detach the battery positive cable, the starter cable and electrical connector from the relay.
9 Pull the relay out.
10 Installation is the reverse of removal. Reconnect the negative battery cable after all the other electrical connections are made.

23 Starter motor - removal and installation

Removal

1 Early GSX-R750, Katana 600/GSX600F, Katana 1100/GSX1100F: Remove the alternator (see Section 27).
2 Late GSX-R1100: Remove the lower fairing (see Chapter 7).
3 Disconnect the cable from the negative terminal of the battery.
4 Remove the nut and disconnect the starter cable from the starter **(see illustration)**.
5 Remove the starter mounting bolts **(see illustration)**.

23.5 Remove the starter mounting bolts

6 Lift the starter out of the engine **(see illustration)**.
7 Check the condition of the O-ring on the end of the starter and replace it if necessary.

Installation

8 Apply a little engine oil to the O-ring and install the starter by reversing the removal procedure.

24 Starter motor - disassembly, inspection and reassembly

1 Remove the starter motor (see Section 23).

24.2 Check for alignment marks where each end cover meets the starter - make your own marks if the factory marks aren't visible

23.6 Lift the starter out of the engine - inspect the O-ring and replace it if necessary

Disassembly

2 Look for a location mark that indicates the position of the housing to each end cover **(see illustration)**. Make your own marks if the factory marks aren't visible.
3 Remove the two long screws and detach both end covers **(see illustration)**. **Note:** *The screws have been secured with thread locking agent. You may have to use an impact driver to remove them. Be sure the screwdriver fits properly in the screw slots.*
4 Remove the shim(s) from each end of the armature **(see illustrations)**. Note their location, number and position so they can be reinstalled in their original locations.
5 Remove the large O-ring from each end of the housing **(see illustration)**.

24.3 Lift the cover off each end

24.4a Take the shim(s) off each end of the starter . . .

24.4b . . . carefully noting their order so you can reinstall them the same way

24.5 The large O-ring at each end of the starter housing should be replaced whenever the starter is disassembled

8

24.6 Pull the armature out of the starter housing

24.7 Slide the brush springs up far enough so the brushes can be slid out of their slots

24.9 Measure the length of the brushes and compare the service limit

6 Pull the armature out of the housing (see illustration).

7 Slide the brush springs up far enough so the brushes can be slipped out of their slots (see illustration).

8 Remove the brush plate from the housing.

Inspection

9 The parts of the starter motor that most likely will require attention are the brushes. Measure the length of the brushes and compare the results to the brush length listed in this Chapter's Specifications (see illustration). If any of the brushes are worn beyond the specified limits, replace the brush holder assembly with a new one. If the brushes are not worn excessively, cracked, chipped, or

otherwise damaged, they may be reused.

10 Inspect the commutator (see illustration) for scoring, scratches and discoloration. The commutator can be cleaned and polished with crocus cloth or 400 grit emery paper. After cleaning, wipe away any residue with a cloth soaked in an electrical system cleaner or denatured alcohol. If the commutator bars are worn down even with the mica separators, undercut the mica with a piece of hacksaw blade. Don't undercut more than the limit listed in this Chapter's Specifications.

11 Using an ohmmeter or a continuity test light, check for continuity between the commutator bars (see illustration). Continuity should exist between each bar and all of the others. Also, check for continuity between the commutator

bars and the armature shaft (see illustration). There should be no continuity between the commutator and the shaft. If the checks indicate otherwise, the armature is defective.

12 Check for continuity between the brush plate and the brushes (see illustration). The meter should read close to 0 ohms. If it doesn't, the brush plate has an open and must be replaced.

13 Using the highest range on the ohmmeter, measure the resistance between the brush holders and the brush plate (see illustration). The reading should be infinite. If there is any reading at all, replace the brush plate.

14 Unclip the seal cover and inspect the seal (and needle roller bearing, if equipped) (see illustration). If the seal lip is worn or if the

24.10 Check the commutator for cracks, discoloring and wear

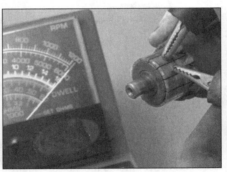

24.11a Continuity should exist between the commutator bars

24.11b There should be no continuity between the commutator bars and the armature shaft

24.12 There should be almost no resistance (0 ohms) between the brushes and the brush plate

24.13 There should be no continuity between the brush plate and the brush holders (the resistance should be infinite)

24.14 Lift the seal cover off to inspect the seal and needle roller bearing (if equipped)

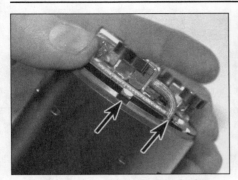

24.15 When installing the brush plate, make sure the brush leads fit into the notches in the plate (arrowed) - also, make sure the tongue on the plate fits into the notch in the housing (arrowed)

bearing is worn or damaged, they should be replaced. Check with a Suzuki dealer to see whether the seal and bearing are available separately; if not, you'll have to replace the end cover.

Reassembly

15 Detach the brush springs from the brush plate (this will make armature installation much easier). Install the brush plate into the housing, routing the brush leads into the notches in the plate (see illustration). Make sure the tongue on the brush plate fits into the notch in the housing.
16 Install the brushes into their holders and slide the armature into place. Install the brush springs (see illustration).
17 Install any shims that were present on each end of the armature shaft. Install the end covers, aligning the protrusions with the notches. Install the two long screws and tighten them securely.

25 Charging system testing - general information and precautions

1 If the performance of the charging system is suspect, the system as a whole should be checked first, followed by testing of the individual components (the alternator and the voltage regulator). Note: Before beginning the checks, make sure the battery is fully charged

27.7 The alternator is secured by three bolts (arrowed)

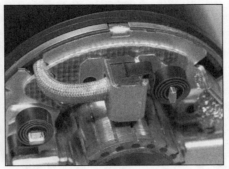

24.16 Seat the end of each brush spring in the groove in the end of the brush

and that all system connections are clean and tight.
2 Checking the output of the charging system and the performance of the various components within the charging system requires the use of special electrical test equipment. A voltmeter or a multimeter is the absolute minimum tool required. In addition, an ohmmeter is generally required for checking the remainder of the system.
3 When making the checks, follow the procedures carefully to prevent incorrect connections or short circuits, as irreparable damage to electrical system components may result if short circuits occur. Because of the special tools and expertise required, it is recommended that the job of checking the charging system be left to a dealer service department or a reputable motorcycle repair shop.

26 Charging system - output test

Caution: Never disconnect the battery cables from the battery while the engine is running. If the battery is disconnected, the alternator and regulator/rectifier will be damaged.
1 To check the charging system output, you will need a voltmeter or a multimeter with a voltmeter function.
2 The battery must be fully charged (charge it from an external source if necessary) and the

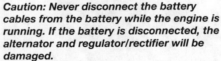

27.8 Remove the O-ring - use a new one during installation

engine must be at normal operating temperature to obtain an accurate reading.
3 Remove the seat (see Chapter 7).
4 Attach the positive (red) voltmeter lead to the positive battery terminal and the negative lead to the negative battery terminal. The voltmeter selector switch (if so equipped) must be in a DC volt range greater than 15 volts.
5 Start the engine. Run it at 5,000 rpm.
6 The charging system output should be above the minimum listed in this Chapter's Specifications.
7 If the output is as specified, the alternator is functioning properly. If the charging system as a whole is not performing as it should, refer to Section 27 and check the voltage regulator.
8 Low voltage output may be the result of damaged windings in the alternator stator coils, worn alternator brushes or wiring problems. Make sure all electrical connections are clean and tight, then refer to Section 27 for specific alternator tests.

27 Alternator - removal, inspection and installation

Removal
Katana 600/GSX600F models
1 Remove the fuel tank, air cleaner and carburetors (see Chapter 3).
2 Remove the fairing (see Chapter 7).
Katana 750/GSX750F models
3 Remove the fuel tank, air cleaner and carburetors (see Chapter 3).
4 Remove the fairing and right frame cover (see Chapter 7).

All models
5 Disconnect the alternator electrical connector.
6 Remove the engine sprocket cover (see Chapter 5).
7 Remove the alternator mounting bolts and lift the alternator out (see illustration).
8 Remove the alternator O-ring (see illustration).

Disassembly and inspection
9 Place the alternator gear in a vise with padded jaws (copper or wood) and loosen the nut (see illustration).

27.9 Hold the gear from turning in a vise with padded jaws and loosen the nut

8

27.10 Remove the nut and washer

27.11a Lift off the gear and inspect the damper . . .

27.11b . . . replace the damper if it's damaged or worn

27.12 Remove the cover nuts and lift the cover off

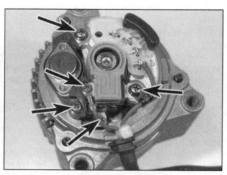

27.13 Remove the brush holder and regulator screws (arrowed) - one of the screws secures a wire and another secures a terminal

10 Remove the nut and washer **(see illustration)**.

11 Remove the alternator gear **(see illustration)**. Inspect the gear damper and replace it if it's worn or damaged **(see illustration)**.

12 Remove the nuts and take off the alternator end cover **(see illustration)**.

13 Remove the brush holder and regulator screws **(see illustration)**.

14 Lift out the brush holder and take the brush assembly out **(see illustrations)**.

15 Measure the length of the brushes **(see illustration)**. If they're worn to less than the minimum listed in this Chapter's Specifications, replace the brush assembly.

16 Lift out the regulator **(see illustration)**.

17 Testing of the regulator requires a variable DC power source, a voltmeter with a 25-volt range, a switch, a 3.4-watt, 12-volt bulb and connecting wires. Identify the regulator terminals **(see illustration)**. Set up a circuit with the regulator and test equipment **(see illustration)**. Set the variable power source to 12 volts and turn the switch on. The bulb should light. When the voltage is increased to 14.5 volts, the bulb should go out. If the regulator doesn't perform properly, replace it.

Assembly and installation

18 Assembly and installation are the reverse of the disassembly steps, with the following additions:

27.14a Lift off the brush holder . . .

27.14b . . . and take out the brush assembly

27.15 Measure the length of the brushes and replace the assembly if they're worn below the minimum listed in this Chapter's Specifications

27.16 Lift off the regulator

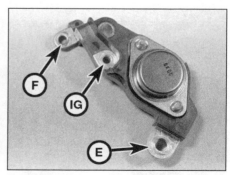

27.17a Identify the regulator terminals . . .

a) Use a new cover O-ring. Tighten the cover nuts securely.
b) Position the alternator on the engine with the wiring connector upwards **(see illustration)**. Tighten the mounting bolts securely.

28 Fairing fan (California models) - check, removal and installation

1 Some California models have an electric fan on the left side of the fairing that blows cooling air onto the carburetors.

Check

2 Remove fairing panels as necessary for access to the fan (see Chapter 7).
3 Follow the wiring harness from the fan to the electrical connector and disconnect the connector.
4 Connect the fan directly to the battery terminals with lengths of wire. If it doesn't run, replace it.

Removal and installation

5 If you haven't already done so, remove the fairing panels and disconnect the electrical connector.
6 Remove the fan mounting screws **(see illustration)**. Take the fan out.
7 Installation is the reverse of removal.

29 Power windshield (Katana 1100/GSX1100F models) - removal and installation

1 Remove the upper and lower fairings (see Chapter 7).

Motor removal

2 Disconnect the motor electrical connector and loosen the coupling screws **(see illustration)**.
3 Remove the motor mounting bolts and take the motor out **(see illustration)**.

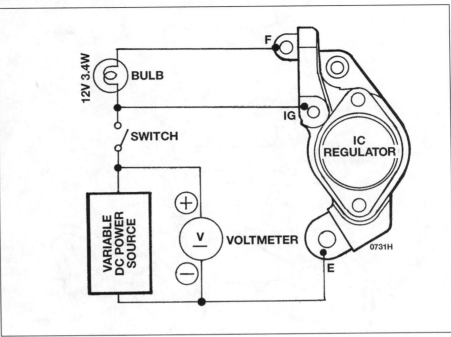

27.17b ... and set up this circuit to test the regulator

27.18 Install the alternator with the wiring connector upward

28.6 The fairing fan is secured by screws (arrowed) (Katana 600/GSX600F shown)

29.2 Loosen the screws (arrowed) that secure the coupling to the motor and shaft

29.3 Remove the motor mounting screws (arrowed) to detach the motor

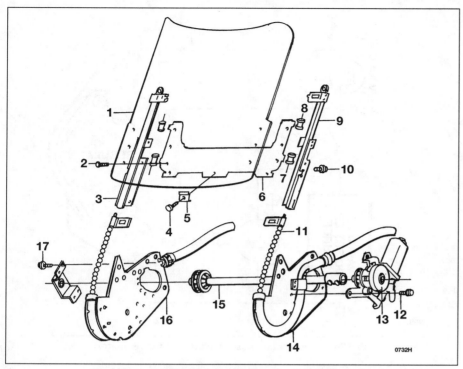

29.5 Power windshield details (Katana 1100/GSX1100F)

1 Windshield	7 Bushing	13 Motor
2 Screw	8 Bushing	14 Drive assembly
3 Guide	9 Guide	15 Drive shaft
4 Screw	10 Bolt	16 Drive assembly
5 Bracket	11 Drive chain	17 Bolt
6 Bracket	12 Bolt	

Windshield assembly removal

4 Unbolt the fairing brace and remove it together with the windshield (see Chapter 7).
5 To remove individual windshield components, remove the fasteners and take them off **(see illustration)**.

Installation

6 Installation is the reverse of the removal steps.

30 Wiring diagrams

Prior to troubleshooting a circuit, check the fuses to make sure they're in good condition. Make sure the battery is fully charged and check the cable connections.

When checking a circuit, make sure all connectors are clean, with no broken or loose terminals or wires. When unplugging a connector, don't pull on the wires - pull only on the connector housings themselves.

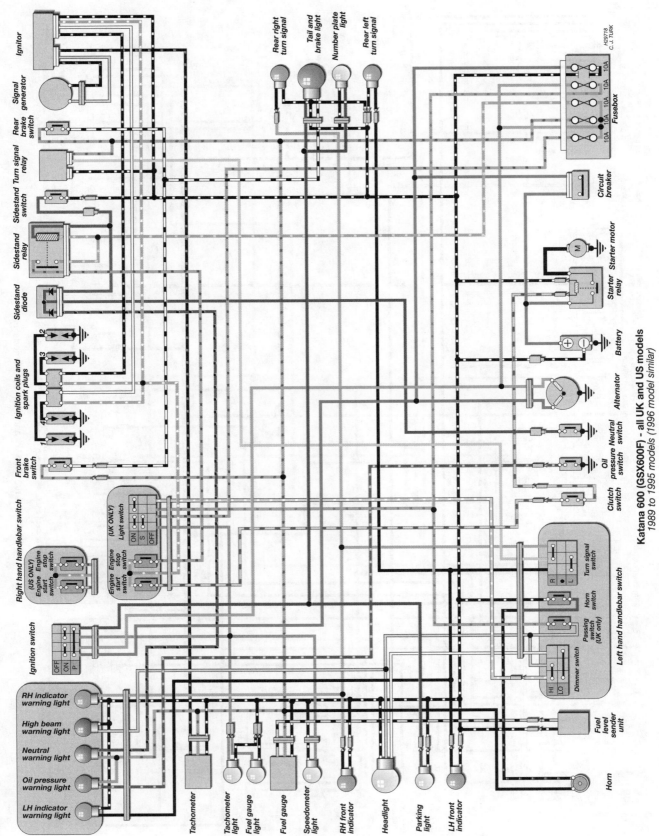

Katana 600 (GSX600F) - all UK and US models
1989 to 1995 models (1996 model similar)

8

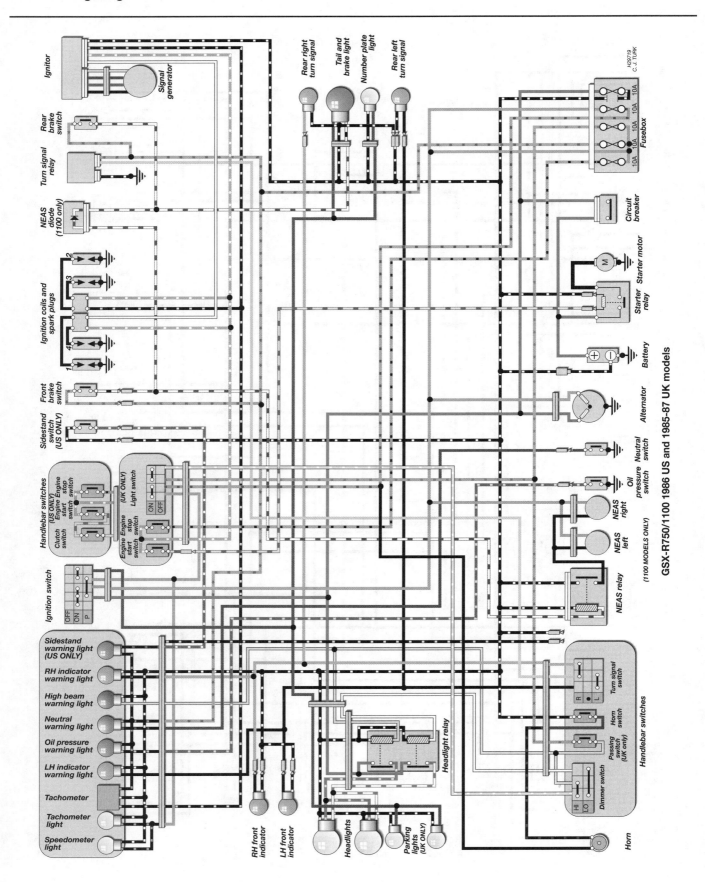

GSX-R750/1100 1986 US and 1985-87 UK models

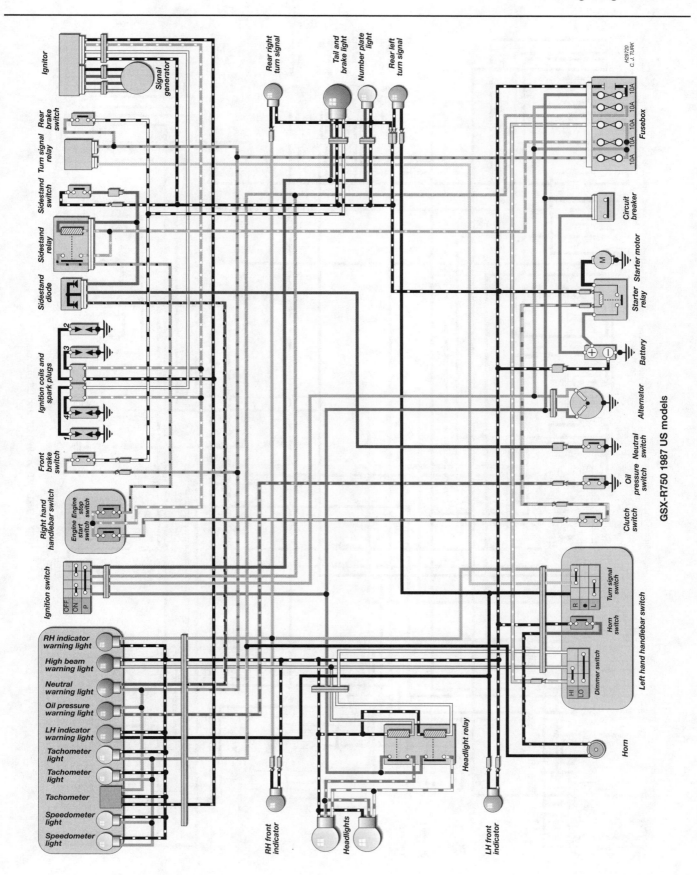

H29720
C. J. TURK

GSX-R750 1987 US models

8

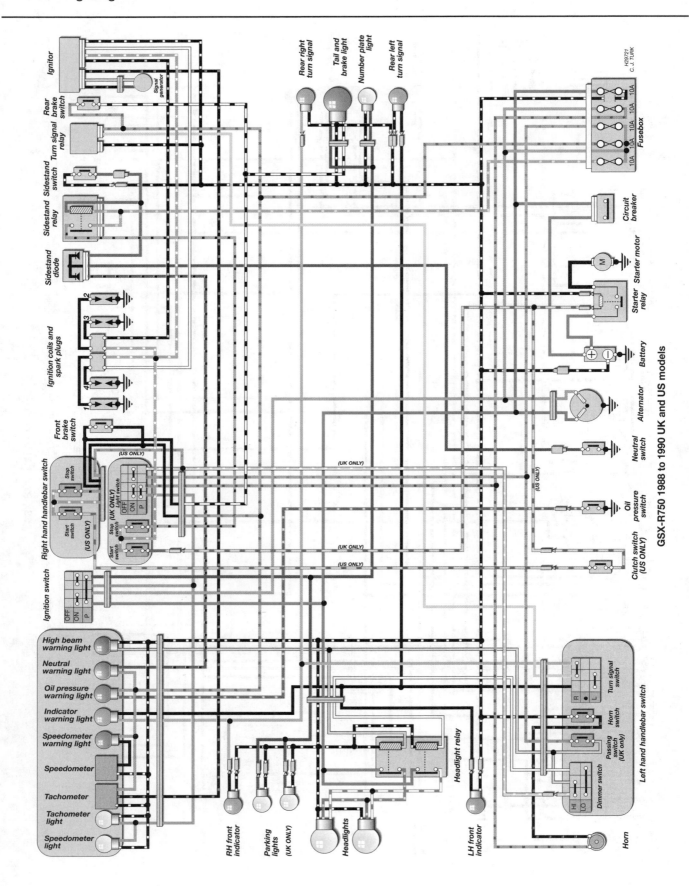

GSX-R750 1988 to 1990 UK and US models

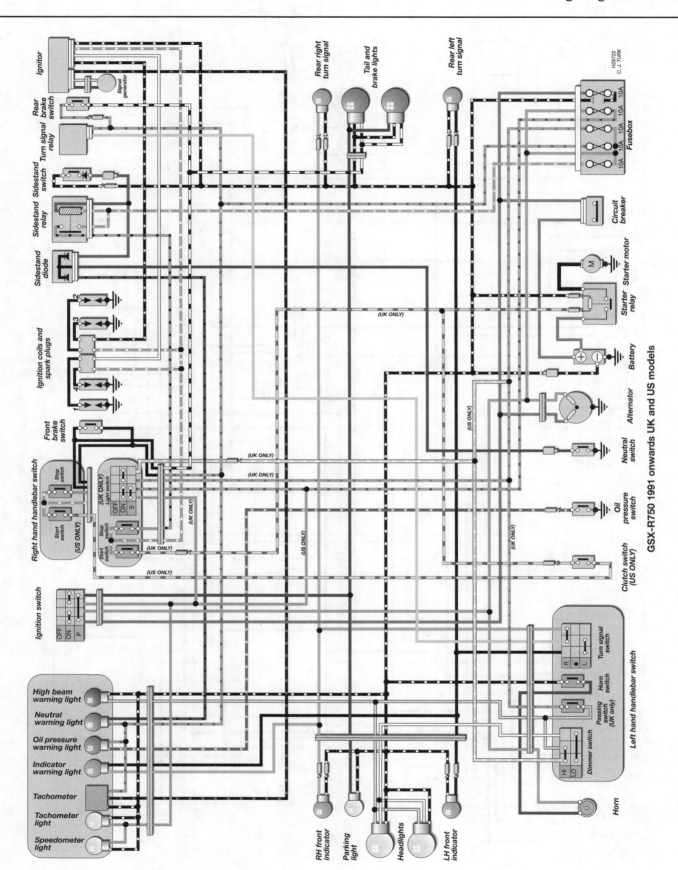

GSX-R750 1991 onwards UK and US models

8

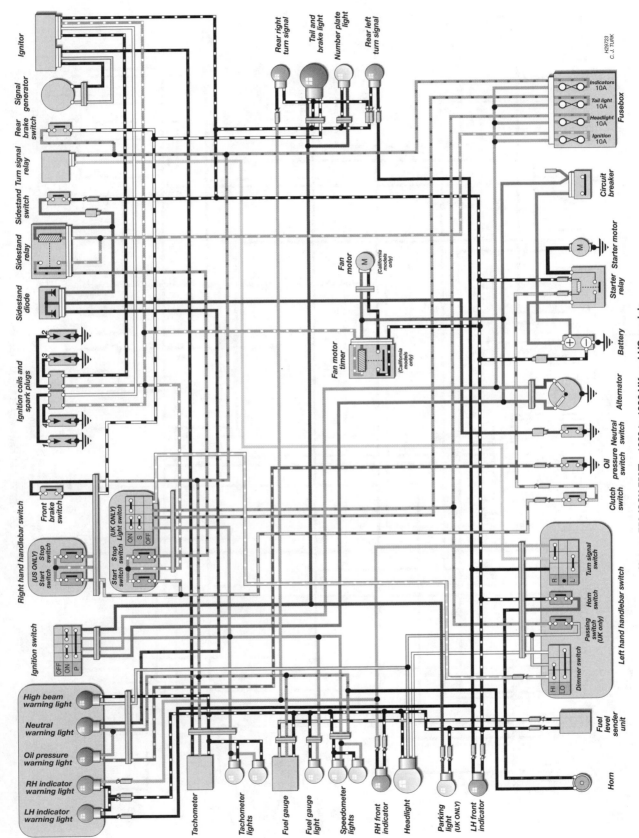

Katana 750 (GSX 750F) - 1989 to 1992 UK and US models

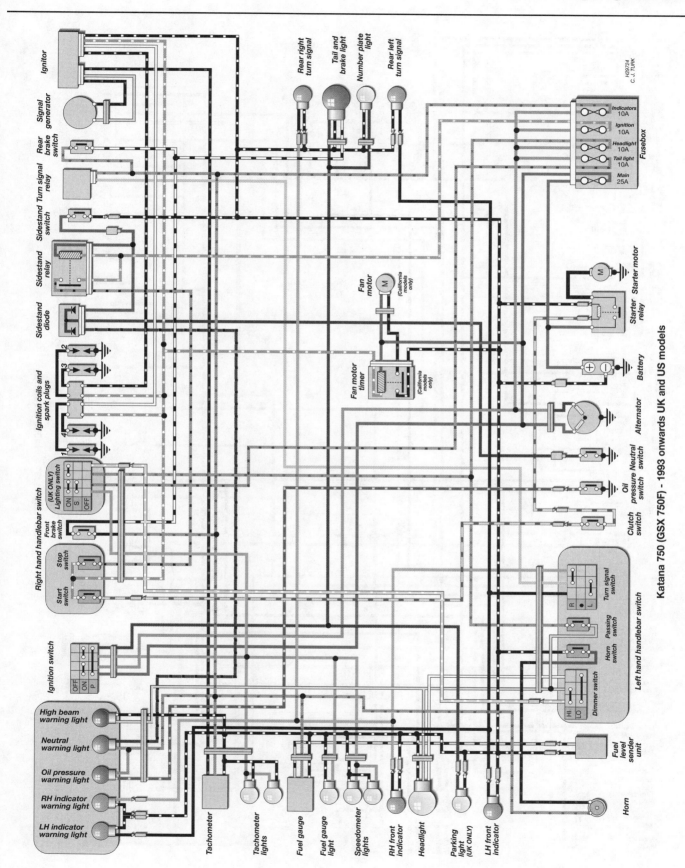

Katana 750 (GSX 750F) - 1993 onwards UK and US models

8

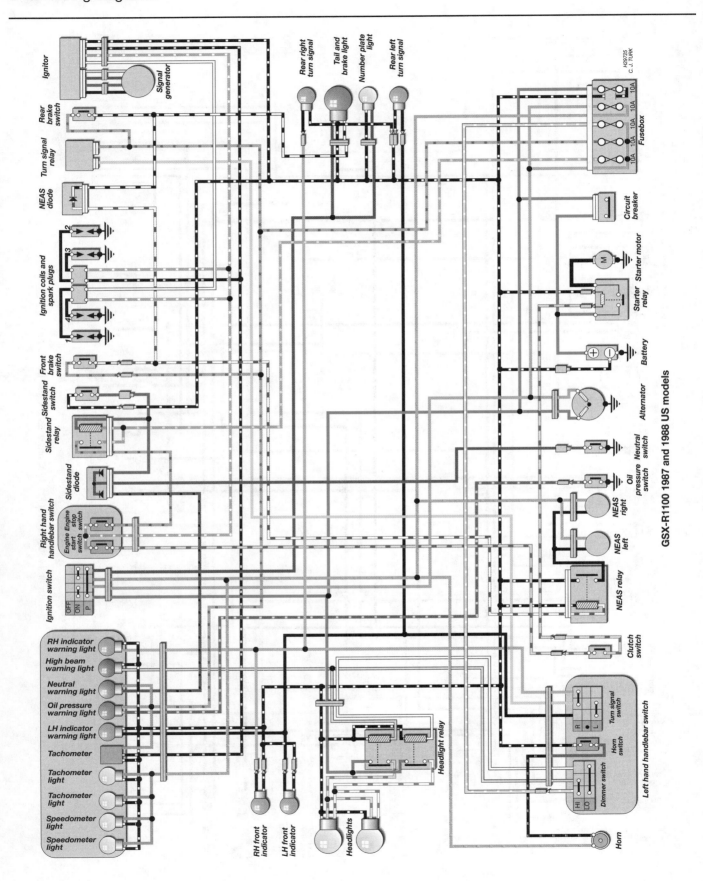

GSX-R1100 1987 and 1988 US models

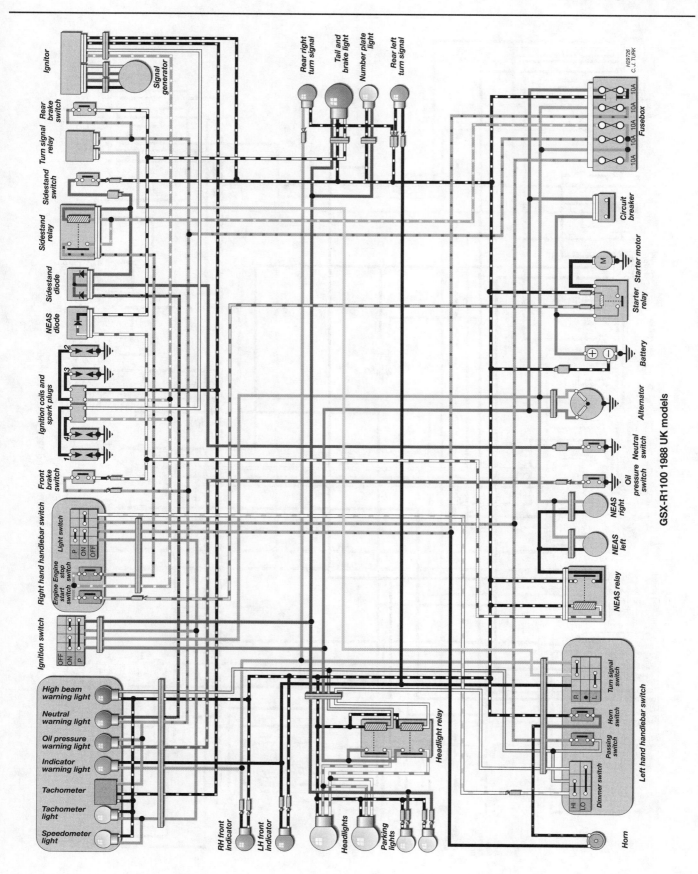

GSX-R1100 1988 UK models

8

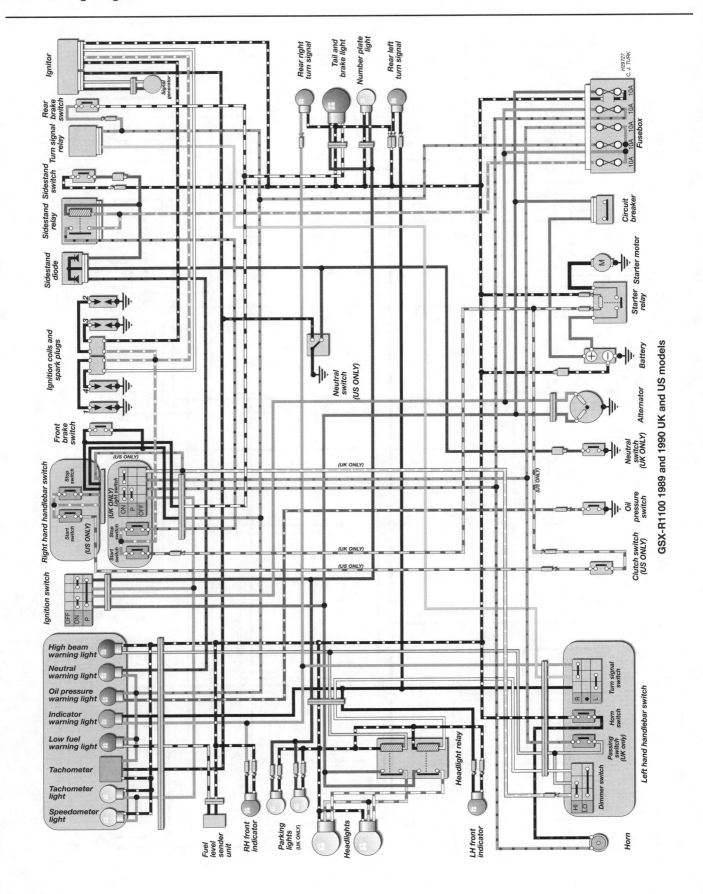

GSX-R1100 1989 and 1990 UK and US models

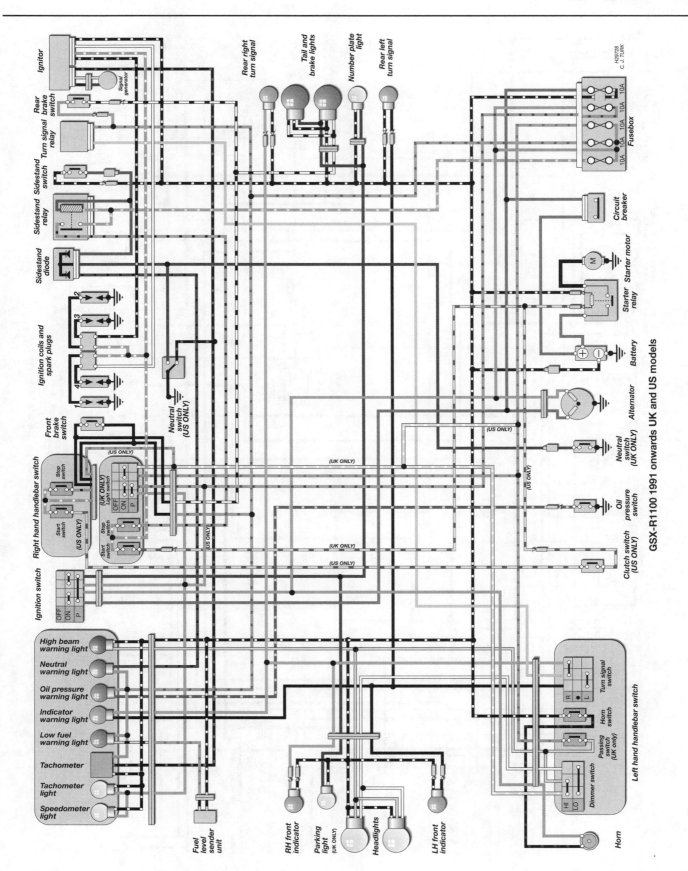

GSX-R1100 1991 onwards UK and US models

8

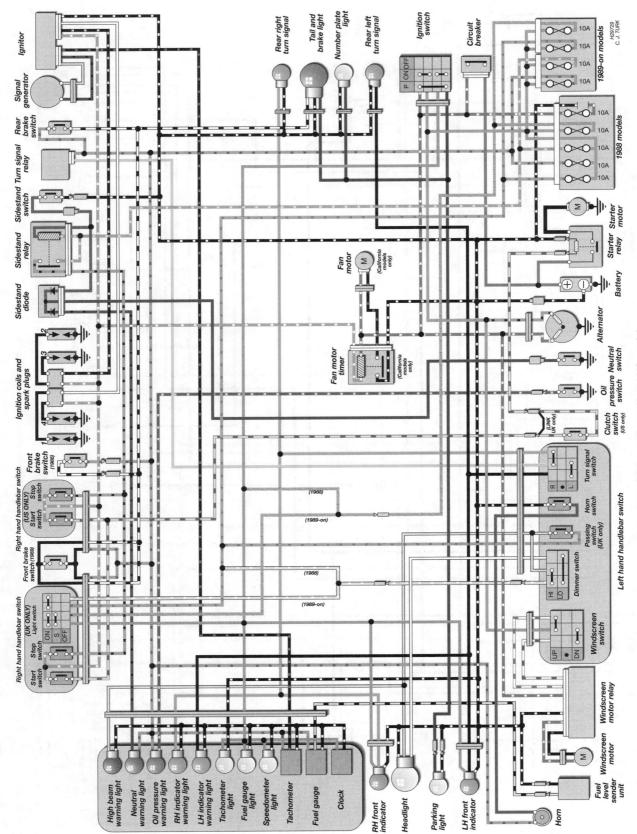

Katana 1100 (GSX 1100F) all UK and US models

Dimensions and weights

Overall length (L)

Katana 600 (GSX600F) . . . . .2110 mm (83.1 inches)
GSX-R750
   1985 (UK) . . . . .2105 mm (82.9 inches)
   1986 and 1987 . . . . .2115 mm (83.3 inches)
   1988 through 1990 .2060 mm (81.1 inches)
   1991 on . . . . .2065 mm (81.3 inches)
Katana 750 (GSX750F) . . . . .2130 mm (83.9 inches)
GSX-R1100
   1985 through 1988 .2115 mm (83.3 inches)
   1989 . . . . .2050 mm (80.7 inches)
   1990 . . . . .2080 mm (81.9 inches)
   1991 on . . . . .2085 mm (82.5 inches)
Katana 1100 (GSX1100F)
   1988 . . . . .2185 mm (86.0 inches)
   1989 on . . . . .2205 mm (86.8 inches)

Wheelbase (W)

Katana 600 (GSX600F) . . . . .1430 mm (56.3 inches)
GSX-R 750
   1985 (UK) . . . . .1435 mm (56.5 inches)
   1986 and 1987 . . . . .1455 mm (57.3 inches)
   1988 (all) and 1989 UK . . . . .1410 mm (55.5 inches)
   1989 on US and 1990 on UK . . . . .1415 mm (55.7 inches)
Katana 750 (GSX750F) . . . . .1470 mm (57.9 inches)
GSX-R1100
   1985 through 1988 .1460 mm (57.5 inches)
   1989 . . . . .1440 mm (56.7 inches)
   1990 on . . . . .1465 mm (57.7 inches)
Katana 1100 (GSX1100F)
   1988 . . . . .1490 mm (58.7 inches)
   1989 on . . . . .1535 mm (60.4 inches)

Dimensions and weights

Overall width

Katana 600 (GSX600F) . . . . .700 mm (27.6 inches)
GSX-R750
   1985 through 1987 .745 mm (29.3 inches)
   1988 through 1990 .730 mm (28.7 inches)
   1991 on . . . . .725 mm (28.5 inches)
Katana 750 (GSX750F) . . . . .730 mm (28.7 inches)
GSX-R1100
   1985 through 1988 .745 mm (29.3 inches)
   1989 on . . . . .755 mm (29.7 inches)
Katana 1100 (GSX1100F) . . . . .765 mm (30.1 inches)

Overall height (H)

Katana 600 (GSX600F) . . . . .1145 mm (45.1 inches)
GSX-R750
   1985 (UK) . . . . .1205 mm (47.4 inches)
   1986 and 1987 . . . . .1215 mm (47.8 inches)
   1988 US, 1988 and 1989 UK . . . . .1130 mm (44.5 inches)
   1989 on US and 1990 on UK . . . . .1140 mm (44.8 inches)
Katana 750 (GSX750F) . . . . .1180 mm (46.5 inches)
GSX-R1100
   1985 through 1988 . . . . .1215 mm (47.8 inches)
   1989 on . . . . .1150 mm (45.3 inches)
Katana 1100 (GSX1100F) . . . . .1290 mm (50.8 inches)*
Windscreen up if equipped with power windscreen

Seat height (S)

Katana 600 (GSX600F) . . . . .780 mm (30.7 inches)
GSX-R750
   1985 through 1987 . . . . .Not specified
   1988 . . . . .785 mm (30.9 inches)
   1989 and 1990 . . . . .795 mm (31.3 inches)
   1991 on . . . . .805 mm (31.7 inches)
Katana 750 (GSX750F) . . . . .790 mm (31.1 inches)
GSX-R1100
   1985 and 1986 . . . . .Not specified
   1987 and 1988 . . . . .795 mm (31.3 inches)
   1989 through 1991 US, 1989 through 1992 UK . . . . . .Not specified
   1992 US . . . . .815 mm (32.1 inches)
Katana 1100 (GSX1100F) . . . . .Not specified

Dry weight

Katana 600 (GSX600F)
  1988
    US except California . . . . .195 kg (429 lbs)
    California . . . . .198 kg (436 lbs)
    UK . . . . .197 kg (434 lbs)
  1989 on
    All except California . . . . .199 kg (438 lbs)
    California . . . . .200 kg (440 lbs)
GSX-R750
  1985 through 1987
    All except California . . . . .176 kg (388 lbs)
    California . . . . .177 kg (390 lbs)
  1988 and 1989
    All except California . . . . .195 kg (429 lbs)
    California . . . . .196 kg (432 lbs)
  1990
    All except California . . . . .193 kg (425 lbs)
    California . . . . .194 kg (428 lbs)
  1991 on
    All except California . . . . .208 kg (459 lbs)
    California . . . . .212 kg (460 lbs)
Katana 750 (GSX750F)
  All except California . . . . .209 kg (461 lbs)
  California . . . . .212 kg (467 lbs)
GSX-R1100
  1985 through 1987
    All except California . . . . .197 kg (434 lbs)
    California . . . . .198 kg (438 lbs)
  1988
    All except California . . . . .438 lbs (199 kg)
    California . . . . .443 lbs (201 kg)
  1989
    All except California . . . . .210 kg (463 lbs)
    California . . . . .212 kg (467 lbs)
  1990
    US except California . . . . .215 kg (474 lbs)
    California . . . . .217 kg (478 lbs)
    UK . . . . .219 kg (482 lbs)
  1991 on
    All except California . . . . .226 kg (498 lbs)
    California . . . . .228 kg (403 lbs)
Katana 1100 (GSX1100F)
  1988
    All except California . . . . .244 kg (537 lbs)
    California . . . . .246 kg (542 lbs)
  1989 on
    US except California . . . . .248 kg (547 lbs)
    California . . . . .250 kg (551 lbs)
    UK . . . . .251 kg (553 lbs)
    Canada . . . . .248 kg (547 lbs)

Buying tools

A toolkit is a fundamental requirement for servicing and repairing a motorcycle. Although there will be an initial expense in building up enough tools for servicing, this will soon be offset by the savings made by doing the job yourself. As experience and confidence grow, additional tools can be added to enable the repair and overhaul of the motorcycle. Many of the specialist tools are expensive and not often used so it may be preferable to hire them, or for a group of friends or motorcycle club to join in the purchase.

As a rule, it is better to buy more expensive, good quality tools. Cheaper tools are likely to wear out faster and need to be renewed more often, nullifying the original saving.

> ⚠️ **Warning: To avoid the risk of a poor quality tool breaking in use, causing injury or damage to the component being worked on, always aim to purchase tools which meet the relevant national safety standards.**

The following lists of tools do not represent the manufacturer's service tools, but serve as a guide to help the owner decide which tools are needed for this level of work. In addition, items such as an electric drill, hacksaw, files, soldering iron and a workbench equipped with a vice, may be needed. Although not classed as tools, a selection of bolts, screws, nuts, washers and pieces of tubing always come in useful.

For more information about tools, refer to the Haynes *Motorcycle Workshop Practice TechBook* (Bk. No. 3470).

Manufacturer's service tools

Inevitably certain tasks require the use of a service tool. Where possible an alternative tool or method of approach is recommended, but sometimes there is no option if personal injury or damage to the component is to be avoided. Where required, service tools are referred to in the relevant procedure.

Service tools can usually only be purchased from a motorcycle dealer and are identified by a part number. Some of the commonly-used tools, such as rotor pullers, are available in aftermarket form from mail-order motorcycle tool and accessory suppliers.

Maintenance and minor repair tools

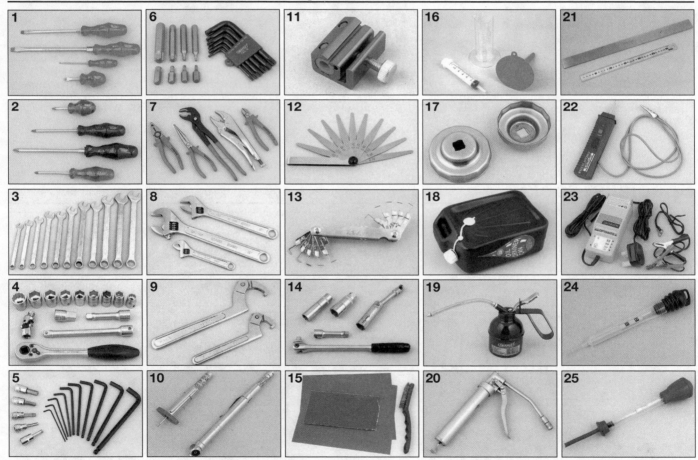

1 Set of flat-bladed screwdrivers
2 Set of Phillips head screwdrivers
3 Combination open-end and ring spanners
4 Socket set (3/8 inch or 1/2 inch drive)
5 Set of Allen keys or bits

6 Set of Torx keys or bits
7 Pliers, cutters and self-locking grips (Mole grips)
8 Adjustable spanners
9 C-spanners
10 Tread depth gauge and tyre pressure gauge

11 Cable oiler clamp
12 Feeler gauges
13 Spark plug gap measuring tool
14 Spark plug spanner or deep plug sockets
15 Wire brush and emery paper

16 Calibrated syringe, measuring vessel and funnel
17 Oil filter adapters
18 Oil drainer can or tray
19 Pump type oil can
20 Grease gun

21 Straight-edge and steel rule
22 Continuity tester
23 Battery charger
24 Hydrometer (for battery specific gravity check)
25 Anti-freeze tester (for liquid-cooled engines)

Repair and overhaul tools

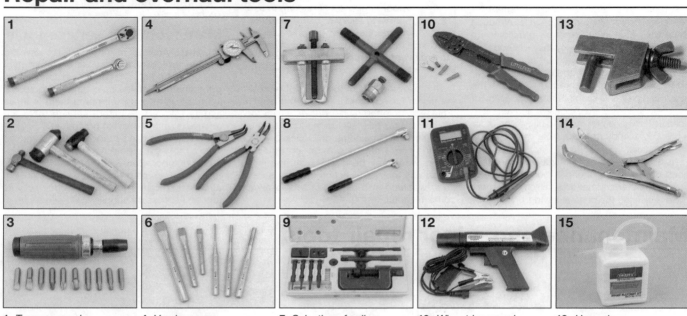

1 Torque wrench
  (small and mid-ranges)
2 Conventional, plastic or
  soft-faced hammers
3 Impact driver set

4 Vernier gauge
5 Circlip pliers (internal and
  external, or combination)
6 Set of cold chisels
  and punches

7 Selection of pullers
8 Breaker bars
9 Chain breaking/
  riveting tool set

10 Wire stripper and
   crimper tool
11 Multimeter (measures
   amps, volts and ohms)
12 Stroboscope (for
   dynamic timing checks)

13 Hose clamp
   (wingnut type shown)
14 Clutch holding tool
15 One-man brake/clutch
   bleeder kit

Specialist tools

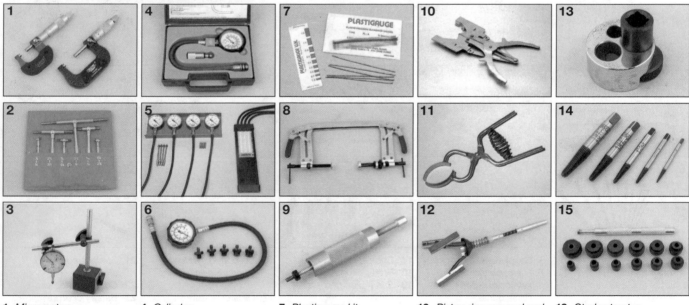

1 Micrometers
  (external type)
2 Telescoping gauges
3 Dial gauge

4 Cylinder
  compression gauge
5 Vacuum gauges (left) or
  manometer (right)
6 Oil pressure gauge

7 Plastigauge kit
8 Valve spring compressor
  (4-stroke engines)
9 Piston pin drawbolt tool

10 Piston ring removal and
   installation tool
11 Piston ring clamp
12 Cylinder bore hone
   (stone type shown)

13 Stud extractor
14 Screw extractor set
15 Bearing driver set

1 Workshop equipment and facilities

The workbench

● Work is made much easier by raising the bike up on a ramp - components are much more accessible if raised to waist level. The hydraulic or pneumatic types seen in the dealer's workshop are a sound investment if you undertake a lot of repairs or overhauls **(see illustration 1.1)**.

1.1 Hydraulic motorcycle ramp

● If raised off ground level, the bike must be supported on the ramp to avoid it falling. Most ramps incorporate a front wheel locating clamp which can be adjusted to suit different diameter wheels. When tightening the clamp, take care not to mark the wheel rim or damage the tyre - use wood blocks on each side to prevent this.
● Secure the bike to the ramp using tie-downs **(see illustration 1.2)**. If the bike has only a sidestand, and hence leans at a dangerous angle when raised, support the bike on an auxiliary stand.

1.2 Tie-downs are used around the passenger footrests to secure the bike

● Auxiliary (paddock) stands are widely available from mail order companies or motorcycle dealers and attach either to the wheel axle or swingarm pivot **(see illustration 1.3)**. If the motorcycle has a centrestand, you can support it under the crankcase to prevent it toppling whilst either wheel is removed **(see illustration 1.4)**.

1.3 This auxiliary stand attaches to the swingarm pivot

1.4 Always use a block of wood between the engine and jack head when supporting the engine in this way

Fumes and fire

● Refer to the Safety first! page at the beginning of the manual for full details. Make sure your workshop is equipped with a fire extinguisher suitable for fuel-related fires (Class B fire - flammable liquids) - it is not sufficient to have a water-filled extinguisher.
● Always ensure adequate ventilation is available. Unless an exhaust gas extraction system is available for use, ensure that the engine is run outside of the workshop.
● If working on the fuel system, make sure the workshop is ventilated to avoid a build-up of fumes. This applies equally to fume build-up when charging a battery. Do not smoke or allow anyone else to smoke in the workshop.

Fluids

● If you need to drain fuel from the tank, store it in an approved container marked as suitable for the storage of petrol (gasoline) **(see illustration 1.5)**. Do not store fuel in glass jars or bottles.

1.5 Use an approved can only for storing petrol (gasoline)

● Use proprietary engine degreasers or solvents which have a high flash-point, such as paraffin (kerosene), for cleaning off oil, grease and dirt - never use petrol (gasoline) for cleaning. Wear rubber gloves when handling solvent and engine degreaser. The fumes from certain solvents can be dangerous - always work in a well-ventilated area.

Dust, eye and hand protection

● Protect your lungs from inhalation of dust particles by wearing a filtering mask over the nose and mouth. Many frictional materials still contain asbestos which is dangerous to your health. Protect your eyes from spouts of liquid and sprung components by wearing a pair of protective goggles **(see illustration 1.6)**.

1.6 A fire extinguisher, goggles, mask and protective gloves should be at hand in the workshop

● Protect your hands from contact with solvents, fuel and oils by wearing rubber gloves. Alternatively apply a barrier cream to your hands before starting work. If handling hot components or fluids, wear suitable gloves to protect your hands from scalding and burns.

What to do with old fluids

● Old cleaning solvent, fuel, coolant and oils should not be poured down domestic drains or onto the ground. Package the fluid up in old oil containers, label it accordingly, and take it to a garage or disposal facility. Contact your local authority for location of such sites or ring the oil care hotline.

OIL CARE
FOLLOW THE CODE
OIL BANK LINE
0800 66 33 66

Note: It is antisocial and illegal to dump oil down the drain. To find the location of your local oil recycling bank, call this number free.

In the USA, note that any oil supplier must accept used oil for recycling.

2 Fasteners -
screws, bolts and nuts

Fastener types and applications

Bolts and screws

● Fastener head types are either of hexagonal, Torx or splined design, with internal and external versions of each type (see illustrations 2.1 and 2.2); splined head fasteners are not in common use on motorcycles. The conventional slotted or Phillips head design is used for certain screws. Bolt or screw length is always measured from the underside of the head to the end of the item (see illustration 2.11).

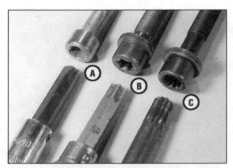

2.1 Internal hexagon/Allen (A), Torx (B) and splined (C) fasteners, with corresponding bits

2.2 External Torx (A), splined (B) and hexagon (C) fasteners, with corresponding sockets

● Certain fasteners on the motorcycle have a tensile marking on their heads, the higher the marking the stronger the fastener. High tensile fasteners generally carry a 10 or higher marking. Never replace a high tensile fastener with one of a lower tensile strength.

Washers (see illustration 2.3)

● Plain washers are used between a fastener head and a component to prevent damage to the component or to spread the load when torque is applied. Plain washers can also be used as spacers or shims in certain assemblies. Copper or aluminium plain washers are often used as sealing washers on drain plugs.

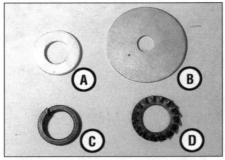

2.3 Plain washer (A), penny washer (B), spring washer (C) and serrated washer (D)

● The split-ring spring washer works by applying axial tension between the fastener head and component. If flattened, it is fatigued and must be renewed. If a plain (flat) washer is used on the fastener, position the spring washer between the fastener and the plain washer.
● Serrated star type washers dig into the fastener and component faces, preventing loosening. They are often used on electrical earth (ground) connections to the frame.
● Cone type washers (sometimes called Belleville) are conical and when tightened apply axial tension between the fastener head and component. They must be installed with the dished side against the component and often carry an OUTSIDE marking on their outer face. If flattened, they are fatigued and must be renewed.
● Tab washers are used to lock plain nuts or bolts on a shaft. A portion of the tab washer is bent up hard against one flat of the nut or bolt to prevent it loosening. Due to the tab washer being deformed in use, a new tab washer should be used every time it is disturbed.
● Wave washers are used to take up endfloat on a shaft. They provide light springing and prevent excessive side-to-side play of a component. Can be found on rocker arm shafts.

Nuts and split pins

● Conventional plain nuts are usually six-sided (see illustration 2.4). They are sized by thread diameter and pitch. High tensile nuts carry a number on one end to denote their tensile strength.

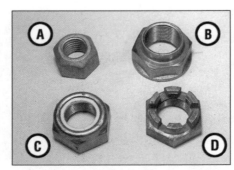

2.4 Plain nut (A), shouldered locknut (B), nylon insert nut (C) and castellated nut (D)

● Self-locking nuts either have a nylon insert, or two spring metal tabs, or a shoulder which is staked into a groove in the shaft - their advantage over conventional plain nuts is a resistance to loosening due to vibration. The nylon insert type can be used a number of times, but must be renewed when the friction of the nylon insert is reduced, ie when the nut spins freely on the shaft. The spring tab type can be reused unless the tabs are damaged. The shouldered type must be renewed every time it is disturbed.
● Split pins (cotter pins) are used to lock a castellated nut to a shaft or to prevent slackening of a plain nut. Common applications are wheel axles and brake torque arms. Because the split pin arms are deformed to lock around the nut a new split pin must always be used on installation - always fit the correct size split pin which will fit snugly in the shaft hole. Make sure the split pin arms are correctly located around the nut (see illustrations 2.5 and 2.6).

2.5 Bend split pin (cotter pin) arms as shown (arrows) to secure a castellated nut

2.6 Bend split pin (cotter pin) arms as shown to secure a plain nut

Caution: If the castellated nut slots do not align with the shaft hole after tightening to the torque setting, tighten the nut until the next slot aligns with the hole - never slacken the nut to align its slot.

● R-pins (shaped like the letter R), or slip pins as they are sometimes called, are sprung and can be reused if they are otherwise in good condition. Always install R-pins with their closed end facing forwards (see illustration 2.7).

2.7 Correct fitting of R-pin. Arrow indicates forward direction

Circlips (see illustration 2.8)

● Circlips (sometimes called snap-rings) are used to retain components on a shaft or in a housing and have corresponding external or internal ears to permit removal. Parallel-sided (machined) circlips can be installed either way round in their groove, whereas stamped circlips (which have a chamfered edge on one face) must be installed with the chamfer facing away from the direction of thrust load **(see illustration 2.9)**.

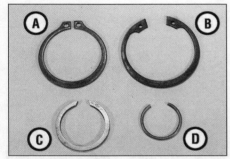

2.8 External stamped circlip (A), internal stamped circlip (B), machined circlip (C) and wire circlip (D)

● Always use circlip pliers to remove and install circlips; expand or compress them just enough to remove them. After installation, rotate the circlip in its groove to ensure it is securely seated. If installing a circlip on a splined shaft, always align its opening with a shaft channel to ensure the circlip ends are well supported and unlikely to catch **(see illustration 2.10)**.

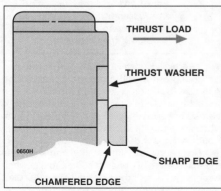

2.9 Correct fitting of a stamped circlip

THRUST LOAD

THRUST WASHER

SHARP EDGE

CHAMFERED EDGE

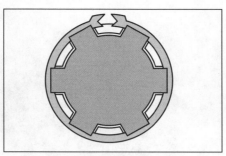

2.10 Align circlip opening with shaft channel

● Circlips can wear due to the thrust of components and become loose in their grooves, with the subsequent danger of becoming dislodged in operation. For this reason, renewal is advised every time a circlip is disturbed.

● Wire circlips are commonly used as piston pin retaining clips. If a removal tang is provided, long-nosed pliers can be used to dislodge them, otherwise careful use of a small flat-bladed screwdriver is necessary. Wire circlips should be renewed every time they are disturbed.

Thread diameter and pitch

● Diameter of a male thread (screw, bolt or stud) is the outside diameter of the threaded portion **(see illustration 2.11)**. Most motorcycle manufacturers use the ISO (International Standards Organisation) metric system expressed in millimetres, eg M6 refers to a 6 mm diameter thread. Sizing is the same for nuts, except that the thread diameter is measured across the valleys of the nut.

● Pitch is the distance between the peaks of the thread **(see illustration 2.11)**. It is expressed in millimetres, thus a common bolt size may be expressed as 6.0 x 1.0 mm (6 mm thread diameter and 1 mm pitch). Generally pitch increases in proportion to thread diameter, although there are always exceptions.

● Thread diameter and pitch are related for conventional fastener applications and the accompanying table can be used as a guide. Additionally, the AF (Across Flats), spanner or socket size dimension of the bolt or nut **(see illustration 2.11)** is linked to thread and pitch specification. Thread pitch can be measured with a thread gauge **(see illustration 2.12)**.

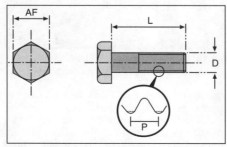

2.11 Fastener length (L), thread diameter (D), thread pitch (P) and head size (AF)

AF

L

D

P

2.12 Using a thread gauge to measure pitch

AF size	Thread diameter x pitch (mm)
8 mm	M5 x 0.8
8 mm	M6 x 1.0
10 mm	M6 x 1.0
12 mm	M8 x 1.25
14 mm	M10 x 1.25
17 mm	M12 x 1.25

● The threads of most fasteners are of the right-hand type, ie they are turned clockwise to tighten and anti-clockwise to loosen. The reverse situation applies to left-hand thread fasteners, which are turned anti-clockwise to tighten and clockwise to loosen. Left-hand threads are used where rotation of a component might loosen a conventional right-hand thread fastener.

Seized fasteners

● Corrosion of external fasteners due to water or reaction between two dissimilar metals can occur over a period of time. It will build up sooner in wet conditions or in countries where salt is used on the roads during the winter. If a fastener is severely corroded it is likely that normal methods of removal will fail and result in its head being ruined. When you attempt removal, the fastener thread should be heard to crack free and unscrew easily - if it doesn't, stop there before damaging something.

● A smart tap on the head of the fastener will often succeed in breaking free corrosion which has occurred in the threads **(see illustration 2.13)**.

● An aerosol penetrating fluid (such as WD-40) applied the night beforehand may work its way down into the thread and ease removal. Depending on the location, you may be able to make up a Plasticine well around the fastener head and fill it with penetrating fluid.

2.13 A sharp tap on the head of a fastener will often break free a corroded thread

● If you are working on an engine internal component, corrosion will most likely not be a problem due to the well lubricated environment. However, components can be very tight and an impact driver is a useful tool in freeing them **(see illustration 2.14)**.

**2.14 Using an impact driver
to free a fastener**

● Where corrosion has occurred between dissimilar metals (eg steel and aluminium alloy), the application of heat to the fastener head will create a disproportionate expansion rate between the two metals and break the seizure caused by the corrosion. Whether heat can be applied depends on the location of the fastener - any surrounding components likely to be damaged must first be removed **(see illustration 2.15)**. Heat can be applied using a paint stripper heat gun or clothes iron, or by immersing the component in boiling water - wear protective gloves to prevent scalding or burns to the hands.

2.15 Using heat to free a seized fastener

● As a last resort, it is possible to use a hammer and cold chisel to work the fastener head unscrewed **(see illustration 2.16)**. This will damage the fastener, but more importantly extreme care must be taken not to damage the surrounding component.

Caution: Remember that the component being secured is generally of more value than the bolt, nut or screw - when the fastener is freed, do not unscrew it with force, instead work the fastener back and forth when resistance is felt to prevent thread damage.

**2.16 Using a hammer and chisel
to free a seized fastener**

Broken fasteners and damaged heads

● If the shank of a broken bolt or screw is accessible you can grip it with self-locking grips. The knurled wheel type stud extractor tool or self-gripping stud puller tool is particularly useful for removing the long studs which screw into the cylinder mouth surface of the crankcase or bolts and screws from which the head has broken off **(see illustration 2.17)**. Studs can also be removed by locking two nuts together on the threaded end of the stud and using a spanner on the lower nut **(see illustration 2.18)**.

2.17 Using a stud extractor tool to remove a broken crankcase stud

2.18 Two nuts can be locked together to unscrew a stud from a component

● A bolt or screw which has broken off below or level with the casing must be extracted using a screw extractor set. Centre punch the fastener to centralise the drill bit, then drill a hole in the fastener **(see illustration 2.19)**. Select a drill bit which is approximately half to three-quarters the

**2.19 When using a screw extractor,
first drill a hole in the fastener . . .**

diameter of the fastener and drill to a depth which will accommodate the extractor. Use the largest size extractor possible, but avoid leaving too small a wall thickness otherwise the extractor will merely force the fastener walls outwards wedging it in the casing thread.

● If a spiral type extractor is used, thread it anti-clockwise into the fastener. As it is screwed in, it will grip the fastener and unscrew it from the casing **(see illustration 2.20)**.

**2.20 . . . then thread the extractor
anti-clockwise into the fastener**

● If a taper type extractor is used, tap it into the fastener so that it is firmly wedged in place. Unscrew the extractor (anti-clockwise) to draw the fastener out.

> ⚠ *Warning: Stud extractors are very hard and may break off in the fastener if care is not taken - ask an engineer about spark erosion if this happens.*

● Alternatively, the broken bolt/screw can be drilled out and the hole retapped for an oversize bolt/screw or a diamond-section thread insert. It is essential that the drilling is carried out squarely and to the correct depth, otherwise the casing may be ruined - if in doubt, entrust the work to an engineer.

● Bolts and nuts with rounded corners cause the correct size spanner or socket to slip when force is applied. Of the types of spanner/socket available always use a six-point type rather than an eight or twelve-point type - better grip

2.21 Comparison of surface drive ring spanner (left) with 12-point type (right)

is obtained. Surface drive spanners grip the middle of the hex flats, rather than the corners, and are thus good in cases of damaged heads **(see illustration 2.21)**.

● Slotted-head or Phillips-head screws are often damaged by the use of the wrong size screwdriver. Allen-head and Torx-head screws are much less likely to sustain damage. If enough of the screw head is exposed you can use a hacksaw to cut a slot in its head and then use a conventional flat-bladed screwdriver to remove it. Alternatively use a hammer and cold chisel to tap the head of the fastener around to slacken it. Always replace damaged fasteners with new ones, preferably Torx or Allen-head type.

HAYNES HiNT

A dab of valve grinding compound between the screw head and screwdriver tip will often give a good grip.

Thread repair

● Threads (particularly those in aluminium alloy components) can be damaged by overtightening, being assembled with dirt in the threads, or from a component working loose and vibrating. Eventually the thread will fail completely, and it will be impossible to tighten the fastener.

● If a thread is damaged or clogged with old locking compound it can be renovated with a thread repair tool (thread chaser) **(see illustrations 2.22 and 2.23)**; special thread

2.22 A thread repair tool being used to correct an internal thread

2.23 A thread repair tool being used to correct an external thread

chasers are available for spark plug hole threads. The tool will not cut a new thread, but clean and true the original thread. Make sure that you use the correct diameter and pitch tool. Similarly, external threads can be cleaned up with a die or a thread restorer file **(see illustration 2.24)**.

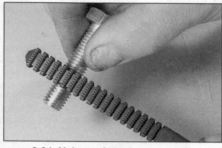

2.24 Using a thread restorer file

● It is possible to drill out the old thread and retap the component to the next thread size. This will work where there is enough surrounding material and a new bolt or screw can be obtained. Sometimes, however, this is not possible - such as where the bolt/screw passes through another component which must also be suitably modified, also in cases where a spark plug or oil drain plug cannot be obtained in a larger diameter thread size.

● The diamond-section thread insert (often known by its popular trade name of Heli-Coil) is a simple and effective method of renewing the thread and retaining the original size. A kit can be purchased which contains the tap, insert and installing tool **(see illustration 2.25)**. Drill out the damaged thread with the size drill specified **(see illustration 2.26)**. Carefully retap the thread **(see illustration 2.27)**. Install the

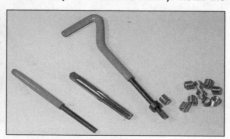

2.25 Obtain a thread insert kit to suit the thread diameter and pitch required

2.26 To install a thread insert, first drill out the original thread . . .

2.27 . . . tap a new thread . . .

2.28 . . . fit insert on the installing tool . . .

2.29 . . . and thread into the component . . .

2.30 . . . break off the tang when complete

insert on the installing tool and thread it slowly into place using a light downward pressure **(see illustrations 2.28 and 2.29)**. When positioned between a 1/4 and 1/2 turn below the surface withdraw the installing tool and use the break-off tool to press down on the tang, breaking it off **(see illustration 2.30)**.

● There are epoxy thread repair kits on the market which can rebuild stripped internal threads, although this repair should not be used on high load-bearing components.

Thread locking and sealing compounds

● Locking compounds are used in locations where the fastener is prone to loosening due to vibration or on important safety-related items which might cause loss of control of the motorcycle if they fail. It is also used where important fasteners cannot be secured by other means such as lockwashers or split pins.

● Before applying locking compound, make sure that the threads (internal and external) are clean and dry with all old compound removed. Select a compound to suit the component being secured - a non-permanent general locking and sealing type is suitable for most applications, but a high strength type is needed for permanent fixing of studs in castings. Apply a drop or two of the compound to the first few threads of the fastener, then thread it into place and tighten to the specified torque. Do not apply excessive thread locking compound otherwise the thread may be damaged on subsequent removal.

● Certain fasteners are impregnated with a dry film type coating of locking compound on their threads. Always renew this type of fastener if disturbed.

● Anti-seize compounds, such as copper-based greases, can be applied to protect threads from seizure due to extreme heat and corrosion. A common instance is spark plug threads and exhaust system fasteners.

3 Measuring tools and gauges

Feeler gauges

● Feeler gauges (or blades) are used for measuring small gaps and clearances (see illustration 3.1). They can also be used to measure endfloat (sideplay) of a component on a shaft where access is not possible with a dial gauge.

● Feeler gauge sets should be treated with care and not bent or damaged. They are etched with their size on one face. Keep them clean and very lightly oiled to prevent corrosion build-up.

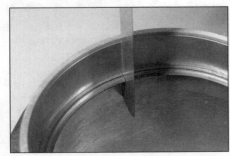

3.1 Feeler gauges are used for measuring small gaps and clearances - thickness is marked on one face of gauge

● When measuring a clearance, select a gauge which is a light sliding fit between the two components. You may need to use two gauges together to measure the clearance accurately.

Micrometers

● A micrometer is a precision tool capable of measuring to 0.01 or 0.001 of a millimetre. It should always be stored in its case and not in the general toolbox. It must be kept clean and never dropped, otherwise its frame or measuring anvils could be distorted resulting in inaccurate readings.

● External micrometers are used for measuring outside diameters of components and have many more applications than internal micrometers. Micrometers are available in different size ranges, eg 0 to 25 mm, 25 to 50 mm, and upwards in 25 mm steps; some large micrometers have interchangeable anvils to allow a range of measurements to be taken. Generally the largest precision measurement you are likely to take on a motorcycle is the piston diameter.

● Internal micrometers (or bore micrometers) are used for measuring inside diameters, such as valve guides and cylinder bores. Telescoping gauges and small hole gauges are used in conjunction with an external micrometer, whereas the more expensive internal micrometers have their own measuring device.

External micrometer

Note: *The conventional analogue type instrument is described. Although much easier to read, digital micrometers are considerably more expensive.*

● Always check the calibration of the micrometer before use. With the anvils closed (0 to 25 mm type) or set over a test gauge (for

3.2 Check micrometer calibration before use

the larger types) the scale should read zero (see illustration 3.2); make sure that the anvils (and test piece) are clean first. Any discrepancy can be adjusted by referring to the instructions supplied with the tool. Remember that the micrometer is a precision measuring tool - don't force the anvils closed, use the ratchet (4) on the end of the micrometer to close it. In this way, a measured force is always applied.

● To use, first make sure that the item being measured is clean. Place the anvil of the micrometer (1) against the item and use the thimble (2) to bring the spindle (3) lightly into contact with the other side of the item (see illustration 3.3). Don't tighten the thimble down because this will damage the micrometer - instead use the ratchet (4) on the end of the micrometer. The ratchet mechanism applies a measured force preventing damage to the instrument.

● The micrometer is read by referring to the linear scale on the sleeve and the annular scale on the thimble. Read off the sleeve first to obtain the base measurement, then add the fine measurement from the thimble to obtain the overall reading. The linear scale on the sleeve represents the measuring range of the micrometer (eg 0 to 25 mm). The annular scale

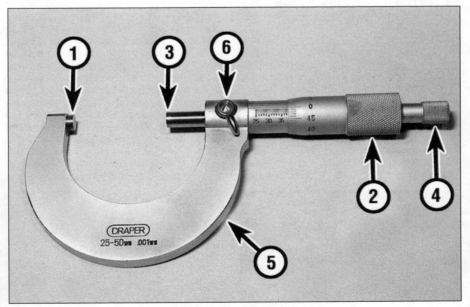

3.3 Micrometer component parts

1 Anvil	3 Spindle	5 Frame
2 Thimble	4 Ratchet	6 Locking lever

on the thimble will be in graduations of 0.01 mm (or as marked on the frame) - one full revolution of the thimble will move 0.5 mm on the linear scale. Take the reading where the datum line on the sleeve intersects the thimble's scale. Always position the eye directly above the scale otherwise an inaccurate reading will result.

In the example shown the item measures 2.95 mm **(see illustration 3.4)**:

Linear scale	2.00 mm
Linear scale	0.50 mm
Annular scale	0.45 mm
Total figure	**2.95 mm**

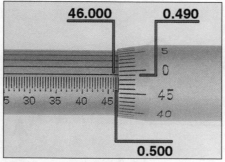

3.5 Micrometer reading of 46.99 mm on linear and annular scales . . .

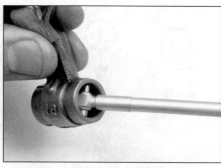

3.7 Expand the telescoping gauge in the bore, lock its position . . .

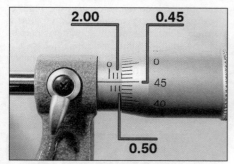

3.4 Micrometer reading of 2.95 mm

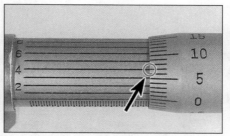

3.6 . . . and 0.004 mm on vernier scale

3.8 . . . then measure the gauge with a micrometer

Most micrometers have a locking lever (6) on the frame to hold the setting in place, allowing the item to be removed from the micrometer.

● Some micrometers have a vernier scale on their sleeve, providing an even finer measurement to be taken, in 0.001 increments of a millimetre. Take the sleeve and thimble measurement as described above, then check which graduation on the vernier scale aligns with that of the annular scale on the thimble **Note:** *The eye must be perpendicular to the scale when taking the vernier reading - if necessary rotate the body of the micrometer to ensure this.* Multiply the vernier scale figure by 0.001 and add it to the base and fine measurement figures.

In the example shown the item measures 46.994 mm **(see illustrations 3.5 and 3.6)**:

Linear scale (base)	46.000 mm
Linear scale (base)	00.500 mm
Annular scale (fine)	00.490 mm
Vernier scale	00.004 mm
Total figure	**46.994 mm**

Internal micrometer

● Internal micrometers are available for measuring bore diameters, but are expensive and unlikely to be available for home use. It is suggested that a set of telescoping gauges and small hole gauges, both of which must be used with an external micrometer, will suffice for taking internal measurements on a motorcycle.

● Telescoping gauges can be used to

measure internal diameters of components. Select a gauge with the correct size range, make sure its ends are clean and insert it into the bore. Expand the gauge, then lock its position and withdraw it from the bore **(see illustration 3.7)**. Measure across the gauge ends with a micrometer **(see illustration 3.8)**.

● Very small diameter bores (such as valve guides) are measured with a small hole gauge. Once adjusted to a slip-fit inside the component, its position is locked and the gauge withdrawn for measurement with a micrometer **(see illustrations 3.9 and 3.10)**.

Vernier caliper

Note: *The conventional linear and dial gauge type instruments are described. Digital types are easier to read, but are far more expensive.*

● The vernier caliper does not provide the precision of a micrometer, but is versatile in being able to measure internal and external diameters. Some types also incorporate a depth gauge. It is ideal for measuring clutch plate friction material and spring free lengths.

● To use the conventional linear scale vernier, slacken off the vernier clamp screws (1) and set its jaws over (2), or inside (3), the item to be measured **(see illustration 3.11)**. Slide the jaw into contact, using the thumb-wheel (4) for fine movement of the sliding scale (5) then tighten the clamp screws (1). Read off the main scale (6) where the zero on the sliding scale (5) intersects it, taking the whole number to the left of the zero; this provides the base measurement. View along the sliding scale and select the division which

3.9 Expand the small hole gauge in the bore, lock its position . . .

3.10 . . . then measure the gauge with a micrometer

lines up exactly with any of the divisions on the main scale, noting that the divisions usually represents 0.02 of a millimetre. Add this fine measurement to the base measurement to obtain the total reading.

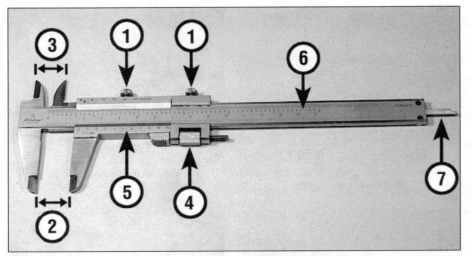

3.11 Vernier component parts (linear gauge)

1 Clamp screws	3 Internal jaws	5 Sliding scale	7 Depth gauge
2 External jaws	4 Thumbwheel	6 Main scale	

In the example shown the item measures 55.92 mm **(see illustration 3.12)**:

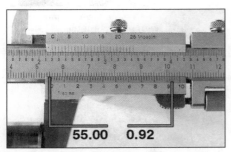

3.12 Vernier gauge reading of 55.92 mm

Base measurement	55.00 mm
Fine measurement	00.92 mm
Total figure	**55.92 mm**

● Some vernier calipers are equipped with a dial gauge for fine measurement. Before use, check that the jaws are clean, then close them fully and check that the dial gauge reads zero. If necessary adjust the gauge ring accordingly. Slacken the vernier clamp screw (1) and set its jaws over (2), or inside (3), the item to be measured **(see illustration 3.13)**. Slide the jaws into contact, using the thumbwheel (4) for fine movement. Read off the main scale (5) where the edge of the sliding scale (6) intersects it, taking the whole number to the left of the zero; this provides the base measurement. Read off the needle position on the dial gauge (7) scale to provide the fine measurement; each division represents 0.05 of a millimetre. Add this fine measurement to the base measurement to obtain the total reading.

In the example shown the item measures 55.95 mm **(see illustration 3.14)**:

Base measurement	55.00 mm
Fine measurement	00.95 mm
Total figure	**55.95 mm**

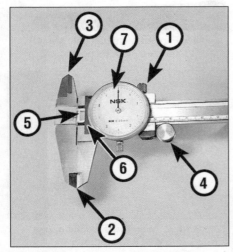

3.13 Vernier component parts (dial gauge)

1 Clamp screw	5 Main scale
2 External jaws	6 Sliding scale
3 Internal jaws	7 Dial gauge
4 Thumbwheel	

3.14 Vernier gauge reading of 55.95 mm

Plastigauge

● Plastigauge is a plastic material which can be compressed between two surfaces to measure the oil clearance between them. The width of the compressed Plastigauge is measured against a calibrated scale to determine the clearance.

● Common uses of Plastigauge are for measuring the clearance between crankshaft journal and main bearing inserts, between crankshaft journal and big-end bearing inserts, and between camshaft and bearing surfaces. The following example describes big-end oil clearance measurement.

● Handle the Plastigauge material carefully to prevent distortion. Using a sharp knife, cut a length which corresponds with the width of the bearing being measured and place it carefully across the journal so that it is parallel with the shaft **(see illustration 3.15)**. Carefully install both bearing shells and the connecting rod. Without rotating the rod on the journal tighten its bolts or nuts (as applicable) to the specified torque. The connecting rod and bearings are then disassembled and the crushed Plastigauge examined.

3.15 Plastigauge placed across shaft journal

● Using the scale provided in the Plastigauge kit, measure the width of the material to determine the oil clearance **(see illustration 3.16)**. Always remove all traces of Plastigauge after use using your fingernails.

Caution: Arriving at the correct clearance demands that the assembly is torqued correctly, according to the settings and sequence (where applicable) provided by the motorcycle manufacturer.

3.16 Measuring the width of the crushed Plastigauge

Dial gauge or DTI (Dial Test Indicator)

● A dial gauge can be used to accurately measure small amounts of movement. Typical uses are measuring shaft runout or shaft endfloat (sideplay) and setting piston position for ignition timing on two-strokes. A dial gauge set usually comes with a range of different probes and adapters and mounting equipment.

● The gauge needle must point to zero when at rest. Rotate the ring around its periphery to zero the gauge.

● Check that the gauge is capable of reading the extent of movement in the work. Most gauges have a small dial set in the face which records whole millimetres of movement as well as the fine scale around the face periphery which is calibrated in 0.01 mm divisions. Read off the small dial first to obtain the base measurement, then add the measurement from the fine scale to obtain the total reading.

In the example shown the gauge reads 1.48 mm **(see illustration 3.17)**:

Base measurement	1.00 mm
Fine measurement	0.48 mm
Total figure	**1.48 mm**

3.17 Dial gauge reading of 1.48 mm

● If measuring shaft runout, the shaft must be supported in vee-blocks and the gauge mounted on a stand perpendicular to the shaft. Rest the tip of the gauge against the centre of the shaft and rotate the shaft slowly whilst watching the gauge reading **(see illustration 3.18)**. Take several measurements along the length of the shaft and record the

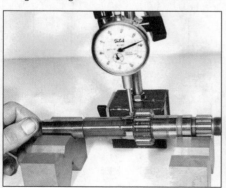

3.18 Using a dial gauge to measure shaft runout

maximum gauge reading as the amount of runout in the shaft. **Note:** *The reading obtained will be total runout at that point - some manufacturers specify that the runout figure is halved to compare with their specified runout limit.*

● Endfloat (sideplay) measurement requires that the gauge is mounted securely to the surrounding component with its probe touching the end of the shaft. Using hand pressure, push and pull on the shaft noting the maximum endfloat recorded on the gauge **(see illustration 3.19)**.

3.19 Using a dial gauge to measure shaft endfloat

● A dial gauge with suitable adapters can be used to determine piston position BTDC on two-stroke engines for the purposes of ignition timing. The gauge, adapter and suitable length probe are installed in the place of the spark plug and the gauge zeroed at TDC. If the piston position is specified as 1.14 mm BTDC, rotate the engine back to 2.00 mm BTDC, then slowly forwards to 1.14 mm BTDC.

Cylinder compression gauges

● A compression gauge is used for measuring cylinder compression. Either the rubber-cone type or the threaded adapter type can be used. The latter is preferred to ensure a perfect seal against the cylinder head. A 0 to 300 psi (0 to 20 Bar) type gauge (for petrol/gasoline engines) will be suitable for motorcycles.

● The spark plug is removed and the gauge either held hard against the cylinder head (cone type) or the gauge adapter screwed into the cylinder head (threaded type) **(see illustration 3.20)**. Cylinder compression is measured with the engine turning over, but not running - carry out the compression test as described in

3.20 Using a rubber-cone type cylinder compression gauge

Fault Finding Equipment. The gauge will hold the reading until manually released.

Oil pressure gauge

● An oil pressure gauge is used for measuring engine oil pressure. Most gauges come with a set of adapters to fit the thread of the take-off point **(see illustration 3.21)**. If the take-off point specified by the motorcycle manufacturer is an external oil pipe union, make sure that the specified replacement union is used to prevent oil starvation.

3.21 Oil pressure gauge and take-off point adapter (arrow)

● Oil pressure is measured with the engine running (at a specific rpm) and often the manufacturer will specify pressure limits for a cold and hot engine.

Straight-edge and surface plate

● If checking the gasket face of a component for warpage, place a steel rule or precision straight-edge across the gasket face and measure any gap between the straight-edge and component with feeler gauges **(see illustration 3.22)**. Check diagonally across the component and between mounting holes **(see illustration 3.23)**.

3.22 Use a straight-edge and feeler gauges to check for warpage

3.23 Check for warpage in these directions

● Checking individual components for warpage, such as clutch plain (metal) plates, requires a perfectly flat plate or piece or plate glass and feeler gauges.

4 Torque and leverage

What is torque?

● Torque describes the twisting force about a shaft. The amount of torque applied is determined by the distance from the centre of the shaft to the end of the lever and the amount of force being applied to the end of the lever; distance multiplied by force equals torque.

● The manufacturer applies a measured torque to a bolt or nut to ensure that it will not slacken in use and to hold two components securely together without movement in the joint. The actual torque setting depends on the thread size, bolt or nut material and the composition of the components being held.

● Too little torque may cause the fastener to loosen due to vibration, whereas too much torque will distort the joint faces of the component or cause the fastener to shear off. Always stick to the specified torque setting.

Using a torque wrench

● Check the calibration of the torque wrench and make sure it has a suitable range for the job. Torque wrenches are available in Nm (Newton-metres), kgf m (kilograms-force metre), lbf ft (pounds-feet), lbf in (inch-pounds). Do not confuse lbf ft with lbf in.

● Adjust the tool to the desired torque on the scale (see illustration 4.1). If your torque wrench is not calibrated in the units specified, carefully convert the figure (see Conversion Factors). A manufacturer sometimes gives a torque setting as a range (8 to 10 Nm) rather than a single figure - in this case set the tool midway between the two settings. The same torque may be expressed as 9 Nm ± 1 Nm. Some torque wrenches have a method of locking the setting so that it isn't inadvertently altered during use.

4.1 Set the torque wrench index mark to the setting required, in this case 12 Nm

● Install the bolts/nuts in their correct location and secure them lightly. Their threads must be clean and free of any old locking compound. Unless specified the threads and flange should be dry - oiled threads are necessary in certain circumstances and the manufacturer will take this into account in the specified torque figure. Similarly, the manufacturer may also specify the application of thread-locking compound.

● Tighten the fasteners in the specified sequence until the torque wrench clicks, indicating that the torque setting has been reached. Apply the torque again to double-check the setting. Where different thread diameter fasteners secure the component, as a rule tighten the larger diameter ones first.

● When the torque wrench has been finished with, release the lock (where applicable) and fully back off its setting to zero - do not leave the torque wrench tensioned. Also, do not use a torque wrench for slackening a fastener.

Angle-tightening

● Manufacturers often specify a figure in degrees for final tightening of a fastener. This usually follows tightening to a specific torque setting.

● A degree disc can be set and attached to the socket (see illustration 4.2) or a protractor can be used to mark the angle of movement on the bolt/nut head and the surrounding casting (see illustration 4.3).

4.2 Angle tightening can be accomplished with a torque-angle gauge . . .

4.3 . . . or by marking the angle on the surrounding component

Loosening sequences

● Where more than one bolt/nut secures a component, loosen each fastener evenly a little at a time. In this way, not all the stress of the joint is held by one fastener and the components are not likely to distort.

● If a tightening sequence is provided, work in the REVERSE of this, but if not, work from the outside in, in a criss-cross sequence (see illustration 4.4).

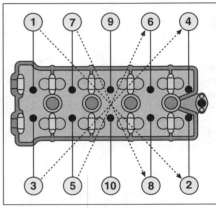

4.4 When slackening, work from the outside inwards

Tightening sequences

● If a component is held by more than one fastener it is important that the retaining bolts/nuts are tightened evenly to prevent uneven stress build-up and distortion of sealing faces. This is especially important on high-compression joints such as the cylinder head.

● A sequence is usually provided by the manufacturer, either in a diagram or actually marked in the casting. If not, always start in the centre and work outwards in a criss-cross pattern (see illustration 4.5). Start off by securing all bolts/nuts finger-tight, then set the torque wrench and tighten each fastener by a small amount in sequence until the final torque is reached. By following this practice,

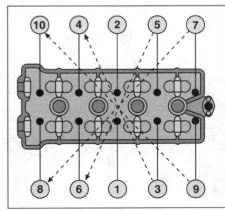

4.5 When tightening, work from the inside outwards

the joint will be held evenly and will not be distorted. Important joints, such as the cylinder head and big-end fasteners often have two- or three-stage torque settings.

Applying leverage

● Use tools at the correct angle. Position a socket wrench or spanner on the bolt/nut so that you pull it towards you when loosening. If this can't be done, push the spanner without curling your fingers around it **(see illustration 4.6)** - the spanner may slip or the fastener loosen suddenly, resulting in your fingers being crushed against a component.

4.6 If you can't pull on the spanner to loosen a fastener, push with your hand open

● Additional leverage is gained by extending the length of the lever. The best way to do this is to use a breaker bar instead of the regular length tool, or to slip a length of tubing over the end of the spanner or socket wrench.
● If additional leverage will not work, the fastener head is either damaged or firmly corroded in place (see *Fasteners*).

5   Bearings

Bearing removal and installation

Drivers and sockets

● Before removing a bearing, always inspect the casing to see which way it must be driven out - some casings will have retaining plates or a cast step. Also check for any identifying markings on the bearing and if installed to a certain depth, measure this at this stage. Some roller bearings are sealed on one side - take note of the original fitted position.
● Bearings can be driven out of a casing using a bearing driver tool (with the correct size head) or a socket of the correct diameter. Select the driver head or socket so that it contacts the outer race of the bearing, not the balls/rollers or inner race. Always support the casing around the bearing housing with wood blocks, otherwise there is a risk of fracture. The bearing is driven out with a few blows on the driver or socket from a heavy mallet. Unless access is severely restricted (as with wheel bearings), a pin-punch is not recommended unless it is moved around the bearing to keep it square in its housing.

● The same equipment can be used to install bearings. Make sure the bearing housing is supported on wood blocks and line up the bearing in its housing. Fit the bearing as noted on removal - generally they are installed with their marked side facing outwards. Tap the bearing squarely into its housing using a driver or socket which bears only on the bearing's outer race - contact with the bearing balls/rollers or inner race will destroy it **(see illustrations 5.1 and 5.2)**.
● Check that the bearing inner race and balls/rollers rotate freely.

5.1 Using a bearing driver against the bearing's outer race

5.2 Using a large socket against the bearing's outer race

Pullers and slide-hammers

● Where a bearing is pressed on a shaft a puller will be required to extract it **(see illustration 5.3)**. Make sure that the puller clamp or legs fit securely behind the bearing and are unlikely to slip out. If pulling a bearing

5.3 This bearing puller clamps behind the bearing and pressure is applied to the shaft end to draw the bearing off

off a gear shaft for example, you may have to locate the puller behind a gear pinion if there is no access to the race and draw the gear pinion off the shaft as well **(see illustration 5.4)**.

> **Caution: Ensure that the puller's centre bolt locates securely against the end of the shaft and will not slip when pressure is applied. Also ensure that puller does not damage the shaft end.**

5.4 Where no access is available to the rear of the bearing, it is sometimes possible to draw off the adjacent component

● Operate the puller so that its centre bolt exerts pressure on the shaft end and draws the bearing off the shaft.
● When installing the bearing on the shaft, tap only on the bearing's inner race - contact with the balls/rollers or outer race with destroy the bearing. Use a socket or length of tubing as a drift which fits over the shaft end **(see illustration 5.5)**.

5.5 When installing a bearing on a shaft use a piece of tubing which bears only on the bearing's inner race

● Where a bearing locates in a blind hole in a casing, it cannot be driven or pulled out as described above. A slide-hammer with knife-edged bearing puller attachment will be required. The puller attachment passes through the bearing and when tightened expands to fit firmly behind the bearing **(see illustration 5.6)**. By operating the slide-hammer part of the tool the bearing is jarred out of its housing **(see illustration 5.7)**.
● It is possible, if the bearing is of reasonable weight, for it to drop out of its housing if the casing is heated as described opposite. If this

5.6 Expand the bearing puller so that it locks behind the bearing . . .

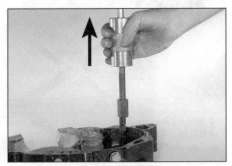

5.7 . . . attach the slide hammer to the bearing puller

method is attempted, first prepare a work surface which will enable the casing to be tapped face down to help dislodge the bearing - a wood surface is ideal since it will not damage the casing's gasket surface. Wearing protective gloves, tap the heated casing several times against the work surface to dislodge the bearing under its own weight **(see illustration 5.8)**.

5.8 Tapping a casing face down on wood blocks can often dislodge a bearing

● Bearings can be installed in blind holes using the driver or socket method described above.

Drawbolts

● Where a bearing or bush is set in the eye of a component, such as a suspension linkage arm or connecting rod small-end, removal by drift may damage the component. Furthermore, a rubber bushing in a shock absorber eye cannot successfully be driven out of position. If access is available to a engineering press, the task is straightforward. If not, a drawbolt can be fabricated to extract the bearing or bush.

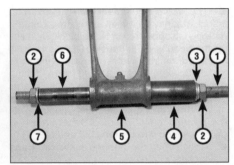

5.9 Drawbolt component parts assembled on a suspension arm

1 Bolt or length of threaded bar
2 Nuts
3 Washer (external diameter greater than tubing internal diameter)
4 Tubing (internal diameter sufficient to accommodate bearing)
5 Suspension arm with bearing
6 Tubing (external diameter slightly smaller than bearing)
7 Washer (external diameter slightly smaller than bearing)

5.10 Drawing the bearing out of the suspension arm

● To extract the bearing/bush you will need a long bolt with nut (or piece of threaded bar with two nuts), a piece of tubing which has an internal diameter larger than the bearing/bush, another piece of tubing which has an external diameter slightly smaller than the bearing/bush, and a selection of washers **(see illustrations 5.9 and 5.10)**. Note that the pieces of tubing must be of the same length, or longer, than the bearing/bush.
● The same kit (without the pieces of tubing) can be used to draw the new bearing/bush back into place **(see illustration 5.11)**.

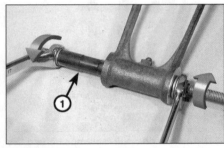

5.11 Installing a new bearing (1) in the suspension arm

Temperature change

● If the bearing's outer race is a tight fit in the casing, the aluminium casing can be heated to release its grip on the bearing. Aluminium will expand at a greater rate than the steel bearing outer race. There are several ways to do this, but avoid any localised extreme heat (such as a blow torch) - aluminium alloy has a low melting point.
● Approved methods of heating a casing are using a domestic oven (heated to 100°C) or immersing the casing in boiling water **(see illustration 5.12)**. Low temperature range localised heat sources such as a paint stripper heat gun or clothes iron can also be used **(see illustration 5.13)**. Alternatively, soak a rag in boiling water, wring it out and wrap it around the bearing housing.

> ⚠ **Warning: All of these methods require care in use to prevent scalding and burns to the hands. Wear protective gloves when handling hot components.**

5.12 A casing can be immersed in a sink of boiling water to aid bearing removal

5.13 Using a localised heat source to aid bearing removal

● If heating the whole casing note that plastic components, such as the neutral switch, may suffer - remove them beforehand.
● After heating, remove the bearing as described above. You may find that the expansion is sufficient for the bearing to fall out of the casing under its own weight or with a light tap on the driver or socket.
● If necessary, the casing can be heated to aid bearing installation, and this is sometimes the recommended procedure if the motorcycle manufacturer has designed the housing and bearing fit with this intention.

● Installation of bearings can be eased by placing them in a freezer the night before installation. The steel bearing will contract slightly, allowing easy insertion in its housing. This is often useful when installing steering head outer races in the frame.

Bearing types and markings

● Plain shell bearings, ball bearings, needle roller bearings and tapered roller bearings will all be found on motorcycles (see illustrations 5.14 and 5.15). The ball and roller types are usually caged between an inner and outer race, but uncaged variations may be found.

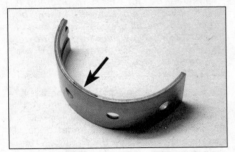

5.14 Shell bearings are either plain or grooved. They are usually identified by colour code (arrow)

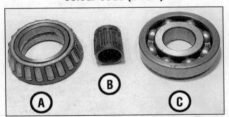

5.15 Tapered roller bearing (A), needle roller bearing (B) and ball journal bearing (C)

● Shell bearings (often called inserts) are usually found at the crankshaft main and connecting rod big-end where they are good at coping with high loads. They are made of a phosphor-bronze material and are impregnated with self-lubricating properties.
● Ball bearings and needle roller bearings consist of a steel inner and outer race with the balls or rollers between the races. They require constant lubrication by oil or grease and are good at coping with axial loads. Taper roller bearings consist of rollers set in a tapered cage set on the inner race; the outer race is separate. They are good at coping with axial loads and prevent movement along the shaft - a typical application is in the steering head.
● Bearing manufacturers produce bearings to ISO size standards and stamp one face of the bearing to indicate its internal and external diameter, load capacity and type (see illustration 5.16).
● Metal bushes are usually of phosphor-bronze material. Rubber bushes are used in suspension mounting eyes. Fibre bushes have also been used in suspension pivots.

5.16 Typical bearing marking

Bearing fault finding

● If a bearing outer race has spun in its housing, the housing material will be damaged. You can use a bearing locking compound to bond the outer race in place if damage is not too severe.
● Shell bearings will fail due to damage of their working surface, as a result of lack of lubrication, corrosion or abrasive particles in the oil (see illustration 5.17). Small particles of dirt in the oil may embed in the bearing material whereas larger particles will score the bearing and shaft journal. If a number of short journeys are made, insufficient heat will be generated to drive off condensation which has built up on the bearings.

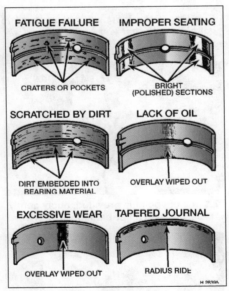

5.17 Typical bearing failures

● Ball and roller bearings will fail due to lack of lubrication or damage to the balls or rollers. Tapered-roller bearings can be damaged by overloading them. Unless the bearing is sealed on both sides, wash it in paraffin (kerosene) to remove all old grease then allow it to dry. Make a visual inspection looking to dented balls or rollers, damaged cages and worn or pitted races (see illustration 5.18).
● A ball bearing can be checked for wear by listening to it when spun. Apply a film of light oil to the bearing and hold it close to the ear - hold the outer race with one hand and spin the inner

5.18 Example of ball journal bearing with damaged balls and cages

5.19 Hold outer race and listen to inner race when spun

race with the other hand (see illustration 5.19). The bearing should be almost silent when spun; if it grates or rattles it is worn.

6 Oil seals

Oil seal removal and installation

● Oil seals should be renewed every time a component is dismantled. This is because the seal lips will become set to the sealing surface and will not necessarily reseal.
● Oil seals can be prised out of position using a large flat-bladed screwdriver (see illustration 6.1). In the case of crankcase seals, check first that the seal is not lipped on the inside, preventing its removal with the crankcases joined.

6.1 Prise out oil seals with a large flat-bladed screwdriver

● New seals are usually installed with their marked face (containing the seal reference code) outwards and the spring side towards the fluid being retained. In certain cases, such as a two-stroke engine crankshaft seal, a double lipped seal may be used due to there being fluid or gas on each side of the joint.

- Use a bearing driver or socket which bears only on the outer hard edge of the seal to install it in the casing - tapping on the inner edge will damage the sealing lip.

Oil seal types and markings

- Oil seals are usually of the single-lipped type. Double-lipped seals are found where a liquid or gas is on both sides of the joint.
- Oil seals can harden and lose their sealing ability if the motorcycle has been in storage for a long period - renewal is the only solution.
- Oil seal manufacturers also conform to the ISO markings for seal size - these are moulded into the outer face of the seal (see illustration 6.2).

6.2 These oil seal markings indicate inside diameter, outside diameter and seal thickness

7 Gaskets and sealants

Types of gasket and sealant

- Gaskets are used to seal the mating surfaces between components and keep lubricants, fluids, vacuum or pressure contained within the assembly. Aluminium gaskets are sometimes found at the cylinder joints, but most gaskets are paper-based. If the mating surfaces of the components being joined are undamaged the gasket can be installed dry, although a dab of sealant or grease will be useful to hold it in place during assembly.
- RTV (Room Temperature Vulcanising) silicone rubber sealants cure when exposed to moisture in the atmosphere. These sealants are good at filling pits or irregular gasket faces, but will tend to be forced out of the joint under very high torque. They can be used to replace a paper gasket, but first make sure that the width of the paper gasket is not essential to the shimming of internal components. RTV sealants should not be used on components containing petrol (gasoline).
- Non-hardening, semi-hardening and hard setting liquid gasket compounds can be used with a gasket or between a metal-to-metal joint. Select the sealant to suit the application: universal non-hardening sealant can be used on virtually all joints; semi-hardening on joint faces which are rough or damaged; hard setting sealant on joints which require a permanent bond and are subjected to high temperature and pressure. **Note:** *Check first if the paper gasket has a bead of sealant*

impregnated in its surface before applying additional sealant.

- When choosing a sealant, make sure it is suitable for the application, particularly if being applied in a high-temperature area or in the vicinity of fuel. Certain manufacturers produce sealants in either clear, silver or black colours to match the finish of the engine. This has a particular application on motorcycles where much of the engine is exposed.
- Do not over-apply sealant. That which is squeezed out on the outside of the joint can be wiped off, whereas an excess of sealant on the inside can break off and clog oilways.

Breaking a sealed joint

- Age, heat, pressure and the use of hard setting sealant can cause two components to stick together so tightly that they are difficult to separate using finger pressure alone. Do not resort to using levers unless there is a pry point provided for this purpose (see illustration 7.1) or else the gasket surfaces will be damaged.
- Use a soft-faced hammer (see illustration 7.2) or a wood block and conventional hammer to strike the component near the mating surface. Avoid hammering against cast extremities since they may break off. If this method fails, try using a wood wedge between the two components.

> **Caution: If the joint will not separate, double-check that you have removed all the fasteners.**

7.1 If a pry point is provided, apply gently pressure with a flat-bladed screwdriver

7.2 Tap around the joint with a soft-faced mallet if necessary - don't strike cooling fins

Removal of old gasket and sealant

- Paper gaskets will most likely come away complete, leaving only a few traces stuck on

Most components have one or two hollow locating dowels between the two gasket faces. If a dowel cannot be removed, do not resort to gripping it with pliers - it will almost certainly be distorted. Install a close-fitting socket or Phillips screwdriver into the dowel and then grip the outer edge of the dowel to free it.

the sealing faces of the components. It is imperative that all traces are removed to ensure correct sealing of the new gasket.
- Very carefully scrape all traces of gasket away making sure that the sealing surfaces are not gouged or scored by the scraper (see illustrations 7.3, 7.4 and 7.5). Stubborn deposits can be removed by spraying with an aerosol gasket remover. Final preparation of

7.3 Paper gaskets can be scraped off with a gasket scraper tool . . .

7.4 . . . a knife blade . . .

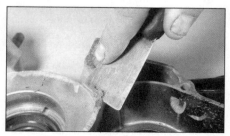

7.5 . . . or a household scraper

7.6 Fine abrasive paper is wrapped around a flat file to clean up the gasket face

7.7 A kitchen scourer can be used on stubborn deposits

the gasket surface can be made with very fine abrasive paper or a plastic kitchen scourer **(see illustrations 7.6 and 7.7)**.

● Old sealant can be scraped or peeled off components, depending on the type originally used. Note that gasket removal compounds are available to avoid scraping the components clean; make sure the gasket remover suits the type of sealant used.

8 Chains

Breaking and joining final drive chains

● Drive chains for all but small bikes are continuous and do not have a clip-type connecting link. The chain must be broken using a chain breaker tool and the new chain securely riveted together using a new soft rivet-type link. Never use a clip-type connecting link instead of a rivet-type link, except in an emergency. Various chain breaking and riveting tools are available, either as separate tools or combined as illustrated in the accompanying photographs - read the instructions supplied with the tool carefully.

 Warning: The need to rivet the new link pins correctly cannot be overstressed - loss of control of the motorcycle is very likely to result if the chain breaks in use.

● Rotate the chain and look for the soft link. The soft link pins look like they have been

8.1 Tighten the chain breaker to push the pin out of the link . . .

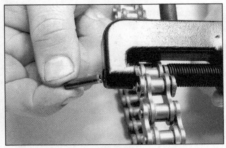

8.2 . . . withdraw the pin, remove the tool . . .

8.3 . . . and separate the chain link

deeply centre-punched instead of peened over like all the other pins **(see illustration 8.9)** and its sideplate may be a different colour. Position the soft link midway between the sprockets and assemble the chain breaker tool over one of the soft link pins **(see illustration 8.1)**. Operate the tool to push the pin out through the chain **(see illustration 8.2)**. On an O-ring chain, remove the O-rings **(see illustration 8.3)**. Carry out the same procedure on the other soft link pin.

Caution: Certain soft link pins (particularly on the larger chains) may require their ends to be filed or ground off before they can be pressed out using the tool.

● Check that you have the correct size and strength (standard or heavy duty) new soft link - do not reuse the old link. Look for the size marking on the chain sideplates **(see illustration 8.10)**.

● Position the chain ends so that they are engaged over the rear sprocket. On an O-ring

8.4 Insert the new soft link, with O-rings, through the chain ends . . .

8.5 . . . install the O-rings over the pin ends . . .

8.6 . . . followed by the sideplate

chain, install a new O-ring over each pin of the link and insert the link through the two chain ends **(see illustration 8.4)**. Install a new O-ring over the end of each pin, followed by the sideplate (with the chain manufacturer's marking facing outwards) **(see illustrations 8.5 and 8.6)**. On an unsealed chain, insert the link through the two chain ends, then install the sideplate with the chain manufacturer's marking facing outwards.

● Note that it may not be possible to install the sideplate using finger pressure alone. If using a joining tool, assemble it so that the plates of the tool clamp the link and press the sideplate over the pins **(see illustration 8.7)**. Otherwise, use two small sockets placed over

8.7 Push the sideplate into position using a clamp

8.8 Assemble the chain riveting tool over one pin at a time and tighten it fully

8.9 Pin end correctly riveted (A), pin end unriveted (B)

the rivet ends and two pieces of the wood between a G-clamp. Operate the clamp to press the sideplate over the pins.

● Assemble the joining tool over one pin (following the maker's instructions) and tighten the tool down to spread the pin end securely **(see illustrations 8.8 and 8.9)**. Do the same on the other pin.

> ⚠ **Warning: Check that the pin ends are secure and that there is no danger of the sideplate coming loose. If the pin ends are cracked the soft link must be renewed.**

Final drive chain sizing

● Chains are sized using a three digit number, followed by a suffix to denote the chain type **(see illustration 8.10)**. Chain type is either standard or heavy duty (thicker sideplates), and also unsealed or O-ring/X-ring type.

● The first digit of the number relates to the pitch of the chain, ie the distance from the centre of one pin to the centre of the next pin **(see illustration 8.11)**. Pitch is expressed in eighths of an inch, as follows:

8.10 Typical chain size and type marking

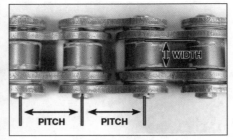

8.11 Chain dimensions

| Sizes commencing with a 4 (eg 428) have a pitch of 1/2 inch (12.7 mm) |
| Sizes commencing with a 5 (eg 520) have a pitch of 5/8 inch (15.9 mm) |
| Sizes commencing with a 6 (eg 630) have a pitch of 3/4 inch (19.1 mm) |

● The second and third digits of the chain size relate to the width of the rollers, again in imperial units, eg the 525 shown has 5/16 inch (7.94 mm) rollers **(see illustration 8.11)**.

9 Hoses

Clamping to prevent flow

● Small-bore flexible hoses can be clamped to prevent fluid flow whilst a component is worked on. Whichever method is used, ensure that the hose material is not permanently distorted or damaged by the clamp.

a) A brake hose clamp available from auto accessory shops **(see illustration 9.1)**.
b) A wingnut type hose clamp **(see illustration 9.2)**.

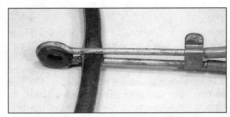

9.1 Hoses can be clamped with an automotive brake hose clamp . . .

9.2 . . . a wingnut type hose clamp . . .

c) Two sockets placed each side of the hose and held with straight-jawed self-locking grips **(see illustration 9.3)**.
d) Thick card each side of the hose held between straight-jawed self-locking grips **(see illustration 9.4)**.

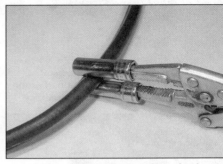

9.3 . . . two sockets and a pair of self-locking grips . . .

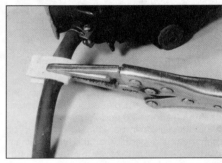

9.4 . . . or thick card and self-locking grips

Freeing and fitting hoses

● Always make sure the hose clamp is moved well clear of the hose end. Grip the hose with your hand and rotate it whilst pulling it off the union. If the hose has hardened due to age and will not move, slit it with a sharp knife and peel its ends off the union **(see illustration 9.5)**.

● Resist the temptation to use grease or soap on the unions to aid installation; although it helps the hose slip over the union it will equally aid the escape of fluid from the joint. It is preferable to soften the hose ends in hot water and wet the inside surface of the hose with water or a fluid which will evaporate.

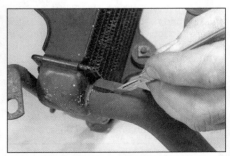

9.5 Cutting a coolant hose free with a sharp knife

Length (distance)

Inches (in)	x 25.4	= Millimetres (mm)	x 0.0394	= Inches (in)
Feet (ft)	x 0.305	= Metres (m)	x 3.281	= Feet (ft)
Miles	x 1.609	= Kilometres (km)	x 0.621	= Miles

Volume (capacity)

Cubic inches (cu in; in^3)	x 16.387	= Cubic centimetres (cc; cm^3)	x 0.061	= Cubic inches (cu in; in^3)
Imperial pints (Imp pt)	x 0.568	= Litres (l)	x 1.76	= Imperial pints (Imp pt)
Imperial quarts (Imp qt)	x 1.137	= Litres (l)	x 0.88	= Imperial quarts (Imp qt)
Imperial quarts (Imp qt)	x 1.201	= US quarts (US qt)	x 0.833	= Imperial quarts (Imp qt)
US quarts (US qt)	x 0.946	= Litres (l)	x 1.057	= US quarts (US qt)
Imperial gallons (Imp gal)	x 4.546	= Litres (l)	x 0.22	= Imperial gallons (Imp gal)
Imperial gallons (Imp gal)	x 1.201	= US gallons (US gal)	x 0.833	= Imperial gallons (Imp gal)
US gallons (US gal)	x 3.785	= Litres (l)	x 0.264	= US gallons (US gal)

Mass (weight)

Ounces (oz)	x 28.35	= Grams (g)	x 0.035	= Ounces (oz)
Pounds (lb)	x 0.454	= Kilograms (kg)	x 2.205	= Pounds (lb)

Force

Ounces-force (ozf; oz)	x 0.278	= Newtons (N)	x 3.6	= Ounces-force (ozf; oz)
Pounds-force (lbf; lb)	x 4.448	= Newtons (N)	x 0.225	= Pounds-force (lbf; lb)
Newtons (N)	x 0.1	= Kilograms-force (kgf; kg)	x 9.81	= Newtons (N)

Pressure

Pounds-force per square inch (psi; lbf/in^2; lb/in^2)	x 0.070	= Kilograms-force per square centimetre (kgf/cm^2; kg/cm^2)	x 14.223	= Pounds-force per square inch (psi; lbf/in^2; lb/in^2)
Pounds-force per square inch (psi; lbf/in^2; lb/in^2)	x 0.068	= Atmospheres (atm)	x 14.696	= Pounds-force per square inch (psi; lbf/in^2; lb/in^2)
Pounds-force per square inch (psi; lbf/in^2; lb/in^2)	x 0.069	= Bars	x 14.5	= Pounds-force per square inch (psi; lbf/in^2; lb/in^2)
Pounds-force per square inch (psi; lbf/in^2; lb/in^2)	x 6.895	= Kilopascals (kPa)	x 0.145	= Pounds-force per square inch (psi; lbf/in^2; lb/in^2)
Kilopascals (kPa)	x 0.01	= Kilograms-force per square centimetre (kgf/cm^2; kg/cm^2)	x 98.1	= Kilopascals (kPa)
Millibar (mbar)	x 100	= Pascals (Pa)	x 0.01	= Millibar (mbar)
Millibar (mbar)	x 0.0145	= Pounds-force per square inch (psi; lbf/in^2; lb/in^2)	x 68.947	= Millibar (mbar)
Millibar (mbar)	x 0.75	= Millimetres of mercury (mmHg)	x 1.333	= Millibar (mbar)
Millibar (mbar)	x 0.401	= Inches of water (inH$_2$O)	x 2.491	= Millibar (mbar)
Millimetres of mercury (mmHg)	x 0.535	= Inches of water (inH$_2$O)	x 1.868	= Millimetres of mercury (mmHg)
Inches of water (inH$_2$O)	x 0.036	= Pounds-force per square inch (psi; lbf/in^2; lb/in^2)	x 27.68	= Inches of water (inH$_2$O)

Torque (moment of force)

Pounds-force inches (lbf in; lb in)	x 1.152	= Kilograms-force centimetre (kgf cm; kg cm)	x 0.868	= Pounds-force inches (lbf in; lb in)
Pounds-force inches (lbf in; lb in)	x 0.113	= Newton metres (Nm)	x 8.85	= Pounds-force inches (lbf in; lb in)
Pounds-force inches (lbf in; lb in)	x 0.083	= Pounds-force feet (lbf ft; lb ft)	x 12	= Pounds-force inches (lbf in; lb in)
Pounds-force feet (lbf ft; lb ft)	x 0.138	= Kilograms-force metres (kgf m; kg m)	x 7.233	= Pounds-force feet (lbf ft; lb ft)
Pounds-force feet (lbf ft; lb ft)	x 1.356	= Newton metres (Nm)	x 0.738	= Pounds-force feet (lbf ft; lb ft)
Newton metres (Nm)	x 0.102	= Kilograms-force metres (kgf m; kg m)	x 9.804	= Newton metres (Nm)

Power

Horsepower (hp)	x 745.7	= Watts (W)	x 0.0013	= Horsepower (hp)

Velocity (speed)

Miles per hour (miles/hr; mph)	x 1.609	= Kilometres per hour (km/hr; kph)	x 0.621	= Miles per hour (miles/hr; mph)

Fuel consumption*

Miles per gallon (mpg)	x 0.354	= Kilometres per litre (km/l)	x 2.825	= Miles per gallon (mpg)

Temperature

Degrees Fahrenheit = (°C x 1.8) + 32   Degrees Celsius (Degrees Centigrade; °C) = (°F - 32) x 0.56

It is common practice to convert from miles per gallon (mpg) to litres/100 kilometres (l/100km), where mpg x l/100 km = 282

A number of chemicals and lubricants are available for use in motorcycle maintenance and repair. They include a wide variety of products ranging from cleaning solvents and degreasers to lubricants and protective sprays for rubber, plastic and vinyl.

● **Contact point/spark plug cleaner** is a solvent used to clean oily film and dirt from points, grime from electrical connectors and oil deposits from spark plugs. It is oil free and leaves no residue. It can also be used to remove gum and varnish from carburettor jets and other orifices.

● **Carburettor cleaner** is similar to contact point/spark plug cleaner but it usually has a stronger solvent and may leave a slight oily reside. It is not recommended for cleaning electrical components or connections.

● **Brake system cleaner** is used to remove grease or brake fluid from brake system components (where clean surfaces are absolutely necessary and petroleum-based solvents cannot be used); it also leaves no residue.

● **Silicone-based lubricants** are used to protect rubber parts such as hoses and grommets, and are used as lubricants for hinges and locks.

● **Multi-purpose grease** is an all purpose lubricant used wherever grease is more practical than a liquid lubricant such as oil. Some multi-purpose grease is coloured white and specially formulated to be more resistant to water than ordinary grease.

● **Gear oil** (sometimes called gear lube) is a specially designed oil used in transmissions and final drive units, as well as other areas where high friction, high temperature lubrication is required. It is available in a number of viscosities (weights) for various applications.

● **Motor oil**, of course, is the lubricant specially formulated for use in the engine. It normally contains a wide variety of additives to prevent corrosion and reduce foaming and wear. Motor oil comes in various weights (viscosity ratings) of from 5 to 80. The recommended weight of the oil depends on the seasonal temperature and the demands on the engine. Light oil is used in cold climates and under light load conditions; heavy oil is used in hot climates and where high loads are encountered. Multi-viscosity oils are designed to have characteristics of both light and heavy oils and are available in a number of weights from 5W-20 to 20W-50.

● **Petrol additives** perform several functions, depending on their chemical makeup. They usually contain solvents that help dissolve gum and varnish that build up on carburettor and inlet parts. They also serve to break down carbon deposits that form on the inside surfaces of the combustion chambers. Some additives contain upper cylinder lubricants for valves and piston rings.

● **Brake and clutch fluid** is a specially formulated hydraulic fluid that can withstand the heat and pressure encountered in brake/clutch systems. Care must be taken that this fluid does not come in contact with painted surfaces or plastics. An opened container should always be resealed to prevent contamination by water or dirt.

● **Chain lubricants** are formulated especially for use on motorcycle final drive chains. A good chain lube should adhere well and have good penetrating qualities to be effective as a lubricant inside the chain and on the side plates, pins and rollers. Most chain lubes are either the foaming type or quick drying type and are usually marketed as sprays. Take care to use a lubricant marked as being suitable for O-ring chains.

● **Degreasers** are heavy duty solvents used to remove grease and grime that may accumulate on engine and frame components. They can be sprayed or brushed on and, depending on the type, are rinsed with either water or solvent.

● **Solvents** are used alone or in combination with degreasers to clean parts and assemblies during repair and overhaul. The home mechanic should use only solvents that are non-flammable and that do not produce irritating fumes.

● **Gasket sealing compounds** may be used in conjunction with gaskets, to improve their sealing capabilities, or alone, to seal metal-to-metal joints. Many gasket sealers can withstand extreme heat, some are impervious to petrol and lubricants, while others are capable of filling and sealing large cavities. Depending on the intended use, gasket sealers either dry hard or stay relatively soft and pliable. They are usually applied by hand, with a brush, or are sprayed on the gasket sealing surfaces.

● **Thread locking compound** is an adhesive locking compound that prevents threaded fasteners from loosening because of vibration. It is available in a variety of types for different applications.

● **Moisture dispersants** are usually sprays that can be used to dry out electrical components such as the fuse block and wiring connectors. Some types can also be used as treatment for rubber and as a lubricant for hinges, cables and locks.

● **Waxes and polishes** are used to help protect painted and plated surfaces from the weather. Different types of paint may require the use of different types of wax polish. Some polishes utilise a chemical or abrasive cleaner to help remove the top layer of oxidised (dull) paint on older vehicles. In recent years, many non-wax polishes (that contain a wide variety of chemicals such as polymers and silicones) have been introduced. These non-wax polishes are usually easier to apply and last longer than conventional waxes and polishes.

About the MOT Test

In the UK, all vehicles more than three years old are subject to an annual test to ensure that they meet minimum safety requirements. A current test certificate must be issued before a machine can be used on public roads, and is required before a road fund licence can be issued. Riding without a current test certificate will also invalidate your insurance.

For most owners, the MOT test is an annual cause for anxiety, and this is largely due to owners not being sure what needs to be checked prior to submitting the motorcycle for testing. The simple answer is that a fully roadworthy motorcycle will have no difficulty in passing the test.

This is a guide to getting your motorcycle through the MOT test. Obviously it will not be possible to examine the motorcycle to the same standard as the professional MOT tester, particularly in view of the equipment required for some of the checks. However, working through the following procedures will enable you to identify any problem areas before submitting the motorcycle for the test.

It has only been possible to summarise the test requirements here, based on the regulations in force at the time of printing. Test standards are becoming increasingly stringent, although there are some exemptions for older vehicles. More information about the MOT test can be obtained from the TSO publications, *How Safe is your Motorcycle* and *The MOT Inspection Manual for Motorcycle Testing*.

Many of the checks require that one of the wheels is raised off the ground. If the motorcycle doesn't have a centre stand, note that an auxiliary stand will be required. Additionally, the help of an assistant may prove useful.

Certain exceptions apply to machines under 50 cc, machines without a lighting system, and Classic bikes - if in doubt about any of the requirements listed below seek confirmation from an MOT tester prior to submitting the motorcycle for the test.

Check that the frame number is clearly visible.

> **HAYNES HiNT**
>
> *If a component is in borderline condition, the tester has discretion in deciding whether to pass or fail it. If the motorcycle presented is clean and evidently well cared for, the tester may be more inclined to pass a borderline component than if the motorcycle is scruffy and apparently neglected.*

Electrical System

Lights, turn signals, horn and reflector

✔ With the ignition on, check the operation of the following electrical components. **Note:** *The electrical components on certain small-capacity machines are powered by the generator, requiring that the engine is run for this check.*

a) *Headlight and tail light. Check that both illuminate in the low and high beam switch positions.*

b) *Position lights. Check that the front position (or sidelight) and tail light illuminate in this switch position.*

c) *Turn signals. Check that all flash at the correct rate, and that the warning light(s) function correctly. Check that the turn signal switch works correctly.*

d) *Hazard warning system (where fitted). Check that all four turn signals flash in this switch position.*

e) *Brake stop light. Check that the light comes on when the front and rear brakes are independently applied. Models first used on or after 1st April 1986 must have a brake light switch on each brake.*

f) *Horn. Check that the sound is continuous and of reasonable volume.*

✔ Check that there is a red reflector on the rear of the machine, either mounted separately or as part of the tail light lens.

✔ Check the condition of the headlight, tail light and turn signal lenses.

Headlight beam height

✔ The MOT tester will perform a headlight beam height check using specialised beam setting equipment **(see illustration 1)**. This equipment will not be available to the home mechanic, but if you suspect that the headlight is incorrectly set or may have been maladjusted in the past, you can perform a rough test as follows.

✔ Position the bike in a straight line facing a brick wall. The bike must be off its stand, upright and with a rider seated. Measure the height from the ground to the centre of the headlight and mark a horizontal line on the wall at this height. Position the motorcycle 3.8 metres from the wall and draw a vertical

Headlight beam height checking equipment

line up the wall central to the centreline of the motorcycle. Switch to dipped beam and check that the beam pattern falls slightly lower than the horizontal line and to the left of the vertical line **(see illustration 2)**.

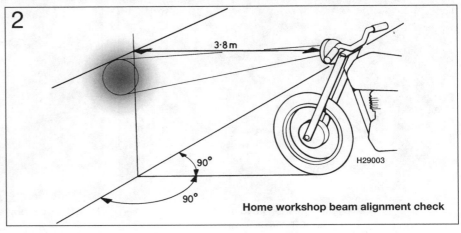

3·8 m

90°

90°

H29003

Home workshop beam alignment check

Exhaust System and Final Drive

Exhaust

✔ Check that the exhaust mountings are secure and that the system does not foul any of the rear suspension components.
✔ Start the motorcycle. When the revs are increased, check that the exhaust is neither holed nor leaking from any of its joints. On a linked system, check that the collector box is not leaking due to corrosion.

✔ Note that the exhaust decibel level ("loudness" of the exhaust) is assessed at the discretion of the tester. If the motorcycle was first used on or after 1st January 1985 the silencer must carry the BSAU 193 stamp, or a marking relating to its make and model, or be of OE (original equipment) manufacture. If the silencer is marked NOT FOR ROAD USE, RACING USE ONLY or similar, it will fail the MOT.

Final drive

✔ On chain or belt drive machines, check that the chain/belt is in good condition and does not have excessive slack. Also check that the sprocket is securely mounted on the rear wheel hub. Check that the chain/belt guard is in place.
✔ On shaft drive bikes, check for oil leaking from the drive unit and fouling the rear tyre.

Steering and Suspension

Steering

✔ With the front wheel raised off the ground, rotate the steering from lock to lock. The handlebar or switches must not contact the fuel tank or be close enough to trap the rider's hand. Problems can be caused by damaged lock stops on the lower yoke and frame, or by the fitting of non-standard handlebars.
✔ When performing the lock to lock check, also ensure that the steering moves freely without drag or notchiness. Steering movement can be impaired by poorly routed cables, or by overtight head bearings or worn bearings. The tester will perform a check of the steering head bearing lower race by mounting the front wheel on a surface plate, then performing a lock to lock check with the weight of the machine on the lower bearing (see illustration 3).
✔ Grasp the fork sliders (lower legs) and attempt to push and pull on the forks (see

Front wheel mounted on a surface plate for steering head bearing lower race check

illustration 4). Any play in the steering head bearings will be felt. Note that in extreme cases, wear of the front fork bushes can be misinterpreted for head bearing play.
✔ Check that the handlebars are securely mounted.
✔ Check that the handlebar grip rubbers are secure. They should by bonded to the bar left end and to the throttle cable pulley on the right end.

Front suspension

✔ With the motorcycle off the stand, hold the front brake on and pump the front forks up and down (see illustration 5). Check that they are adequately damped.

Checking the steering head bearings for freeplay

Hold the front brake on and pump the front forks up and down to check operation

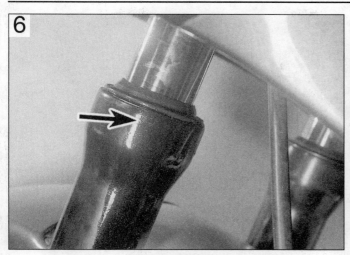

Inspect the area around the fork dust seal for oil leakage (arrow)

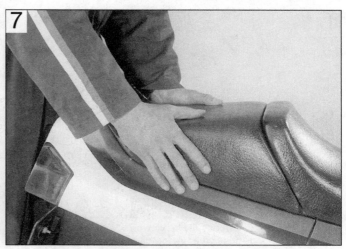

Bounce the rear of the motorcycle to check rear suspension operation

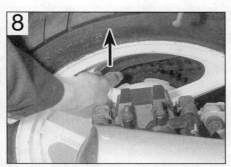

Checking for rear suspension linkage play

✔ Inspect the area above and around the front fork oil seals (see illustration 6). There should be no sign of oil on the fork tube (stanchion) nor leaking down the slider (lower leg). On models so equipped, check that there is no oil leaking from the anti-dive units.

✔ On models with swingarm front suspension, check that there is no freeplay in the linkage when moved from side to side.

Rear suspension

✔ With the motorcycle off the stand and an assistant supporting the motorcycle by its handlebars, bounce the rear suspension (see illustration 7). Check that the suspension components do not foul on any of the cycle parts and check that the shock absorber(s) provide adequate damping.

✔ Visually inspect the shock absorber(s) and check that there is no sign of oil leakage from its damper. This is somewhat restricted on certain single shock models due to the location of the shock absorber.

✔ With the rear wheel raised off the ground, grasp the wheel at the highest point and attempt to pull it up (see illustration 8). Any play in the swingarm pivot or suspension linkage bearings will be felt as movement. Note: Do not confuse play with actual suspension movement. Failure to lubricate suspension linkage bearings can lead to bearing failure (see illustration 9).

✔ With the rear wheel raised off the ground, grasp the swingarm ends and attempt to move the swingarm from side to side and forwards and backwards - any play indicates wear of the swingarm pivot bearings (see illustration 10).

Worn suspension linkage pivots (arrows) are usually the cause of play in the rear suspension

Grasp the swingarm at the ends to check for play in its pivot bearings

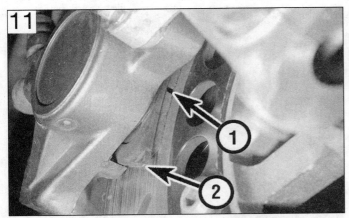

Brake pad wear can usually be viewed without removing the caliper. Most pads have wear indicator grooves (1) and some also have indicator tangs (2)

On drum brakes, check the angle of the operating lever with the brake fully applied. Most drum brakes have a wear indicator pointer and scale.

Brakes, Wheels and Tyres

Brakes

✔ With the wheel raised off the ground, apply the brake then free it off, and check that the wheel is about to revolve freely without brake drag.

✔ On disc brakes, examine the disc itself. Check that it is securely mounted and not cracked.

✔ On disc brakes, view the pad material through the caliper mouth and check that the pads are not worn down beyond the limit (see illustration 11).

✔ On drum brakes, check that when the brake is applied the angle between the operating lever and cable or rod is not too great (see illustration 12). Check also that the operating lever doesn't foul any other components.

✔ On disc brakes, examine the flexible hoses from top to bottom. Have an assistant hold the brake on so that the fluid in the hose is under pressure, and check that there is no sign of fluid leakage, bulges or cracking. If there are any metal brake pipes or unions, check that these are free from corrosion and damage. Where a brake-linked anti-dive system is fitted, check the hoses to the anti-dive in a similar manner.

✔ Check that the rear brake torque arm is secure and that its fasteners are secured by self-locking nuts or castellated nuts with split-pins or R-pins (see illustration 13).

✔ On models with ABS, check that the self-check warning light in the instrument panel works.

✔ The MOT tester will perform a test of the motorcycle's braking efficiency based on a calculation of rider and motorcycle weight. Although this cannot be carried out at home, you can at least ensure that the braking systems are properly maintained. For hydraulic disc brakes, check the fluid level, lever/pedal feel (bleed of air if its spongy) and pad material. For drum brakes, check adjustment, cable or rod operation and shoe lining thickness.

Wheels and tyres

✔ Check the wheel condition. Cast wheels should be free from cracks and if of the built-up design, all fasteners should be secure. Spoked wheels should be checked for broken, corroded, loose or bent spokes.

✔ With the wheel raised off the ground, spin the wheel and visually check that the tyre and wheel run true. Check that the tyre does not foul the suspension or mudguards.

✔ With the wheel raised off the ground, grasp the wheel and attempt to move it about the axle (spindle) (see illustration 14). Any play felt here indicates wheel bearing failure.

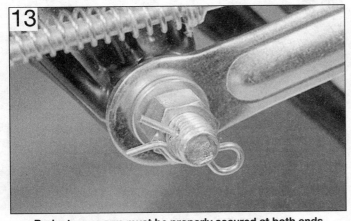

Brake torque arm must be properly secured at both ends

Check for wheel bearing play by trying to move the wheel about the axle (spindle)

Checking the tyre tread depth

Tyre direction of rotation arrow can be found on tyre sidewall

Castellated type wheel axle (spindle) nut must be secured by a split pin or R-pin

Two straightedges are used to check wheel alignment

✔ Check the tyre tread depth, tread condition and sidewall condition **(see illustration 15)**.

✔ Check the tyre type. Front and rear tyre types must be compatible and be suitable for road use. Tyres marked NOT FOR ROAD USE, COMPETITION USE ONLY or similar, will fail the MOT.

✔ If the tyre sidewall carries a direction of rotation arrow, this must be pointing in the direction of normal wheel rotation **(see illustration 16)**.

✔ Check that the wheel axle (spindle) nuts (where applicable) are properly secured. A self-locking nut or castellated nut with a split-pin or R-pin can be used **(see illustration 17)**.

✔ Wheel alignment is checked with the motorcycle off the stand and a rider seated. With the front wheel pointing straight ahead, two perfectly straight lengths of metal or wood and placed against the sidewalls of both tyres **(see illustration 18)**. The gap each side of the front tyre must be equidistant on both sides. Incorrect wheel alignment may be due to a cocked rear wheel (often as the result of poor chain adjustment) or in extreme cases, a bent frame.

General checks and condition

✔ Check the security of all major fasteners, bodypanels, seat, fairings (where fitted) and mudguards.

✔ Check that the rider and pillion footrests, handlebar levers and brake pedal are securely mounted.

✔ Check for corrosion on the frame or any load-bearing components. If severe, this may affect the structure, particularly under stress.

Sidecars

A motorcycle fitted with a sidecar requires additional checks relating to the stability of the machine and security of attachment and swivel joints, plus specific wheel alignment (toe-in) requirements. Additionally, tyre and lighting requirements differ from conventional motorcycle use. Owners are advised to check MOT test requirements with an official test centre.

Preparing for storage

Before you start

If repairs or an overhaul is needed, see that this is carried out now rather than left until you want to ride the bike again.

Give the bike a good wash and scrub all dirt from its underside. Make sure the bike dries completely before preparing for storage.

Engine

● Remove the spark plug(s) and lubricate the cylinder bores with approximately a teaspoon of motor oil using a spout-type oil can **(see illustration 1)**. Reinstall the spark plug(s). Crank the engine over a couple of times to coat the piston rings and bores with oil. If the bike has a kickstart, use this to turn the engine over. If not, flick the kill switch to the OFF position and crank the engine over on the starter **(see illustration 2)**. If the nature on the ignition system prevents the starter operating with the kill switch in the OFF position,

remove the spark plugs and fit them back in their caps; ensure that the plugs are earthed (grounded) against the cylinder head when the starter is operated **(see illustration 3)**.

 Warning: It is important that the plugs are earthed (grounded) away from the spark plug holes otherwise there is a risk of atomised fuel from the cylinders igniting.

HAYNES HINT *On a single cylinder four-stroke engine, you can seal the combustion chamber completely by positioning the piston at TDC on the compression stroke.*

● Drain the carburettor(s) otherwise there is a risk of jets becoming blocked by gum deposits from the fuel **(see illustration 4)**.

● If the bike is going into long-term storage, consider adding a fuel stabiliser to the fuel in the tank. If the tank is drained completely, corrosion of its internal surfaces may occur if left unprotected for a long period. The tank can be treated with a rust preventative especially for this purpose. Alternatively, remove the tank and pour half a litre of motor oil into it, install the filler cap and shake the tank to coat its internals with oil before draining off the excess. The same effect can also be achieved by spraying WD40 or a similar water-dispersant around the inside of the tank via its flexible nozzle.

● Make sure the cooling system contains the correct mix of antifreeze. Antifreeze also contains important corrosion inhibitors.

● The air intakes and exhaust can be sealed off by covering or plugging the openings. Ensure that you do not seal in any condensation; run the engine until it is hot,

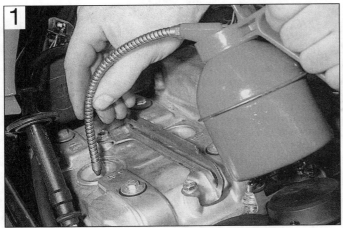

Squirt a drop of motor oil into each cylinder

Flick the kill switch to OFF . . .

. . . and ensure that the metal bodies of the plugs (arrows) are earthed against the cylinder head

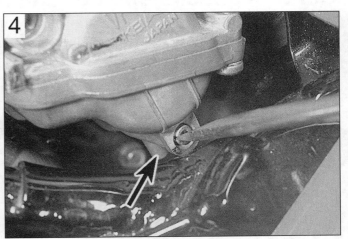

Connect a hose to the carburettor float chamber drain stub (arrow) and unscrew the drain screw

Exhausts can be sealed off with a plastic bag

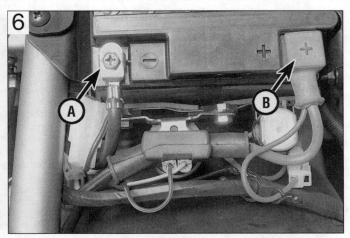

Disconnect the negative lead (A) first, followed by the positive lead (B)

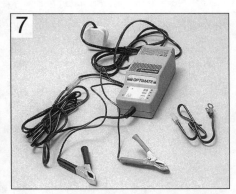

Use a suitable battery charger - this kit also assess battery condition

then switch off and allow to cool. Tape a piece of thick plastic over the silencer end(s) **(see illustration 5)**. Note that some advocate pouring a tablespoon of motor oil into the silencer(s) before sealing them off.

Battery

● Remove it from the bike - in extreme cases of cold the battery may freeze and crack its case **(see illustration 6)**.

● Check the electrolyte level and top up if necessary (conventional refillable batteries). Clean the terminals.
● Store the battery off the motorcycle and away from any sources of fire. Position a wooden block under the battery if it is to sit on the ground.
● Give the battery a trickle charge for a few hours every month **(see illustration 7)**.

Tyres

● Place the bike on its centrestand or an auxiliary stand which will support the motorcycle in an upright position. Position wood blocks under the tyres to keep them off the ground and to provide insulation from damp. If the bike is being put into long-term storage, ideally both tyres should be off the ground; not only will this protect the tyres, but will also ensure that no load is placed on steering head or wheel bearings.
● Deflate each tyre by 5 to 10 psi, no more or the beads may unseat from the rim, making subsequent inflation difficult on tubeless tyres.

Pivots and controls

● Lubricate all lever, pedal, stand and footrest pivot points. If grease nipples are fitted to the rear suspension components, apply lubricant to the pivots.
● Lubricate all control cables.

Cycle components

● Apply a wax protectant to all painted and plastic components. Wipe off any excess, but don't polish to a shine. Where fitted, clean the screen with soap and water.
● Coat metal parts with Vaseline (petroleum jelly). When applying this to the fork tubes, do not compress the forks otherwise the seals will rot from contact with the Vaseline.
● Apply a vinyl cleaner to the seat.

Storage conditions

● Aim to store the bike in a shed or garage which does not leak and is free from damp.
● Drape an old blanket or bedspread over the bike to protect it from dust and direct contact with sunlight (which will fade paint). This also hides the bike from prying eyes. Beware of tight-fitting plastic covers which may allow condensation to form and settle on the bike.

Getting back on the road

Engine and transmission

● Change the oil and replace the oil filter. If this was done prior to storage, check that the oil hasn't emulsified - a thick whitish substance which occurs through condensation.
● Remove the spark plugs. Using a spout-type oil can, squirt a few drops of oil into the cylinder(s). This will provide initial lubrication as the piston rings and bores comes back into contact. Service the spark plugs, or fit new ones, and install them in the engine.

● Check that the clutch isn't stuck on. The plates can stick together if left standing for some time, preventing clutch operation. Engage a gear and try rocking the bike back and forth with the clutch lever held against the handlebar. If this doesn't work on cable-operated clutches, hold the clutch lever back against the handlebar with a strong elastic band or cable tie for a couple of hours **(see illustration 8)**.
● If the air intakes or silencer end(s) were blocked off, remove the bung or cover used.
● If the fuel tank was coated with a rust

Hold clutch lever back against the handlebar with elastic bands or a cable tie

preventative, oil or a stabiliser added to the fuel, drain and flush the tank and dispose of the fuel sensibly. If no action was taken with the fuel tank prior to storage, it is advised that the old fuel is disposed of since it will go off over a period of time. Refill the fuel tank with fresh fuel.

Frame and running gear

● Oil all pivot points and cables.
● Check the tyre pressures. They will definitely need inflating if pressures were reduced for storage.
● Lubricate the final drive chain (where applicable).
● Remove any protective coating applied to the fork tubes (stanchions) since this may well destroy the fork seals. If the fork tubes weren't protected and have picked up rust spots, remove them with very fine abrasive paper and refinish with metal polish.
● Check that both brakes operate correctly. Apply each brake hard and check that it's not possible to move the motorcycle forwards, then check that the brake frees off again once released. Brake caliper pistons can stick due to corrosion around the piston head, or on the sliding caliper types, due to corrosion of the slider pins. If the brake doesn't free after repeated operation, take the caliper off for examination. Similarly drum brakes can stick due to a seized operating cam, cable or rod linkage.
● If the motorcycle has been in long-term storage, renew the brake fluid and clutch fluid (where applicable).
● Depending on where the bike has been stored, the wiring, cables and hoses may have been nibbled by rodents. Make a visual check and investigate disturbed wiring loom tape.

Battery

● If the battery has been previously removal and given top up charges it can simply be reconnected. Remember to connect the positive cable first and the negative cable last.
● On conventional refillable batteries, if the battery has not received any attention, remove it from the motorcycle and check its electrolyte level. Top up if necessary then charge the battery. If the battery fails to hold a charge and a visual checks show heavy white sulphation of the plates, the battery is probably defective and must be renewed. This is particularly likely if the battery is old. Confirm battery condition with a specific gravity check.
● On sealed (MF) batteries, if the battery has not received any attention, remove it from the motorcycle and charge it according to the information on the battery case - if the battery fails to hold a charge it must be renewed.

Starting procedure

● If a kickstart is fitted, turn the engine over a couple of times with the ignition OFF to distribute oil around the engine. If no kickstart is fitted, flick the engine kill switch OFF and the ignition ON and crank the engine over a couple of times to work oil around the upper cylinder components. If the nature of the ignition system is such that the starter won't work with the kill switch OFF, remove the spark plugs, fit them back into their caps and earth (ground) their bodies on the cylinder head. Reinstall the spark plugs afterwards.
● Switch the kill switch to RUN, operate the choke and start the engine. If the engine won't start don't continue cranking the engine - not only will this flatten the battery, but the starter motor will overheat. Switch the ignition off and try again later. If the engine refuses to start, go through the fault finding procedures in this manual. **Note:** *If the bike has been in storage for a long time, old fuel or a carburettor blockage may be the problem. Gum deposits in carburettors can block jets - if a carburettor cleaner doesn't prove successful the carburettors must be dismantled for cleaning.*

● Once the engine has started, check that the lights, turn signals and horn work properly.
● Treat the bike gently for the first ride and check all fluid levels on completion. Settle the bike back into the maintenance schedule.

This Section provides an easy reference-guide to the more common faults that are likely to afflict your machine. Obviously, the opportunities are almost limitless for faults to occur as a result of obscure failures, and to try and cover all eventualities would require a book. Indeed, a number have been written on the subject.

Successful troubleshooting is not a mysterious 'black art' but the application of a bit of knowledge combined with a systematic and logical approach to the problem. Approach any troubleshooting by first accurately identifying the symptom and then checking through the list of possible causes, starting with the simplest or most obvious and progressing in stages to the most complex.

Take nothing for granted, but above all apply liberal quantities of common sense.

The main symptom of a fault is given in the text as a major heading below which are listed the various systems or areas which may contain the fault. Details of each possible cause for a fault and the remedial action to be taken are given, in brief, in the paragraphs below each heading. Further information should be sought in the relevant Chapter.

1 Engine doesn't start or is difficult to start

- ☐ Starter motor does not rotate
- ☐ Starter motor rotates but engine does not turn over
- ☐ Starter works but engine won't turn over (seized)
- ☐ No fuel flow
- ☐ Engine flooded
- ☐ No spark or weak spark
- ☐ Compression low
- ☐ Stalls after starting
- ☐ Rough idle

2 Poor running at low speed

- ☐ Spark weak
- ☐ Fuel/air mixture incorrect
- ☐ Compression low
- ☐ Poor acceleration

3 Poor running or no power at high speed

- ☐ Firing incorrect
- ☐ Fuel/air mixture incorrect
- ☐ Compression low
- ☐ Knocking or pinging
- ☐ Miscellaneous causes

4 Overheating

- ☐ Engine overheats
- ☐ Firing incorrect
- ☐ Fuel/air mixture incorrect
- ☐ Compression too high
- ☐ Engine load excessive
- ☐ Lubrication inadequate
- ☐ Miscellaneous causes

5 Clutch problems

- ☐ Clutch slipping
- ☐ Clutch not disengaging completely

6 Gear shifting problems

- ☐ Doesn't go into gear, or lever doesn't return
- ☐ Jumps out of gear
- ☐ Overshifts

7 Abnormal engine noise

- ☐ Knocking or pinging
- ☐ Piston slap or rattling
- ☐ Valve noise
- ☐ Other noise

8 Abnormal driveline noise

- ☐ Clutch noise
- ☐ Transmission noise
- ☐ Chain or final drive noise

9 Abnormal frame and suspension noise

- ☐ Front end noise
- ☐ Shock absorber noise
- ☐ Disc brake noise

10 Oil pressure indicator light comes on

- ☐ Engine lubrication system
- ☐ Electrical system

11 Excessive exhaust smoke

- ☐ White smoke
- ☐ Black smoke
- ☐ Brown smoke

12 Poor handling or stability

- ☐ Handlebar hard to turn
- ☐ Handlebar shakes or vibrates excessively
- ☐ Handlebar pulls to one side
- ☐ Poor shock absorbing qualities

13 Braking problems

- ☐ Brakes are spongy, don't hold
- ☐ Brake lever pulsates
- ☐ Brakes drag

14 Electrical problems

- ☐ Battery dead or weak
- ☐ Battery overcharged

1 Engine doesn't start or is difficult to start

Starter motor does not rotate

☐ Engine stop switch Off.
☐ Fuse blown. Check fuse block (Chapter 8).
☐ Battery voltage low. Check and recharge battery (Chapter 8).
☐ Starter motor defective. Make sure the wiring to the starter is secure. Make sure the starter relay clicks when the start button is pushed. If the relay clicks, then the fault is in the wiring or motor.
☐ Starter relay faulty. Check it according to the procedure in Chapter 8.
☐ Starter button not contacting. The contacts could be wet, corroded or dirty. Disassemble and clean the switch (Chapter 8).
☐ Wiring open or shorted. Check all wiring connections and harnesses to make sure that they are dry, tight and not corroded. Also check for broken or frayed wires that can cause a short to ground (see wiring diagram, Chapter 8).
☐ Ignition switch defective. Check the switch according to the procedure in Chapter 8. Replace the switch with a new one if it is defective.
☐ Engine stop switch defective. Check for wet, dirty or corroded contacts. Clean or replace the switch as necessary (Chapter 8).
☐ Faulty starter lockout switch (if equipped). Check the wiring to the switch and the switch itself according to the procedures in Chapter 8.

Starter motor rotates but engine does not turn over

☐ Starter motor clutch defective. Inspect and repair or replace (Chapter 2).
☐ Damaged idler or starter gears. Inspect and replace the damaged parts (Chapter 2).

Starter works but engine won't turn over (seized)

☐ Seized engine caused by one or more internally damaged components. Failure due to wear, abuse or lack of lubrication. Damage can include seized valves, valve lifters, camshaft, pistons, crankshaft, connecting rod bearings, or transmission gears or bearings. Refer to Chapter 2 for engine disassembly.

No fuel flow

☐ No fuel in tank.
☐ Fuel tap vacuum hose broken or disconnected.
☐ Tank cap air vent obstructed. Usually caused by dirt or water. Remove it and clean the cap vent hole.
☐ Fuel tap clogged. Remove the tap and clean it and the filter (Chapter 4).
☐ Fuel line clogged. Pull the fuel line loose and carefully blow through it.
☐ Inlet needle valve clogged. For all of the valves to be clogged, either a very bad batch of fuel with an unusual additive has been used, or some other foreign material has entered the tank. Many times after a machine has been stored for many months without running, the fuel turns to a varnish-like liquid and forms deposits on the inlet needle valves and jets. The carburetors should be removed and overhauled if draining the float bowls doesn't solve the problem.

Engine flooded

☐ Float level too high. Check and adjust as described in Chapter 3.
☐ Inlet needle valve worn or stuck open. A piece of dirt, rust or other debris can cause the inlet needle to seat improperly, causing excess fuel to be admitted to the float bowl. In this case, the float chamber should be cleaned and the needle and seat inspected. If the needle and seat are worn, then the leaking will persist and the parts should be replaced with new ones (Chapter 3).
☐ Starting technique incorrect. Under normal circumstances (i.e., if all the carburetor functions are sound) the machine should start with little or no throttle. When the engine is cold, the choke should be operated and the engine started without opening the throttle. When the engine is at operating temperature, only a very slight amount of throttle should be necessary. If the engine is flooded, turn the fuel tap off and hold the throttle open while cranking the engine. This will allow additional air to reach the cylinders. Remember to turn the gas back on after the engine starts.

No spark or weak spark

☐ Ignition switch Off.
☐ Engine stop switch turned to the Off position.
☐ Battery voltage low. Check and recharge battery as necessary (Chapter 8).
☐ Spark plug dirty, defective or worn out. Locate reason for fouled plug(s) using spark plug condition chart and follow the plug maintenance procedures in Chapter 1.
☐ Spark plug cap or secondary (HT) wiring faulty. Check condition. Replace either or both components if cracks or deterioration are evident (Chapter 4).
☐ Spark plug cap not making good contact. Make sure that the plug cap fits snugly over the plug end.
☐ IC igniter defective. Check the unit, referring to Chapter 4 for details.
☐ Signal generator defective. Check the unit, referring to Chapter 4 for details.
☐ Ignition coil(s) defective. Check the coils, referring to Chapter 4.
☐ Ignition or stop switch shorted. This is usually caused by water, corrosion, damage or excessive wear. The switches can be disassembled and cleaned with electrical contact cleaner. If cleaning does not help, replace the switches (Chapter 8).
☐ Wiring shorted or broken between:
   a) Ignition switch and engine stop switch (or blown fuse)
   b) IC igniter and engine stop switch
   c) IC igniter and ignition coil
   d) Ignition coil and plug
   e) IC igniter and signal generator
☐ Make sure that all wiring connections are clean, dry and tight. Look for chafed and broken wires (Chapters 4 and 8).

1 Engine doesn't start or is difficult to start (continued)

Compression low

☐ Spark plug loose. Remove the plug and inspect the threads. Reinstall and tighten to the specified torque (Chapter 1).

☐ Cylinder head not sufficiently tightened down. If the cylinder head is suspected of being loose, then there's a chance that the gasket or head is damaged if the problem has persisted for any length of time. The head bolts should be tightened to the proper torque in the correct sequence (Chapter 2).

☐ Improper valve clearance. This means that the valve is not closing completely and compression pressure is leaking past the valve. Check and adjust the valve clearances (Chapter 1).

☐ Cylinder and/or piston worn. Excessive wear will cause compression pressure to leak past the rings. This is usually accompanied by worn rings as well. A top end overhaul is necessary (Chapter 2).

☐ Piston rings worn, weak, broken, or sticking. Broken or sticking piston rings usually indicate a lubrication or carburetion problem that causes excess carbon deposits or seizures to form on the pistons and rings. Top end overhaul is necessary (Chapter 2).

☐ Piston ring-to-groove clearance excessive. This is caused by excessive wear of the piston ring lands. Piston replacement is necessary (Chapter 2).

☐ Cylinder head gasket damaged. If the head is allowed to become loose, or if excessive carbon build-up on the piston crown and combustion chamber causes extremely high compression, the head gasket may leak. Retorquing the head is not always sufficient to restore the seal, so gasket replacement is necessary (Chapter 2).

☐ Cylinder head warped. This is caused by overheating or improperly tightened head bolts. Machine shop resurfacing or head replacement is necessary (Chapter 2).

☐ Valve spring broken or weak. Caused by component failure or wear; the spring(s) must be replaced (Chapter 2).

☐ Valve not seating properly. This is caused by a bent valve (from over-revving or improper valve adjustment), burned valve or seat (improper carburetion) or an accumulation of carbon deposits on the seat (from carburetion, lubrication problems). The valves must be cleaned and/or replaced and the seats serviced if possible (Chapter 2).

Stalls after starting

☐ Improper choke action. Make sure the choke rod is getting a full stroke and staying in the "out" position. Adjustment of the cable slack is covered in Chapter 1.

☐ Ignition malfunction. See Chapter 4.

☐ Carburetor malfunction. See Chapter 3.

☐ Fuel contaminated. The fuel can be contaminated with either dirt or water, or can change chemically if the machine is allowed to sit for several months or more. Drain the tank and float bowls (Chapter 3).

☐ Intake air leak. Check for loose carburetor-to-intake manifold connections, loose or missing vacuum gauge access port cap or hose, or loose carburetor top (Chapter 3).

☐ Engine idle speed incorrect. Turn idle speed adjuster screw until the engine idles at the specified rpm (Chapters 1 and 3).

Rough idle

☐ Ignition malfunction. See Chapter 4.

☐ Idle speed incorrect. See Chapter 1.

☐ Carburetors not synchronized. Adjust carburetors with vacuum gauge or manometer set as described in Chapter 1.

☐ Carburetor malfunction. See Chapter 3.

☐ Fuel contaminated. The fuel can be contaminated with either dirt or water, or can change chemically if the machine is allowed to sit for several months or more. Drain the tank and float bowls (Chapter 3).

☐ Intake air leak. Check for loose carburetor-to-intake manifold connections, loose or missing vacuum gauge access port cap or hose, or loose carburetor top (Chapter 3).

☐ Air cleaner clogged. Service or replace air filter element (Chapter 1).

2 Poor running at low speed

Spark weak

☐ Battery voltage low. Check and recharge battery (Chapter 8).

☐ Spark plug fouled, defective or worn out. Refer to Chapter 1 for spark plug maintenance.

☐ Spark plug cap or high tension wiring defective. Refer to Chapters 1 and 5 for details on the ignition system.

☐ Spark plug cap not making contact.

☐ Incorrect spark plug. Wrong type, heat range or cap configuration. Check and install correct plugs listed in Chapter 1. A cold plug or one with a recessed firing electrode will not operate at low speeds without fouling.

☐ IC igniter defective. See Chapter 4.

☐ Signal generator defective. See Chapter 4.

☐ Ignition coil(s) defective. See Chapter 4.

Fuel/air mixture incorrect

☐ Pilot screw(s) out of adjustment (Chapters 1 and 3).

☐ Pilot jet or air passage clogged. Remove and overhaul the carburetors (Chapter 3).

☐ Air bleed holes clogged. Remove carburetor and blow out all passages (Chapter 3).

☐ Air cleaner clogged, poorly sealed or missing.

☐ Air cleaner-to-carburetor boot poorly sealed. Look for cracks, holes or loose clamps and replace or repair defective parts.

☐ Fuel level too high or too low. Adjust the floats (Chapter 3).

☐ Fuel tank air vent obstructed. Make sure that the air vent passage in the filler cap is open.

☐ Carburetor intake manifolds loose. Check for cracks, breaks, tears or loose clamps or bolts. Repair or replace the rubber boots.

Poor acceleration

☐ Carburetors leaking or dirty. Overhaul the carburetors (Chapter 3).

☐ Timing not advancing. The signal generator or the IC igniter may be defective. If so, they must be replaced with new ones, as they can't be repaired.

☐ Carburetors not synchronized. Adjust them with a vacuum gauge set or manometer (Chapter 1).

☐ Engine oil viscosity too high. Using a heavier oil than that recommended in Chapter 1 can damage the oil pump or lubrication system and cause drag on the engine.

☐ Brakes dragging. Usually caused by debris which has entered the brake piston sealing boot, or from a warped disc or bent axle. Repair as necessary (Chapter 6).

2 Poor running at low speed (continued)

Compression low

☐ Spark plug loose. Remove the plug and inspect the threads. Reinstall and tighten to the specified torque (Chapter 1).

☐ Cylinder head not sufficiently tightened down. If the cylinder head is suspected of being loose, then there's a chance that the gasket and head are damaged if the problem has persisted for any length of time. The head bolts should be tightened to the proper torque in the correct sequence (Chapter 2).

☐ Improper valve clearance. This means that the valve is not closing completely and compression pressure is leaking past the valve. Check and adjust the valve clearances (Chapter 1).

☐ Cylinder and/or piston worn. Excessive wear will cause compression pressure to leak past the rings. This is usually accompanied by worn rings as well. A top end overhaul is necessary (Chapter 2).

☐ Piston rings worn, weak, broken, or sticking. Broken or sticking piston rings usually indicate a lubrication or carburetion problem that causes excess carbon deposits or seizures to form on the pistons and rings. Top end overhaul is necessary (Chapter 2).

☐ Piston ring-to-groove clearance excessive. This is caused by excessive wear of the piston ring lands. Piston replacement is necessary (Chapter 2).

☐ Cylinder head gasket damaged. If the head is allowed to become loose, or if excessive carbon build-up on the piston crown and combustion chamber causes extremely high compression, the head gasket may leak. Retorquing the head is not always sufficient to restore the seal, so gasket replacement is necessary (Chapter 2).

☐ Cylinder head warped. This is caused by overheating or improperly tightened head bolts. Machine shop resurfacing or head replacement is necessary (Chapter 2).

☐ Valve spring broken or weak. Caused by component failure or wear; the spring(s) must be replaced (Chapter 2).

☐ Valve not seating properly. This is caused by a bent valve (from over-revving or improper valve adjustment), burned valve or seat (improper carburetion) or an accumulation of carbon deposits on the seat (from carburetion, lubrication problems). The valves must be cleaned and/or replaced and the seats serviced if possible (Chapter 2).

3 Poor running or no power at high speed

Firing incorrect

☐ Air filter restricted. Clean or replace filter (Chapter 1).

☐ Spark plug fouled, defective or worn out. See Chapter 1 for spark plug maintenance.

☐ Spark plug cap or secondary (HT) wiring defective. See Chapters 1 and 4 for details of the ignition system.

☐ Spark plug cap not in good contact. See Chapter 4.

☐ Incorrect spark plug. Wrong type, heat range or cap configuration. Check and install correct plugs listed in Chapter 1. A cold plug or one with a recessed firing electrode will not operate at low speeds without fouling.

☐ IC igniter defective. See Chapter 4.

☐ Ignition coil(s) defective. See Chapter 4.

Fuel/air mixture incorrect

☐ Main jet clogged. Dirt, water or other contaminants can clog the main jets. Clean the fuel tap filter, the float bowl area, and the jets and carburetor orifices (Chapter 3).

☐ Main jet wrong size. The standard jetting is for sea level atmospheric pressure and oxygen content.

☐ Throttle shaft-to-carburetor body clearance excessive. Refer to Chapter 3 for inspection and part replacement procedures.

☐ Air bleed holes clogged. Remove and overhaul carburetors (Chapter 3).

☐ Air cleaner clogged, poorly sealed, or missing.

☐ Air cleaner-to-carburetor boot poorly sealed. Look for cracks, holes or loose clamps, and replace or repair defective parts.

☐ Fuel level too high or too low. Adjust the float(s) (Chapter 3).

☐ Fuel tank air vent obstructed. Make sure the air vent passage in the filler cap is open.

☐ Carburetor intake manifolds loose. Check for cracks, breaks, tears or loose clamps or bolts. Repair or replace the rubber boots (Chapter 2).

☐ Fuel tap clogged. Remove the tap and clean it and the filter (Chapter 1).

☐ Fuel line clogged. Pull the fuel line loose and carefully blow through it.

Knocking or pinging

☐ Carbon build-up in combustion chamber. Use of a fuel additive that will dissolve the adhesive bonding the carbon particles to the crown and chamber is the easiest way to remove the build-up. Otherwise, the cylinder head will have to be removed and decarbonized (Chapter 2).

☐ Incorrect or poor quality fuel. Old or improper grades of fuel can cause detonation. This causes the piston to rattle, thus the knocking or pinging sound. Drain old fuel and always use the recommended fuel grade.

☐ Spark plug heat range incorrect. Uncontrolled detonation indicates the plug heat range is too hot. The plug in effect becomes a glow plug, raising cylinder temperatures. Install the proper heat range plug (Chapter 1).

☐ Improper air/fuel mixture. This will cause the cylinder to run hot, which leads to detonation. Clogged jets or an air leak can cause this imbalance. See Chapter 3.

Miscellaneous causes

☐ Throttle valve doesn't open fully. Adjust the cable slack (Chapter 1).

☐ Clutch slipping. On cable-operated clutches, caused by a cable that is improperly adjusted, snagging or damaged. On all models, may be caused by loose or worn clutch components. Refer to Chapters 1 and 2 for cable adjustment and clutch overhaul procedures.

☐ Timing not advancing.

☐ Engine oil viscosity too high. Using a heavier oil than the one recommended in Chapter 1 can damage the oil pump or lubrication system and cause drag on the engine.

☐ Brakes dragging. Usually caused by debris which has entered the brake piston sealing boot, or from a warped disc or bent axle. Repair as necessary.

3 Poor running or no power at high speed (continued)

Compression low

☐ Spark plug loose. Remove the plug and inspect the threads. Reinstall and tighten to the specified torque (Chapter 1).

☐ Cylinder head not sufficiently tightened down. If the cylinder head is suspected of being loose, then there's a chance that the gasket and head are damaged if the problem has persisted for any length of time. The head bolts should be tightened to the proper torque in the correct sequence (Chapter 2).

☐ Improper valve clearance. This means that the valve is not closing completely and compression pressure is leaking past the valve. Check and adjust the valve clearances (Chapter 1).

☐ Cylinder and/or piston worn. Excessive wear will cause compression pressure to leak past the rings. This is usually accompanied by worn rings as well. A top end overhaul is necessary (Chapter 2).

☐ Piston rings worn, weak, broken, or sticking. Broken or sticking piston rings usually indicate a lubrication or carburetion problem that causes excess carbon deposits or seizures to form on the pistons and rings. Top end overhaul is necessary (Chapter 2).

☐ Piston ring-to-groove clearance excessive. This is caused by excessive wear of the piston ring lands. Piston replacement is necessary (Chapter 2).

☐ Cylinder head gasket damaged. If the head is allowed to become loose, or if excessive carbon build-up on the piston crown and combustion chamber causes extremely high compression, the head gasket may leak. Retorquing the head is not always sufficient to restore the seal, so gasket replacement is necessary (Chapter 2).

☐ Cylinder head warped. This is caused by overheating or improperly tightened head bolts. Machine shop resurfacing or head replacement is necessary (Chapter 2).

☐ Valve spring broken or weak. Caused by component failure or wear; the spring(s) must be replaced (Chapter 2).

☐ Valve not seating properly. This is caused by a bent valve (from over-revving or improper valve adjustment), burned valve or seat (improper carburetion) or an accumulation of carbon deposits on the seat (from carburetion, lubrication problems). The valves must be cleaned and/or replaced and the seats serviced if possible (Chapter 2).

4 Overheating

Engine overheats

☐ Engine oil level low. Check and add oil (Chapter 1).

☐ Wrong type of oil. If you're not sure what type of oil is in the engine, drain it and fill with the correct type (Chapter 1).

☐ Air leak at carburetor intake boots. Check and tighten or replace as necessary (Chapter 3).

☐ Float level low. Check and adjust if necessary (Chapter 3).

☐ Worn oil pump or clogged oil passages. Check oil pressure (Chapter 2). Replace pump or clean passages as necessary.

☐ Carbon build-up in combustion chambers. Use of a fuel additive that will dissolve the adhesive bonding the carbon particles to the piston crowns and chambers is the easiest way to remove the build-up. Otherwise, the cylinder head will have to be removed and decarbonized (Chapter 2).

Firing incorrect

☐ Spark plug fouled, defective or worn out. See Chapter 1 for spark plug maintenance.

☐ Incorrect spark plug.

☐ Faulty ignition coil(s) (Chapter 4).

Fuel/air mixture incorrect

☐ Main jet clogged. Dirt, water and other contaminants can clog the main jets. Clean the fuel tap filter, the float bowl area and the jets and carburetor orifices (Chapter 3).

☐ Main jet wrong size. The standard jetting is for sea level atmospheric pressure and oxygen content.

☐ Air cleaner poorly sealed or missing.

☐ Air cleaner-to-carburetor boot poorly sealed. Look for cracks, holes or loose clamps and replace or repair.

☐ Fuel level too low. Adjust the float(s) (Chapter 3).

☐ Fuel tank air vent obstructed. Make sure that the air vent passage in the filler cap is open.

☐ Carburetor intake manifolds loose. Check for cracks, breaks, tears or loose clamps or bolts. Repair or replace the rubber boots (Chapter 2).

Compression too high

☐ Carbon build-up in combustion chamber. Use of a fuel additive that will dissolve the adhesive bonding the carbon particles to the piston crown and chamber is the easiest way to remove the build-up. Otherwise, the cylinder head will have to be removed and decarbonized (Chapter 2).

☐ Improperly machined head surface or installation of incorrect gasket during engine assembly. Check Specifications (Chapter 2).

Engine load excessive

☐ Clutch slipping. On cable clutches, can be caused by an out of adjustment or snagging cable. On all models, can be caused by damaged, loose or worn clutch components. Refer to Chapters 1 and 2 for adjustment and overhaul procedures.

☐ Engine oil level too high. The addition of too much oil will cause pressurization of the crankcase and inefficient engine operation. Check Specifications and drain to proper level (Chapter 1).

☐ Engine oil viscosity too high. Using a heavier oil than the one recommended in Chapter 1 can damage the oil pump or lubrication system as well as cause drag on the engine.

☐ Brakes dragging. Usually caused by debris which has entered the brake piston sealing boot, or from a warped disc or bent axle. Repair as necessary.

Lubrication inadequate

☐ Engine oil level too low. Friction caused by intermittent lack of lubrication or from oil that is "overworked" can cause overheating. The oil provides a definite cooling function in the engine. Check the oil level (Chapter 1).

☐ Poor quality engine oil or incorrect viscosity or type. Oil is rated not only according to viscosity but also according to type. Some oils are not rated high enough for use in this engine. Check the Specifications section and change to the correct oil (Chapter 1).

Miscellaneous causes

☐ Modification to exhaust system. Most aftermarket exhaust systems cause the engine to run leaner, which make them run hotter. When installing an accessory exhaust system, always rejet the carburetors.

5 Clutch problems

Clutch slipping

- ☐ No clutch lever play (cable clutch only). Adjust clutch lever free play according to the procedure in Chapter 1.
- ☐ Friction plates worn or warped. Overhaul the clutch assembly (Chapter 2).
- ☐ Steel plates worn or warped (Chapter 2).
- ☐ Clutch springs broken or weak. Old or heat-damaged (from slipping clutch) springs should be replaced with new ones (Chapter 2).
- ☐ Worn or warped clutch plates. Replace (Chapter 2).
- ☐ Clutch inner cable hanging up (cable clutch models). Caused by a frayed inner cable or kinked outer cable. Replace the cable. repair of a frayed cable is not advised.
- ☐ Clutch release mechanism defective. Replace any defective parts (Chapter 2).
- ☐ Clutch hub or housing unevenly worn. This causes improper engagement of the discs. Replace the damaged or worn parts (Chapter 2).

Clutch not disengaging completely

- ☐ Clutch lever play excessive (cable clutch only). Adjust (Chapter 1).
- ☐ Worn master or slave cylinder (hydraulic clutch only). Inspect and overhaul or replace (Chapter 2).

- ☐ Clutch plates warped or damaged. This will cause clutch drag, which in turn will cause the machine to creep. Overhaul the clutch assembly (Chapter 2).
- ☐ Clutch spring tension uneven. Usually caused by a sagged or broken spring. Check and replace the springs (Chapter 2).
- ☐ Engine oil deteriorated. Old, thin, worn out oil will not provide proper lubrication for the discs, causing the clutch to drag. Replace the oil and filter (Chapter 1).
- ☐ Engine oil viscosity too high. Using a heavier oil than recommended in Chapter 1 can cause the plates to stick together, putting a drag on the engine. Change to the correct weight oil (Chapter 1).
- ☐ Clutch housing seized on shaft. Lack of lubrication, severe wear or damage can cause the housing to seize on the shaft. Overhaul of the clutch, and perhaps transmission, may be necessary to repair the damage (Chapter 2).
- ☐ Clutch release mechanism defective. Worn or damaged release mechanism parts can stick and fail to apply force to the pressure plate. Overhaul the clutch cover components (Chapter 2).
- ☐ Loose clutch hub nut. Causes housing and hub misalignment putting a drag on the engine. Engagement adjustment continually varies. Overhaul the clutch assembly (Chapter 2).

6 Gear shifting problems

Jumps out of gear

- ☐ Shift fork(s) worn. Overhaul the transmission (Chapter 2).
- ☐ Gear groove(s) worn. Overhaul the transmission (Chapter 2).
- ☐ Gear dogs or dog slots worn or damaged. The gears should be inspected and replaced. No attempt should be made to service the worn parts.

Overshifts

- ☐ Pawl spring weak or broken (Chapter 2).
- ☐ Shift drum stopper lever not functioning (Chapter 2).
- ☐ Overshift limiter broken or distorted (Chapter 2).

Doesn't go into gear or lever doesn't return

- ☐ Clutch not disengaging. See Section 5.

- ☐ Shift fork(s) bent or seized. Often caused by dropping the machine or from lack of lubrication. Overhaul the transmission (Chapter 2).
- ☐ Gear(s) stuck on shaft. Most often caused by a lack of lubrication or excessive wear in transmission bearings and bushings. Overhaul the transmission (Chapter 2).
- ☐ Shift drum binding. Caused by lubrication failure or excessive wear. Replace the drum and bearings (Chapter 2).
- ☐ Shift lever return spring weak or broken (Chapter 2).
- ☐ Shift lever broken. Splines stripped out of lever or shaft, caused by allowing the lever to get loose or from dropping the machine. Replace necessary parts (Chapter 2).
- ☐ Shift mechanism pawl broken or worn. Full engagement and rotary movement of shift drum results. Replace shaft assembly (Chapter 2).
- ☐ Pawl spring broken. Allows pawl to "float", causing sporadic shift operation. Replace spring (Chapter 2).

7 Abnormal engine noise

Knocking or pinging

☐ Carbon build-up in combustion chamber. Use of a fuel additive that will dissolve the adhesive bonding the carbon particles to the piston crown and chamber is the easiest way to remove the build-up. Otherwise, the cylinder head will have to be removed and decarbonized (Chapter 2).

☐ Incorrect or poor quality fuel. Old or improper fuel can cause detonation. This causes the pistons to rattle, thus the knocking or pinging sound. Drain the old gas and always use the recommended grade fuel (Chapter 3).

☐ Spark plug heat range incorrect. Uncontrolled detonation indicates that the plug heat range is too hot. The plug in effect becomes a glow plug, raising cylinder temperatures. Install the proper heat range plug (Chapter 1).

☐ Improper air/fuel mixture. This will cause the cylinders to run hot and lead to detonation. Clogged jets or an air leak can cause this imbalance. See Chapter 3.

Piston slap or rattling

☐ Cylinder-to-piston clearance excessive. Caused by improper assembly. Inspect and overhaul top end parts (Chapter 2).

☐ Connecting rod bent. Caused by over-revving, trying to start a badly flooded engine or from ingesting a foreign object into the combustion chamber. Replace the damaged parts (Chapter 2).

☐ Piston pin or piston pin bore worn or seized from wear or lack of lubrication. Replace damaged parts (Chapter 2).

☐ Piston ring(s) worn, broken or sticking. Overhaul the top end (Chapter 2).

☐ Piston seizure damage. Usually from lack of lubrication or overheating. Replace the pistons and bore the cylinders, as necessary (Chapter 2).

☐ Connecting rod bearing and/or piston pin-end clearance excessive. Caused by excessive wear or lack of lubrication. Replace worn parts.

Valve noise

☐ Incorrect valve clearances. Adjust the clearances by referring to Chapter 1.

☐ Valve spring broken or weak. Check and replace weak valve springs (Chapter 2).

☐ Camshaft or cylinder head worn or damaged. Lack of lubrication at high rpm is usually the cause of damage. Insufficient oil or failure to change the oil at the recommended intervals are the chief causes. Since there are no replaceable bearings in the head, the head itself will have to be replaced if there is excessive wear or damage (Chapter 2).

Other noise

☐ Cylinder head gasket leaking.

☐ Exhaust pipe leaking at cylinder head connection. Caused by improper fit of pipe(s) or loose exhaust flange. All exhaust fasteners should be tightened evenly and carefully. Failure to do this will lead to a leak.

☐ Crankshaft runout excessive. Caused by a bent crankshaft (from over-revving) or damage from an upper cylinder component failure. Can also be attributed to dropping the machine on either of the crankshaft ends.

☐ Engine mounting bolts loose. Tighten all engine mount bolts to the specified torque (Chapter 2).

☐ Crankshaft bearings worn (Chapter 2).

☐ Camshaft chain tensioner defective. Replace according to the procedure in Chapter 2.

☐ Camshaft chain, sprockets or guides worn (Chapter 2).

8 Abnormal driveline noise

Clutch noise

☐ Clutch housing/friction plate clearance excessive (Chapter 2).

☐ Loose or damaged clutch pressure plate and/or bolts (Chapter 2).

Transmission noise

☐ Bearings worn. Also includes the possibility that the shafts are worn. Overhaul the transmission (Chapter 2).

☐ Gears worn or chipped (Chapter 2).

☐ Metal chips jammed in gear teeth. Probably pieces from a broken clutch, gear or shift mechanism that were picked up by the gears. This will cause early bearing failure (Chapter 2).

☐ Engine oil level too low. Causes a howl from transmission. Also affects engine power and clutch operation (Chapter 1).

Final drive noise

☐ Chain not adjusted properly (Chapter 1).

☐ Primary sprocket or rear sprocket loose. Tighten fasteners (Chapter 5).

☐ Sprocket(s) worn. Replace sprocket(s). (Chapter 4).

☐ Rear sprocket warped. Replace (Chapter 5).

☐ Wheel coupling worn. Replace coupling (Chapter 5).

9 Abnormal frame and suspension noise

Front end noise

- [ ] Low fluid level or improper viscosity oil in forks. This can sound like "spurting" and is usually accompanied by irregular fork action (Chapter 5).
- [ ] Spring weak or broken. Makes a clicking or scraping sound. Fork oil, when drained, will have a lot of metal particles in it (Chapter 5).
- [ ] Steering head bearings loose or damaged. Clicks when braking. Check and adjust or replace as necessary (Chapter 5).
- [ ] Fork clamps loose. Make sure all fork clamp pinch bolts are tight (Chapter 5).
- [ ] Fork tube bent. Good possibility if machine has been dropped. Replace tube with a new one (Chapter 5).
- [ ] Front axle or axle clamp bolt loose. Tighten them to the specified torque (Chapter 6).

Shock absorber noise

- [ ] Fluid level incorrect. Indicates a leak caused by defective seal. Shock will be covered with oil. Replace shock (Chapter 5).
- [ ] Defective shock absorber with internal damage. This is in the body of the shock and can't be remedied. The shock must be replaced with a new one (Chapter 5).

- [ ] Bent or damaged shock body. Replace the shock with a new one (Chapter 5).

Brake noise

- [ ] Squeal caused by pad shim not installed or positioned correctly (Chapter 6).
- [ ] Squeal caused by dust on brake pads. Usually found in combination with glazed pads. Clean using brake cleaning solvent (Chapter 6).
- [ ] Contamination of brake pads. Oil, brake fluid or dirt causing brake to chatter or squeal. Clean or replace pads (Chapter 6).
- [ ] Pads glazed. Caused by excessive heat from prolonged use or from contamination. Do not use sandpaper, emery cloth, carborundum cloth or any other abrasive to roughen the pad surfaces as abrasives will stay in the pad material and damage the disc. A very fine flat file can be used, but pad replacement is suggested as a cure (Chapter 6).
- [ ] Disc warped. Can cause a chattering, clicking or intermittent squeal. Usually accompanied by a pulsating lever and uneven braking. Replace the disc (Chapter 6).
- [ ] Loose or worn wheel bearings. Check and replace as needed (Chapter 6).

10 Oil pressure indicator light comes on

Electrical system

- [ ] Oil pressure switch defective. Check the switch according to the procedure in Chapter 8. Replace it if it is defective.
- [ ] Oil pressure indicator light circuit defective. Check for pinched, shorted, disconnected or damaged wiring (Chapter 8).

Engine lubrication system

- [ ] Engine oil pump defective (Chapter 2).

- [ ] Engine oil level low. Inspect for leak or other problem causing low oil level and add recommended oil (Chapters 1 and 2).
- [ ] Engine oil viscosity too low. Very old, thin oil or an improper weight of oil used in the engine. Change to correct oil (Chapter 1).
- [ ] Camshaft or journals worn. Excessive wear causing drop in oil pressure. Replace cam and/or cylinder head. Abnormal wear could be caused by oil starvation at high rpm from low oil level or improper weight of type of oil (Chapter 1).
- [ ] Crankshaft and/or bearings worn. Same problems as paragraph 4. Check and replace crankshaft and/or bearings (Chapter 2).

11 Excessive exhaust smoke

White smoke

- [ ] Piston oil ring worn. The ring may be broken or damaged, causing oil from the crankcase to be pulled past the piston into the combustion chamber. Replace the rings with new ones (Chapter 2).
- [ ] Cylinders worn, cracked, or scored. Caused by overheating or oil starvation. The cylinders will have to be rebored and new pistons installed.
- [ ] Valve oil seal damaged or worn. Replace oil seals with new ones (Chapter 2).
- [ ] Valve guide worn. Perform a complete valve job (Chapter 20).
- [ ] Engine oil level too high, which causes the oil to be forced past the rings. Drain oil to the proper level (Chapter 10).
- [ ] Head gasket broken between oil return and cylinder. Causes oil to be pulled into the combustion chamber. Replace the head gasket and check the head for warpage (Chapter 2).
- [ ] Abnormal crankcase pressurization, which forces oil past the rings. Clogged breather or hoses usually the cause (Chapter 3).

Black smoke

- [ ] Air cleaner clogged. Clean or replace the element (Chapter 1).
- [ ] Main jet too large or loose. Compare the jet size to the Specifications (Chapter 3).
- [ ] Choke stuck, causing fuel to be pulled through choke circuit (Chapter 3).
- [ ] Fuel level too high. Check and adjust the float level as necessary (Chapter 3).
- [ ] Inlet needle held off needle seat. Clean the float bowls and fuel line and replace the needles and seats if necessary (Chapter 3).
- [ ] Brown smoke
- [ ] Main jet too small or clogged. Lean condition caused by wrong size main jet or by a restricted orifice. Clean float bowl and jets and compare jet size to Specifications (Chapter 3).
- [ ] Fuel flow insufficient. Fuel inlet needle valve stuck closed due to chemical reaction with old fuel. Float level incorrect. Restricted fuel line. Clean line and float bowl and adjust floats if necessary.
- [ ] Carburetor intake manifolds loose (Chapter 3).
- [ ] Air cleaner poorly sealed or not installed (Chapter 1).

12 Poor handling or stability

Handlebar hard to turn

☐ Steering stem locknut too tight (Chapter 5).
☐ Bearings damaged. Roughness can be felt as the bars are turned from side-to-side. Replace bearings and races (Chapter 5).
☐ Races dented or worn. Denting results from wear in only one position (e.g., straight ahead), from a collision or hitting a pothole or from dropping the machine. Replace races and bearings (Chapter 5).
☐ Steering stem lubrication inadequate. Causes are grease getting hard from age or being washed out by high pressure car washes. Disassemble steering head and repack bearings (Chapter 5).
☐ Steering stem bent. Caused by a collision, hitting a pothole or by dropping the machine. Replace damaged part. Don't try to straighten the steering stem (Chapter 5).
☐ Front tire air pressure too low (Chapter 1).

Handlebar shakes or vibrates excessively

☐ Tires worn or out of balance (Chapter 6).
☐ Swingarm bearings worn. Replace worn bearings by referring to Chapter 6.
☐ Rim(s) warped or damaged. Inspect wheels for runout (Chapter 6).
☐ Wheel bearings worn. Worn front or rear wheel bearings can cause poor tracking. Worn front bearings will cause wobble (Chapter 6).
☐ Handlebar clamp bolts loose (Chapter 5).
☐ Steering stem or fork clamps loose. Tighten them to the specified torque (Chapter 5).
☐ Motor mount bolts loose. Will cause excessive vibration with increased engine rpm (Chapter 2).

Handlebar pulls to one side

☐ Frame bent. Definitely suspect this if the machine has been dropped. May or may not be accompanied by cracking near the bend. Replace the frame (Chapter 5).
☐ Wheel out of alignment. Caused by improper location of axle spacers or from bent steering stem or frame (Chapter 5).
☐ Swingarm bent or twisted. Caused by age (metal fatigue) or impact damage. Replace the arm (Chapter 5).
☐ Steering stem bent. Caused by impact damage or by dropping the motorcycle. Replace the steering stem (Chapter 5).
☐ Fork leg bent. Disassemble the forks and replace the damaged parts (Chapter 6).
☐ Fork oil level uneven. Check and add or drain as necessary (Chapter 1).

Poor shock absorbing qualities

☐ Too hard:
Fork oil level excessive (Chapter 5).
Fork oil viscosity too high. Use a lighter oil (see the Specifications in Chapter 1).
Fork tube bent. Causes a harsh, sticking feeling (Chapter 5).
Shock shaft or body bent or damaged (Chapter 5).
Fork internal damage (Chapter 5).
Shock internal damage.
Tire pressure too high (Chapters 1 and 6).
☐ Too soft:
Fork or shock oil insufficient and/or leaking (Chapter 5).
Fork oil level too low (Chapter 5).
Fork oil viscosity too light (Chapter 5).
Fork springs weak or broken (Chapter 5).

13 Braking problems

Brakes are spongy, don't hold

☐ Air in brake line. Caused by inattention to master cylinder fluid level or by leakage. Locate problem and bleed brakes (Chapter 6).
☐ Pad or disc worn (Chapters 1 and 6).
☐ Brake fluid leak. See paragraph 1.
☐ Contaminated pads. Caused by contamination with oil, grease, brake fluid, etc. Clean or replace pads. Clean disc thoroughly with brake cleaner (Chapter 6).
☐ Brake fluid deteriorated. Fluid is old or contaminated. Drain system, replenish with new fluid and bleed the system (Chapter 6).
☐ Master cylinder internal parts worn or damaged causing fluid to bypass (Chapter 6).
☐ Master cylinder bore scratched by foreign material or broken spring. Repair or replace master cylinder (Chapter 6).
☐ Disc warped. Replace disc (Chapter 6).

Brake lever or pedal pulsates

☐ Disc warped. Replace disc (Chapter 6).
☐ Axle bent. Replace axle (Chapter 5).
☐ Brake caliper bolts loose (Chapter 6).

☐ Brake caliper shafts damaged or sticking, causing caliper to bind. Lube the shafts or replace them if they are corroded or bent (Chapter 6).
☐ Wheel warped or otherwise damaged (Chapter 6).
☐ Wheel bearings damaged or worn (Chapter 6).

Brakes drag

☐ Master cylinder piston seized. Caused by wear or damage to piston or cylinder bore (Chapter 6).
☐ Lever balky or stuck. Check pivot and lubricate (Chapter 6).
☐ Brake caliper binds. Caused by inadequate lubrication or damage to caliper shafts (Chapter 6).
☐ Brake caliper piston seized in bore. Caused by wear or ingestion of dirt past deteriorated seal (Chapter 6).
☐ Brake pad damaged. Pad material separated from backing plate. Usually caused by faulty manufacturing process or from contact with chemicals. Replace pads (Chapter 6).
☐ Pads improperly installed (Chapter 6).
☐ Rear brake pedal free pay insufficient (Chapter 1).

14 Electrical problems

Battery dead or weak

- [ ] Battery faulty. Caused by sulfated plates which are shorted through sedimentation or low electrolyte level. Also, broken battery terminal making only occasional contact (Chapter 8).
- [ ] Battery cables making poor contact (Chapter 8).
- [ ] Load excessive. Caused by addition of high wattage lights or other electrical accessories.
- [ ] Ignition switch defective. Switch either grounds internally or fails to shut off system. Replace the switch (Chapter 8).
- [ ] Regulator/rectifier defective (Chapter 8).
- [ ] Stator coil open or shorted (Chapter 8).
- [ ] Wiring faulty. Wiring grounded or connections loose in ignition, charging or lighting circuits (Chapter 8).

Battery overcharged

- [ ] Regulator/rectifier defective. Overcharging is noticed when battery gets excessively warm or boils over (Chapter 8).
- [ ] Battery defective. replace battery with a new one (Chapter 8).
- [ ] Battery amperage too low, wrong type or size. Install manufacturer's specified amp-hour battery to handle charging load (Chapter 8).

Checking engine compression

● Low compression will result in exhaust smoke, heavy oil consumption, poor starting and poor performance. A compression test will provide useful information about an engine's condition and if performed regularly, can give warning of trouble before any other symptoms become apparent.

● A compression gauge will be required, along with an adapter to suit the spark plug hole thread size. Note that the screw-in type gauge/adapter set up is preferable to the rubber cone type.

● Before carrying out the test, first check the valve clearances as described in Chapter 1.

1 Run the engine until it reaches normal operating temperature, then stop it and remove the spark plug(s), taking care not to scald your hands on the hot components.

2 Install the gauge adapter and compression gauge in No. 1 cylinder spark plug hole **(see illustration 1)**.

Screw the compression gauge adapter into the spark plug hole, then screw the gauge into the adapter

3 On kickstart-equipped motorcycles, make sure the ignition switch is OFF, then open the throttle fully and kick the engine over a couple of times until the gauge reading stabilises.

4 On motorcycles with electric start only, the procedure will differ depending on the nature of the ignition system. Flick the engine kill switch (engine stop switch) to OFF and turn the ignition switch ON; open the throttle fully and crank the engine over on the starter motor for a couple of revolutions until the gauge reading stabilises. If the starter will not operate with the kill switch OFF, turn the ignition switch OFF and refer to the next paragraph.

5 Install the spark plugs back into their suppressor caps and arrange the plug electrodes so that their metal bodies are earthed (grounded) against the cylinder head; this is essential to prevent damage to the ignition system as the engine is spun over **(see illustration 2)**. Position the plugs well

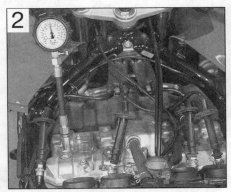

All spark plugs must be earthed (grounded) against the cylinder head

away from the plug holes otherwise there is a risk of atomised fuel escaping from the combustion chambers and igniting. As a safety precaution, cover the top of the valve cover with rag. Now turn the ignition switch ON and kill switch ON, open the throttle fully and crank the engine over on the starter motor for a couple of revolutions until the gauge reading stabilises.

6 After one or two revolutions the pressure should build up to a maximum figure and then stabilise. Take a note of this reading and on multi-cylinder engines repeat the test on the remaining cylinders.

7 The correct pressures are given in Chapter 2 Specifications. If the results fall within the specified range and on multi-cylinder engines all are relatively equal, the engine is in good condition. If there is a marked difference between the readings, or if the readings are lower than specified, inspection of the top-end components will be required.

8 Low compression pressure may be due to worn cylinder bores, pistons or rings, failure of the cylinder head gasket, worn valve seals, or poor valve seating.

9 To distinguish between cylinder/piston wear and valve leakage, pour a small quantity of oil into the bore to temporarily seal the piston rings, then repeat the compression tests **(see illustration 3)**. If the readings show

Bores can be temporarily sealed with a squirt of motor oil

a noticeable increase in pressure this confirms that the cylinder bore, piston, or rings are worn. If, however, no change is indicated, the cylinder head gasket or valves should be examined.

10 High compression pressure indicates excessive carbon build-up in the combustion chamber and on the piston crown. If this is the case the cylinder head should be removed and the deposits removed. Note that excessive carbon build-up is less likely with the used on modern fuels.

Checking battery open-circuit voltage

 Warning: The gases produced by the battery are explosive - never smoke or create any sparks in the vicinity of the battery. Never allow the electrolyte to contact your skin or clothing - if it does, wash it off and seek immediate medical attention.

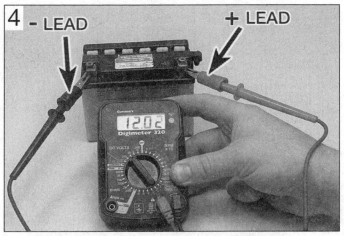

Measuring open-circuit battery voltage

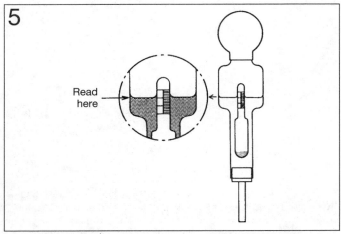

Float-type hydrometer for measuring battery specific gravity

● Before any electrical fault is investigated the battery should be checked.

● You'll need a dc voltmeter or multimeter to check battery voltage. Check that the leads are inserted in the correct terminals on the meter, red lead to positive (+ve), black lead to negative (-ve). Incorrect connections can damage the meter.

● A sound fully-charged 12 volt battery should produce between 12.3 and 12.6 volts across its terminals (12.8 volts for a maintenance-free battery). On machines with a 6 volt battery, voltage should be between 6.1 and 6.3 volts.

1 Set a multimeter to the 0 to 20 volts dc range and connect its probes across the battery terminals. Connect the meter's positive (+ve) probe, usually red, to the battery positive (+ve) terminal, followed by the meter's negative (-ve) probe, usually black, to the battery negative terminal (-ve) **(see illustration 4)**.

2 If battery voltage is low (below 10 volts on a 12 volt battery or below 4 volts on a six volt battery), charge the battery and test the voltage again. If the battery repeatedly goes flat, investigate the motorcycle's charging system.

Checking battery specific gravity (SG)

⚠ *Warning: The gases produced by the battery are explosive - never smoke or create any sparks in the vicinity of the battery. Never allow the electrolyte to contact your skin or clothing - if it does, wash it off and seek immediate medical attention.*

● The specific gravity check gives an indication of a battery's state of charge.

● A hydrometer is used for measuring specific gravity. Make sure you purchase one which has a small enough hose to insert in the aperture of a motorcycle battery.

● Specific gravity is simply a measure of the electrolyte's density compared with that of water. Water has an SG of 1.000 and fully-charged battery electrolyte is about 26% heavier, at 1.260.

● Specific gravity checks are not possible on maintenance-free batteries. Testing the open-circuit voltage is the only means of determining their state of charge.

1 To measure SG, remove the battery from the motorcycle and remove the first cell cap. Draw

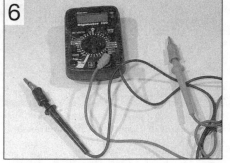

Digital multimeter can be used for all electrical tests

some electrolyte into the hydrometer and note the reading **(see illustration 5)**. Return the electrolyte to the cell and install the cap.

2 The reading should be in the region of 1.260 to 1.280. If SG is below 1.200 the battery needs charging. Note that SG will vary with temperature; it should be measured at 20°C (68°F). Add 0.007 to the reading for every 10°C above 20°C, and subtract 0.007 from the reading for every 10°C below 20°C. Add 0.004 to the reading for every 10°F above 68°F, and subtract 0.004 from the reading for every 10°F below 68°F.

3 When the check is complete, rinse the hydrometer thoroughly with clean water.

Checking for continuity

● The term continuity describes the uninterrupted flow of electricity through an electrical circuit. A continuity check will determine whether an **open-circuit** situation exists.

● Continuity can be checked with an ohmmeter, multimeter, continuity tester or battery and bulb test circuit **(see illustrations 6, 7 and 8)**.

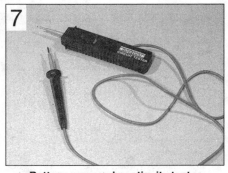

Battery-powered continuity tester

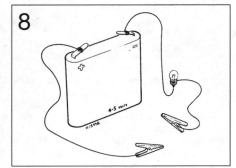

Battery and bulb test circuit

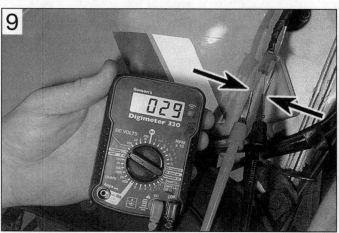

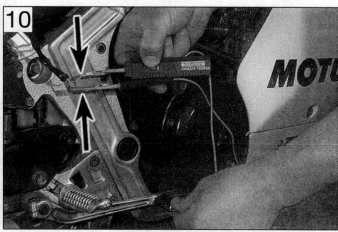

Continuity check of front brake light switch using a meter - note split pins used to access connector terminals

Continuity check of rear brake light switch using a continuity tester

● All of these instruments are self-powered by a battery, therefore the checks are made with the ignition OFF.

● As a safety precaution, always disconnect the battery negative (-ve) lead before making checks, particularly if ignition switch checks are being made.

● If using a meter, select the appropriate ohms scale and check that the meter reads infinity (∞). Touch the meter probes together and check that meter reads zero; where necessary adjust the meter so that it reads zero.

● After using a meter, always switch it OFF to conserve its battery.

Switch checks

1 If a switch is at fault, trace its wiring up to the wiring connectors. Separate the wire connectors and inspect them for security and condition. A build-up of dirt or corrosion here will most likely be the cause of the problem - clean up and apply a water dispersant such as WD40.

2 If using a test meter, set the meter to the ohms x 10 scale and connect its probes across the wires from the switch **(see illustration 9)**. Simple ON/OFF type switches, such as brake light switches, only have two

wires whereas combination switches, like the ignition switch, have many internal links. Study the wiring diagram to ensure that you are connecting across the correct pair of wires. Continuity (low or no measurable resistance - 0 ohms) should be indicated with the switch ON and no continuity (high resistance) with it OFF.

3 Note that the polarity of the test probes doesn't matter for continuity checks, although care should be taken to follow specific test procedures if a diode or solid-state component is being checked.

4 A continuity tester or battery and bulb circuit can be used in the same way. Connect its probes as described above **(see illustration 10)**. The light should come on to indicate continuity in the ON switch position, but should extinguish in the OFF position.

Wiring checks

● Many electrical faults are caused by damaged wiring, often due to incorrect routing or chaffing on frame components.

● Loose, wet or corroded wire connectors can also be the cause of electrical problems, especially in exposed locations.

1 A continuity check can be made on a single length of wire by disconnecting it at each end

and connecting a meter or continuity tester across both ends of the wire **(see illustration 11)**.

2 Continuity (low or no resistance - 0 ohms) should be indicated if the wire is good. If no continuity (high resistance) is shown, suspect a broken wire.

Checking for voltage

● A voltage check can determine whether current is reaching a component.

● Voltage can be checked with a dc voltmeter, multimeter set on the dc volts scale, test light or buzzer **(see illustrations 12 and 13)**. A meter has the advantage of being able to measure actual voltage.

● When using a meter, check that its leads are inserted in the correct terminals on the meter, red to positive (+ve), black to negative (-ve). Incorrect connections can damage the meter.

● A voltmeter (or multimeter set to the dc volts scale) should always be connected in parallel (across the load). Connecting it in series will destroy the meter.

● Voltage checks are made with the ignition ON.

Continuity check of front brake light switch sub-harness

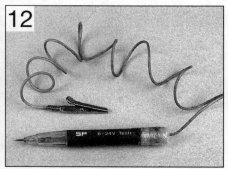

A simple test light can be used for voltage checks

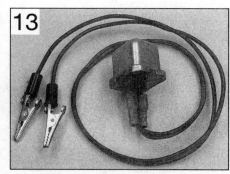

A buzzer is useful for voltage checks

Checking for voltage at the rear brake light power supply wire using a meter . . .

1 First identify the relevant wiring circuit by referring to the wiring diagram at the end of this manual. If other electrical components share the same power supply (ie are fed from the same fuse), take note whether they are working correctly - this is useful information in deciding where to start checking the circuit.

2 If using a meter, check first that the meter leads are plugged into the correct terminals on the meter (see above). Set the meter to the dc volts function, at a range suitable for the battery voltage. Connect the meter red probe (+ve) to the power supply wire and the black probe to a good metal earth (ground) on the motorcycle's frame or directly to the battery negative (-ve) terminal **(see illustration 14)**. Battery voltage should be shown on the meter

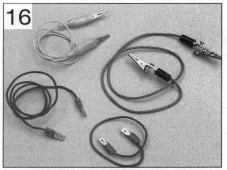

A selection of jumper wires for making earth (ground) checks

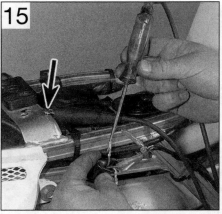

. . . or a test light - note the earth connection to the frame (arrow)

with the ignition switched ON.

3 If using a test light or buzzer, connect its positive (+ve) probe to the power supply terminal and its negative (-ve) probe to a good earth (ground) on the motorcycle's frame or directly to the battery negative (-ve) terminal **(see illustration 15)**. With the ignition ON, the test light should illuminate or the buzzer sound.

4 If no voltage is indicated, work back towards the fuse continuing to check for voltage. When you reach a point where there is voltage, you know the problem lies between that point and your last check point.

Checking the earth (ground)

● Earth connections are made either directly to the engine or frame (such as sensors, neutral switch etc. which only have a positive feed) or by a separate wire into the earth circuit of the wiring harness. Alternatively a short earth wire is sometimes run directly from the component to the motorcycle's frame.

● Corrosion is often the cause of a poor earth connection.

● If total failure is experienced, check the security of the main earth lead from the negative (-ve) terminal of the battery and also the main earth (ground) point on the wiring harness. If corroded, dismantle the connection and clean all surfaces back to bare metal.

1 To check the earth on a component, use an insulated jumper wire to temporarily bypass its earth connection **(see illustration 16)**. Connect one end of the jumper wire between the earth terminal or metal body of the component and the other end to the motorcycle's frame.

2 If the circuit works with the jumper wire installed, the original earth circuit is faulty. Check the wiring for open-circuits or poor connections. Clean up direct earth connections, removing all traces of corrosion and remake the joint. Apply petroleum jelly to the joint to prevent future corrosion.

Tracing a short-circuit

● A short-circuit occurs where current shorts to earth (ground) bypassing the circuit components. This usually results in a blown fuse.

● A short-circuit is most likely to occur where the insulation has worn through due to wiring chafing on a component, allowing a direct path to earth (ground) on the frame.

1 Remove any bodypanels necessary to access the circuit wiring.

2 Check that all electrical switches in the circuit are OFF, then remove the circuit fuse and connect a test light, buzzer or voltmeter (set to the dc scale) across the fuse terminals. No voltage should be shown.

3 Move the wiring from side to side whilst observing the test light or meter. When the test light comes on, buzzer sounds or meter shows voltage, you have found the cause of the short. It will usually shown up as damaged or burned insulation.

4 Note that the same test can be performed on each component in the circuit, even the switch.

A

ABS (Anti-lock braking system) A system, usually electronically controlled, that senses incipient wheel lockup during braking and relieves hydraulic pressure at wheel which is about to skid.

Aftermarket Components suitable for the motorcycle, but not produced by the motorcycle manufacturer.

Allen key A hexagonal wrench which fits into a recessed hexagonal hole.

Alternating current (ac) Current produced by an alternator. Requires converting to direct current by a rectifier for charging purposes.

Alternator Converts mechanical energy from the engine into electrical energy to charge the battery and power the electrical system.

Ampere (amp) A unit of measurement for the flow of electrical current. Current = Volts ˆ Ohms.

Ampere-hour (Ah) Measure of battery capacity.

Angle-tightening A torque expressed in degrees. Often follows a conventional tightening torque for cylinder head or main bearing fasteners **(see illustration)**.

Antifreeze A substance (usually ethylene glycol) mixed with water, and added to the cooling

Angle-tightening cylinder head bolts

system, to prevent freezing of the coolant in winter. Antifreeze also contains chemicals to inhibit corrosion and the formation of rust and other deposits that would tend to clog the radiator and coolant passages and reduce cooling efficiency.

Anti-dive System attached to the fork lower leg (slider) to prevent fork dive when braking hard.

Anti-seize compound A coating that reduces the risk of seizing on fasteners that are subjected to high temperatures, such as exhaust clamp bolts and nuts.

API American Petroleum Institute. A quality standard for 4-stroke motor oils.

Asbestos A natural fibrous mineral with great heat resistance, commonly used in the composition of brake friction materials. Asbestos is a health hazard and the dust created by brake systems should never be inhaled or ingested.

ATF Automatic Transmission Fluid. Often used in front forks.

ATU Automatic Timing Unit. Mechanical device for advancing the ignition timing on early engines.

ATV All Terrain Vehicle. Often called a Quad.

Axial play Side-to-side movement.

Axle A shaft on which a wheel revolves. Also known as a spindle.

B

Backlash The amount of movement between meshed components when one component is held still. Usually applies to gear teeth.

Ball bearing A bearing consisting of a hardened inner and outer race with hardened steel balls between the two races.

Bearings Used between two working surfaces to prevent wear of the components and a build-up of heat. Four types of bearing are commonly used on motorcycles: plain shell bearings, ball bearings, tapered roller bearings and needle roller bearings.

Bevel gears Used to turn the drive through 90°. Typical applications are shaft final drive and camshaft drive **(see illustration)**.

Bevel gears are used to turn the drive through 90°

BHP Brake Horsepower. The British measurement for engine power output. Power output is now usually expressed in kilowatts (kW).

Bias-belted tyre Similar construction to radial tyre, but with outer belt running at an angle to the wheel rim.

Big-end bearing The bearing in the end of the connecting rod that's attached to the crankshaft.

Bleeding The process of removing air from an hydraulic system via a bleed nipple or bleed screw.

Bottom-end A description of an engine's crankcase components and all components contained there-in.

BTDC Before Top Dead Centre in terms of piston position. Ignition timing is often expressed in terms of degrees or millimetres BTDC.

Bush A cylindrical metal or rubber component used between two moving parts.

Burr Rough edge left on a component after machining or as a result of excessive wear.

C

Cam chain The chain which takes drive from the crankshaft to the camshaft(s).

Canister The main component in an evaporative emission control system (California market only); contains activated charcoal granules to trap vapours from the fuel system rather than allowing them to vent to the atmosphere.

Castellated Resembling the parapets along the top of a castle wall. For example, a castellated wheel axle or spindle nut.

Catalytic converter A device in the exhaust system of some machines which converts certain pollutants in the exhaust gases into less harmful substances.

Charging system Description of the components which charge the battery, ie the alternator, rectifer and regulator.

Circlip A ring-shaped clip used to prevent endwise movement of cylindrical parts and shafts. An internal circlip is installed in a groove in a housing; an external circlip fits into a groove on the outside of a cylindrical piece such as a shaft. Also known as a snap-ring.

Clearance The amount of space between two parts. For example, between a piston and a cylinder, between a bearing and a journal, etc.

Coil spring A spiral of elastic steel found in various sizes throughout a vehicle, for example as a springing medium in the suspension and in the valve train.

Compression Reduction in volume, and increase in pressure and temperature, of a gas, caused by squeezing it into a smaller space.

Compression damping Controls the speed the suspension compresses when hitting a bump.

Compression ratio The relationship between cylinder volume when the piston is at top dead centre and cylinder volume when the piston is at bottom dead centre.

Continuity The uninterrupted path in the flow of electricity. Little or no measurable resistance.

Continuity tester Self-powered bleeper or test light which indicates continuity.

Cp Candlepower. Bulb rating common found on US motorcycles.

Crossply tyre Tyre plies arranged in a criss-cross pattern. Usually four or six plies used, hence 4PR or 6PR in tyre size codes.

Cush drive Rubber damper segments fitted between the rear wheel and final drive sprocket to absorb transmission shocks **(see illustration)**.

Cush drive rubbers dampen out transmission shocks

D

Degree disc Calibrated disc for measuring piston position. Expressed in degrees.

Dial gauge Clock-type gauge with adapters for measuring runout and piston position. Expressed in mm or inches.

Diaphragm The rubber membrane in a master cylinder or carburettor which seals the upper chamber.

Diaphragm spring A single sprung plate often used in clutches.

Direct current (dc) Current produced by a dc generator.

Decarbonisation The process of removing carbon deposits - typically from the combustion chamber, valves and exhaust port/system.

Detonation Destructive and damaging explosion of fuel/air mixture in combustion chamber instead of controlled burning.

Diode An electrical valve which only allows current to flow in one direction. Commonly used in rectifiers and starter interlock systems.

Disc valve (or rotary valve) A induction system used on some two-stroke engines.

Double-overhead camshaft (DOHC) An engine that uses two overhead camshafts, one for the intake valves and one for the exhaust valves.

Drivebelt A toothed belt used to transmit drive to the rear wheel on some motorcycles. A drivebelt has also been used to drive the camshafts. Drivebelts are usually made of Kevlar.

Driveshaft Any shaft used to transmit motion. Commonly used when referring to the final driveshaft on shaft drive motorcycles.

E

Earth return The return path of an electrical circuit, utilising the motorcycle's frame.

ECU (Electronic Control Unit) A computer which controls (for instance) an ignition system, or an anti-lock braking system.

EGO Exhaust Gas Oxygen sensor. Sometimes called a Lambda sensor.

Electrolyte The fluid in a lead-acid battery.

EMS (Engine Management System) A computer controlled system which manages the fuel injection and the ignition systems in an integrated fashion.

Endfloat The amount of lengthways movement between two parts. As applied to a crankshaft, the distance that the crankshaft can move side-to-side in the crankcase.

Endless chain A chain having no joining link. Common use for cam chains and final drive chains.

EP (Extreme Pressure) Oil type used in locations where high loads are applied, such as between gear teeth.

Evaporative emission control system Describes a charcoal filled canister which stores fuel vapours from the tank rather than allowing them to vent to the atmosphere. Usually only fitted to California models and referred to as an EVAP system.

Expansion chamber Section of two-stroke engine exhaust system so designed to improve engine efficiency and boost power.

F

Feeler blade or gauge A thin strip or blade of hardened steel, ground to an exact thickness, used to check or measure clearances between parts.

Final drive Description of the drive from the transmission to the rear wheel. Usually by chain or shaft, but sometimes by belt.

Firing order The order in which the engine cylinders fire, or deliver their power strokes, beginning with the number one cylinder.

Flooding Term used to describe a high fuel level in the carburettor float chambers, leading to fuel overflow. Also refers to excess fuel in the combustion chamber due to incorrect starting technique.

Free length The no-load state of a component when measured. Clutch, valve and fork spring lengths are measured at rest, without any preload.

Freeplay The amount of travel before any action takes place. The looseness in a linkage, or an assembly of parts, between the initial application of force and actual movement. For example, the distance the rear brake pedal moves before the rear brake is actuated.

Fuel injection The fuel/air mixture is metered electronically and directed into the engine intake ports (indirect injection) or into the cylinders (direct injection). Sensors supply information on engine speed and conditions.

Fuel/air mixture The charge of fuel and air going into the engine. See **Stoichiometric ratio**.

Fuse An electrical device which protects a circuit against accidental overload. The typical fuse contains a soft piece of metal which is calibrated to melt at a predetermined current flow (expressed as amps) and break the circuit.

G

Gap The distance the spark must travel in jumping from the centre electrode to the side electrode in a spark plug. Also refers to the distance between the ignition rotor and the pickup coil in an electronic ignition system.

Gasket Any thin, soft material - usually cork, cardboard, asbestos or soft metal - installed between two metal surfaces to ensure a good seal. For instance, the cylinder head gasket seals the joint between the block and the cylinder head.

Gauge An instrument panel display used to monitor engine conditions. A gauge with a movable pointer on a dial or a fixed scale is an analogue gauge. A gauge with a numerical readout is called a digital gauge.

Gear ratios The drive ratio of a pair of gears in a gearbox, calculated on their number of teeth.

Glaze-busting see **Honing**

Grinding Process for renovating the valve face and valve seat contact area in the cylinder head.

Gudgeon pin The shaft which connects the connecting rod small-end with the piston. Often called a piston pin or wrist pin.

H

Helical gears Gear teeth are slightly curved and produce less gear noise that straight-cut gears. Often used for primary drives.

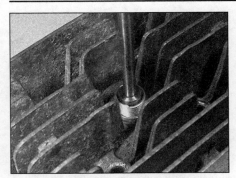

Installing a Helicoil thread insert in a cylinder head

Helicoil A thread insert repair system. Commonly used as a repair for stripped spark plug threads **(see illustration)**.

Honing A process used to break down the glaze on a cylinder bore (also called glaze-busting). Can also be carried out to roughen a rebored cylinder to aid ring bedding-in.

HT High Tension Description of the electrical circuit from the secondary winding of the ignition coil to the spark plug.

Hydraulic A liquid filled system used to transmit pressure from one component to another. Common uses on motorcycles are brakes and clutches.

Hydrometer An instrument for measuring the specific gravity of a lead-acid battery.

Hygroscopic Water absorbing. In motorcycle applications, braking efficiency will be reduced if DOT 3 or 4 hydraulic fluid absorbs water from the air - care must be taken to keep new brake fluid in tightly sealed containers.

I

lbf ft Pounds-force feet. An imperial unit of torque. Sometimes written as ft-lbs.

lbf in Pound-force inch. An imperial unit of torque, applied to components where a very low torque is required. Sometimes written as in-lbs.

IC Abbreviation for Integrated Circuit.

Ignition advance Means of increasing the timing of the spark at higher engine speeds. Done by mechanical means (ATU) on early engines or electronically by the ignition control unit on later engines.

Ignition timing The moment at which the spark plug fires, expressed in the number of crankshaft degrees before the piston reaches the top of its stroke, or in the number of millimetres before the piston reaches the top of its stroke.

Infinity (∞) Description of an open-circuit electrical state, where no continuity exists.

Inverted forks (upside down forks) The sliders or lower legs are held in the yokes and the fork tubes or stanchions are connected to the wheel axle (spindle). Less unsprung weight and stiffer construction than conventional forks.

J

JASO Quality standard for 2-stroke oils.

Joule The unit of electrical energy.

Journal The bearing surface of a shaft.

K

Kickstart Mechanical means of turning the engine over for starting purposes. Only usually fitted to mopeds, small capacity motorcycles and off-road motorcycles.

Kill switch Handebar-mounted switch for emergency ignition cut-out. Cuts the ignition circuit on all models, and additionally prevent starter motor operation on others.

km Symbol for kilometre.

kph Abbreviation for kilometres per hour.

L

Lambda (λ) sensor A sensor fitted in the exhaust system to measure the exhaust gas oxygen content (excess air factor).

Lapping see **Grinding**.

LCD Abbreviation for Liquid Crystal Display.

LED Abbreviation for Light Emitting Diode.

Liner A steel cylinder liner inserted in a aluminium alloy cylinder block.

Locknut A nut used to lock an adjustment nut, or other threaded component, in place.

Lockstops The lugs on the lower triple clamp (yoke) which abut those on the frame, preventing handlebar-to-fuel tank contact.

Lockwasher A form of washer designed to prevent an attaching nut from working loose.

LT Low Tension Description of the electrical circuit from the power supply to the primary winding of the ignition coil.

M

Main bearings The bearings between the crankshaft and crankcase.

Maintenance-free (MF) battery A sealed battery which cannot be topped up.

Manometer Mercury-filled calibrated tubes used to measure intake tract vacuum. Used to synchronise carburettors on multi-cylinder engines.

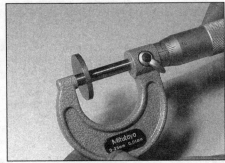

Tappet shims are measured with a micrometer

Micrometer A precision measuring instrument that measures component outside diameters **(see illustration)**.

MON (Motor Octane Number) A measure of a fuel's resistance to knock.

Monograde oil An oil with a single viscosity, eg SAE80W.

Monoshock A single suspension unit linking the swingarm or suspension linkage to the frame.

mph Abbreviation for miles per hour.

Multigrade oil Having a wide viscosity range (eg 10W40). The W stands for Winter, thus the viscosity ranges from SAE10 when cold to SAE40 when hot.

Multimeter An electrical test instrument with the capability to measure voltage, current and resistance. Some meters also incorporate a continuity tester and buzzer.

N

Needle roller bearing Inner race of caged needle rollers and hardened outer race. Examples of uncaged needle rollers can be found on some engines. Commonly used in rear suspension applications and in two-stroke engines.

Nm Newton metres.

NOx Oxides of Nitrogen. A common toxic pollutant emitted by petrol engines at higher temperatures.

O

Octane The measure of a fuel's resistance to knock.

OE (Original Equipment) Relates to components fitted to a motorcycle as standard or replacement parts supplied by the motorcycle manufacturer.

Ohm The unit of electrical resistance. Ohms = Volts ÷ Current.

Ohmmeter An instrument for measuring electrical resistance.

Oil cooler System for diverting engine oil outside of the engine to a radiator for cooling purposes.

Oil injection A system of two-stroke engine lubrication where oil is pump-fed to the engine in accordance with throttle position.

Open-circuit An electrical condition where there is a break in the flow of electricity - no continuity (high resistance).

O-ring A type of sealing ring made of a special rubber-like material; in use, the O-ring is compressed into a groove to provide the

Oversize (OS) Term used for piston and ring size options fitted to a rebored cylinder.

Overhead cam (sohc) engine An engine with single camshaft located on top of the cylinder head.

Overhead valve (ohv) engine An engine with the valves located in the cylinder head, but with the camshaft located in the engine block or crankcase.

Oxygen sensor A device installed in the exhaust system which senses the oxygen content in the exhaust and converts this information into an electric current. Also called a Lambda sensor.

P

Plastigauge A thin strip of plastic thread, available in different sizes, used for measuring clearances. For example, a strip of Plastigauge is laid across a bearing journal. The parts are assembled and dismantled; the width of the crushed strip indicates the clearance between journal and bearing.

Polarity Either negative or positive earth (ground), determined by which battery lead is connected to the frame (earth return). Modern motorcycles are usually negative earth.

Pre-ignition A situation where the fuel/air mixture ignites before the spark plug fires. Often due to a hot spot in the combustion chamber caused by carbon build-up. Engine has a tendency to 'run-on'.

Pre-load (suspension) The amount a spring is compressed when in the unloaded state. Preload can be applied by gas, spacer or mechanical adjuster.

Premix The method of engine lubrication on older two-stroke engines. Engine oil is mixed with the petrol in the fuel tank in a specific ratio. The fuel/oil mix is sometimes referred to as "petroil".

Primary drive Description of the drive from the crankshaft to the clutch. Usually by gear or chain.

PS Pfedestärke - a German interpretation of BHP.

PSI Pounds-force per square inch. Imperial measurement of tyre pressure and cylinder pressure measurement.

PTFE Polytetrafluroethylene. A low friction substance.

Pulse secondary air injection system A process of promoting the burning of excess fuel present in the exhaust gases by routing fresh air into the exhaust ports.

Q

Quartz halogen bulb Tungsten filament surrounded by a halogen gas. Typically used for the headlight (see illustration).

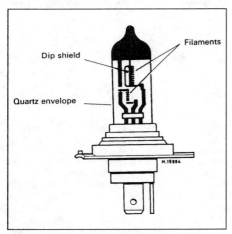

Quartz halogen headlight bulb construction

R

Rack-and-pinion A pinion gear on the end of a shaft that mates with a rack (think of a geared wheel opened up and laid flat). Sometimes used in clutch operating systems.

Radial play Up and down movement about a shaft.

Radial ply tyres Tyre plies run across the tyre (from bead to bead) and around the circumference of the tyre. Less resistant to tread distortion than other tyre types.

Radiator A liquid-to-air heat transfer device designed to reduce the temperature of the coolant in a liquid cooled engine.

Rake A feature of steering geometry - the angle of the steering head in relation to the vertical (see illustration).

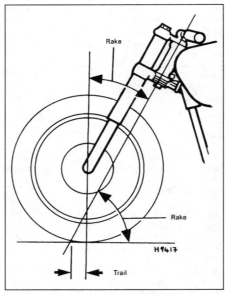

Steering geometry

Rebore Providing a new working surface to the cylinder bore by boring out the old surface. Necessitates the use of oversize piston and rings.

Rebound damping A means of controlling the oscillation of a suspension unit spring after it has been compressed. Resists the spring's natural tendency to bounce back after being compressed.

Rectifier Device for converting the ac output of an alternator into dc for battery charging.

Reed valve An induction system commonly used on two-stroke engines.

Regulator Device for maintaining the charging voltage from the generator or alternator within a specified range.

Relay A electrical device used to switch heavy current on and off by using a low current auxiliary circuit.

Resistance Measured in ohms. An electrical component's ability to pass electrical current.

RON (Research Octane Number) A measure of a fuel's resistance to knock.

rpm revolutions per minute.

Runout The amount of wobble (in-and-out movement) of a wheel or shaft as it's rotated. The amount a shaft rotates 'out-of-true'. The out-of-round condition of a rotating part.

S

SAE (Society of Automotive Engineers) A standard for the viscosity of a fluid.

Sealant A liquid or paste used to prevent leakage at a joint. Sometimes used in conjunction with a gasket.

Service limit Term for the point where a component is no longer useable and must be renewed.

Shaft drive A method of transmitting drive from the transmission to the rear wheel.

Shell bearings Plain bearings consisting of two shell halves. Most often used as big-end and main bearings in a four-stroke engine. Often called bearing inserts.

Shim Thin spacer, commonly used to adjust the clearance or relative positions between two parts. For example, shims inserted into or under tappets or followers to control valve clearances. Clearance is adjusted by changing the thickness of the shim.

Short-circuit An electrical condition where current shorts to earth (ground) bypassing the circuit components.

Skimming Process to correct warpage or repair a damaged surface, eg on brake discs or drums.

Slide-hammer A special puller that screws into or hooks onto a component such as a shaft or bearing; a heavy sliding handle on the shaft bottoms against the end of the shaft to knock the component free.

Small-end bearing The bearing in the upper end of the connecting rod at its joint with the gudgeon pin.

Spalling Damage to camshaft lobes or bearing journals shown as pitting of the working surface.

Specific gravity (SG) The state of charge of the electrolyte in a lead-acid battery. A measure of the electrolyte's density compared with water.

Straight-cut gears Common type gear used on gearbox shafts and for oil pump and water pump drives.

Stanchion The inner sliding part of the front forks, held by the yokes. Often called a fork tube.

Stoichiometric ratio The optimum chemical air/fuel ratio for a petrol engine, said to be 14.7 parts of air to 1 part of fuel.

Sulphuric acid The liquid (electrolyte) used in a lead-acid battery. Poisonous and extremely corrosive.

Surface grinding (lapping) Process to correct a warped gasket face, commonly used on cylinder heads.

T

Tapered-roller bearing Tapered inner race of caged needle rollers and separate tapered outer race. Examples of taper roller bearings can be found on steering heads.

Tappet A cylindrical component which transmits motion from the cam to the valve stem, either directly or via a pushrod and rocker arm. Also called a cam follower.

TCS Traction Control System. An electronically-controlled system which senses wheel spin and reduces engine speed accordingly.

TDC Top Dead Centre denotes that the piston is at its highest point in the cylinder.

Thread-locking compound Solution applied to fastener threads to prevent slackening. Select type to suit application.

Thrust washer A washer positioned between two moving components on a shaft. For example, between gear pinions on gearshaft.

Timing chain See **Cam Chain**.

Timing light Stroboscopic lamp for carrying out ignition timing checks with the engine running.

Top-end A description of an engine's cylinder block, head and valve gear components.

Torque Turning or twisting force about a shaft.

Torque setting A prescribed tightness specified by the motorcycle manufacturer to ensure that the bolt or nut is secured correctly. Undertightening can result in the bolt or nut coming loose or a surface not being sealed. Overtightening can result in stripped threads, distortion or damage to the component being retained.

Torx key A six-point wrench.

Tracer A stripe of a second colour applied to a wire insulator to distinguish that wire from another one with the same colour insulator. For example, Br/W is often used to denote a brown insulator with a white tracer.

Trail A feature of steering geometry. Distance from the steering head axis to the tyre's central contact point.

Triple clamps The cast components which extend from the steering head and support the fork stanchions or tubes. Often called fork yokes.

Turbocharger A centrifugal device, driven by exhaust gases, that pressurises the intake air. Normally used to increase the power output from a given engine displacement.

TWI Abbreviation for Tyre Wear Indicator. Indicates the location of the tread depth indicator bars on tyres.

U

Universal joint or U-joint (UJ) A double-pivoted connection for transmitting power from a driving to a driven shaft through an angle. Typically found in shaft drive assemblies.

Unsprung weight Anything not supported by the bike's suspension (ie the wheel, tyres, brakes, final drive and bottom (moving) part of the suspension).

V

Vacuum gauges Clock-type gauges for measuring intake tract vacuum. Used for carburettor synchronisation on multi-cylinder engines.

Valve A device through which the flow of liquid, gas or vacuum may be stopped, started or regulated by a moveable part that opens, shuts or partially obstructs one or more ports or passageways. The intake and exhaust valves in the cylinder head are of the poppet type.

Valve clearance The clearance between the valve tip (the end of the valve stem) and the rocker arm or tappet/follower. The valve clearance is measured when the valve is closed. The correct clearance is important - if too small the valve won't close fully and will burn out, whereas if too large noisy operation will result.

Valve lift The amount a valve is lifted off its seat by the camshaft lobe.

Valve timing The exact setting for the opening and closing of the valves in relation to piston position.

Vernier caliper A precision measuring instrument that measures inside and outside dimensions. Not quite as accurate as a micrometer, but more convenient.

VIN Vehicle Identification Number. Term for the bike's engine and frame numbers.

Viscosity The thickness of a liquid or its resistance to flow.

Volt A unit for expressing electrical "pressure" in a circuit. Volts = current x ohms.

W

Water pump A mechanically-driven device for moving coolant around the engine.

Watt A unit for expressing electrical power. Watts = volts x current.

Wear limit see **Service limit**

Wet liner A liquid-cooled engine design where the pistons run in liners which are directly surrounded by coolant (**see illustration**).

Wet liner arrangement

Wheelbase Distance from the centre of the front wheel to the centre of the rear wheel.

Wiring harness or loom Describes the electrical wires running the length of the motorcycle and enclosed in tape or plastic sheathing. Wiring coming off the main harness is usually referred to as a sub harness.

Woodruff key A key of semi-circular or square section used to locate a gear to a shaft. Often used to locate the alternator rotor on the crankshaft.

Wrist pin Another name for gudgeon or piston pin.